THE WAR IN UKRAINE AND EUROPEAN SECURITY

Global Affairs and Diplomacy

WAR STUDIES UNIVERSITY
and
UNIVERSITY OF BUCKINGHAM

THE WAR IN UKRAINE AND EUROPEAN SECURITY

Global Affairs and Diplomacy

Edited By
Andrzej Soboń, Julian Richards,
Vassilis Kappis, Marzena Żakowska

Hero, an imprint of Legend times group Ltd
51 Gower Street
London WC1E 6HJ
United Kingdom
www.hero-press.com

The right of the editors to be identified as the editors of this work has
been asserted in accordance with the Copyright, Designs and Patents
Act 1988. British Library Cataloguing in Publication Data available.

Technical Editor: Urszula Jaśkiewicz, Maja Grochalska, Bartosz
Mlyczyński and Małgorzata Zeniuk

Cover design by Ewa Wiśniewska

Print ISBN: 978-1-917163-45-3

TABLE OF CONTENTS

LIST OF FIGURES AND TABLES

CHAPTER 1

CHAPTER 2

Chapter 8

Chapter 10

LIST OF ABBREVIATIONS

AESA	Active Electronically Scanned Array
AI	Artificial Intelligence
BSR	The Black Sea Region
BTC	Baku-Tbilisi-Ceyhan
CAATSA	Countering America Adversaries Through Sanctions Act
CAGR	Compound Annual Growth Rate
CAT	Convention Against Torture
CCS	Communications System
CCW	Certain Conventional Weapon
CIA	Central Intelligence Agency
CIS	Commonwealth of Independent States
COMINT	Communications Intelligence
COP-DKP	Air Operations Center- Command Air Component
DA-ASAT	Direct-Ascent Anti-satellite
DARPA	The Advanced Research Projects Agency
DNR	Donetsk People's Republic
DOD	Department of Defence
ECHR	European Convention on Human Rights
ECtHR	European Court of Human Rights
EDC	European Defence Community
EDI	European Deterrence Initiative
EEAS	European Eternal Action Service
EEC	European Economic Community
EKV	Exo-Atmospheric Kill Vehicle
ELINT	Electronic Intelligence

EU	European Union
EUISS	European Union For Security Studies
FAO	Food and Agriculture Organization of the United Nations
FISINT	Foreign Instrumentation Signals Intelligence
FPV	First-Person-View
FSB	Federal Security Service
FTI	Fixed Target Indication
GEOINT	Geospatial Intelligence
GMTI	Ground Targets
HUMINT	Human Intelligence
ICC	International Criminal Court
ICCPR	International Covenant on Civil and Political Rights
ICJ	International Court of Justice
IHL	International Humanitarian Law
INF	Intermediate-Range Nuclear Forces
ISAF	International Security Assistance Force
ISS	International Space Station
IT	Information Technology
LEO	Low Earth Orbit
LNR	Luhansk People's Republic
LOI	Letter of Intent
MASINT	Measurement and Signature Intelligence
MERICS	Mercator Institute of China Studies
MNF	Multinational Force
NACC	North Atlantic Cooperation Council
NAFTA	North American Free Trade Agreement
NATINAMDS	NATO Integrated Air and Missile Defence System
NATO	The North Atlantic Treaty Organisation
NATO StratCom COE	NATO Strategic Communications Centre of Excellence
NAVWAR	Navigation Warfare
NGO	Non-Governmental Organization
NRF	NATO Response Force
PAROS	Prevention of an Arms Race in Outer Space
PAX	Personnel

PFP	Partnership For Peace
POW	Prisoners of War
RADINT	Radar Intelligence
RAP	Readiness Action Plan
RPO	Rendezvous And Proximity Operations
SACEUR	Supreme Allied Commander Europe
SAR	Synthetic-Aperture Radar
SBU	Ukraine's Secret Service
SGC	Southern Gas Corridor
SIGINT	Signal Intelligence
SME	Small and Medium-Sized Enterprise
SSA	Space Situational Awareness
SSN	Space Surveillance Network
SSU	Security Service of Ukraine
StratCom	NATO strategic communications
SVR	Foreign Intelligence Service
TOT	Temporarily Occupied Territory
TPP	Trans-Pacific Partnership
UAV	Unmanned Aerial Vehicle
UN	United Nations
USCYBERCOM	U.S. Cyber Command
UWC	Ukrainian World Congress
VJTF	Very High Readiness Joint Task Force

Acknowledgement

We express our sincere thankfulness for the contribution and recommendations to the program of Post Diploma Studies of Global Affairs and Diplomacy (GAD). We are grateful to the following Guest Speakers for sharing with the GAD Students knowledge and professional experience:

Prof. Omar ASHOUR
Professor at Doha Institute for Graduate Studies and Director of the Strategic Studies Unit at the Arab Centre for Research and Policy Studies, Quatar

Prof. Gawdet BAHGAT
Professor of Middle East Studies at National Defence University, USA

Dr. Lech DRAB
Visiting Professor at the War Studies University and Director of the Department of Military Foreign Affairs at the Ministry of National Defence of Poland

Prof. Larry GOODSON
Professor of Middle East Studies at U.S. Army War College

Dr. Byron HARPER
Deputy Director of the Partnership Directorate at the NATO Special Operations Headquarters (NSHQ) in Mons, Belgium

Dr. Richard A. LACQUEMENT Jr.
Professor of the Military Profession and Director of the National Security Policy Program, U.S. Army War College

Prof. Daivd LAST
Associate Professor of Political Science at the Royal Military College of Canada, a Commonwealth Scholar and Fulbright Research Chair, Secretary of the International Society of Military Sciences

Sönke MARAHRENS
Col (GS) Director Strategy & Defence, The European Centre of Excellence for Countering Hybrid Threats

Dr. Inez MIYAMOTO
Professor of Cybersecurity, Transnational Crimes, Supply Chain Security, Resilience Development at Daniel K. Inouye Asia-Pacific Center for Security Studies

Prof. Robert PERSON
Associate Professor of International Relations at the United States Military Academy and director of West Point's curriculum in International Affairs

Dr. Johann SCHMID
Professor at Centre for Military History and Social Sciences of the Bundeswehr (ZMSBw) in Potsdam and non-resident fellow at the Institute for Peace Research and Security Policy at the University of Hamburg

Dr. John P. SULLIVAN
Research Fellow at Arizona State University Future Security Initiative and Instructor in the Safe Communities Institute (SCI) at the Sol Price School of Public Policy, University of Southern California specialized in emergency operations, transit policing, counterterrorism, and intelligence

Lieutenant Colonel Rafał WIECZOREK
Polish Special Operations Forces NATO Special Operation Headquarters, Mons, Belgium

Foreword

Julian Richards

The chapters in this Volume represent the research outputs of the fourth cohort of students on the Postgraduate Diploma in Global Affairs and Diplomacy, delivered jointly by the War Studies University in Poland, and the University of Buckingham in the United Kingdom. As the war in Ukraine grinds on into its second year, the collected analyses presented here represent an extraordinary and critical set of reflections on this – the most significant security crisis in the European continent since the end of the Cold War.

The war in Ukraine has marked a critical juncture in global and regional security. The reverberations of this conflict extend well beyond the borders of Eastern Europe, challenging the existing international order and the assumptions of security frameworks that have underpinned peace in Europe since the latter stages of the twentieth century. The invasion of Ukraine by Russia is not only a devastating humanitarian crisis, but also a geopolitical event with wide-ranging implications for military strategy, international diplomacy, and global security policy.

This Volume, titled *The War in Ukraine and European Security*, offers an essential examination of the many dimensions of this conflict. The authors of the chapters bring to the fore various perspectives on how this war is reshaping both the European and global security landscapes. Each chapter provides critical insight into different aspects of the conflict: from military strategies employed by NATO, to the challenges of hybrid warfare, and the broader implications for global arms races and space militarization.

The importance of this analysis cannot be overstated. As the conflict in Ukraine continues, the ripple effects will undoubtedly be felt across various international arenas – be it the reconfiguration of alliances, a new Cold War dynamic, or the reshaping of defence policies in Europe and beyond. This volume helps illuminate these pressing concerns by offering a timely and in-depth understanding of the situation, particularly for scholars, policymakers, and military practitioners.

I would like to extend my gratitude to the authors who have contributed their expertise and perspectives to this comprehensive body of work. Their efforts in analyzing this rapidly evolving situation will undoubtedly contribute to the discourse on conflict resolution and strategic foresight. I also thank the team at the War Studies University for assembling and supporting such important research.

Professor Julian Richards
Dean of Humanities and Social Sciences,
Director of the Centre for Security and Intelligence Studies
University of Buckingham, United Kingdom

Introduction

Andrzej Soboń

The war in Ukraine, which began in 2014 and intensified with Russia's full-scale invasion in 2022, has dramatically shifted the geopolitical landscape of Europe and the world. The repercussions of this conflict have been felt across military, political, and humanitarian domains, forcing a reevaluation of security frameworks and military strategies globally. This volume, *The War in Ukraine and European Security*, explores these wide-ranging impacts through the contributions of leading scholars and experts in global affairs and diplomacy.

The book opens with an examination of NATO's Eastern Flank by Magdalena BUGAJNY, analyzing the vulnerabilities faced by countries bordering Russia and how NATO's current deterrence mechanisms are functioning. This chapter sheds light on the urgent need for improvements in defence strategies to ensure security in the region. Next, Szymon BOGUSKI discusses the use of incendiary weapons in the Ukrainian conflict, focusing on their legality under International Humanitarian Law (IHL). His analysis provides a critical assessment of the humanitarian impact of these weapons and highlights violations of legal frameworks. Moving to the technological domain, Irena DIAMENTOWICZ explores the role of artificial intelligence on the battlefield, with a focus on its use in Ukraine. Ethical considerations surrounding AI in military operations are also examined, alongside real-time applications in conflict zones. Jarosław DRYGOWSKI then presents a linguistic analysis of Vladimir Putin's 2022 Victory Day speech. His study reveals how persuasive strategies and language are used to shape narratives and garner support for Russia's military actions. The focus shifts to the actions of the Security Service of Ukraine during the defence of Kyiv in the contribution by Krzysztof GÓRECKI. This chapter provides a detailed look at Ukraine's intelligence and security operations during the initial stages of the invasion. Maciej GRUNT offers insights into the implications of the 2022 U.S. midterm elections for NATO and Ukraine. This chapter explores how potential shifts in U.S. foreign policy could impact NATO's collective security strategies. Dawid KUFEL examines the role of hybrid warfare in the conflict between Russia and Ukraine prior to the full-scale invasion. His analysis covers the use of non-traditional forms of warfare, including cyberattacks and information warfare, to destabilize Ukraine. In his chapter, Jarosław ŁĘSKI delves into the geopolitical rivalry between Turkey and Russia in the Black Sea region, analyzing the implications for regional security and the broader geopolitical competition in the area. Strategic communications play a key role in warfare, and Agata MAZUREK addresses NATO's communication strategies during the war in Ukraine. She explores the dilemmas and challenges faced by NATO in effectively communicating its role and actions during the conflict. Tomasz MĄCZKA investigates Russia's potential to undermine U.S. supremacy through strategic alliances. His chapter explores the global ramifications of Russia's efforts to shift international power dynamics in its favor. From a historical perspective, Rafał OLENDER examines how the war in Ukraine fits into the broader context of global and regional security. This chapter provides a long-term view of how the conflict might reshape international relations. The impact of the war on the arms race in space is the focus of Łukasz POKRYWACKI'S chapter. He discusses the militarization of space and the new security challenges posed by technological advancements in space weaponry. In his contribution, Wiktor SATKOWSKI explores how the conflict has led to significant changes in the management of Polish airspace. This chapter highlights the strategic importance of airspace management in defending NATO's Eastern Flank. Finally, Mikołaj SCHULZ delves into the role of HUMINT (human intelligence) in the Ukraine war, showing how intelligence-gathering has influenced military outcomes during the conflict.

Through this comprehensive exploration, this volume not only illuminates the immediate impacts of the war but also serves as a valuable resource for policymakers, military professionals, and scholars. By presenting a variety of perspectives – from military strategy and intelligence operations to legal and ethical concerns – this book offers a thorough understanding of how the war in Ukraine is reshaping the regional and world's security landscape.

I extend my sincerest appreciation to all the authors who

contributed their expertise and insights to this Volume. Their comprehensive analyses and carefully considered perspectives have greatly deepened the understanding of the war in Ukraine, shedding light on its far-reaching implications for both regional and global security.

Colonel Prof. Andrzej Soboń
Dean of the National Security Faculty
War Studies University
Warsaw, Poland

CHAPTER 1

The NATO's Eastern Flank deterrence

Magdalena Bugajny

Abstract

This chapter examines the deterrence efforts of NATO's Eastern Flank, focusing on the vulnerabilities faced by the countries bordering Russia, especially in light of recent Russian actions in Ukraine. The study explores how NATO's deterrence mechanisms have historically kept Russia at bay and addresses the implications of Russia's increasing military aggression, aimed at reclaiming former territories. Moreover, it highlights the significant challenges NATO faces, such as the lack of immediate readiness among the most vulnerable member states to counter a potential Russian invasion before NATO intervention. Through a comparative analysis of the military capabilities of these Eastern European nations, the chapter finds that their current levels of preparedness are insufficient to withstand an attack long enough for NATO forces to respond. This insufficiency presents a significant threat to the integrity of the region's defence. The aim of this chapter is to analyze the deterrence strategies of NATO and provide insights into necessary improvements for maintaining security along the Eastern Flank. The findings underscore the need for enhancing military capabilities and readiness among these NATO members to ensure their defence until broader NATO involvement is possible.

Keywords: NATO's Eastern Flank, regional deterrence, interoperability.

Introduction

The Russian aggression on the Ukraine put Europe in difficult situation. A democratic country willing to become a part of united, strong and secured Europe was attacked, because a different actor decided that this course of action may weaken him. The aggression put in motion multinational organizations with NATO on the top of them. It started discussions about the actions to be taken towards Russia and about the amount of support to be provided to the Ukraine. It also started disputes about how the rest of this part of Europe is prepared for a possible Russian attack. Inside NATO it intensified discussion about how to strengthen the existing coalition. It seemed to be vital especially for the countries in the vicinity of Russia. The example of that is the statement of Lithuania's Minister of Foreign Affairs Gabrielius Landsbergis: *Today, more than ever, we need decisions on the NATO eastern flank's credible defence. The Alliance must be ready to defend every inch of its territory on land, in air and at sea from the very first minutes of a possible conflict* (Landsbergis, 2022). The reason why governments of these countries want more NATO efforts is that they are more vulnerable to Russia then the rest of the coalition.

The constant evaluation of NATO's defence and deterrence is an important issue for the Alliance. Nevertheless, we need to remember that the strength of the existing coalition relies on the defence and deterrence of its several Regions. Having in mind that the NATO's Eastern Flank is mostly vulnerable to possible Russian attack it seems appropriate to focus on that Region. It leads to the adoption of the main research question: Does the NATO's Eastern Flank deterrence need evaluation? To find the answer to that question it was necessary to take few steps. First one was about describing the level of threat from the Russian side, by pointing the vulnerabilities of the Region. Secondly it was vital to point the problem connected with NATO's reaction time on its eastern flank, in case of military aggression in that region. The last step was to estimate the existing level of military preparation of countries of NATO's Eastern flank for a possible Russian attack, by comparing their manpower and equipment assets with Russian side. The study focused on eight countries which build the NATO's Eastern Flank: Estonia, Latvia, Lithuania, Poland, Slovakia, Hungary, Romania and Bulgaria. The research method comprises the analysis, which was used to examine the publications and studies, on the subject, source documents, and press articles. Comparative analysis of the potentials of countries pointed to this study led to synthesis explained in conclusions.

Undertaking research on this topic is important because the literature on the subject includes a lot of items on the vulnerabilities of described region towards Russia, such as the book by Tim Marshall *'Prisoners of Geography'*, or the article by Yasmeen Serhan *'Who is Vladimir Putin's Revisionist History For?'*, but without explanation, how this affects the Regional deterrence. Scholars also made efforts to study approach of smaller groups of countries to maintain a credible deterrence posture, such as the analysis by Centre for Strategic and Budgetary *'Deterrence and defence in the Baltic Region.'*, but focusing on NATO's deterrence as a whole and not on Regional one. It is important to comprehensively analyse if the level of NATO's Eastern flank deterrence is robust. Moreover, the question that the author tries to answer after a detailed analysis of the spheres that response to regional deterrence is: How can the countries significantly strengthen the deterrence of the Region?

Vulnerability of the Region

East part of Europe was always vulnerable to Russia and that fact did not change over the years. There is more than one reason for that state of affairs. One of the most important ones is Russian revisionism. *When Putin speaks of Russia today, he speaks of a country whose greatness is defined by its past – namely, its imperial history and its victory during World War II – which he believes must guide its present* (Serhan, 2022). He described the demise of the Soviet Union as *the greatest geopolitical tragedy of the century* (NBC News, 2005) and therefore his greatest ambition is to rebuild Russian influences on the periphery, which were lost. That would strengthen the position of Russia as a leader in the region and enable it to become a global power of the new international order. *By restoring Russia's control over its former territories, Putin not only corrects what he sees as a historic wrong but also cements his place in Russian history as the leader who restored the country to its rightful status* (Serhan, 2022). That kind of posture is a great threat for all former Soviet Union member states and for all other countries in the vicinity of Russia as well.

Figure 1.1. East European Plain

Source: Wikipedia, East European Plain (n.d.) https://simple.wikipedia.org/wiki/East_European_ Plain.

Likewise, the Russian view on the world the geographical rules also did not change over the years. As an American publicist Tim Marshall pointed in his book *The map Ivan the Terrible confronted is the same one Vladimir Putin is faced with to this day* (Marshall, 2019). Countries mostly vulnerable to Russia from the geographical point of view are the ones which lay on the East European Plain - also called the Russian Plain. According to the Great Soviet Encyclopaedia, it spreads from Scandinavian Mountains on the west-north to Sudetes and Carpathian Mountains on the west-south and Ural Mountains on the east and from coasts of Barents Sea and North Sea on the North and coasts of Black Sea and Caspian Sea on the south (Marshall, 2019). This terrain is the mountain-free part of the European landscape and mountains and seas became its external boundaries. In Poland, the vast European Plain is only three hundred miles wide. From this point it begins to broaden and at Russia's borders it is more than two thousand miles wide. Effective protection of that long border with no big natural obstacles to overcome requires a lot of effort and for Russia which sees the American-friendly part of Europe as a threat it is not a comfortable position. *Poland represents a relatively narrow corridor into which Russia could drive its armed forces if necessary and thus prevent an enemy from advancing toward Moscow* (Marshall, 2019) and the protection of mountains and seas from the west side of the country would be most appreciated for Russia.

NATO's challenge

It is clear that east part of Europe always was vulnerable to Russia. It still is. One of the most functional solutions to that state was evolution of NATO. NATO as a collective security system in which its independent member states agreed to defend each other against attacks by third parties seemed to keep the Russia's attempts at bay and outside NATO borders. However, looking at vulnerabilities mentioned above especially the one connected with Russian revisionism and having in mind the war in the Ukraine there is still place for the assumption that one day Russia may change its attitude and the NATO's deterrence may not be enough. In June 2022 during the NATO Summit in Madrid *Allied leaders agreed on a fundamental shift in NATO's deterrence and defence, with strengthened forward defences, enhanced battlegroups in the eastern part of the Alliance, and an increase in the number of high readiness forces* (NATO, 2022). Even with those changes there is still a question connected with time needed for NATO to respond.

From the very beginning of its existence NATO never had to respond to an attack to European Country. It means we had never a chance to see how fast would alliance deal with opponent on the European Continent. What we know are the timelines given by The Readiness Action Plan (RAP) – a comprehensive package of assurance and adaptation measures. According to this document the Alliance can quickly deploy *technologically advanced multinational force made up of land, air, maritime and Special Operations Forces components able to react to the full range of security challenges from crisis management to collective defence – The NATO Response Force (NRF)* (NATO, 2022). The NRF has the overarching purpose of being able to provide a rapid military response and it comprises around 40,000 troops. About half of it is the Very High Readiness Joint Task Force (VJTF) – element ready to move within two to three days. The NRF are based in their home countries. Overall command of the NRF belongs to the Supreme Allied Commander Europe (SACEUR). Operational command of the NRF alternates annually between Allied Joint Force Commands in Naples, Italy and Brunssum, the Netherlands. Allies assume the lead role for the VJTF on a rotational basis, with one Ally designated as the lead country and other Allies participating (NATO, 2022).

These measures are a part of the baseline of the Alliance's deterrence and defence posture. The problem connected with possible Russian attack on neighbouring country is the time. All the steps that need to be taken before the NATO forces appear in the operational area takes time and that is the time when country under attack needs to deal with the opponent isolated. First step takes time between the awareness of the attack and the green light to send the troops. NRF are multinational force, the alliance is multinational organization. Thinking about agreement between all the allies to send troops we have to have regard to the possible delays. Second step is about preparing NRF before the deployment. *Before use, the NRF will be tailored (adjusted in size and capability) to match the demands of any specific operation to which it is committed.* (NATO, 2022). Even with VJTF and their readiness within two to three days it is still two-three days plus time necessary to make a decision before the reinforcement arrives. This means an attacked country will be forced to deal with the opponent isolated at least couple of days.

Mentioned above scenario does not include most of air domain, while NATO Air Policing – a peacetime mission – aims to preserve the security of Alliance airspace. It is a collective task and involves the continuous presence – 24 hours a day,

365 days a year – of fighter aircraft and crews, which are ready to react quickly to possible airspace violations (NATO, 2022). Still, it is about land domain, and in unfavourable circumstances it may be enough for attacked country to lose advantage. Having that in mind it is wise to consider how the countries of NATO's Eastern Flank are prepared to protect their land before the Article 5 of North-Atlantic Treaty starts working. The research on that field will analyse two areas: available military manpower and military equipment. These areas do not cover the whole issue. To determine a country's position on that field is to consider also other factors like armed forces organisation, capabilities, military posture, etc. but selected areas are the most measurable ones and the comparison of these numbers serves well the discussion about the level of readiness to respond to armed attack. The next two chapters shows the numbers of manpower and equipment of all Eastern Flank countries and Russia, but also summarise the numbers for the whole Region with the purpose of a discussion about the regional deterrence.

Manpower

While we reflect upon military manpower it is understandable to start with its sources and a total population of a country becomes the biggest determinant on that matter. Russia ranks number 9 in the list of countries by population. The biggest country of NATO's Eastern Flank is Poland and it ranks 38 and the smallest one like Estonia or Latvia places themselves in the second half of that list (Wikipedia, 2023). Therefore it is not possible for one of the countries of eastern flank to be competitive with Russia on that matter. It has an enormous advantage in all statistics which has its sources in total population: available manpower, fit-for-service and manpower reaching military age annually (Table 1.1). The country closest to Russia from the manpower perspective is Poland but the numbers are more than three times higher for the opponent. But as for the whole region the advantage of Russia is not that overwhelming. Still the numbers are bigger for the opponent like two to one (see Table 1.1).

Numbers above lead to the most important factor – total military personnel. In Table 1.2 we can see how look the numbers in active, reserve an para-military sector which gave the total sum of available military personnel. The proportion at the bottom of the table shows a great gap between Region and Russia. The biggest difference is as it comes to reserve forces, which is connected with poor politics of those countries on that matter.

Table 1.1. Manpower: NATO's Eastern Flank and Russia

MANPOWER	Total population	Available manpower	Fit-for-service	Reaching Mil Age Annually
ESTONIA	1 211 524	593 647	462 802	13 327
LATVIA	1 842 226	829 002	663 201	16 580
LITHUANIA	2 683 546	1 744 305	1 360 558	37 570
POLAND	38 093 101	18 665 619	15 313 427	457 117
SLOVAKIA	5 431 252	2 769 939	2 297 420	59 744
HUNGARY	9 699 577	4 558 801	3 734 337	116 395
ROMANIA	18 519 899	9 630 347	7 889 477	203 719
BULGARIA	6 873 253	3 230 429	2 646 202	61 859
REGION	74 654 801	34 232 859	27 986 885	966 311
RUSSIA	142 021 981	69 590 771	46 583 210	1 278 198
REG: RUS	0,53	0,49	0,60	0,76

Source: Author's elaboration based on globalfirepower.com

This is a serious problem to be taken into considerations, while it may be the easiest way to increase numbers of total military personnel for the Region. The next in line is para-military factor. The statistics counts only the units which are armed. Five of eight countries of the Region have number of para-military forces equals to zero. For countries in the vicinity of Russia it may be a good idea to broaden the prospect of military aware and trained society.

Table 1.2. Military personnel: NATO's Eastern Flank and Russia

MILITARY PERSONNEL	TOTAL	Active	Reserve	Para-military
ESTONIA	24 700	7 200	17 500	0
LATVIA	22 100	6 600	15 500	0
LITHUANIA	44 250	23 000	7 100	14 150
POLAND	195 350	114 050	67 000	14 300
SLOVAKIA	17 950	17 950	0	0
HUNGARY	52 150	32 150	20 000	0
ROMANIA	183 500	71 500	55 000	57 000
BULGARIA	39 950	36 950	3 000	0
REGION	579 950	309 400	185 100	85 450
RUSSIA	3 249 000	1 190 000	1 500 000	559 000
REG: RUS	0,18	0,26	0,12	0,15

Source: Author's elaboration based on: Chipman *et. al.,* 2023.

The last one factor – number of active forces – is built as a resultant of proportions of forces for different components (Table 1.3). Those proportions look similar (0,23-0,30), with one exception – navy forces (0,13). One important factor is that Russia as a country with a vast land cannot use its all manpower for an armed conflict on its west border and as a country with a great access to the sea the navy personnel will be signed to particular regions.

Therefore, the great advantage of Russia in number of navy forces is not significant. From regional perspective the most important factors are numbers of air and land forces. And those reinforced with high number of reserve forces (if achieved) would be enough for regional defence.

The one important thing about military manpower is that Russia as a country engaged in a war has generated a great number of military personnel. Therefore, even if the proportion between Region and Russia for the fit-for-service power is 0,60 (which means well for the Eastern Flank), the total military personnel is 3 times smaller (0,23) which means that Russia has already engaged a bigger percentage of its population for military

Table 1.3. Active personnel: NATO's Eastern Flank and Russia

ACTIVE PERSONNEL	TOTAL	Air Foces	Land Forces	Navy Forces	Other
ESTONIA	7 200	400	4 100	400	2 300
LATVIA	6 600	500	1 800	500	3 800
LITHUANIA	23 000	1 500	14 500	700	6 300
POLAND	114 050	14 300	58 500	6 000	35 250
SLOVAKIA	17 950	4 000	10 300	0	3 650
HUNGARY	32 150	5 750	26 700	0	0
ROMANIA	71 500	11 700	35 500	6 800	17 500
BULGARIA	36 950	8 500	17 000	4 450	7 000
REGION	309 400	46 650	168 400	18 850	75 800
RUSSIA	1 190 000	165 000	550 000	145 000	330 000
REG: RUS	0,26	0,28	0,30	0,13	0,23

Source: Author's elaboration based on: Chipman *et. al.,* 2023.

purposes. This is the direction eastern Flank should fallow. It would be hard to do this by increasing the number of active forces, but it is possible to achieve with the number of reserve and paramilitary forces.

Military equipment

Having high numbers of heavy equipment does not equal having high military capabilities, but not having it especially when the adversary does, mean that the opponent has an advantage from the starting point. Russia has got a substantial number of aircraft and helicopters in their inventory (Table 1.4 and 1.5). There is an overwhelming difference in numbers between assets of Russian Federation and countries in the Region. Unfortunately, the lack of numbers of aircraft in countries in the region equals small position towards Russia as a whole Region. Russia has got an overwhelming advantage over the Region as it comes to attack aircraft and helicopters and it needs to be taken into considerations especially when it comes to three Baltic States with no fighting aircraft available. The additional problematic field is connected with Badlands bombing range – strategic bombers. Russian Long-range Aviation Command is equipped in 76 of them with nuclear land attack cruise missiles and Aerospace Forces has got 137 with capability to carry such missiles. As for the countries in the region, none has a capability or assets on that field. Even if US provides a nuclear umbrella to all allies it still means the countries in the Region are dependent on quick respond of their allies and not capable of dealing with the problem by their own.

Table 1.4. Aircraft assets: NATO's Eastern Flank and Russia

AIRCRAFT	Badlands Bombing Range	Fighter	Fighter Ground Attack	Attack	Anti-Submarine Warfare	Trans-port	Training
ESTONIA	0	0	0	0	0	3	1
LATVIA	0	0	0	0	0	4	0
LITHUANIA	0	0	0	0	0	6	0
POLAND	0	28	66	0	0	54	40
SLOVAKIA	0	11	0	0	0	5	8
HUNGARY	0	0	14	0	0	4	8
ROMANIA	0	17	22	0	0	12	32
BULGARIA	0	14	0	6	0	7	12
REGION	0	70	102	6	0	95	101
RUSSIA	213	252	455	297	44	495	266
REG: RUS	0:213	0,28	0,22	0,02	0:44	0,19	0,40

Source: Author's elaboration based on: Chipman *et. al.*, 2023.

The lack of aircraft and helicopters will make the Region dependant on NATO air assets for a long time. Fortunately, the mentioned before air policing mission makes the airspace of all NATO countries safer and ready for any possible violation on that domain. The next advantage of air policing programme is reaction time. The continuous presence of fighter aircraft and crews makes NATO ready to react as quick as it is possible to air-space violations. Still, it should not equal restfulness, especially not for the countries with the smallest number of air assets.

Table 1.5. Helicopters: NATO's Eastern Flank and Russia

HELICOPTERS	Attack	Multi-Role	Anti-Submarine Warfare	Transport	Training
ESTONIA	0	3	0	2	0
LATVIA	0	2	0	6	0
LITHUANIA	0	3	0	3	0
POLAND	28	72	8	109	0
SLOVAKIA	15	13	0	9	0
HUNGARY	8	20	0	2	0
ROMANIA	0	29	0	24	0
BULGARIA	6	5	0	18	0
REGION	57	147	8	18	0
RUSSIA	369	0	52	354	69
REG: RUS	0,15	147:0	0,15	0,05	0:69

Source: Author's elaboration based on: Chipman *et. al.,* 2023.

They need to take steps to systematically reduce the level of dependence on allies. It is vital to make the Region become fully capable of dealing with potential violations in air domain. The region which is highly vulnerable for potential Russian attack cannot afford to be dependent on other actors in air domain which is vital for achieving advantage on the ground.

Table 1.6. Navy: NATO's Eastern Flank and Russia

NAVY	SUBMARINES	Principal coastal combatants	Patrol and coastal combatants	Mine warfare	Amphibious
ESTONIA	0	0	6	4	3
LATVIA	0	0	13	4	0
LITHUANIA	0	0	7	4	2
POLAND	1	2	23	21	10
SLOVAKIA	0	0	0	0	0
HUNGARY	0	0	0	0	0

Table 1.6. Navy: NATO's Eastern Flank and Russia (continued)

NAVY	SUBMA-RINES	Principal coastal combatants	Patrol and coastal combatants	Mine warfare	Amphibious
ROMANIA	0	3	24	11	0
BULGARIA	0	3	4	9	+
REGION	1	8	77	53	15
RUSSIA	50	31	226	43	47
RUS:REG	1:50				

Source: Author's elaboration based on: Chipman *et. al.,* 2023.

The second domain is maritime domain. When we look at the numbers of naval assets (Table 1.6) the difference between Russia and Region seems enormous. We need to remember though that more realistic numbers come from the comparison between fleets of different seas. It is wise to understand how Russian assets are spread to different Military Districts just as well as the manpower. From the regional perspective in the area of interest lays the Western district.

Table 1.7. Navy: NATO's Eastern Flank and Russian Baltic Fleet

NAVY	SUB-MARINES	Principal surface combatant	Patrol and coastal combatants	Mine warfare	Amphibious
ESTONIA	0	0	2	4	0
LATVIA	0	0	13	4	0
LITHUANIA	0	0	7	4	2
POLAND	1	2	23	21	10
3B+P	1	2	45	33	12
Baltic Fleet	1	6	65	11	13
RUS: REG	1	0,33	0,69	3	0,92

Source: Author's elaboration based on: Chipman *et. al.,* 2023.

Russian Baltic Fleet should be then compared with the assets of countries which have access to the Baltic Sea: Estonia, Latvia, Lithuania and Poland. Table 1.7 shows the sum of these country's naval assets and their proportion with Russian assets on this area.

The only problematic field stand for principal surface combatants, but considering the other NATO countries in the region of the Baltic Sea this is not a problem to be bothered.

From the regional perspective and possible Russian attack to neighbouring country the most important domain is land. Next 3 tables present the numbers of the most important assets as it comes to land domain: vehicles, artillery and air defence equipment. Table 1.8 shows the number of different kind vehicles in chosen countries. The biggest disproportion between Region and Russia is for the armoured personnel carriers (0,33) Similar proportion stands for the infantry vehicles (0,35) but those are not overwhelming numbers. The statistic looks better for tanks (0,58) and for reconnaissance vehicles (0,85). The numbers of equipment for the whole Region may be sufficient, but the problem is that not all of the countries own all these kinds of vehicles. A considerable lack of tanks in three Baltic states which are the most vulnerable points of the Eastern Flank should be seen as area to be fixed. The lack of reconnaissance vehicles however may be covered by high numbers of infantry fighting vehicles and vice versa.

Table 1.8. Vehicles: NATO's Eastern Flank and Russia

VEHICLES	Tanks	Recce vehicles	Infantry fighting vehicles	Armoured personnel carriers
ESTONIA	0	0	44	136
LATVIA	3	170	0	8
LITHUANIA	0	0	30	236
POLAND	647	407	1 567	450
SLOVAKIA	30	18	216	101
HUNGARY	56	0	121	322
ROMANIA	377	0	241	749
BULGARIA	90	0	160	120
REGION	1 203	595	2 379	2 122
RUSSIA	2 070	700	6 880	6350+
REG: RUS	0,58	0,85	0,35	0,33

Source: Author's elaboration based on: Chipman *et. al.,* 2023.

As for the artillery assets the proportion differs even more between different kind of equipment. The biggest disproportion is for the self-propelled artillery and the smallest is for towed artillery. Having in mind the advantages of self-propelled artillery over the towed one and looking at the numbers of Russian assets it would be better for the Region to invest more in that first kind (see Table 1.9). The key advantage of self-propelled over towed artillery is that it can be brought into action much faster. Before one can use the towed artillery, it has to stop, unlimber and set up the guns. To move, the guns must be limbered up again and brought to the new location. Self-propelled platforms have a slight range advantage over comparative towed artillery platforms, but also the advantage of being operated by a smaller and better-protected crew that can reload and fire at an improved rate. That gives an advantage on the battlefield. The countries in the Region have three times less self-propelled artillery than the Russia and that should be fixed especially in the countries where there is more towed artillery then the self-propelled one. The disproportion between Region and Russia for Multiple Rocket Launcher is not great, but there is the same problem as for tanks – there are countries which do not poses those and it is important for each of the countries to become fully armed.

Table 1.9. Artillery: NATO's Eastern Flank and Russia

ARTILLERY	Self-propelled artillery	Towed artillery	Multiple Rocket Launcher	Mortars
ESTONIA	6	36	0	126
LATVIA	59	23	0	53
LITHUANIA	16	18	0	84
POLAND	424	0	179	170
SLOVAKIA	30	0	30	0
HUNGARY	2	31	0	+
ROMANIA	40	447	206	443
BULGARIA	48	24	24	80
REGION	625	579	439	956
RUSSIA	2176+	789+	944+	1529+
REG: RUS	0,29	0,73	0,47	0,62

Source: Author's elaboration based on: Chipman *et. al.*, 2023.

The last land category – air defence assets – shows the problem as it comes for almost all kind of air defence assets. Long-range and medium-range air defence assets gives the enormous disproportion between every country in the Region and Russia (Table 1.10).

Table 1.10. Air Defence: NATO's Eastern Flank and Russia

AIR DEFENCE	Long-range	Medium-range	Short-range	Point-defence	Self-propelled Guns	Towed guns
ESTONIA	0	0	0	+	0	+
LATVIA	0	0	0	+	0	+
LITHUANIA	0	0	4	+	0	0
POLAND	1	0	40	143+	22	355
SLOVAKIA	0	0	+	+	0	0
HUNGARY	0	0	0	16	0	0
ROMANIA	8	13	48	48	41	24+
BULGARIA	20	0	+	+	100	300
REGION	29	13	92	64	163	655
RUSSIA	970+	430	132+	900+	576+	+
REG: RUS	0,03	0,03	0,70	0,07	0,28	-

Source: Author's elaboration based on: Chipman *et. al.*, 2023.

As for short-range assets individuals who possess such equipment are three times wicker on that field then Russia. Unfortunately, the sum of these assets in the whole region does not look good either. The actual problem is not about the comparison of the air defence assets of the Region with the Russian side but comparison with Russian artillery and air attack assets. Russia is equipped in those in a very great scale and the Easter Flank of NATO is not capable of dealing with those numbers alone. Almost all countries in the Region should consider a purchase of those systems.

Regional deterrence

The analysis of the numbers connected with manpower and equipment showed that the individual capacity to counter Russian aggression from its very beginning does not exist. The same numbers revealed that countries as a Region in many aspects are capable to confront Russia. The problem is that this is only a statistic and a real capacity comes from an interoperability. NATO's Eastern Flank is still only a set of countries with different tactics and equipment. Even if all these countries are members of NATO the differences between them are still great. The head of the Estonian Defence Forces, Lieutenant General Martin Herem in his speech about three Baltic States said that they "need to take more regional approach" (Van Tol, I. *et al.*, 2022). It would be even better if all countries of NATO's Eastern Flank took that kind of approach. The regional cooperation between NATO members on the Eastern Flank with purpose to resist potential threat from Russian side might be the answer for the low level of deterrence in that part of NATO.

That kind of coalition should focus on interoperability in land domain but should also include in some circumstances maritime and air domain. Inside NATO improvement of the ability of forces to work together started since the Alliance was founded in 1949. NATO defines interoperability as: *the ability for Allies to act together coherently, effectively and efficiently to achieve tactical, operational and strategic objectives. Specifically, interoperability enables forces, units and/or systems to operate together, allowing them to communicate and to share common doctrine and procedures, along with each other's infrastructure and bases* (NATO, 2022). Still it is easier to make Allies to act together coherently, effectively and efficiently when the group of countries is smaller. It does not mean the countries of Eastern Flank should not be a part of this process inside NATO. It only meant that they should focus more on improvement of this ability within themselves to achieve common tactical, operational and strategic objectives.

This Regional interoperability should mean multiple dimensions: technical, procedural, human and information. It should include hardware, equipment, armaments and systems especially as it comes to fire support and air-control systems. It does not require common military equipment, but the equipment that can share common facilities and is able to interact, connect, exchange data and communicate. Therefore, the rational priorities for the defence budgets and cooperation as it comes for purchasing new kinds of equipment would be appreciated. The Regional approach should focus on integration of the command structures, by establishment of allied commands and multinational units working on interoperable defence plans. Such planning will result in more purposeful capability development, and more effectively planned allied reinforcement to the Region. The doctrines and procedures within NATO already exist. Now it is about achieving the same level of standardization and training between all the countries of Eastern Flank to have a coherent set of deployable, interoperable and sustainable forces equipped, trained, and commanded to operate together and with other members of NATO.

Such alliance should work at the same rules as Article 5 of NATO, but with the purpose of reducing the time needed to reinforce the attacked country. This concept does not exclude quick deployment of air forces of western NATO countries, which would be appropriate and significant correspondingly to the current state of air assets within the countries in the Region. Still countries in the Region needs to increase their air capabilities. Moreover, for the deterrence measures this kind of alliance still needs to be bolstered by constant or rotational presence of NATO powers in the countries located in the Region. Even if partially achieved, this model allows to increase the capabilities of chosen countries to conduct effective regional defence and that will give the other parties time for adequate and organized military response.

Conclusions

The level of deterrence for whole NATO should be considered as a sum of deterrence of its Regions. Russian revisionism and regional geography make NATO's Eastern flank a region mostly vulnerable to Russian attack, which means it should have the highest level of deterrence. Unfortunately, the analysis conducted on that matter revealed it does not look that way. The chapter devoted to NATO's reaction time revealed that NATO as multinational organisation needs time to deploy its land forces after the attack on one on its members, but it is time that attacked country cannot afford, therefore it needs to be prepared to deal with the aggression for at least two to three days before the reinforcement comes. If these countries show that they are not capable of dealing with such problem it might be an encouraging impulse for the opponent.

Chapters devoted to military strength showed that as it comes to military manpower and equipment there is no individual actor on this side of Europe who could effortlessly oppose Russian Federation at the beginning of possible conflict when it will act alone. The analysis confirmed that countries in the Region are not sufficient as it comes to air assets – not as individuals and not as a

Region as a whole, therefore the NATO reactions connected with air policing mission are indispensable. Looking at the strength in maritime domain in Baltic Sea Region it would be wise to consider the purchase of principal surface combatants. The most important land domain shows that as for the vehicles and artillery the problem is that some countries do not poses an important equipment such as tanks and Multiple Rocket Launchers. The biggest problem stands for air defence assets. It should be the primary objective for all countries of Eastern Flank for the next years. Again, the military strength is not only the sum of these areas but those are good points to start with.

Based on these analyses the author believes that the regional deterrence is not sufficient while it relays on individual capabilities of countries in the Region and NATO reinforcement, which would take time. One of the solutions to change that state of affairs is for the countries of NATO's Eastern Flank is to become more interoperable within the region. It is vital for these countries to look at the problem from regional perspective – less generic than NATO's and wider then purely national. This interoperability must include all dimensions: technical, procedural, human and information. As a fully interoperable coalition of countries their strength can give enough time to other NATO allies to respond appropriately. Allies who can act together coherently, effectively and efficiently show that they can defend their Region and this rise the level of deterrence.

References

Chipman, J. *et al.* (2023) *The military balance. The annual assessment of global military capabilities and defence economics.* The International Institute for Strategic Studies.

Landsbergis G. (2022) The next NATO summit in Madrid should properly assess the changes security environment and threars posed by Russia. Available at https:// keliauk. urm.lt/en/news/view/lithuanias-foreign-minister-gabrielius-landsbergis-the-next-nato-summit-in-madrid-should-properly-assess-the-changed-security-environment-and-threats-posed-by-russia.

Marshall, T. (2019) Prisoners of Geography. Elliott & Thompson Limited.

NBC News (2005). Available at: https://www.nbcnews.com/id/wbna7632057.

North Atlantic Treaty Organization (2022) NATO Response Force. Available at https:// www.nato.int/cps/en/natohq/topics_49755.

Serhan, Y. (2022) Who is Vladimir Putin's Revisionist History For?.

Available at: https:// www.theatlantic.com/international/archive/2022/02/putin-russia-ukraine-revisionist-history/622936/.

Van Tol, I. *et al.* (2022) Deterrence and defence in the Baltic Region. New realities, Centre for Strategic and Budgetary.

Wikipedia (2023) NATO. Available at: https://en.wikipedia.org/wiki/NATO.

Wikipedia (2023) List of countries and dependencies by population. Available at: https:// en.wikipedia.org/wiki/List_of_countries_and_dependencies_by_population.

Wikipedia (2023). Available at: https://simple.wikipedia.org/wiki/East_European_Plain.

CHAPTER 2

Exploring the legality of incendiary weapons in Ukraine's war within the light of humanitarian law

Szymon Boguski

Abstract

This chapter delves into the legal discourse surrounding the use of incendiary weapons in the ongoing conflict in Ukraine, particularly in the context of International Humanitarian Law (IHL). It examines the legality of these weapons following the 2014 annexation of Crimea and the rise of pro-Russian separatist movements in Eastern Ukraine. The study explores the 1980 Convention on Certain Conventional Weapons and its Protocol III, which regulates the use of incendiary weapons in conflict, analyzing their applicability in the Ukraine war. Through careful examination, the chapter determines that the use of incendiary weapons violates IHL, highlighting their indiscriminate impact on civilians and civilian objects. Findings emphasize the need for stricter enforcement of IHL, alongside efforts to strengthen international legal frameworks, to ensure the protection of civilians in armed conflicts. This chapter aims to contribute to the understanding of the legal implications of incendiary weapons and their devastating humanitarian consequences.

Keywords: International Humanitarian Law, incendiary weapons, Ukraine's conflict, civilian protection, legal framework, IHL compliance

Introduction

The historical context of the conflict in Ukraine sets the stage for an in-depth exploration of the legality of incendiary weapons under the realm of International Humanitarian Law (IHL). The ongoing conflict in Ukraine, which began in 2014, has not only led to a significant loss of life and displacement of civilians but has also ignited debates concerning the adherence to IHL principles.

This conflict emerged following Russia's annexation of Crimea in 2014 and the subsequent pro-Russian separatist movements in Eastern Ukraine (BBC News, 2014). The separatist groups, backed by Russia, declared independence in regions like Donetsk and Luhansk, leading to a complex and multifaceted struggle for sovereignty, territorial integrity, and political influence. The conflict's evolution has been marked by key milestones, including the downing of Malaysia Airlines Flight MH17 in 2014, which increased international scrutiny and involvement. This eventually led to various parties being involved in hostilities, including Ukrainian government forces, separatist militias, and international actors. The international community's response to the conflict has been diverse. Diplomatic efforts, such as the Minsk agreements, aimed to negotiate a ceasefire and a political resolution, but have had limited success. Sanctions were imposed on Russia by Western countries in response to its involvement in the conflict. Humanitarian aid initiatives were also launched to assist the displaced civilians and mitigate the humanitarian crisis.

The use of incendiary weapons within this context has garnered increasing attention, raising pertinent questions about their legality and compatibility with IHL. As the conflict has unfolded, allegations of the deployment of incendiary weapons have surfaced, particularly in the context of urban warfare. This has prompted the need for a comprehensive analysis of these weapons' adherence to established international norms. Given the titular issue, pertinent research themes have been invoked. Initially, this article addresses the historical context, definition and classifications of incendiary agents. Subsequently, the discourse expands to delineate the ramifications of incendiary weaponry on human beings, specifically: thermal traumas, toxicological implications arising from combustion by-products, detrimental consequences for equipment and armament, and adverse effects on the environment milieu.

The primary objective of this research is to conduct a meticulous appraisal of employment of incendiary weapons within military operations, with emphasis on their usage during the combat operation and in particular in Ukraine's war, contextualized within the framework of International Humanitarian Law (IHL) and the stipulations encompassed within the 1980 Convention on Certain Conventional Weapons and its Protocol III. The Convention and its associated Protocol endeavour to modulate the deployment of incendiary weapons (ICRS, 2023). Such assessment inherently considers the expansive repercussions for the civilian populace and the broader humanitarian spectrum. Incendiary armament possesses the potential to inflict profound and non-discriminatory devastation, impacting both belligerents and the non-combatant populace alike. Protocol III refers to one on of the Protocols to the Geneva Conventions that specially deals with the restriction of the use of incendiary weapons. Since its adoption in 1980, it has been an essential instrument in IHL, outlining the rules of war regarding the use of such weapons. However, Protocol III is not without its limitations. Over the years, evolving technological and strategic realities have exposed certain gaps in the Protocol's provisions. By 2022, the international debate intensified over these inadequacies, spurred by increasing reports of incendiary weapons use in conflict zones. The resultant outcry underscored the urgency for nations to revisit and fortify the Protocol. This evolving conversation has significant implications for global security, military strategy, and the overall commitment of nations to uphold humanitarian principles in warfare. In this context, this article delves deep in the nuances of Protocol III, its constraints, and the path forward in international consensus.

By meticulously probing the historical underpinnings of the Ukrainian conflict and is multifaceted dynamics, this investigation aims to elucidate the jurisprudential dimensions associated with deployment of incendiary weaponry. Such a scholarly endeavour is imperative not solely for grasping the proximate ramification of these armaments, but also for facilitating and enriched dialogue on the expensive applications of IHL tenets within the milieu of modern-day armed confrontations.

A brief history of incendiary weapons

Weapons of incendiary type have been known since ancient times. Already during the Peloponnesian Wars, the army of the Athenian leader Thucydides, using the so-called Greek fire – a mixture of tar and natural flammable substances (most likely saltpetre and turpentine) – was able to destroy the wooden fortifications of Delium in 424 BC (Partington, 1999, p. 1-2). This weapon was significantly improved during the Byzantine period, where it became a military secret of the highest classification and contributed many times to repelling invasions of Constantinople (Haldane, 1998, p. 138). It was used, among other things, to set fire to the decks of contemporary warships. In later periods, incendiary substances became a constant element of artillery ammunition, used in land operations (especially in sieges) and naval ones. Fire – due to its scale of destruction and its impact on combatants and civilians – was important in the tactics and strategy of the ancient and medieval periods (Rogers, 2010, p. 50). Under the influence of changes in the construction of fortifications and buildings, and the emergence at the turn of the 18th and 19th centuries of massive ground forces, the concept of using incendiary weapons changed: these substances were to strike the infantry of the enemy (Łabędzki, 2007). For this purpose, quasi-rocket means and the first flamethrowers were introduced. The breakthrough in the widespread use of incendiary weapons was the introduction of incendiary bombs to the equipment of air forces. Such measures allowed – through the use of aviation – to attack built-up areas and also expanded the possibility of strikes on the deep rear of the enemy. Incendiary weapons thus became weapons for the destruction of infrastructure and built-up areas again. On May 31, 1915, during an attack on London, a German zeppelin used explosive charges containing powdered magnesium for the first time, causing fires in the central districts of the city (Department of the Army Technical Manual, 1984, p. 2-10). The first such strikes made the international community aware of the possibility of using this method as a fundamental element of terrorist bombings, targeting civilians (Castle, 2015, p. 20). Incendiary bombs became – besides conventional demolition bombs – a basic element of bomber aviation equipment. The substance used was thermite, which reached very high combustion temperatures and caused immediate ignition. The German Luftwaffe, even before the war in Spain, and also during the invasion of Poland in 1939, used alternating demolition and incendiary bombs to increase the range of damage and limit the possibility of effective rescue operations (Patterson, 2007, p. 47-48). Thermite bombs became the main means of air raids during World War II, llied air forces during massive aerial strikes in urban areas in Nazi Germany and Japan used the phenomenon of so-called firestorms, which devastated urban buildings (Garon, 2016, p. 3). Victims of firestorm attacks often died from suffocation, caused by a lack of oxygen consumed by fires. During the attack on Tokyo in 1945, M-47 incendiary bombs and M-69 fuel-air explosives caused more fatalities than the atomic bombing of Hiroshima (Tannemwald, 2007, p. 80-81). After World War II, incendiary weapons were still used in combat operations by aviation (during the civil war in Greece, the Korean War, the French intervention in Indochina) (Barnaby & Huisken, 1975, p. 205; Deane, 1999, p. 149). It is well known for its widespread use by the US Air Force during the conflict in Vietnam, where napalm served as the basic anti-infantry weapon in tropical vegetation conditions. There are also reports of the use of MK-77 kerosene bombs with reduced fuel by the US Marine Corps aviation during Operation "Iraqi Freedom" (Neer, 2013, p. 233). In the summer of 2016, the UN and NGOs drew attention to the possible use of incendiary bombs in Aleppo by the Syrian Air Force and the supporting Russian combat aircraft (Anadolu Agency, 2106). Later, incendiary weapons were used during the conflict in Ukraine, which is the main theme of this article.

Definition and classification of incendiary agents

Incendiary agents are chemical compounds or mixtures capable of releasing a large amount of heat during combustion and producing high temperatures, able to ignite other materials and objects and harm people and animals due to their properties. The primary harming factor of incendiary agents is thermal energy. In this context, fuels and flammable materials are considered incendiary agents. Only some of them, with specific properties, can be used for military purposes (Szewczuk, 1961, p. 16):

- Burning temperatures of around 1300 K or higher;
- High heat of combustion value;
- Sufficiently long combustion time;
- Relatively easy ignitability;
- Safety during preparation, storage, and transport;
- Resistance to extinguishing agents.

High combustion temperature is necessary to heat a targeted object above its ignition temperature and ignite it. Even to ignite easily flammable materials (straw, hay, wood), a temperature of several hundred Kelvins is required (approximately 500-600K), and for moist wood, petroleum, oils, and similar materials, even 600-800 K.

The heat produced during combustion is transferred to the environment, with only a small portion being used to heat the targeted object. Hence, the temperature produced by the incendiary agent should be 2-3 times higher than the target's temperature. Given the limited number of flammable objects in future battlefields (due to armoured combat equipment, earthen, concrete structures, etc.), incendiary agents with combustion temperatures of 1300K and higher are required.

The high calorific value allows for rapid heating of an object to its ignition temperature. It should be noted that not all the heat from a burning incendiary agent is transferred to an object in direct contact with it. Some thermal energy radiates into the environment or is carried away by emitted gases and smoke. Every flammable material has its specific heat capacity. This means it needs more or less heat to warm up to a certain temperature. Materials with a high calorific value include:

- Some gases, e.g., hydrogen;
- Solids like clay, magnesium, and phosphorus;
- Liquids such as petroleum and oils.

Intensive burning and burn time are mutually exclusive factors. If the burn rate is high, burn duration is typically shorter and vice versa. In practice, an incendiary agent with a burn temperature of 1300 K – 2300 K should burn for about 10 minutes over the largest possible surface. The larger the surface affected by the incendiary agent, the more energy is transferred to the surroundings, making it easier to ignite a target.

Incendiary agents must also be easily ignitable but should not spontaneously ignite before their combat application, i.e., during preparation or transport.

Some incendiary agents (like phosphorus) require special protection against self-ignition when exposed to atmospheric air; they are dissolved in an organic solvent or stored underwater. Once stored this way, they can be kept for an extended period. If the solvent evaporates or is removed, phosphorus will self-ignite upon contact with air.

Safety while working with incendiary agents and their storage stability are fully understood requirements. Handling such substances not only increases production costs due to the need for strict safety conditions and special equipment but also limits their production volume. Instability during storage prevents stockpiling and requires moving production activities from industry to the military.

Civilian incendiary agents should also have properties that make extinguishing as challenging as possible. Hence, sodium is often used; its burning is sustained by water, the most common extinguishing agent.

Out of the vast number of substances and mixtures that are fuels and flammable mixtures, only some meet the specified requirements and are used as combat incendiary agents. They can be classified based on criteria like:

- Physical state;
- Chemical composition;
- Burn rate;
- Heat of combustion, and others.

For military purposes, incendiary agents are most often divided according to their chemical composition and physical state (MON, 1974, p. 7).

Due to their chemical composition, incendiary agents are divided into two groups. The first group consists of agents that do not contain oxidizers in their composition. Atmospheric oxygen is essential for their combustion. The second group comprises agents containing oxidizers in their formula. They burn without the need for air.

The first group includes elements like sodium, potassium, magnesium, aluminium, their alloys, and chemical mixtures containing petroleum and its derivatives – gasoline, kerosene, benzol, oils, and their mixtures, as well as phosphorus and organic metal compounds. Combustion of these incendiary agents is characterized by the emission of a large number of gases heated to high temperatures and an intense flame that enhances the ignition effect. It is possible to extinguish these incendiary agents by cutting off the air supply.

The second group consists of metal and metal oxide mixtures, as well as oxygen-rich salts. The oxidizers in the incendiary agents provide the necessary oxygen for combustion. The amount of oxygen contained in the oxidizer usually ensures the complete combustion of the flammable substance (metal). Extinguishing such incendiary agents is very challenging because cutting off the air supply does not stop the combustion process.

Based on their physical state, incendiary agents used to attack people, equipment, armaments, and terrain features are divided into solid and liquid.

Solid incendiary agents create point sources of fire. Their striking power is limited as most of the thermal energy released during combustion is focused on a small area. Liquid incendiary agents create surface sources of fire. They have the ability to spray and spill at their point of use, creating one or several fire centres over a large area.

The incendiary effect of weapon on humans

Incendiary weapons affect people mainly through thermal and psychological shock and can cause poisoning from toxic gases.

Thermal injuries

Thermal injuries are various kinds of burns. The severity of a burn depends on several factors, including the size of the burn, its location, and the age and general health of the person burned. The primary factors for classifying burns are their depth and extent. Therefore, burns are often divided into:

- first-degree – reddening and swelling of the skin;
- second-degree – blisters form;
- third-degree "A" – the true skin is charred, leaving remnants of the epidermis capable of regeneration;
- third-degree "B" – all layers of the skin are necrotic;
- fourth-degree – not only the skin but also deep tissues such as muscles or bones are affected.

Surface burns include first, second, and third "A" degree burns. Deep burns include third "B" and fourth-degree burns. In practice, we often deal with a combination of different degrees of burns. Unlike burns resulting from the thermal radiation of a nuclear explosion, napalm burns are due to prolonged exposure to a thermal agent on the skin and are therefore deep. Determining burn depth within the first few hours is usually impossible, so it's crucial to understand the extent of the injury. Burn sizes are expressed as a percentage of total skin area. The "rule of nines" is used to determine burn extent (Konupka, 1962, p. 110). It assumes that in an adult, the head and neck area accounts for 9%, each arm for 9%, the front torso for 18%, the back torso for 18%, each leg for 18%, and the groin and genitals for 1% of the total body surface area.

It's important to note that an adult's hand represents about 1% of the body's total skin surface. Thus, we can estimate the size of a burn by simple comparison. Injuries covering more than 30% of the body are life-threatening. First and second-degree burns are relatively harmless as they usually heal without scarring within 14 days. Third and fourth-degree burns make spontaneous healing lengthy and limited. If the area affected by second and third-degree burns exceeds 10-15% of the body, the body reacts with what is called burn disease.

During this disease, four stages can be distinguished: shock, acute toxaemia (poisoning), septic toxaemia (infection), and the recovery period. The most severe conditions usually occur in cases of burns to the upper respiratory tract.

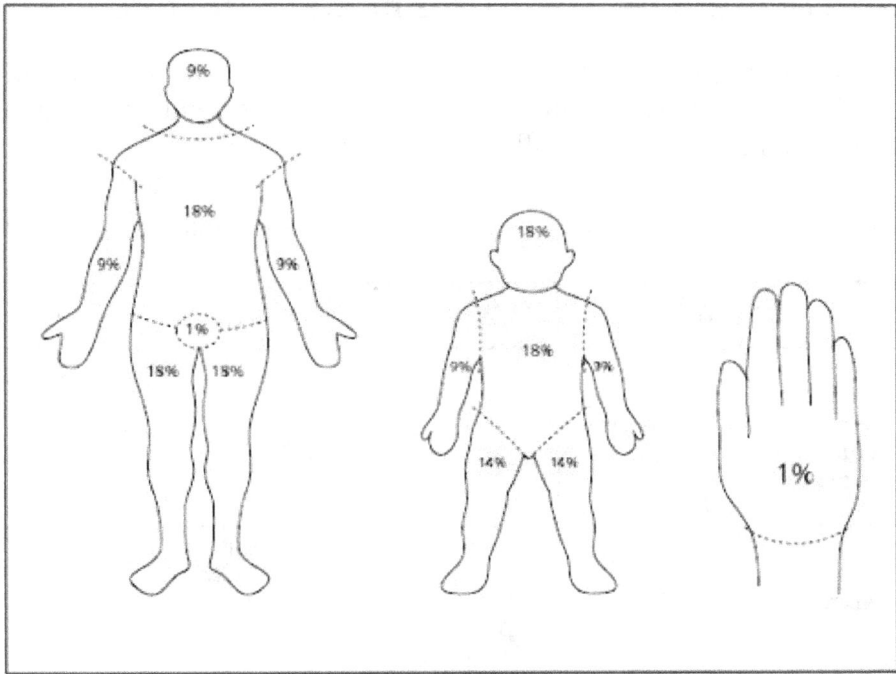

Figure 2.1. The principle of determining the percentage extent of burns on the body surface

Source: *The Royal Children's Hospital Melbourne* (n.d.), https://www.rch.org.au/trauma-service/manual/Burns/.

Common causes are flames, hot or heated air, and toxic combustion products. Thermal injury from heated air can occur even up to 100 meters away when downwind and 40-50 meters when upwind from a burning object. The air temperature in the direct flame zone can reach 800K, and between individual napalm burn sites, it can be 400K. The destructive effect of such air can last up to 10 minutes. Increased humidity promotes respiratory tract burns, and inhaling smoke further deteriorates healing conditions, leading to changes in lung tissue, such as congestion, swelling, and purulent complications. This also further reduces respiratory efficiency. Typical symptoms of burns include sore throat when swallowing, cough, dry mouth, voice distortion, shortness of breath, and difficulty breathing. Concurrent skin and respiratory burns are among the most dangerous (Boszkiewicz, 1982, p. 110).

Intoxication by Toxic Combustion Products

The burning process, depending on its substrates and conditions in which it occurs, produces a range of products that are toxic or poisonous to the body, as illustrated in Table 2.1.

Table 2.1. Toxicity of some combustion products found in fire smoke

Name			Toxicity		
Substances formed in the combustion process	Burning agents	Dose type	The mass of the poisoning agent	Route of entry into the body	Type of organisms for which the dose has been affected
Acetaldehyde	wool, cotton, paper	TD LD LD	60 mg 500 mg/kg 1900 mg/kg	subcutaneously intraperitoneally orally	rats rats rats
Acrolein	napalm, petroleum distillation products	LD TC LC	46 mg/kg 504 mg/kg 24 mg/m³	orally through the skin inhalation	rats mice mice
Alumina _	aluminum, electron	LC	500 mg/m³	inhalation	mice
Ammonia	wool, silk, melanin, resins	LC	2000 ppm	inhalation	rats
Benzene	Fuel	TD	48 mg/kg	through the skin	mice
Soot	napalm, petroleum distillation products	LD	4080 mg/kg 120 mg/kg	orally subcutaneously	rats rats
Carbon monoxide	napalm, petroleum distillation products, plastic masses	LC	2000 ppm	inhalation	mice
Chlorine	polyvinyl chloride	TC	5 ppm	inhalation	People
Hydrogen chloride	polyvinyl chloride	LC	1000 mg/m³	inhalation	rabbits

Table 2.1. (Continued)

Name			Toxicity		
Substances formed in the combustion process	Burning agents	Dose type	The mass of the poisoning agent	Route of entry into the body	Type of organisms for which the dose has been affected
hydrogen cyanide	wool, silk, polyurethane, phenolic and melanin resins	LC	5000 ppm	inhalation	People
hydrogen sulfide	wool, silk	LC	1500 mg/m³	inhalation	rats
Magnesium oxide	electron, magnesium	TC	400 mg/m³	inhalation	People
Nitrogen oxides	nitrocellulose	LC	250 mg/kg	inhalation	mice
Octafluoro-io-butylene	polyfluoro-carbonates	LD	180 mg/kg	–	rats
Phosgene	polyvinyl chloride	LC	500 ppm	inhalation	rats
Phosphines	phosphorus (in the absence of air)	LC	8 ppm	inhalation	People
Phosphoric acid	phosphorus (air access)	TC LD	100 mg/m³ 1.4 mg/kg	inhalation orally	People People
Sodium hydroxide	sodium	LD	500 mg/kg	orally	rabbits
Uranium oxide	depleted uranium	LD	6 mg/kg	intraperitoneally	mice

Source: Nowak, Incendiary Weapons, MON Publishing, 1986, p. 185-186.

The most dangerous combustion product, almost always present in fire smoke, is carbon monoxide. It arises from incomplete combustion of organic substances. It is particularly dangerous because it penetrates through absorbers and filter-inserts of regular gas masks. The toxicity of carbon monoxide is illustrated by the numerical data in Table 2.2.

Table 2.2. Carbon monoxide toxicity and degrees of poisoning resulting from its inhalation

The concentration of carbon monoxide in the air in percent	Degree of poisoning
0.001–0.03	Symptoms of paralysis after exposure for several hours
0.1–0.2	Intermediate degree poisoning after exposure 0.5–1 hour
0.2–0.3	Severe poisoning after exposure 0.5–1 hour
0.4–0.5	Fatal shock within 5–30 minutes
Above 0.5	Death in 1–5 minutes

Source: Nowak, Incendiary Weapons, MON Publishing, 1986, p. 187

Carbon monoxide poses a significant danger when its concentration in the air exceeds 0.2-1%, which is common in burning buildings. Carbon dioxide is toxicologically less dangerous than its monoxide counterpart, but when its concentration in the air reaches 3-5%, soldiers may lose combat ability due to hypoxia, which can even be fatal. This phenomenon can occur, for instance, during the combustion of a large amount of napalm since burning 1 kg of this agent requires 3.5 kg of oxygen, equivalent to 11.7 m3 of air.

Using any incendiary weapon, exerts psychological pressure on the opposing soldiers due to the presence of fire. The potential for painful death or mutilation, which is a real threat at that moment, strongly impacts the imagination. There are documented instances of entire units succumbing to panic and frantic escapes, significantly increasing the casualty toll (Nowikow & Koniukow, 1959, s.26).

It's essential to recognize that the sudden, unexpected engulfment by fire of our surroundings – flames, smoke restricting visibility, temperature, and accompanying fire sounds (loud crackling, the rumble of burning, smoke, etc.) – are potent stress factors that can easily induce terror. The accompanying shock is a natural, innate defensive reaction of the body. However, this state doesn't last long. As a person becomes accustomed to stress, the shock subsides. In some cases, it leads to calmness, while in others, it results in feelings of fear or even panic. Fear arises when an individual subconsciously assesses the situation as life-threatening. To inoculate soldiers against such situations, they should be familiarized with it, for example, by conducting sessions and systematically training unconditional reflexes, which can assist trainees in scenarios involving extensive use of incendiary weapons and widespread fires (Grabowoj & Kadjuk, Moskwa, 1983).

Damaging Impact on Equipment and Armament

As a result of the impact of incendiary weapons on combat vehicles and transportation means, they typically lose their functional properties completely. This is not so much due to direct damage to the vehicles, but because of the damage to the equipment that allows for their effective operation. The most flammable components include seats, covers, tarpaulins, tires, and other combustible items found in vehicle trunks and on combat vehicles. Such an initiated fire can quickly engulf the entire vehicle, and as a result, ignite the fuel tanks or even cause them to explode. This further facilitates the spread of the fire and introduces additional chaos.

The effectiveness of using napalm against armoured combat vehicles is clearly dependent on whether the vehicles are grouped close together, are in motion, or are stationary. Effective targeting of vehicles and their crews also largely depends on whether hatches and other openings are open or closed. With an active engine, the critical elements are the vents and openings through which air is drawn into the engine, as the fire can penetrate through them to the engine or the engine compartment. Inside the compartment, destruction occurs by burning through electrical wires and damaging plastic and rubber components. The engine can also be immobilized due to a lack of sufficient oxygen in the air.

Inside a tank with a turned-off engine and covered hatches, it is relatively safe; the most vulnerable to fire are the rubber components, and with open hatches, the combat compartment. Inside the combat compartment, the fire poses a threat by potentially igniting ammunition and explosives. During an ammunition explosion, both the crew and anyone nearby can be affected.

Of course, when discussing the devastating effects of incendiary weapons, one cannot overlook their impact on the natural environment. Incendiary agents interacting with the natural environment can cause fires. Depending on the terrain cover in the area of their use, there can be fires in settlements, forests, cereals, and grasses (Winogorskij, 1967).

International Humanitarian Law

Within the same legal framework, a regime of rules for the use of incendiary weapons is established, which undoubtedly causes "serious injury" with long-term consequences in the form of life-threatening or health-threatening burns, so it is possible to comply with the classification of these weapons as non-compliant Criterion of Article 23(e) of the Fourth Hague Convention (or other earlier customary norms). In contrast to chemical weapons, however, prewar states considered incendiary weapons to be legitimate means of warfare for two reasons (Bender, 1998, p. 290). First, it's not forbidden by any standard that directly references it. According to the principle established by the Permanent Court of International Justice in the Lotus case, State conduct not expressly prohibited by norms of international law is permissible (*Justia Law*, 1927, p. 23). Second, state practice shows that different types of grenades, bombs, hand grenades or flamethrowers were frequently used in World War I and World War II (Hannikainen, Hanski & Rosas, 1992, p. 50). Another topic is the use of incendiary bombs in so-called area explosions, which has attracted considerable attention due to the violation of the principle of distinction. Even shortly after the war, there was no investigation into whether incendiary weapons would in any way violate norms of customary international law. Only the air war in Vietnam and existing media coverage of the conflict, showing the consequences of the use of napalm, drew international attention to the legality of this weapon of war (Sossai, 2016, p. 198). A survey of the use of incendiary weapons conducted by the UN Secretary-General on behalf of UN member states in the mid-1970s revealed considerable variation in the applicable legal framework. While all countries have strongly condemned the use of aerial bombing in so-called indiscriminate bombing, which includes simultaneous attacks on civilians and military targets, there has been no such unity in the use of incendiary substances against military personnel. Some countries, such as the United States or the United Kingdom, have stated that napalm should not be used on military personnel in a manner that causes undue suffering. It was also emphasized that the provisions on air operations in the Petersburg Declaration are somewhat outdated, given the usual practice of using such weapons by air forces during World War II (Respect for Human Rights in Armed Conflict: Current Rules of International Law Regarding Air Operations) Certain weapons are prohibited or restricted. Survey prepared by the Secretariat of the United Nations General Assembly, 1973, A/9215, p. 143. The status of projectiles weighing more than 400 grams, such as incendiary bombs, remains unclear. The 1975 UN General Assembly Resolution (3255) recommended that Member States should consider whether napalm and other incendiary weapons should be included in a separate prohibitive or restrictive treaty regime because they failed to meet the requirements of "excessive suffering" (napalm and other incendiary weapons weapons) standards. Other incendiary weapons and all aspects of their possible use, General Assembly resolution 3255 (XXIX)). The wording of the resolution is telling in this regard and shows the conservatism of the international community (Asamoah, 1966, p. 107).

Limitations of Protocol III and required actions

The utilization of incendiary weaponry is governed by the Convention on Certain Conventional Weapons' Protocol III, which is the sole instrument worldwide to do so. This protocol prohibits the use of incendiary weapons on "concentrations of civilians" and "forests or other kinds of plant cover" (available at: https://ihl-databases. icrc.org/applic/ihl/ihl.nsf/). Nonetheless, Protocol III's legal and normative efficacy is restricted by two significant exceptions. The existing definition found in Article 1 of the protocol fails to include multipurpose munitions like white phosphorus. Instead, the definition is based on the intent behind the weapons' design, specifically their primary function of causing burn injury to persons or setting objects alight. This neglects to take into consideration the actual effects of said weapons. (Convention on Certain Conventional Weapons Protocol III on Prohibitions or Restrictions on the Use of Incendiary Weapons, adopted October 10, 1980, entered into force December 2, 1983, art. 1, available at: https://ihl-databases.icrc.org/ applic/ihl/ihl.nsf/).

Within the context of weaponry, it is important to note that some items may not be covered under conventional regulations. Take for instance, white phosphorus, a substance which has been engineered to produce a thick smokescreen. If utilized, however, it can leave devastating burns that have the potential to reignite when exposed to oxygen. This peculiar exception was raised in "Incendiary Weapons: Recent Use and Growing Opposition", a report published in November 2014 (available at https://www. hrw.org/ news/2014/11/10/incendiary-weapons-recent-use-and-growing-opposition). It high-lights that certain classifications of ammunitions may exclude themselves from convention due to their intended use, which is usually based on the manufacturer's or user's representation. The report "From Condemnation to Concrete Action: A Five-Year Review of www.hrw. Incendiary Weapons," published in November 2015, supports this view (available at: https://org/news/2015/11/05/ condemnation-concrete-action-five-year-review-incendiary-weapons). The restrictions imposed on incendiary weapons have nuanced differences depending on their method of delivery. While Article 2 of the Convention on Certain Conventional Weapons prohibits the use of air-based incendiary weapons on concentrations of civilians, ground-launched models have slightly weaker regulations. Specifically, ground-based attacks are permissible only if the military objective is unambiguously separated from the civilians present and reasonable care is taken to minimize bystander damage. Despite these provisions, research suggests that incendiary weapons – regardless of their launch method – lead to significant harm to non-combatants. In November 2014, a report titled "Incendiary Weapons: Recent Use and Growing Opposition" highlighted the inconsistency of protocols in different modes of delivery, indicating their inadequacy in ensuring civilians' protection. Despite previous concerns raised by civil society organizations, such as Human Rights Watch and PAX, the issue has recently resurfaced in a joint statement addressing incendiary weapons during the UN General Assembly First Committee in October 2021 (available at https://www.hrw.org/news/2021/10/08/ statement-incendiary-weapons-un-general-assembly-first-committee) and these groups continue to advocate for the improvement of protocols surrounding incendiary weapons. Incendiary weapons and those with incendiary effects have been condemned by the

International Committee of the Red Cross, who have emphasized the negative impact they have on individuals. The committee has urged states to reevaluate their stance on Protocol III regarding incendiary weapons, as documented in their statement at the CCW Meeting of High Contracting Parties in Geneva on November 14, 2019. To further support this stance, individuals who have undergone or treated individuals with burns have called for more comprehensive legislation pertaining to incendiary weapons. Released in November 2021, an open letter on incendiary weapons garnered support from several healthcare professionals and burn survivor organizations across 7 countries (available at https://humanitariandisarmament.org/initiatives/open-letter-on-incendiary-weapons/). As the sole agents with decision-making abilities in the CCW, it is of paramount importance that states take measures to curb any further harm to civilians. This also means they hold the sole power to ratify legally binding global treaties. Concerns have been raised by an increasing number of states regarding the employment of incendiary weapons. Nonetheless, there still remains an absence of tangible outcomes (Human Rights Watch, 2021, p. 2). It is essential for the High Contracting Parties of the CCW to commence a dialogue concerning the inadequacy of Protocol III, denounce the usage of incendiary weapons, and acknowledge the destruction they cause. Additionally, it is imperative to resolve the protocol's inconsistencies by embracing an effects-oriented definition and prohibiting the employment of both air and ground-based incendiary weaponry in areas of concentrated habitation. Ultimately, a universal ban on incendiary weapons would be highly beneficial for civilian populations. The consensus mechanism inherent in the CCW affords a select few states the power to obstruct forward momentum, effectively derailing efforts to revise the protocol and sparking debates on the very legitimacy of discussing it at all. Interestingly, the protocol had been tabled for discussion during the 2017-2018 CCW state party's meetings, yet it was stricken from the agenda in 2019 due to opposition from a handful of High Contracting Parties. It is imperative that these specific nations recognize the disproportionately severe humanitarian impact that incendiary weapons wield and yield to renewed discourse on Protocol III within the CCW. Within the realm beyond the CCW, there are opportunities for states to advance the delegitimization of incendiary weapons.

One illustration of this is evidenced by the proposal laid out by the European Parliament in December 2018 that outlined a roster of weapon types to be disallowed from the European Defence Fund, of which "incendiary weapons including white phosphorus" were listed. However, regrettably, this fragment was ultimately omitted from the final enactment as stated in 'The European Defence Fund and its Impact on the EU Defence Industry' report published in May 2021 (available at: https://vigeo-eiris.com/wp-content/ uploads/ 2021/05/European DefenceFund.pdf).

Incendiary weapons in combat operations

Incendiary weapons, like other types of conventional weapons, can be used to attack enemy troops and facilities. Their specific features, which offer the possibility of simultaneous attack on people, equipment, or objects in a particular area, attacking people, equipment, or objects by causing fires in the environment, and psychologically degrading the enemy's combat capability, should be taken into account. The properties of incendiary weapons influence their use principles.

Past wars' experience using incendiary weapons clearly indicates that positive results can be expected when adhering to principles like surprise, mass use, concentration of effort, thorough preparation, and collaboration.

Surprise means using incendiary weapons unexpectedly for the enemy, creating a situation that makes it hard for them to act. Achieving surprise involves covert preparation, choosing the right time and area for strikes, and using stealth for troop positioning. The element of surprise is enhanced by using tactics like covert artillery positioning, low-altitude air operations, and the use of cassette ammunition.

Mass use involves using incendiary weapons on a large scale in areas where they can be most effective. Concentrating effort means focusing on the most critical targets with all available incendiary resources. This approach prevents the scattering of forces and resources, ensuring favourable situations. The decision to use incendiary weapons is typically made by the commander in charge.

Thorough preparation largely determines the effectiveness of incendiary weapons. Each target must be meticulously assessed, which might require the expertise of specialists, including engineers, statisticians, architects, mathematicians, and even fire brigade experts. This preparation should determine target nature, surrounding terrain, vulnerability to ignition, meteorological conditions, and the incendiary ammunition's properties.

Collaboration means coordinating efforts of all forces equipped with incendiary weapons and synchronizing the use of incendiary weapons with troops that exploit their effects. This coordination ensures the maximum effectiveness of used incendiary agents and guarantees the freedom and safety of troops. Coordination matters are typically determined by the commanding level that plans both troop operations and the use of incendiary agents.

The destructive action of incendiary weapons is linked to the combustion process, during which complex physicochemical processes occur. Combustion, in its broadest sense, is referred to when a physicochemical process occurs, where, as a result of a rapid chemical reaction between fuel and oxidizer, a large amount of energy is released. In everyday life, the concept of combustion usually pertains to processes where substances combine with oxygen, accompanied by the release of light and heat. This process is most common and significant. For combustion and the occurrence of fire, the following are essential:

- materials capable of burning, known as fuels;

- pure oxygen or air;

- a specific temperature to which the fuel must be heated to ignite (Encyklopedia Powszechna, 1975, p. 437).

Usage of incendiary weapons in Ukraine

In Ukraine, a worrisome discovery of fresh instances of incendiary weapon use in 2014 has emerged. Human Rights Watch researchers, on field missions conducted in August and October of that year, were able to establish that incendiary weapons were utilized in both Ilovaisk (a town located 30 kilometres away from Donetsk) and Luhansk (a small village situated in the southern part of Donetsk). Three homes were engulfed in flames as residents of Ilovaisk testified to witnessing weapons that resembled celebratory fireworks falling onto the northwest section of the town on three separate nights. During a period of heavy fighting between Ukrainian forces and Russia-supported rebels, a resident recalls an attack that may have occurred after August 14th but the precise date remains elusive. During research, abandoned firing positions were discovered by Human Rights Watch in a field situated about 18 kilometres south-southwest of Ilovaisk. These positions contained several 122mm Grad 9M22S rockets which had misfired. Of note, these rockets had been equipped with incendiary warheads, specifically containing 180 hexagonal incendiary capsules. These capsules burn for two minutes and were identified as the 9N510 variant. The remnants of these incendiary capsules were also found in the field. During our time in Luhansk in August, locals reported a fireworks-like display that covered the village on the night of July 25-26. These events left remnants that were difficult to extinguish. Despite Human Rights Watch finding pieces of hexagonal capsules from incendiary weapons at both sites, it remains uncertain whether the fires that destroyed numerous homes were due to the so-called "fireworks" or Grad rockets launched during the same time. The perpetrators of the attacks in both Ilovaisk and Luhansk, however, have yet to be identified by Human Rights Watch. Interestingly, although white phosphorus did not play a role in the incidents in Ilovaisk and Luhansk, it has been utilized in the ongoing conflict in Ukraine in two distinguishable manners. An area formerly used as a battlefield was being cleaned up by a team linked to the rebel faction when they reported destroying white phosphorus rounds. There is no substantiated evidence for this report from Human Rights Watch, however, it is noteworthy as it highlights the risk associated with white phosphorus. This danger may not only manifest during an attack, but also afterwards if the rounds do not function as intended. Additionally, pro-Kremlin media outlets provided flawed evidence in order to support the accusations that Ukrainian forces utilized white phosphorus ammunition. It was evident from the incident that the Kremlin was relentless in discrediting the Ukrainian administration, while simultaneously acknowledging that the use of white phosphorus weapons was subject to widespread criticism. On June 11, 2014, a pro-Kremlin news source known as LifeNews reported that insurgents with pro-Russia tendencies alleged the deployment of white phosphorus weapons during an assault on a village adjacent to the former separatist fortress in Slovyansk. The

LifeNews agency appeared to validate this claim by releasing video footage of a phosphorescent material descending from above. Amidst accusations of using banned and forbidden weaponry, Russia vehemently criticized Ukraine on June 12. Specifically, Russia claimed Ukraine had deployed white phosphorus, spurring backlash from the international community. However, the allegations were quickly debunked by Human Rights Watch, whose experts asserted that no incendiary weapon was used in the attack in question. Despite the lack of evidence, the uproar over the use of white phosphorus demonstrates a growing consensus that such weapons are unacceptable. In recent times, particularly since 2022, the global community has observed a discernible decline in the incendiary weapons in the armed conflict in Ukraine. This trend, however, does not signal their complete eradication from modern warfare. Even with diminished deployment, the applications of substances like white phosphorus remains contentious issue. Notwithstanding the recorded decline in the use of these weapons, the topic remains a prominent subject of debate and security in scientific and diplomatic circles, emphasizing the unceasing relevance of the issue in international area.

International debate

Debate surrounding the utilization of incendiary weapons in regions such as Syria, Ukraine, Gaza, Afghanistan, Yemen, and other locations has been a recurrent topic at annual CCW meetings since 2010. Concerns about the use of white phosphorus and incendiary weapons have been publicly expressed by at least 36 countries, the European Union, and other international actors over the past ten years. The renewed momentum for revisiting Protocol III led to its inclusion in the CCW's Meeting of States Parties in 2017, as more nations began to support the cause. Sadly, this issue was not included in the agendas for 2019 and 2020 due to the pressure from a few countries, most prominently Russia. At their November 2019 meeting, CCW state parties did not have a specific agenda item dedicated to the topic at hand. Nevertheless, they managed to find ways to engage with it. During the "General Exchange of Views" or under the "Status of Implementation of and Compliance with the Convention and its Protocols" Agenda

Item 12, those who wished to speak were free to do so. Of the 17 states who participated in the discussions regarding incendiary weapons, almost all voiced concerns over their use and called for dedicated deliberations. The discussion on CCW Protocol III was obstructed by Russia and the United States, who prevented the establishment of dedicated time for deliberations on the topic in 2020. Nonetheless, the persistence of some states prompted the acknowledgment of requests to reintroduce an agenda item on the protocol in the final report, a departure from the previous year. A total of 13 states and the European Union expressed reservations or censured the usage of incendiary weapons targeting civilians since the onset of the Syrian conflict in 2019, as highlighted in the report. During the 2018 CCW, only a select number of voices were heard discussing the issue at hand, but the recent discussions have allowed for new perspectives to be heard. Out of the 13 states that participated, a significant 5 of them had not contributed to the topic previously. The main point of discussion among these states was the detrimental effect that incendiary weapons have on humanity. The notion of suffering caused by incendiary weapons remained a key concern for numerous delegations during the meeting. Austria expressed its deep concern over the use of such weapons and the suffering they cause. Likewise, New Zealand emphasized the dire consequences these weapons bring upon innocent civilians. The European Union remained horrified by the situation in Syria, which it believes has resulted in inexcusable human suffering. Additionally, Australia, Belgium, Chile, Costa Rica, Germany, Ireland, Jordan, Mexico, Sweden, Switzerland, and the United Kingdom united with these countries in their objection towards incendiary weapons. The subsequent report of the meeting reflected these opinions. During the 2019 annual meeting of the CCW, numerous delegations expressed apprehension about the rising instances of incendiary weapons being utilized against non-combatants. Consequently, they vehemently denounced their use against civilians or any other entity that is inconsistent with applicable International Humanitarian Law rules, such as those found in Protocol III. In total, 256 states spoke up and emphasized the importance of further discussions and preventive measures regarding incendiary weapons. Amongst these states, six called for Protocol III to be added to the agenda of the 2020 annual meeting. The eradication of Protocol III issues from the CCW agenda due to opposition by a single High Contracting Party, saddened the European Union, comprised of 28 member states and three others, prompting them to request for its inclusion in 2020. Meanwhile, Mexico, troubled by the utilization of incendiary weapons, felt that additional discussion was imperative considering the humanitarian conditions triggered by the deployment of these weapons' contrary to the responsibilities of parties and legal gaps that exist. Protocol III was lacking the attention it required, prompting New Zealand to urge its addition to the CCW's 2020 annual meeting. In addition, it suggested an informal gathering to ponder the universalisation, implementation, and adequacy of Protocol III within the context of the humanitarian concerns associated with incendiary weapons. This meeting wouldn't take place during the formal Meeting of States Parties but would provide scope for in-depth dialogues. Emphasizing the significance of the 2021 Review Conference, Switzerland suggested to consider Protocol III at the event. Furthermore, 261 International and nongovernmental organizations expressed their support for continuing the discussions. The International Committee of the Red Cross called for immediate accession to the protocol and encouraged states to provide reports on their policies and operational practices pertaining to the use of incendiary weapons. Such reports would then be used to better determine the efficacy of Protocol III and customary international law. The Protocol III discussion was subject to the input of several civil society organizations, such as Human Rights Watch, Mines Action Canada, and PAX. These organizations urged for significant deliberations and the implementation of improvements to the protocol. In the end, the official report incorporated the opinions of states parties who had advocated for further dialogue. According to the report, there were differing perspectives among delegations in terms of reviving a specific agenda item on Protocol III. Some argued that the item was essential, while others believed it was unnecessary. The need for amending the existing Protocol III and tightening its loopholes has been highlighted by a number of countries, which are concerned about the arbitrary and outdated distinctions within the protocol. The call for such amendments has been reiterated by at least four countries in 2019 alone. Austria, for instance, has suggested that strengthening Protocol III would help curb the insidious damage inflicted by weapons. Chile has pointed out the limitations of the current protocol, owing to its exclusion of multipurpose weapons and differing treatment of surface-launched and air-dropped incendiary weapons.

Conclusion

In the panorama of contemporary conflict, as exemplified starkly by the situation in Ukraine, the grievous toll exacted by incendiary weapons has emerged as an exigent point of international contemplation. The repercussions, especially when examining the deployment of agents such as white phosphorus, resonate with an acute intensity, emphasizing the imperativeness of enhanced legal structures to govern their use. This amplifies the collective responsibility resting upon the shoulders of the signatories of the 2014 CCW Meeting of States Parties. They must not only ardently condemn recent invocations of incendiary weaponry but also be invigorated towards a rigorous re-evaluation and fortification of Protocol III.

This urgent need for introspection and reform is further underscored by a proposition to integrate dedicated segments on incendiary weaponry within the concluding summaries of significant diplomatic engagements, a practice resonating with precedents set in earlier summits. Navigating the labyrinthine challenge of these especially lethal armaments, notorious for their indiscriminate and expansive maleficence, fundamentally requires an international consensus that champions amendments to Protocol III.

Current research offers a disquieting revelation: even in the face of overwhelming evidence highlighting the dire human conse-quences, the manufacture and strategic employment of incendiary weapons, notably white phosphorus, remain unabated. While Protocol III of the Convention on Certain Conventional Weapons is poised as the preeminent regulatory beacon, its present form exhibits glaring loopholes. These vulnerabilities in the existing protocol, alarmingly, provide tacit permissions, allowing the per-sistence of specific incendiary manifestations, often culminating in civilian tragedies.

Addressing these aforementioned loopholes demands an evolution in our regulatory lexicon. Transitioning towards an effects-oriented characterization is pivotal, particularly when contending with adaptable munitions like white phosphorus. Concurrently, the international legal framework must ardently advocate for, and institutionalize, prohibitive measures against the deployment of both airborne and ground-based incendiary apparatuses within demographically dense regions.

The discourse culminates in an emphatic and pressing overture to the High Contracting Parties of the CCW. This appeal encapsulates a multi-pronged objective: to initiate exhaustive and critical dialogues that holistically assess the contemporaneous adequacy of Protocol III, to articulate an unambiguous denunciation of the continued reliance on incendiary weaponry, and to acutely recognize the potential for devastation that such weaponry harbours. The recalibration of Protocol III must be firmly grounded in an effects-based framework, thereby encapsulating even multifaceted ammunition. Furthermore, the narrative should veer towards a comprehensive interdiction against incendiary operations in urban and populated environs. Only by addressing these vital tenets can we aspire to curtail the rampant, indiscriminate destruction wrought by incendiary weapons, thereby safeguarding the countless innocent lives ensnared in the throes of conflict.

References

Anadolu Agency (2016) UN concerned by reports of incendiary bombs in Syria. Available at: http://aa.com.tr/en/anadolu-post/un-concerned-by-reports-of-incendiary-bombs-in-syria/597342 .

Asamoah O. (1966) The legal significance of the declaration of the General Assembly of United Nation.

Austria (2019) Statement to the CCW Meeting of High Contracting Parties, Geneva.

Barnaby F. & Huisken R. (1975) *Arms uncontrolled*. London.

BBC News (2014) Ukraine crisis: Timeline. https://www.bbc.com/news/world-middle-east-26248275.

Bender R. (1998) *Launching and operating satellites: legal issues*. The Hague.

Boszkiewicz T. (1982) „Termiczne oparzenia wojenne". *Przegląd Obrony Kraju,* no. 1.

CCW Meeting of High Contracting Parties (2019) *Final Report CCW/ MSP/2019/9*.

Deane H. (1999) *The Korean War 1945-1953*. San Franciso.

Department of the Army Technical Manual (1984) *Military explosives*.

Encyklopedia Powszechna (1975) Spalanie.

Garon S. (2016) "Defending civilians against aerial bombardment: a comparative / transnational history of Japanese, German and British home fronts", *The Asia- Pacific Journal*, vol. 14. no. 2.

Grabowoj I. D. & Kadjuk W.K. (1983) *Zażigatielnoje oružije i zaszczita ot niego*.

Haldane D. (1998) "The fire-ship of Al-Salih Ayyub and Muslim use of Greek fire", in Kagay D. J., Villalon L. J. A (eds.) *The circle of war in the Middle Ages: essays on medieval military and naval history*. Suffolk.

Hannikainen L., Hanski R. & Rosas A. (1992) *Implementing humanitarian law applicable in armed conflicts: the case of Finland*. Dordrecht.

Human Rights Watch (2014) Incendiary Weapons: Recent Use and Growing Opposition. Available at: https://www.hrw.org/ news/2014/11/10/incendiary-weapons-recent-use-and-growing-opposition.

Human Rights Watch (2021) Incendiary Weapons: Assessing the Problem. Available at: https://www.hrw.org/sites/default/files/ media_2021/02/IW_final2.pdf.

Human Rights Watch (2021) Statement on Incendiary Weapons, UN General Assembly First Committee. Available at: https://www.hrw. org/news/2021/10/08/statement-incendiary-weapons-un-general-assembly-first-committee.

Convention on Certain Conventional Weapons Protocol III on Prohibitions or Restrictions on the Use of Incendiary Weapons, adopted October 10, 1980, entered into force December 2, 1983, art. 1. Available at: https://ihldatabases.icrc.org/applic/ihl/ihl.nsf/.

Protocol III on Prohibitions or Restrictions on the Use of Incendiary Weapons. available at: https: https://ihl-databases.icrc.org/en/ ihl-treaties/ccw-protocol-iii-1980.

International Committee of the Red Cross (1980) Protocol on Prohibitions or Restrictions on the Use of Incendiary Weapons (Protocol III). Available at: https://ihl-databases.icrc.org/en/ihl-treaties/ ccw-protocol-iii-1980.

Justia Law (1927) The S.S. Lotus (France v. Turkey) series A, Nr 10, 1927. Available at: https://law.justia.com/cases/foreign/international/1927-pcij-series-a-no-10.html.

Konupka F. (1962) *Walka Ogniem.*

Łabędzki J. (2007) *Szkolenie Obronne. Materiały do studiowania, z. 2: Broń zapalająca.*

Mexico (2019) Statement to the CCW Meeting of High Contracting Parties, Geneva.

MON (1974) Działanie wojsk w warunkach masowych pożarów.

Neer R. M. (2013) Napalm: an American biography.

New Zealand (2019) Statement to the CCW Meeting of High Contracting Parties, Geneva.

Nowak I. (1986) *Incendiary Weapons.* MON Publishing.

Nowikow M.W. & Koniukow W.I. (1959) *Środki zapalające i motacze ognia.*

Partington J.R. (1999) *A history of Greek fire and gunpowder.*

Patterson I. (2007) *Guernica and total war.*

Rogers C. (2010) The Oxford Encyclopaedia of Medieval Warfare and Military Technology, vol. 1.

Russian Envoy to UN Calls Attention to Reports Claiming White Phosphorus Use in Ukraine, Voice of Russia. Available at: https://www.tert.am/en/news/2014/06/13/chur/1317699

Sossai M. (2016) "Conventional weapons", in Linvoja R., McCormack T. (eds.) *Routledge handbook of the law of armed conflict*, New York.

Switzerland (2019) Statement to the CCW Meeting of High Contracting Parties, Geneva.

Szewczuk M.K (1961) *Zażigatielnyje sriedstwa i zaszczita ot nich.*

Tannenwald N. (2007) *The nuclear taboo: the United States and the non-use of nuclear weapons since 1945.* Cambridge.

The Royal Children's Hospital Melbourne (n.d.) Burns. Available at: https://www.rch.org.au/ trauma-service/manual/Burns/.

UN General Assembly (1975) Napalm and other incendiary weapons and all aspects of their possible use. Available at: https://digitallibrary.un.org/record/189997?ln=en.

United Nations General Assembly (1973) Respect for human rights in armed conflict: existing rules of international law concerning the prohibition or restriction of use of specific weapons.

United States (1946) *Strategic Bomber Survey (Pacific), Summary Report*. Washington: Government Printing Office.

Winogorskij, J.P. (1967) Lesnyje pożary i borba z nimi. *Vojennyj Viestnik*, vol 8.

CHAPTER 3

Artificial Intelligence on the frontlines: Overview of AI applications on the Ukraine battlefield and ethical considerations of using it in military operations

Irena Diamentowicz

Abstract

This chapter addresses the growing significance of Artificial Intelligence (AI) in modern warfare, particularly on the battlefield during the Ukraine-Russia war. The chapter explores how AI is used to enhance military capabilities, from providing security and intelligence to enabling autonomous weapons, drones, and decision-making technologies. The aim of the chapter is to present how AI is applied on the Ukraine battlefield, examining examples of its usage in combat and analyzing the ethical implications of AI in military operations. The research methodology includes a review of open-source materials, expert interviews, and analysis, recognizing that some data remains confidential due to the ongoing nature of the conflict. The findings suggest that while AI has the potential to revolutionize military strategies, its advancement also brings forth ethical dilemmas concerning the autonomy of weapons and the need for human oversight. The chapter also highlights the challenges of international regulations aimed at restricting AI's use in warfare, noting that some countries may not comply with such limitations, ultimately driving others to continue their own AI developments. The analysis suggests that the future of AI in warfare will continue to shape military dominance and the nature of war itself. Finally, the study raises questions about the implications of AI's increasing role in armed conflicts and the potential consequences for international security.

Keywords: Artificial Intelligence, Ukraine-Russia war, drones, intelligence, IT technology, resistance.

Introduction

Looking back on our history one can easily notice that the battlefield has always been thought as a direct and violent armed conflict. Today, the rapid development in IT technology has brought the drastic change in the perception of war. As one can see that on examples of Ukraine-Russia war, the enormous power on frontlines is in the hands of IT departments, the frontline bases are occupied by tech people in control of the technology that is deployed on the battlefield. The dominance is no longer on the side that has more strength in hands or bigger army with more powerful artillery but the dominance is on the side that is more advanced in the IT technology, whose machine learning is more progressive, and whose algorithms are more sophisticated. The war between Russia and Ukraine is being perceived by many as the first war where AI and autonomous weapons have such significant impact on the battlefield. This conflict is defined by many military and IT experts as the first war of IT technology in the history of humankind.

In the first section of this chapter the history of AI development in military is presented. The growing potential of AI is reflected in the statistics for the AI investments, and based on those statistics the forecast for the future of AI is being discussed. In addition, the most common modern applications for AI on the battlefield are explained. The second section concentrates on the live examples of the AI application in the ongoing Ukraine-Russia war. The potential dangers of further development of AI in military and most probable outcomes of it are highlighted. The last section raises the concern on the ethical considerations of using AI in warfare, discusses the attempts for banning or limiting the use of AI in the course of war and the potential consequences of this circumspection in the reality of war.

As the discussed conflict is still ongoing, the real data analysis and statistics for the effectiveness of AI use are not presented. The statistics on using AI, the effectiveness of using it and detailed descriptions of functioning of AI based technology are strictly state confidential, however, the contains the observation-based opinions of multiple IT and military experts.

The study are going to give answer to the following

questions: *What is potential future of the nature of war? What are the possible outcomes of the discussed conflict? What are the perspectives for imposing the limitations or even bans for AI application in military? Are those limitations reasonable peculiarly being aware that some states will not obey them?*

Background on Artificial Intelligence and its military uses

Artificial Intelligence (AI) is the concept encompassing the creation of computer systems capable of executing tasks typically associated with human intelligence. These tasks span a range from interpreting visual data and recognizing speech to making decisions and facilitating language translation. The growing sophistication of AI systems is increasingly demonstrating their practical value across various aspects of daily life. This encompasses everything from automated responses in customer service to the functionality of intelligent speakers. Particularly noteworthy is the advancement in using AI for autonomous systems and decision-making processes. Over time, it has improved to the point where it can now do more difficult tasks and has almost completely replaced the requirement for human input in some circumstances. AI has also a wide range of applications in the military, from data processing to combat simulation, it has enormous potential to assist war fighters in their duties, and military applications of AI have grown to be a hot topic of discussion. The usage of AI has advanced dramatically in the last year alone, both in terms of capabilities and accessibility, such as in the area of generative AI. To retain security and a competitive technical edge, the military must keep up with these innovations. It is important to consider how the military is using AI now and how it might be using it in the future because, as AI becomes more important, military superiority won't be determined by the size of an army but by the performance of its algorithms (Sentient Digital Inc, 2023).

AI "has the potential to be a transformative national security technology, comparable to nuclear weapons, aircraft, computers, and biotech," according to some observers. This might spark a military revolution and possibly redefine what it means to be defended. Some continue to be more cautious. They contend that concentrating on the far-off possibility of radical change "may well divert from developing a more nuanced understanding of slower and subtler, but equally significant, changes." The potential for AI to be used in the armed forces is unquestionably "present in all domains [...] and all levels of warfare," according to practically all defence experts (NATO Parliamentary Assembly, 2019).

Development of AI use in military

While tracing back the history of artificial intelligence it can easily be spotted how rapid was the development of AI in military.

- 1958: The Advanced Research Projects Agency (DARPA) is created by the US Department of Defence to support research and development of military and industrial initiatives. Additionally, research towards teaching computers to mimic basic human reasoning began in the 1960s.

- 1991: The American military employs an AI program to plan the transportation of supplies, personnel and to address other logistical issues. It employs intelligent agents to support decision support systems at the European Commands and U.S. Transportation, and it immediately began saving the military millions of dollars.

- 2014: The "Third Offset Strategy," unveiled by the US Department of Defence, asserts that the upcoming generation of warfare will be characterized by quick developments in AI.

- 2015: Steven Hawking, Elon Musk, and Steve Wozniak together with 3,000 researchers in AI and robotics appeal for a ban of the development of autonomous weapons.

- 2016: The budget for investment in AI, big data, and cloud computing is expanded from $5.6 billion in 2011 to $7.4 billion in 2016 by the U.S. Department of Defence. Sea Hunter, an autonomous unmanned surface vehicle launched in 2016. It can operate at sea without any crew member for long periods of time. But in 2017 DoD establishes the directive that requires a human operator to be in the loop when taking a human life by autonomous weapons systems.

- 2017: 22 nations demand complete ban on lethal automated weaponry as the result of the debate on a potential ban on „killer robots" at the United Nations' Convention on Conventional Weapons. A report from Harvard's Belfer Center suggests that AI may have impact that is comparable to nuclear weapons. China's "Next Generation Artificial Intelligence Development Plan" states a goal of "world domination in AI by 2030." (Military Embedded Systems, 2019).

- 2023: In light of China's ambition to be the global leader in AI area by 2030, the US Department of Defence is giving investments in this field top priority (Albon, 2023).

Forecast for AI use in military

Recent statistics about Artificial Intelligence (AI) are showing how potent it is. It is expected that the AI market will grow to almost $60 billion, the productivity of business will increase by 40%, and by 2030, global GDP will increase by $15.7 trillion because of AI. This is one of the reasons why national security has such an interest in AI, – if it is changing the world, it can also be a fundamental change for military applications. Military defence strategies and personnel can benefit from artificial intelligence as well as commercial businesses do (National Security Technology Accelerator, 2023).

Based on the research conducted by Vantage Market Research (presented on Figure 3.1), the Global Artificial Intelligence in Military Market valued at USD 6.76 Billion in the year 2022 is projected to reach a value of USD 17.60 Billion by the year 2030.

The growth is mainly attributed to:

- the increase in the development of AI integrated systems;
- adoption of cloud-based high-performance computers and applications;
- government initiatives and funding for the defence sector;
- increasing adoption of AI in AI-powered cybersecurity and growth in the threat of cyber-attacks;
- integration of quantum computing in AI;
- the rise in the acceptance of AI in predictive maintenance in military platforms;
- companies are exploring cost-effective and innovative hardware solutions that can efficiently improve the performance of AI also rhythm in the military sector (VANTAGE Market Research, 2022).

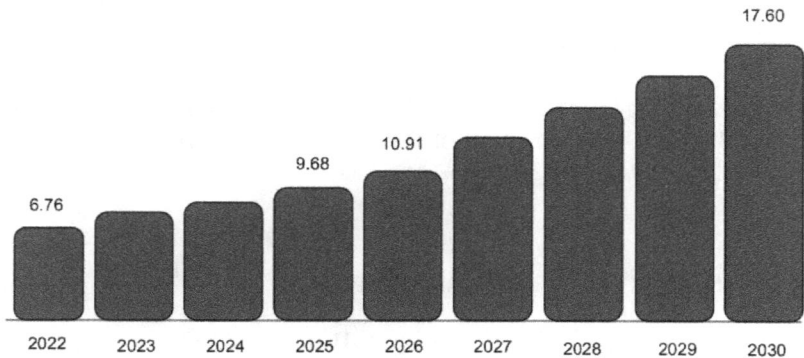

Figure 3.1. Artificial Intelligence in Military Market size, 2022 to 2030 (USD Billion)

Source: VANTAGE Market Research, 2022.

Based on the research, North America region holds the largest share of AI in Military Market. The growth of the region is mainly attributed to increasing investments in AI technologies by countries such as Canada and US in the region. Majorly US is gradually investing in AI systems to maintain combat superiority and overcome the risk of possible threats to computer networks, and the US is planning to increase its spending on AI in the military to acquire a competitive edge over other country.

The Asia Pacific is expected to witness the fastest growing CAGR in the Global AI in Military Market during the forecast period. The growth of this region is attributed to rapid military transformations and increasing demand for AI from emerging economies like India and China. The advancements in AI-based weapons in China have contributed to the growth of the market in this region (VANTAGE Market Research, 2022).

Overview on the use of AI in modern military operations

To preserve innocent lives on the battlefields, swift decision-making, adaptable strategies, and high levels of productivity are required. Such levels of efficiency require time, research, and resources. Due to its ability to handle computational complexity,

AI is ideal for use in military applications. Even under extreme pressure and stress, it can still run an algorithm. Additionally, because it lacks human emotions, it makes decisions far more quickly. Also, it can decide at a much faster speed... without human emotions (National Security Technology Accelerator, 2023).

Humans generally act in an environment of incomplete information. Sometimes, plenty of information is available. In military and strategic affairs, this is decidedly not the case. Political and military leaders must act in the well-known 'fog of war'. Information and decision support by AI systems is thus of high interest to military and strategic decision makers. Such systems can substantially increase both the pace and the quality of the processing, exploiting, and disseminating of information, as well as of human and machine decision-making (NATO Parliamentary Assembly, 2019). The volumes of data the military collects are huge and the computer assistance is required to process it. This is obviously much easier and more effective way to make use of the information. It analyses the data and presents it in an understandable and condensed way. This is how military leadership can make actionable decisions based on facts. The decisions are taken much faster and without any biases even under enormous stress and pressure (National Security Technology Accelerator, 2023).

AI-enabled information and decision support systems can, for example:

- vastly improve the reaction times of defensive systems against fast-acting weapon systems, such as hypersonic missiles, cyberattacks, or directed-energy weapons;

- deliver actionable information faster to decision makers, which could potentially deliver a decisive edge on adversaries;

- quickly discover cyber intrusions by detecting evasive malicious codes or by scanning for suspicious patterns of behaviour rather than for specific code; and

- help identify attempts to manipulate citizens through disinformation campaigns (NATO Parliamentary Assembly, 2019).

By employing AI in the military the benefits can be accrued in the following fields:

- Training: AI is widely used in military trainings, providing the military personnel with detailed individualized instructions. Military simulations are growing more realistic so that soldiers can get better prepared for the times of war.

- Threat Monitoring: the frontline is usually a very dangerous place, so AI is taking care of the safety of the soldiers identifying the dangers faster and giving the soldiers instructions on how to proceed in the given situation. The military vehicles of today are equipped with intelligent sensors. AI can be coupled with drones so that the information on threats and possible risks is transmitted to reaction teams immediately.

- Target recognition: it is much easier for the military to pinpoint the location of targets when the systems are equipped with AI. Using machine learning and collected data, the systems may track targets, analyse mission approaches, predict enemy activity, and aggregate environmental data (National Security Technology Accelerator, 2023).

- Warfare systems such as weapons, sensors, navigation, aviation support, and surveillance can employ AI in order to make operations more efficient and less reliant on human input. Taking away the need for full human control of warfare systems reduces the impact of human error and frees up humans' bandwidth for other essential tasks.

- Swarm intelligence for drone operations: These swarms of drones are inherently much more effective than a singular drone for several reasons. When a drone receives vital information, it can act upon it or communicate it to other drones in the swarm. These swarms can be used in simulations, as well as actual training operations and have the ability to make decisions in a variety of situations, with the swarm having an overarching objective but the individual drones having the ability to act independently and creatively towards it.

AI-controlled swarms of drones are actually programmed to act in the same manner that swarms of insects act in nature. They are able to communicate the distance, direction, and elevation of a target, as well as any potential dangers, just as a bee does. The ability to use AI-powered drone swarms to put this powerful collective intelligence to work towards military objectives represents a critical frontier in the military applications of AI.

Strategic decision making: AI's algorithms are able to collect and process data from numerous different sources to aid in decision making, especially in high-stress situations. It is also able to neutralize prejudices that may come with human input, with the caveat that AI may not yet have a fully developed understanding of human ethical concerns and there is a danger of AI learning from the biases that may exist in materials in its database. The combination of humans' ethical understanding and AI's quick analytical abilities can speed up the decision-making process.

Geospatial Intelligence: combines the human ability to envision, discover, record, comprehend, and track events on the ground by using sensors from drones, aircraft, and satellites. It's collected every day by private and government satellites and drones and with cell-phone cameras, and, when reviewed by trained analysts, it can reveal locational, environmental, military, and social information in denied areas of the world (Ard, 2022).

Data processing and research: AI can be helpful for quickly filtering through data and selecting the most valuable information. It can also aid in grouping information from various datasets. This can allow military personnel to identify patterns more efficiently, draw more accurate conclusions, and create plans of action based on a more complete view of the situation.

Transportation: AI is able to play a role in the transportation of ammunition, goods, armaments, and troops. AI can lower transportation costs and reduce the need for human input by, for example, plotting the most efficient route to travel under current conditions.

Casualty care and evacuation: soldiers and medics have to make decisions in high-stress situations, AI may assist as it uses an algorithm and large medical database that is able to access data containing medical trauma cases, which include diagnoses, vital sign sets, medications given, treatments, and outcomes. It then takes this data, combined with manually entered information in order to provide indications, warnings, and suggestions for treatment. AI is not qualified to make medical decisions but it can provide rapid analysis to give humans more information on which to base their decisions (Sentient Digital Inc, 2023).

AI Applications in the Ukraine-Russia war

Ukraine has always had a significant yet perhaps underestimated contribution to the international security system. The country is currently in the centre of a revived great-power rivalry that, as many observers say, will have significant influence on international affairs for many years. A critical turning point for European security was reached with Russia's invasion of Ukraine in February 2022, which marked a major escalation of the eight-year-old conflict that started with Russia's takeover of Crimea. Many defence and international policy specialists viewed the conflict as a significant strategic error by Russian President Vladimir Putin a year after hostilities started. Many observers believe that there is little chance of a diplomatic solution in the months to come and instead recognize the possibility of a deadly escalation, which might involve the use of a nuclear weapon by Russia. Ukraine's efforts to join Western political organizations, such as the European Union (EU) and the North Atlantic Treaty Organization (NATO), have been accelerated by the war.

In 2014 when Russia invaded Crimea and started supporting separatists in the southeast of the country in the Donbas region, Ukraine turned into a battlefield. This was the first time since World War II, that the European state annexed the territory of another. The Donbas conflict, the worst in Europe since the Balkan Wars of the 1990s, claimed the lives of over 14,000 people between 2014 and 2021. The conflicts clearly signaled the end of the United States' unipolar era of world domination and the beginning of a new era of great-power rivalry. Russia launched a full-scale invasion of Ukraine in February 2022 with the intention of displacing Volodymyr Zelenskyy's Western-aligned administration (Masters, 2023).

Using an array of weapons technology, the Russian military has pummeled wide areas in Ukraine with airstrikes and has conducted major rocket and artillery bombardments, resulting in large numbers of casualties. On the eve of the war, the military forces of Russia and Ukraine were very imbalanced in the Russians' favour with vastly superior firepower and troops (Euronews, 2022). Ukraine's military fought back with the equipment it had on hand: Soviet-era aircraft, tanks, armoured vehicles and artillery, and a scattering of Western-supplied weapons such as Javelin anti-tank missiles. Within weeks, shipments of military support from Ukraine's allies began to arrive and helped bend the trajectory of a war that already seemed to be going badly for the Russian military (Doyle, 2023).

Tens of billions of dollars of weapons have flowed from European and North American countries into Ukraine. Rifles. Bullets. Missiles. Artillery pieces. At first, those nations insisted that the weapons were "defensive," designed to help Ukraine fight off a marauding Russian Army that had stormed, unprovoked, across the border. One year later, as the battered but still potent Russian military prepares for a renewed offensive, the types of weapons heading into Ukraine have changed dramatically. Now, what's flowing in from the West are armoured vehicles, long-range rockets and advanced tanks.

The distinction between offensive and defensive weapons was always a little arbitrary. Now, though, Ukraine will have the ability to play offense and potentially drive Russia out of their country using some of the best weapons in the world. That means the stakes for all sides have increased substantially (Axe, 2023).

The use of AI in the ongoing war

Artificial intelligence and machine learning technologies are often costly, labour-intensive, and occasionally raise ethical controversies. However, they are being developed and utilized worldwide, particularly in times of war. Military applications of artificial intelligence and machine learning encompass surveillance and various types of intelligence gathering (geospatial, signals, etc.), humanitarian aid and disaster relief, command and control, logistics, and more (Bodniak, 2022).

In this chapter the reader will discover some of the key AI empowered technologies that have been and are in use in, as it seems to be, the most technologically advanced war that humanity has ever seen.

Unmanned Aerial Vehicle (UAV)

An unmanned aerial vehicle (UAV), commonly known as a drone, is an aircraft without a human pilot on board. The flight of UAVs may operate with various degrees of autonomy: either under remote control by a human operator or autonomously by onboard computers referred to as an autopilot. Drones originated mostly in military applications. The Global Drone Market Size Reached USD 7705.8 Million in 2021-2022. The Global Drone Market is to Reach the Value of USD 17520 Million by the End of 2030 (MarketWatch, 2023).

Drones are at the heart of precision fire. In 1970s the films were returned from droned by parachute. Starting from 1980s it was already possible to transmit data in real time but only on condition that the drone stayed in the right line of sight. Now the skies are thick with them: during the battle for Bakhmut there were 50 up at any one time. Around 86% of all Ukrainian targets are derived from drones, says T.J. Holland, the top enlisted soldier in America's XVIII Airborne Corps. In the first six months of the war, Russian artillery units that had their own drones, rather than relying on those from headquarters, could strike targets within three to five minutes of detecting them. Those without drones took around half an hour—with lower accuracy (Joshi, 2023). With the integration of Artificial Intelligence (AI), drones have become even more versatile, efficient, and accurate in performing complex tasks. AI algorithms enable drones to perform tasks such as object recognition, navigation, and data analysis with greater speed and accuracy (Akash, 2023).

In July 2022, the Ukrainian World Congress (UWC) and the Ministry of Digital Transformation of Ukraine signed a Memorandum of Cooperation to support the UNITED24 fundraising platform for the "Army of Drones" project. This is a complex program that involves drone procurement, delivery, maintenance and replacement, as well as pilot training. The project will raise funds to purchase professional unmanned drone systems for aerial reconnaissance. They are vital equipment that Ukraine's defenders need in order to fight off the Russian invasion. The Drone Army will allow the defenders of Ukraine to constantly monitor an enormous 2 470 km frontline and support an effective response to enemy attacks (Ukrainian World Congress, 2023).

The critical role of drones on the battlefield has helped fuel a wartime boom in domestic production. Over the past six months, the number of Ukrainian companies producing UAVs has increased more than fivefold. The full-scale Russian invasion of Ukraine is fast evolving into the world's first war of robots. In order to win, Ukraine needs large quantities of drones in every conceivable category (Fedorov, 2023).

Many of Ukraine's innovations in drone warfare were made in sheds, offices, small industrial premises, and in the trenches themselves. Soldiers jury-rigged drones to carry grenades or mortar bombs; engineers and designers helped refine the systems,

3D-printing harnesses that used, for example, light-activated mechanisms that could be fitted to the underside of DJI Mavic drones, turning the UAV's auxiliary lights into a trigger. Mykhailo Fedorov, Ukraine Minister for Digital Transformation recounts a recent visit to a base on the front line near Zaporizhzhia. "The base is like an underground IT company. Everything is on screens with satellite connections, drone videos," he says, with evident satisfaction. "The way people look and the way people talk, it's just an IT company. A year ago, before the invasion, you wouldn't see that." (Wired, 2023).

John Hudson and Kostiantyn Khudov in their article to Washington Post describe the following tests on drones they have witnessed: – a drone carrying a bomb lost contact with its human operator in an open test field in rural Ukraine after being attacked by electronic jamming gear. However, the drone drove toward its intended target and destroyed it instead of crashing to the ground. The drone relied on new AI algorithms that allow to stabilize the drone and keep it locked on a predetermined target while accounting for the electromagnetic interference that Russia is now frequently using in the war. A substantial improvement over current drones that monitor precise coordinates, AI capabilities enable the drone to accomplish its task even if its target moves. Such AI technology, under development by a growing number of Ukrainian drone companies, is one of several innovative leaps underway in Kyiv's domestic drone market that are accelerating and democratizing the lethality of unmanned warfare – especially crucial for Ukraine's outgunned military, which is fighting a larger and better-equipped Russian enemy.

More than 200 Ukrainian companies involved in drone production are now working hand-in-glove with military units on the front lines to tweak and augment drones to improve their ability to kill and spy on the enemy. The improvements in speed, flight range, payload capacity and other capabilities are having an immediate impact on the battlefield, enabling Ukraine to destroy Russian vehicles, blow up surveillance posts and even wreck parts of Russian President Vladimir Putin's prized Crimean Bridge in an operation last week involving explosive-laden naval drones (Hudson, 2023).

However, initially underestimated, the development of drone technology was quickly picked up also by the Russian side. The

Ukrainians, with a culture of startups and tech knowledge have been far ahead in this arms race, but with official support Russia network of artisanal drone makers is now catching up – and may exceed Ukrainian production. Russian volunteers have also been producing FPV drones. So far their efforts have appeared crude and smaller scale than their Ukrainian counterpart. That may be changing. Russian FPV drones have reportedly been highly effective during the Ukrainian counterattack, typically targeting vehicles while they attempt to traverse minefields (Hambling, 2023). AI empowered targeting system for UAVs was created by a Russian company manufacturing the Gadfly first-person-view (FPV) kamikaze drone as reported by its designer, Ivanov, in RIA Novosti on 14 August. The aiming system employs a neural network to analyse, identify and assist in attacking both stationary and mobile targets with an accuracy rate of 90%. The drone has already completed numerous tests and is prepared for the use in Ukraine for additional testing. A new version of the Gadfly was introduced in August 2023 with modifications to its electronics, rotors and some 'curiosities', according to Ivanov. It is possible that the 'curiosities' referred to included additional computers to enable the drone to use AI on the edge. The targeting of FPV drones is reliant upon a strong and stable connection that enables the user to direct the drone onto the selected target without the video stream being interrupted. If the Gadfly has been modified to carry a neural network with computer vision without negatively impacting its payload, it would theoretically make it more resistant to jamming and video stream interference. This in turn would make the drone more survivable and potentially more lethal. However, a lot depends on the training of the model and its ability to account for different target sets (Cranny-Evans, 2023).

According to AI researchers, military analysts and combatants the longer the war lasts the higher is the probability for the use of drones to detect, chose and attack targets without human assistance. Semi-autonomous attack drones are already being used in Ukraine, as well as anti-drone weapons empowered with AI. Although still unproven, Russia claims to have AI weaponry as well. This is just a matter of time before the AI weaponry will be deployed by one side or another. Ukraine's digital transformation minister, Mykhailo Fedorov, admits that the use of fully autonomous killer drones is quite natural and simply inevitable direction for the war. Lt. Col.Yaroslav Honchar, one of the founders of Aerorozvidka – combat drone innovation nonprofit, notes that machines are simply faster at processing information and making choices than humans are. He adds that, although for the time being, the use of fully independent lethal weapons is prohibited in Ukraine, there is possibility that this may change soon.

Autonomous AI can be obtained by Russia from Iran. While terrorizing citizens and destroying Ukrainian power stations, Iran's long-range, exploding Shahed-136 drones are not particularly intelligent however Iran claims to have more drones with AI in its expanding arsenal. According to the Western drone producers, Ukraine could easily transform its semi-autonomous weapons drones into completely independent drones in order to better withstand battlefield interference. Those drones include the US-made Switchblade 600 and the Polish Warmate, which both currently require a human to choose targets over a live video feed. AI finishes the job. The drones, technically known as "loitering munitions," can hover for minutes over a target, awaiting a clean shot. Using catalogued photos, drones can already identify objects like armoured trucks. However, there is debate over whether the technology is trustworthy enough to guarantee that the machines won't malfunction and kill civilians.

The amount of AI empowered drones is increasing. They have been exported by Israel for many years. When waiting for anti-aircraft radar to turn on, Israeli radar-killing Harpy may hover over them for up to nine hours. Beijing's Blowfish-3 unmanned armed helicopter is another such. Russia has been developing the Poseidon, an AI drone with a nuclear tip. A ground robot with a 50-caliber machine gun is currently undergoing tests in Denmark. However Honchar believes Russia, whose attacks on Ukrainian civilians have shown little regard for international law, would have used autonomous killer drones by now if the Kremlin had them.

The defence ministries of Ukraine and Russia were asked if they would use autonomous weapons offensively – and whether they would agree not to use them if the other side similarly agreed. Neither responded (Bajak, 2023).

CIA chief technology officer, Nand Mulchandani, has invented the term "software defined warfare". This term reflects the vision of software as an inevitable part of the defence architecture that is required for the future warfighting systems. The common idea of these concepts is genuinely networked battlefield, where information flows at the speed of light to link sensors to shooters as well as the full range of deployed forces and platforms. Not only the rapid advancement of technology was the source of this vision of future battlefield but also concerns over geopolitical competition and uncertainties on what near-peer rivals may be able to implement in the near future. The Russia-Ukraine war falls short of these future scenarios. Yet it clearly brings these futurist visions of warfare closer to reality. The conflict is an unprecedented testing ground for AI. In some areas, its use has been clear (Fontes & Kamminga, 2023).

Counter-drone systems

The importance of AI in developing anti-drone technology has become more significant as the expansion of UAVs constantly increases and the ability to detect and identify the drones in the real-time is one of the greatest difficulties. Contrary to usual radar systems, that, quite often, have troubles to differ between drones and, for example, birds, AI empowered systems can process huge volumes of data from numerous cameras, sensors, radars to be able to identify and track drones. By training the machine learning algorithms the system learns the specific traces of different drone models, therefore is able to distinguish between authorized and unauthorized UAVs. When the drone is identified, the AI anti-drone systems analyse its movements and predict its next steps, which, in result, makes it much more easy to remove the threat by deploying counter-drones, electronic jamming or employing directed energy weapons. Equipped with advanced sensors and AI algorithms, counter-drones can quickly detect, track, and neutralize rogue UAVs without the need for human intervention. This not only reduces the response time to potential threats but also minimizes the risk of human error in high-pressure situations (Frąckiewicz, 2023).

The AI powered anti-drone systems can also be found on the Ukraine battlefield. In his interview to Forbes magazine, the spokesman of Marss, a global technology company developing intelligent turnkey solutions to protect lives and assets, has confirmed that MARSS NiDAR system is helping to protect critical infrastructure and personnel in Ukraine, and is operating in a number of Ukrainian locations. MARSS –is a sophisticated complete packaged interceptor system which combines networked sensors and interceptors in box launchers. MARSS interceptors are quadcopters which destroy targets by ramming them. AI is a key part of the system: the interceptors have a smart vision system to recognize and track targets, and possess "dogfight maneuverability" to pursue and destroy incoming drones. The product of U.S. startup Anduril, Anvil, is also reported to be deployed in Ukraine. A suite of sensors powered by Anduril's AI Lattice system detects, locates and tracks threats, passing details to Anvil interceptors. The 12-pound Anvil has backwards-facing propellers and a reinforced frame to withstand the force of impact. With a speed of over 100 mph, Anvil will smash apart any drone, it hits, large or small. Launch boxes, each containing two interceptors, are positioned around the area to be defended (Hambling, 2022). In addition, Utah-based Fortem Technologies has supplied the Ukrainian military with drone-hunting systems that combine small radars and unmanned aerial vehicles, both powered by AI. The radars are designed to identify enemy drones, which the UAVs then disable by firing nets at them – all without human assistance (Bajak, 2023).

The advanced Israeli interception system "Smart Shooter" was installed on light aircraft and drones in Ukraine to fight down the Iranian kamikaze drones. This is a high-tech individual fire control system that employs radar to locate its target. With unmatched accuracy, it can identify, locate, and hit ground and air targets. It operates under the "one shot, one hit" tenet with the assistance of artificial intelligence (Tiwari, 2022).

It is also worth mentioning that apart from the western supplies Ukraine put also great emphasis on developing its own anti-drone technology. A Ukrainian-made long-range anti-drone rifle is one of the latest weapons to emerge from Russia's ongoing invasion of its neighbour (UAS Vision, 2022). The weapon, manufactured by Kvertus Technology in the Ukrainian city of Ivano-Frankivsk, has a range of up to three kilometers, or around 1.8 miles, and can operate for up to 30 minutes at a time, according to the company. While both Russia and Ukraine have used older anti-aircraft guns to shoot down drones, anti-drone guns disrupt drones without physically damaging them (Shoaib, 2023). As was stated by Kvertus' director of technology Yaroslav Filimonov, rifles are not damaging the drone. With communication lost, it just loses coordination and doesn't know where to go. The drone lands where it is jammed, or can be carried away by the wind because it's uncontrollable. Because the downed drones are unharmed, they give Ukrainian soldiers recovering them a wealth of potential intelligence (UAS Vision, 2022). Ukrainian forces can then take the drone and read its data to gain valuable information about it, such as where it came from and any images it might have taken, Filimonov said.

Zvook

Russian cruise missiles fly under Ukraine's radars, making them hard to shoot down. During World War I, this problem was solved by sharp-eared soldiers taking turns listening in to the sounds of incoming missiles. The Ukrainian military-tech startup Zvook used AI to replace the soldiers: its acoustic stations help Ukraine's air defence cover its "blind" areas.

In an interview with the Guardian, Defence Minister Oleksii Reznikov said Ukraine's air defence systems had increased their efficiency from 50% at the beginning of the war to 80% in December 2022. To break the country's successful defence, Russian troops constantly change their military tactics and use both Iranian Shahed-drones and missiles when launching strikes to exhaust Ukraine's surveillance systems.

The Ukrainian Army retaliates to the new challenges with strengthened complexes, which include modern high-tech systems. One of them is the Zvook AI project ("Zvook" is "sound" in the Ukrainian language) that helps identify and destroy Russian cruise missiles, helicopters, drones, and fighter jets at low and medium altitudes (Mukhina, 2023). The system uses Machine Learning. Zvook was trained on a sound database containing the sound of cars, trucks, flies, cows, human voices, and Russian missiles that account for about 0.1% of the data. The sound data originate mainly from the internet, data on enemy aircraft noise (mostly of close rocket fly-bys) were recorded with the help of the military. The Zvook algorithm identifies the aircraft within the mass of non-threatening sound and notifies the military in such a case. Engineers constantly train the algorithm and add more sound data to the database.

Hardware-wise, Zvook sensors consist of acoustic mirrors and a microphone. The mirrors focus the signal for the microphone to better discern the sounds. By comparing data from different sensors, Zvook can identify the type, as well as estimate a missile's speed and direction. The sensors are decentralized and operate as a network which accounts for a resistant effect and therefore make it harder to destroy (Andriushchenko, 2022).

Currently, the Ukrainian Air Defence Forces can predict the routes of cruise missiles by analysing tracks of previous missile strikes. Zvook, in cooperation with air defence, covers "blind" areas and conducts reconnaissance. Since the start of the Zvook project, the team has increased the accuracy of intercepting missiles from 50% to 100% by installing acoustic devices throughout Ukraine and collecting data from actual missile launches (Mukhina, 2023). As for now 64 acoustic sensors are installed and plans are to instal a lot more (Financial Times, 2023).

The team behind the project is built around people from technology, telecommunication, and the military. Its founders are co-founder of Respeecher, a world-(in) famous Ukrainian company that uses Artificial Intelligence to mimic celebrity voices, CEO of i3 Engineering, a Ukrainian company providing Smart Home solutions, a serviceman from the 125th brigade of the territorial defence forces (Andriushchenko, 2022).

Geospacial intelligence

Geospatial intelligence (GEOINT) has emerged as a critical tool in navigating through crisis situations, as evidenced by its role in the ongoing conflict in Ukraine. As the country continues to grapple with the challenges posed by Russian aggression, the use of GEOINT has become increasingly important in providing valuable insights into the evolving situation on the ground. This technology, which involves the collection, analysis, and dissemination of geospatial data, has proven to be indispensable in helping decision-makers better understand the complex dynamics at play in this volatile region.

One of the primary ways in which GEOINT has been utilized in Ukraine is through the monitoring of troop movements and military activities. By analysing satellite imagery and other geo-spatial data, analysts have been able to track the movement of Russian forces, providing valuable information on their locations, capabilities, and intentions. This has been crucial in helping Ukrainian forces prepare for potential attacks and respond more effectively to Russian aggression.

Moreover, GEOINT has played a significant role in assessing the damage caused by the conflict, particularly in terms of infra-structure and civilian casualties. By examining high-resolution satellite imagery, analysts have been able to identify destroyed buildings, damaged roads, and other signs of destruction, allowing for a more accurate assessment of the human and economic toll of the fighting. This information has been invaluable in guiding humanitarian efforts and ensuring that aid is directed to the area most in need (Frąckiewicz, 2023).

It has many advantages: Geospatial intelligence can monitor the conflict and the social changes in Ukraine in near-real time. It cannot be jammed like radio or television signals, or turned off like Russia has started to do with social media. It can also track humanitarian issues such as refugee flows and refugee camp con-struction, as well as systemic destruction of cities or Ukrainian infrastructure. It can also play a part in any future peace nego-tiations, treaty monitoring, and potential war crimes, as well as identify any environmental disaster that may result from the invasion (Ard, 2022)

SPRINGFIELD, Virginia – The National Geospatial-Intelligence Agency and The Global Disinformation Lab at the University of Texas in Austin have collaborated through NGA's open-source Tearline program to study displaced persons activ-ity from a GEOINT perspective in Ukraine. This research, begun in May, and continued in November, followed displaced persons activity in Ukraine through open-source reporting and commer-cial imagery. The research found that Russian media inflated the daily number of Ukrainian refugees entering Russia, by as much as thousands per day, and that Russia reallocated filtration site resources based on anticipated flows of displaced persons.

According to the U.S. State Department, Russian officials and proxy authorities in Russia-controlled areas of Ukraine are undertaking a monumental effort to "filter" the population as a means of suppressing Ukrainian resistance and enforcing loyalty among the remaining population (National Geospatial-Intelligence Agency, 2022).

Satellite data has been employed by both civilian and military entities in unprecedented ways throughout the conflict in Ukraine. On March 1, 2022, the Ministry of Digital Transformation of Ukraine appealed to global remote sensing firms and organizations to provide synthetic-aperture radar (SAR) data to support the Ukrainian Armed Forces. SAR technology is a form of EO data that is particularly useful in the context of war because it can penetrate cloud cover and provide imagery in different kinds of weather conditions. Space companies such as Planet, Maxar Technologies, MDA, and the Finnish microsatellite manufacturer ICEYE are all playing a critical role in boosting Ukraine's defence capabilities (Bosc & Haines, 2022).

One of the leading providers of GEOINT for both defence and commercial purposes is Maxar Technologies, which has a long history of working with the US Department of Defence. Maxar has been releasing imagery of Ukraine throughout the war, even from before the invasion began when Russian troops were massing in concentration areas over the border. From satellite images of those troops on the border, to columns of armour and tanks moving through the countryside towards Kyiv, a convoy 64 km (40 miles) long attempting resupply, mass graves outside Mariupol, and the town's theatre, bombed into oblivion despite satellite imagery clearly showing the word 'children' written into the ground outside. And the wider world and media, too, have, like never before, also had access to the same GEOINT imagery as the military.

A strategically-contested aspect of the conflict in Ukraine has been its agriculture, specifically its wheat crop, and satellite imagery has provided vital GEOINT in this regard crucial for Ukraine's Government of world markets. Earth-observing satellites are constantly acquiring imagery across Ukraine's, currently, daily-changing landscape and analysts are deciphering the impacts of human conflict on the country's built, agricultural and natural environment. NASA's Harvest research team, for example, has been using GEOINT imagery and economic data to track how the

Russia-Ukraine conflict is disrupting the global food system. In the early days of the conflict, food security specialists wondered if Ukrainian farmers would be able to harvest the wheat and barley they had planted the previous autumn – food for the population and Army, and income to buy more weaponry... or not.

The NASA Harvest team combines satellite observations and modelling to assess the planting, growth, and harvest of key commodity crops. NASA Harvest's analysis showed that 94% of the winter crop was harvested, including 88% of winter crops in areas not controlled by Ukraine. And while the UN-brokered Black Sea Grain Initiative freed up vessels from a few Black Sea ports for some 5.4 million tonnes of Ukrainian grain to reach global markets, GEOINT and economic data analysis showed that Russia benefited from a large amount of the 26.6 million tonnes harvested. This represents a financial loss to Kyiv of at least USD 1 Bn. This detailed analysis would not have been possible without the use of high-quality images from space (Guest, 2023).

As the conflict in Ukraine continues to evolve, the role of geospatial intelligence in navigating through crisis situations is likely to become even more pronounced. By providing timely, accurate, and actionable information, GEOINT has the potential to significantly enhance decision-making and improve the effectiveness of military, humanitarian, and diplomatic efforts (Frąckiewicz, 2023).

Facial recognition technology by Clearview AI

The global facial recognition market grew from $5.43 billion in 2022 to $6.28 billion in 2023 and is expected to grow to $11.35 billion in 2027. The growing importance of the surveillance industry is expected to drive the facial recognition market. The increasing incidences of cyberattacks, terrorist activities, and identity thefts across the globe have increased surveillance (The Business Research Company, 2023).

Clearview, facial recognition software, allows a law enforcement customer to upload a photo of a face and find matches in a database of billions of images it has collected. It then provides links to where matching images appear online. It is considered one of the most powerful and accurate facial recognition companies in the world (Derico, 2022). This software has been deployed on a massive scale in Ukraine-Russia war. This is the first military conflict where this kind of IT solutions are in use. The authorities of Ukraine are using Clearview AI facial recognition tool since March 2022. The software allows to identify dead soldiers, to uncover Russian assailants and combat misinformation (Fontes & Kamminga, 2023).

Clearview company has listed the benefits and examples of using facial recognition tool during the war in Ukraine:

- Checkpoint security: clearview AI database contains over 2 billion publicly available images from the Russian social media site, Vkontakte. This was one of the greatest sources for identifying potential Russian soldiers and infiltrators at checkpoints.

- Identifying & detaining Russian infiltrators: M.Fedorov, Ukraine Minister of Digital Transformation gives a very interesting example of Clearview AI use. As he says, one of the patients in a Ukrainian hospital claimed to be a Ukrainian soldier who suffered on post traumatic amnesia. The doctor sent his pictures to the authorities and the patient was identified in a matter of minutes. His social network profile was found, which clearly showed that that patient was a Russian soldier. He was brought to responsibility.

- War crime investigations: photos and videos are checked for social-media accounts. According to Ukrainian police, around 7500 suspects have been identified till current moment. Indictments have been issued against 127 Russian military personnel.

- Identification of deceased people was also part of the campaign on informing the Russian society, especially Russian families about their deceased family members. At the beginning of the war Russian propaganda claimed that "no one dies" in the "special operation" in Ukraine therefore, with this campaign Ukraine tried to dispel the Russian myth to make the Russians aware of the reality of ongoing war. Identification of the dead Russians provides an opportunity to obtain information like who exactly was in this area about the unit and the crimes committed (Clearview AI, n.d.).

Since the beginning of the full-scale war in Ukraine, Clearview software has helped to significantly improve the effectiveness of the fight against crimes under the jurisdiction of the border agency. In particular, with the use of Clearview AI, border guards were able to identify more than 10,000 people, including: captured citizens of Ukraine; persons involved in the illegal transportation of children from the TOT (Temporarily Occupied Territory of

Ukraine) to the Russian Federation; servicemen of the Russian Federation and members of the Russian National Defence Force; Russian propagandists who provide material support for the occupying forces and are involved in the information war against Ukraine; collaborators and traitors of Ukraine; persons involved in criminal and administrative offenses, etc. (Ministry of Internal Affairs, 2023).

In the interview to AIN Capital – an online publication dedicated to the growing Central and Eastern European tech ecosystem – the CEO of Clearview, Hoan Ton-That is saying that Ukrainian Board Guard Service were able to identify 50 people involved in the recent human trafficking of Ukrainian children put up for adoption in Russia, more than 700 civilian prisoners of war, and over 3,900 servicemen of the Russian Federation. The National Police of Ukraine also worked a lot with Clearview to identify war criminals. In previous wars, there was little or no way to identify who the person committing war crimes was. Now we have photo and video footage. So for the first time, there is an option to run the search and find a VK profile or other related information. And after the verification, they know who did this. To the question on the accuracy of the technology Hoan Ton-That answers that there were photos of dead Russian soldiers with faces and bodies mutilated to the point of being unrecognizable but still, Clearview was able to match those with social media profiles.

There is another thing to it because with this level of deanonymization if you are on the Russian side, you might just start thinking – do you really want to go to war if they know who you are? This might be the very first-time war criminals have nowhere to hide.

Also, Clearview could be used to find missing and kidnapped kids. We have a feature that gives an alert when a particular missing child has another photo appears on the internet (Yarova, 2023).

Ukraine is the first major conflict that we've seen the use of facial recognition technology in such scale, but it is far from the last," Peter Singer, a security scholar at New America, a think tank in Washington said. "It will be increasingly hard for future warriors to keep their identity secret, just as for regular civilians walking down your own city streets" (Hill, 2022).

Who is winning the technology battle war in Ukraine?

Today's Ukraine is often described as a testing ground for new military technologies, but it is important to stress that Ukrainians are active participants in this process who are in many instances leading the way with new innovations. The scale of Russia's invasion and the intensity of the fighting mean that concepts can often go from the drawing board to the battlefield in a matter of months or sometimes even days. Luckily, Ukraine has the tech talent and flexibility to make the most of these conditions.

Russian preparations for the current full-scale invasion of Ukraine have been underway for much of the past two decades and have focused on traditional military thinking with an emphasis on armour, artillery, and air power. In contrast, the rapidly modernizing Ukrainian military has achieved a technological leap in less than twelve months. Since the invasion began, Ukraine has demonstrated a readiness to innovate that the more conservative Russian military simply cannot match (Fedorov, 2023).

The war in Ukraine is showing to be a unique environment for testing AI. Maj Gen (Retd.) Robin Fontes asserts that Ukraine is a laboratory where the future form of warfare is being made. And this is not a marginal activity, according to him, this implacable and unparalleled attempt to refine AI-enhanced and AI-enabled systems for immediate deployment. And this is the way for AI warfare in the future. They have pointed out how aerial systems, autonomous ships, undersea drones for mine hunting, and uncrewed ground vehicles have been deployed and how the combined use of aerial and sea drones in the October attack on Russia's Black Sea flagship vessel, the Admiral Makarov, was perceived and implemented. AI is heavily used in systems that connect target and object recognition with satellite imagery.

In addition, this war is also unique from a different perspective – foreign geospatial intelligence companies express outstanding willingness to support Ukraine with enabling AI-enhanced systems that transform satellite imagery into intelligence, surveillance, and reconnaissance advantages. Palantir Technologies, Planet Labs, BlackSky Technology, and Maxar Technologies provided its AI software to analyze how the war has unfolded, understand troop movements, and conduct battlefield damage assessments. As per request from Ukrainian government and defence forces, parts of the data are shared almost instantly with them (Nanda, 2023). Elon Musk's SpaceX company provided Ukraine with the access to Starlink – satellite internet constellation. This means that soldier has the connectivity and intelligence that were restricted only for the brigade commanders in the past. No complex equipment is required. One can use his regular laptop to watch the live feed of the battlefield, complete with Russian jets on the move.

At the tactical level, Russia has waged a form of networked warfare. After a sluggish start, it now uses computerised command and control to knit together drones and artillery batteries. It also has good human intelligence (i.e., spies) and satellites of its own. But the war has shown that intelligence is not enough: you also have to use it well. Russia's air force failed to pick off Ukraine's air defences in the first days of fighting not just because of poor training and preparation, but because it took two days, and sometimes longer, for Russian military intelligence to send target information to a command centre in Moscow and onwards to warplanes. The targets were typically long gone by then. Even now, 16 months on, the Russian army struggles to find and strike moving targets.

Ukrainian planners, in contrast, waged "data-driven combat" at a level of "speed and precision that NATO has not yet achieved", concludes a report by Nico Lange, a former chief of staff at Germany's defence ministry. Firms such as Palantir, an American tech company, have used cutting-edge AI to help Ukraine find high-value targets. But data-driven warfare can be quietly prosaic, too. A Ukrainian police officer explains that last year his units were locating Russian troops simply by intercepting 1,000 conversations a day (the figure is now higher). If they found a general, the details were shared in an ad hoc WhatsApp group. "We were connected to the people who were literally bombing" (Joshi, 2023).

Mykhailo Fedorov, Ukraine's Minister of Digital Transformation acknowledged that Russia was also aware of the importance of technology on the battlefield, and was actively developing and improving its own. Every day, there are new UAVs on the battlefield from both sides and it is visible what kind of drones Russia have. Ukraine side receive, disassemble and study those drones. He said the government was planning investments in new technology projects to encourage further competition and innovation (Arhirova, 2023).

"We have to be innovative because we would like to survive" – the head of the Victory Drones Volunteer project said. Russia is also very strong in battlefield technology for many of the same reasons. It has that long tradition of technical education, and it's used it well on the battlefield. Russians were much better prepared and equipped for this war. The only thing we can do as a counter-action is to use resources we have in more efficient ways. Unfortunately, the Russians have superiority, not only in fighter jets, but they have the superiority in technologies. First of all, because they have supply chains from China. And the second point, western technologies in Russian rockets, in Russian missiles, in Russian UAV systems. They also have used drones in very large numbers, whether it's reconnaissance or attack. They've taken vast numbers of Iranian-built, low-cost attack drones and sent them flying into Ukrainian cities. They have not been vastly successful at hitting targets, necessarily. But they are successful at depleting Ukraine's more expensive air defence systems (Financial Times, 2023).

Everyone is learning from the war, including Russia. Consider infantry tactics. Russia now sends small packets of "disposable" infantry, a handful of men at a time, often under the influence of amphetamines, to "skirmish…until killed", exposing Ukrainian positions. Larger groups of better-trained assault infantry then move in, backed by armour, mortars and artillery. If a position is taken, it is fortified within 12 hours. "The speed with which Russian infantry dig, and the scale at which they improve their fighting positions, is noteworthy," said Mr Watling, Senior Research Fellow for Land Warfare at the Royal United Services Institute and Mr Reynolds, Research Fellow for Land Warfare at RUSI. Russian engineers have built fortifications and bridges and laid minefields.

Russian gunnery is improving. Drones can be connected to artillery batteries via the Strelets computer system, letting Ukrainian targets be struck within minutes of detection. One tactic, say the authors, "is for the Russians to withdraw from a position that is being assaulted and then saturate it with fire once Ukrainian troops attempt to occupy it." Such "fire pockets" are one of the biggest risks to Ukraine's counter-offensive. Russian tanks also make better use of camouflage. They fight at dusk and dawn when their temperature signature is less obvious. Russia's reactive armour, which explodes outward, has "proven highly effective", with some tanks surviving multiple hits.

Russian air defences, much derided on social media, are increasingly connected, allowing them to share data on incoming threats. They are shooting down a significant proportion of strikes by GMLRS – the GPS-guided rockets, fired from American HIMARS launchers – that played havoc with Russian headquarters last year. Russia has been pulling command-and-control centres farther back, dispersing and hardening them and wiring physical cables to brigades closer to the front. Meanwhile Russia's air force, an irrelevance for much of the war, is making more use of glide bombs, in which a guidance kit is fitted to older "dumb" munitions. That poses a growing threat to Ukrainian troops moving south.

Russia's army is beset by problems, including poor recruitment and a lack of modern equipment. Its elite units have been decimated. It is unlikely to have serious offensive capability for the rest of this year. The recent short-lived mutiny of Yevgeny Prigozhin's Wagner mercenaries will not have boosted morale. Yet the army remains a formidable obstacle. "There is evidence of a centralised process for identifying shortcomings in employment and the development of mitigations," conclude the RUSI authors. Major-General Viktor Nikolyuk, in charge of army training for Ukraine, says: "It is impossible to say that the enemy does not know how to fight. We learned a lot from them, too, [on] tactics" (The Economist, 2023).

As announced by Mykhailo Fedorov, now they are working on the project Army of Robots. This is not only the technology that does the reconnaissance and can hit the target but it is the technology that can shoot, technology that can evacuate from the battlefield. Today the goal number one is to produce enough technology to win the war but in the future Ukraine will be able to export the military technology all over the world. Many technical products related to Miltech have been created so far and not just created, but also tested and polished through the course of war. This is the formula that will allow Ukraine to maintain the interest of the western investors because they will see there are results on the battlefield there is demand for these products and they need to invest because there is market.

The Ukrainian government aspires to turn their country into something like Israel, with super sophisticated military technology. However, the reality is that Ukraine is decades behind Israel in terms of building up the depth of scientific and technological knowledge, or the financial ecosystem that nurtures these companies, or the exchange of scientific knowledge with partners, particularly the United States (Financial Times, 2023).

Lessons from the war: While Russian forces continued to mismanage their technology, Ukraine was mastering theirs. This provides the key lesson for the West. The mere existence of cutting-edge technology and high-tech weapons does not provide a military with a guarantee of success. Western militaries can look to Ukraine for an example of how to integrate technologies and weapons to remain agile and adaptable. At the same time, they can look to Russia as an example of the dangers of lack of competence and poor command and control.

Ukraine is a window into future warfare. The next wars will also hinge on which side can better use all levels of technology and integrate them into a coherent strategy. Technology is a game changer, but only for those who make the best use of it (Jones, 2023).

Ethical Considerations for using AI in Warfare

The decision to use a lethal weapon in battle against combatants has always been a decision made by a human being. That may soon change. Modern advancements in artificial intelligence, machine image recognition and robotics have poised some of the world's largest militaries on the edge of a new future, where weapon systems may find and kill people on the battlefield without human involvement. Russia, China and the United States are all working on autonomous platforms that pair weapons with sensors and targeting computers; Britain and Israel are already using weapons with autonomous characteristics: missiles and drones that can seek and attack an adversary's radar, vehicle or ship without a human command triggering the immediate decision to fire.

Under what circumstances can and should militaries delegate the decision to take a human life to machines? It's a moral leap that has raised fundamental questions about the nature of warfare and that military planners, human rights organizations, defence officials, research analysts and ethicists have yet to reach a consensus on (Atherton, 2018).

International powers need to start regulating AI warfare now, before it begins to dominate the battlefield. The consequences of lethal AI's unrestrained use, in the absence of rules and norms governing it, would be highly destabilizing. AI has, to varying degrees, existed in weapons systems for many years. The United States' armed drones, a hallmark of the "War on Terror," are a familiar example. However, a key characteristic of these systems is their limited level of autonomy. Humans are deeply involved in the decision-making process, providing guidance on targeting and authorizing attacks. The issue begins when AI weapons systems are developed to operate with greater autonomy, independently making decisions. This degree of advanced AI is still off in the future, but the issues it could cause are already discernible. Given a mission and let loose, autonomous weapons will be suitable for tasks such as assassinations, subduing populations or certain ethnic groups, and destabilizing nations (Knipfer, 2017).

Fully autonomous weapons would be a fundamental paradigm shift in warfare. In deploying fully autonomous weapons, militaries would be introducing onto the battlefield a highly lethal system that they cannot control or recall once launched. They would be sending this weapon into an environment that they do not control where it is subject to enemy hacking and manipulation. In the event of failures, the damage fully autonomous weapons could cause would be limited only by the weapons' range, endurance, ability to sense targets, and magazine capacity. Additionally, militaries rarely deploy weapons individually. Flaws in any one system are likely to be replicated in entire squadrons and fleets of autonomous weapons, opening the door to what John Borrie described as "incidents of mass lethality." This is fundamentally different from human mistakes, which tend to be idiosyncratic (Scharre, 2018).

From the global perspective, discussions of AI-enabled lethal autonomous weapon systems have called for pre-emptive global bans on these advanced technological weapons. Due to the ethical concerns regarding the lethal autonomous weapon systems. Opponents of the lethal weapon systems highlight numerous ethical challenges such as operational risks, disintegrated accountability, and the proportionality of use during armed conflict. Correspondingly, entities of more than "30 countries and 165 nongovernmental organizations" have endorsed a global ban. Although the US Government does not currently support a ban on lethal autonomous weapon systems, senior leaders of the government may see the criticality and utility of maintaining the capability of lethal autonomous weapon systems through the virtues lens (Steinhoff, 2023).

As part of its digital strategy, the EU wants to regulate artificial intelligence (AI) to ensure better conditions for the development and use of this innovative technology. In April 2021, the European Commission proposed the first EU regulatory framework for AI. It says that AI systems that can be used in different applications are analysed and classified according to the risk they pose to users. The different risk levels will mean more or less regulation. Once approved, these will be the world's first rules on AI. Parliament's priority is to make sure that AI systems used in the EU are safe, transparent, traceable, non-discriminatory and environmentally friendly. AI systems should be overseen by people, rather than by automation, to prevent harmful outcomes (European Parliament News , 2023).

AI offers numerous benefits to be taken advantage of, yet there are also certain challenges and potential risks due to the specific features of the technology and how it can be used in different contexts. This duality of AI, the balance of advantages and risks, may be especially amplified in a military or defence context. Just as AI can be used as a tool to optimize the lethal capacity of systems, as in the case of kamikaze drones, it can also be used to save the lives of civilians and soldiers and defend against numerous threats, including physical and cybersecurity attacks.

Military applications of AI are often deployed in high-stake situations, introducing new factors that need to be accounted for or raising the bar of existing ones. For instance, there are not only ethical risks surrounding human rights, moral responsibility and accountability, but also significant operational and domain-specific risks such as the reliability of such systems in extreme situations and the severe consequences should they be vulnerable to attacks. In perhaps no other domain is it more crucial to rely on safe, robust and trustworthy AI systems.

Yet, today, there are no formal certification processes,

universally applicable standards or governance frameworks assuring such characteristics of AI in military contexts. International discussions are increasingly focusing on those issues more seriously. The REAIM2023 conference on Responsible AI in the Military Domain, organised by the Government of the Netherlands and co-hosted by the Republic of Korea in February, marked an important step towards international discussion. The conference attracted participants from over 80 countries, various stakeholders and institutions to begin discussion about the challenges of AI in military uses. Governance frameworks for responsible application of AI in the military domain was among the areas of focus. During its presentation on this topic, the European External Action Service (EEAS) highlighted the lack of international, multilateral agreements or any existing governance framework that covers the use of AI in the military. Although countries like France and the US are exploring the military use of AI at a strategy level and NATO has already adopted its own AI Strategy, most countries have not taken such steps yet and current efforts are still far off from comprehensive multilateral frameworks (such as the UN Treaty on the prohibition of nuclear weapons, for instance) which are crucial for ensuring continued global safety, peace and security (Rönnback, 2023).

Over 3,000 robotics and artificial intelligence experts have called for a ban on offensive autonomous weapons, and are joined by over sixty nongovernmental organizations (NGOs) in the Campaign to Stop Killer Robots. Science and technology luminaries such as Stephen Hawking, Elon Musk, and Apple cofounder Steve Wozniak have spoken out against autonomous weapons, warning they could spark a "global AI arms race." Can an arms race be prevented, or is one already under way? If it's already happening, can it be stopped? Humanity's track record for controlling dangerous technology is mixed; attempts to ban weapons that were seen as too dangerous or inhumane date back to antiquity. Many of these attempts have failed, including early-twentieth-century attempts to ban submarines and airplanes. Even those that have succeeded, such as the ban on chemical weapons, rarely stop rogue regimes such as Bashar al-Assad's Syria or Saddam Hussein's Iraq. If an international ban cannot stop the world's most odious regimes from building killer robot armies, we may someday face our darkest nightmares brought to life (Scharre, 2018).

AI technology poses challenges for arms control for a variety of reasons. AI technology is diffuse, and many of its applications are dual use. As an emerging technology, its full potential has yet to be realized—which may hinder efforts to control it. Verification of any AI arms control agreement would also be challenging; states would likely need to develop methods of ensuring that other states are in compliance to be comfortable with restraining their own capabilities. These hurdles, though significant, are not insurmountable in all instances. Under certain conditions, arms control may be feasible for some military AI applications. Even while states compete in military AI, they should seek opportunities to reduce its risks, including through arms control measures where feasible (Scharre, 2022).

In his article to European AI Alliance, Head of The Expert Committee on Artificial Intelligence of Ukraine in 2020-2022 Vitaliy Goncharuk, discusses how the war and its real challenges have influenced his understanding of the regulation of AI, especially taking into account such a radical event as a war.

In December 2020, the Cabinet of Ministers of Ukraine approved the AI development concept and its implementation plan. This was preceded by a year of public discussions of this document and significant changes to the original document, as civil society organizations and activists mainly defended human rights, privacy and ethics, and not issues of security or the use of AI in case of war. The problem was that among the experts who were trying to regulate AI, there were a lot of experts on ethics, human rights and privacy, and very few of those who practically understood how AI works, its limitations, etc.

During the development of the document, a lot of incomprehensible (unqualified) people in AI tried to wedge themselves into the process. All these characters in every possible way delayed the adoption of the document for various reasons...mainly based on ethics and human rights. With the beginning of the war, many of these people declared a public pro-russian position. Now we can clearly say that these were Russian agents, whose goal was simply to reduce all normal initiatives to zero.

Questions about the use of AI for military purposes should not be removed but discussed separately. During the development process, we tried to create an ideal document that wouldn't have any complaints from the public. Because of this, many things had to be removed from defence and cybersecurity sections. Looking back, Goncharuk claims it was a mistake because it was necessary to design a document for two scenarios – "peacetime" and "wartime". In this case, all useful developments would be applied in the case of "Plan B" and there would be no need to compromise in them "as for peacetime".

The data privacy for small countries and AI regulation requirements should be different than for large countries. Since the beginning of the war in 2022, the bulk of the work on creating AI systems in Ukraine, which are now used for military purposes, has been taken over by the private sector – activists or private companies. Small and medium-sized countries don't have the resources to create state AI systems in advance for such crises. It's not difficult to understand that a lot of systems were created without taking into account the requirements of privacy, etc., because the goal was to survive. If these activists and private companies strictly followed the laws, then perhaps Ukraine would not be so good on the battlefield right now.

When discussing AI regulation, Vitaliy Goncharuk often sees a desire mostly of activists and civil society representatives to regulate the industry and protect everything and everyone as fully as possible. But as soon as he brought into the discussion the issue of competition with other countries and the fact that the Western world can't afford to lose competition in AI to China and Russia, this argument allowed them to switch their opponents from dogmatism to the search for a compromise and practical solutions.

The case with Ukraine and the active use of AI by both sides shows how important it is to find practical solutions that allow the country to develop AI, but not compete with regulations. The main thing that the war showed is that it can't be won with piles of documents on the regulation of AI – the war can only be won with really developed AI technologies, developed infrastructure and qualified engineering and management personnel. Therefore, if Western countries want to compete with China and other potential adversaries, then it is worth significantly revising the balance of investment between regulation and direct investment in technology development, as well as removing players with a conflict of interest from the regulatory process (Goncharuk, 2023).

Conclusions

The role of artificial intelligence on the battlefield is far from being marginal. While observing the unfold of events in the war in Ukraine, it is easy to notice that AI is steadily moving to the central stage of the battle, it is on the way to shift the main focus of war from conventional warfare to the war between the IT solutions. The more sophisticated software is incorporated into military technology, the more advanced smart solutions are in use by military personnel the more chances one side has to dominate the opponent.

As the presented statistics show the role of AI is increasing constantly. The investment into AI solutions are growing tremendously. The biggest actors on the globe have started the rivalry to take the role of the global leader in AI sphere thus the infusion of AI into almost all dimensions of our lives is rather inescapable. When it comes to military sphere the AI is of great support due to its ability to assist in transporting the wounded soldiers from the battlefield, ability to instruct on how to apply the first aid, ability to transmit the information on impending danger as well as being an irreplaceable element in military training simulations.

When it comes to the dark side of AI application in military, the biggest concerns are raised on the fully autonomous weapons. Among other functionalities, the autonomous weapons will be able to make the independent decision on attack based on its own assessment of the situation on the battlefield. Lack of human intervention may lead to serious threats that some experts compare to the danger posed by nuclear weapon.

There are clear signals from both side of Ukraine-Russia war that they are progressing on developing fully autonomous weapons, and both sides claim that the use of this kind of weapon is inevitable at some point in the future.

The development of AI can be summarized by the following quotes – "Artificial intelligence is the future, not only for Russia, but for all humankind. It comes with colossal opportunities, but also threats that are difficult to predict. Whoever becomes the leader in this sphere will become the ruler of the world. When one party's drones are destroyed by drones of another, it will have no other choice but to surrender" said Russian president V. Putin (Vincent, 2017). When it comes to Ukrainian side, the following statement of the head of the Victory Drones Volunteer project can be posted "We have to be innovative because we would like to survive" (Financial Times, 2023).

Considering the ethical dilemma of using AI in weaponry there are at least two predicaments to look into. The first is that the bans or limitations on AI application in military can be imposed but there is high probability some states will not obey. And in case one actor is developing such powerful weapon, the others have no other choice as to proceed in the same direction so that in case of danger they will be able to protect themselves.

The second point is that the war time is completely different reality than the peace time. The war time is being ruled by much different set of principles than time of peace. Due to this impediment, we cannot expect that the restrictions that are imposed during the peace time will be respected during the war.

References

Akash, S. (2023) What is the role of artificial intelligence in drone technology? *Analytics Insight.* Available at: https://www.analyticsinsight.net/what-is-the-role-of-artificial-intelligence-in-drone-technology/#:~:text=With%20the%20integration%20of%20Artificial,with%20greater%20speed%20and%20accuracy.

Albon, C. (2023) Pentagon updates autonomous weapons policy to account for AI advances. *Defence News.* Available at: https://www.defencenews.com/artificial-intelligence/2023/01/25/pentagon-updates-autonomous-weapons-policy-to-account-for-ai-advances/.

Andriushchenko, Y. (2022) Zvook Ukraine air defence. *Algorithm Watch.* Available at: https://algorithmwatch.org/en/zvook-ukraine-air-defence/.

Ard, M.J.O. (2022) Geospatial intelligence: Insights from Michael Ard and John O'Connor. *Johns Hopkins University.* Available at: https://hub.jhu.edu/2022/03/14/michael-ard-john-oconnor-geospatial-intelligence/.

Arhirova, H. (2023) Ukraine war drones technology. *The Associated Press.* Available at: https://apnews.com/article/ukraine-war-drones-technology-fe5dae6a8faba0d-46fa829a549592127.

Atherton, K.D. (2018) Autonomous robots and weapons. *New York Times*. Available at: https://www.nytimes.com/2018/11/15/magazine/autonomous-robots-weapons.html.

Axe, D. (2023) Ukraine's tanks and the future of warfare. *The New York Times*.Available at: https://www.nytimes.com/2023/02/20/opinion/ukraine-russia-tanks-offensive.html.

Bajak, F.H. (2023) Drone advances in Ukraine could herald battlefield dawn of autonomous killer robots. *Times of Israel*. Available at: https://www.timesofisrael.com/drone-advances-in-ukraine-could-herald-battlefield-dawn-of-autonomous-killer-robots/.

Bodniak, O. (2022) *Viyna z rosiyeyu: yak ukrayintsi vykorystovuyut shtuchniy intelekt*. ZAHID.NET. Available at: https://zaxid.net/viyna_z_rosiyeyu_yak_ukrayintsi_vikoristovuyut_shtuchniy_intelekt_n1549819.

Bosc, R. & Haines, M. (2022) The role of geospatial technology in the conflict in Ukraine. *The German Marshall Fund of the United States*. Available at: https://www.gmfus.org/news/geospatial-technologys-role-conflict-ukraine.

Clearview AI (n.d.) *Ukraine*. Available at: https://www.clearview.ai/ukraine.

Cranny-Evans, S. (2023) Russia claims to have developed AI-based aiming system for Gadfly FPV drone. *Shephard*. Available at: https://www.shephardmedia.com/news/landwarfareintl/russia-claims-to-have-developed-ai-based-aiming-system-for-gadfly-fpv-drone/.

Derico, J.C. (2022) *BBC.com*. Available at: https://www.bbc.com/news/technology-65057011.

Doyle, G. (2023) *UKRAINE CRISIS: ARMS*. Reuters.Available at: https://www.reuters.com/graphics/UKRAINE-CRISIS/ARMS/lgvdkoygnpo/.

Euronews (2022) *Ukraine war: what weapons tech is being used in Russia's invasion*. euronews.next.Available at: https://www.euronews.com/next/2022/03/07/ukraine-war-what-weapons-tech-is-being-used-in-russia-s-invasion.

European Parliament News (2023) *EU AI Act: first regulation on artificial intelligence*. Available at: https://www.europarl.europa.eu/news/en/headlines/society/20230601STO93804/eu-ai-act-first-regulation-on-artificial-intelligence.

Fedorov, M. (2023) Tech innovation helps Ukraine even the odds against Russia's military might. *Atlantic Council*. Available at: https://

www.atlanticcouncil.org/blogs/ukrainealert/tech-innovation-helps-ukraine-even-the-odds-against-russias-military-might/.

Financial Times (2023) *Financial Times*. Available at: https://www.youtube.com/watch?v=voPCPhzmL10&ab_channel=FinancialTimes.

Fontes, R. & Kamminga, J. (2023) Ukraine: A living lab for AI warfare. *National Defence*. Available at: https://www.nationaldefencemagazine.org/articles/2023/3/24/ukraine-a-living-lab-for-ai-warfare.

Frąckiewicz, M. (2023) Navigating through crisis: the role of geospatial intelligence Ukraine. *TS2 SPACE*. Available at: https://ts2.space/en/navigating-through-crisis-the-role-of-geospatial-intelligence-in-ukraine/.

Frąckiewicz, M. (2023) The role of artificial intelligence in advancing anti-drone technology. *TS2*. Available at: https://ts2.space/en/the-role-of-artificial-intelligence-in-advancing-anti-drone-technology/.

Goncharuk, V. (2023) War in Ukraine and AI regulation: Some controversial takeaways. *European Commission*. Available at: https://futurium.ec.europa.eu/en/european-ai-alliance/blog/war-ukraine-and-ai-regulation-some-controversial-takeaways.

Guest, T. (2023) Understanding the view imagery in geospatial intelligence. *European Security & Defence*. Available at: https://euro-sd.com/2023/03/articles/30037/understanding-the-view-imagery-in-geospatial-intelligence/ .

Hambling, D. (2022) Shahed catchers: Ukraine's interceptor drones to bring down Russian kamikazes. *Forbes*. Available at: https://www.forbes.com/sites/davidhambling/2022/11/02/shahed-catchers-ukraines-interceptor-drones-to-bring-down-russian-kamikazes/?sh=5e3a71c267b6.

Hambling, D. (2023) Russia prepares avalanche of FPV kamikaze drones. *Forbes*. Available at: https://www.forbes.com/sites/davidhambling/2023/07/26/russia-prepares-avalanche-of-fpv-kamikaze-drones/?sh=338193381ca2.

Hill, K. (2022) Facial recognition technology in Ukraine. *The New York Times*. Available at: https://www.nytimes.com/2022/04/07/technology/facial-recognition-ukraine-clearview.html .

Hudson, J. & Khudov, K. (2023) Drones and AI in the Ukraine war: Innovation at the forefront. *Washington Post*. Available at: https://www.washingtonpost.com/world/2023/07/26/drones-ai-ukraine-war-innovation/.

Jones, L. (2023) Lesson from a year at war: In contrast to the Russians, Ukrainians master a mix of high and low-end technology on the battlefield. *The Conversation*. Available at: https://theconversation.com/lesson-from-a-year-at-war-in-contrast-to-the-russians-ukrainians-master-a-mix-of-high-and-low-end-technology-on-the-battlefield-197853.

Joshi, S. (2023) The war in Ukraine shows how technology is changing the battlefield. *The Economist*. Available at: https://www.economist.com/special-report/2023/07/03/the-war-in-ukraine-shows-how-technology-is-changing-the-battlefield.

Knipfer, C. (2017) AI weapons: International regulations needed – but too late. *Diplomatic Courier*. Available at: https://www.diplomaticourier.com/posts/ai-weapons-international-regulations-needed-late.

MarketWatch (2023) Global drone market 2023-2030: Booming industry expected to surpass USD 17.52 million. *MarketWatch*. Available at: https://www.marketwatch.com/press-release/global-drone-market-2023-2030-booming-industry-expected-to-surpass-usd-17520-million-2023-05-04.

Masters, J. (2023) Ukraine conflict: A crossroads for Europe and Russia. *Council on Foreign Relations*. Available at: https://www.cfr.org/backgrounder/ukraine-conflict-crossroads-europe-and-russia.

Military Embedded Systems (2019) Artificial intelligence timeline. *Military Embedded Systems*. Available at: https://militaryembedded.com/ai/machine-learning/artificial-intelligence-timeline#:~:text=1991%3A,to%20solve%20other%20logistical%20problems.

Ministry of Internal Affairs (2023) CEO of American company Clearview AI to continue cooperation with MVS. *Ministry of Internal Affairs*. Available at: https://mvs.gov.ua/news/ceo-amerikanskoyi-kompaniyi-clearview-ai-produkt-iakoyi-identifikuvav-okupantiv-ta-zradnikiv-prodovzit-spivpraciu-z-mvs.

Mukhina, O. (2023) Hear and destroy: Ukrainian artificial intelligence project Zvook helps shoot down Russian missiles. *EUROMAIDAN Press*. Available at: https://euromaidanpress.com/2023/03/03/hear-and-destroy-ukrainian-artificial-intelligence-project-zvook-helps-shoot-down-russian-missiles/.

Nanda, P. (2023) From AI, internet satellites to naval drones: War in Ukraine. *The Eurasian Times*. Available at: https://www.eurasiantimes.com/from-ai-internet-satellites-to-naval-drones-war-in-ukraine/ .

National Geospatial-Intelligence Agency (2022) Tearline research highlights displaced Ukrainians. *National Geospatial-Intelligence*

*Agency.*Availableat:https://www.nga.mil/news/1671720903204_Tearline_research_highlights_displaced_Ukrainians.html.

National Security Technology Accelerator (2023) How artificial intelligence is changing the future of military defence strategies. *National Security Technology Accelerator.* Available at: https://nstxl.org/how-artificial-intelligence-is-changing-the-future-of-military-defence-strategies/.

NATO Parliamentary Assembly (2019) Artificial intelligence: An evolving challenge. *NATO Parliamentary Assembly.* Available at: https://www.nato-pa.int/download-file?filename=/sites/default/files/2019-10/REPORT%20149%20STCTTS%2019%20E%20rev.%201%20fin-%20ARTIFICIAL%20INTELLIGENCE.pdf.

Rönnback, R. (2023) Challenges in governing AI for military purposes and spill-over effects: AI Act. *European AI Alliance.* Available at: https://futurium.ec.europa.eu/en/european-ai-alliance/blog/challenges-governing-ai-military-purposes-and-spill-over-effects-ai-act.

Scharre, P. (2022) *Artificial Intelligence and Arms Control.* Center for a New American Security. Available at: https://www.cnas.org/publications/reports/artificial-intelligence-and-arms-control.

Scharre, P. (2018) *Army of None: Autonomous Weapons and the Future of War.* 1st ed. New York | London: W. W. Norton & Company.

Sentient Digital Inc (2023) The most useful military applications of AI. *Sentient Digital Inc.* Available at: https://sdi.ai/blog/the-most-useful-military-applications-of-ai/.

Shoaib, A. (2023) Ukraine's anti-drone guns: Recovering intelligence from downed Russian drones. *Insider.* Available at: https://www.businessinsider.com/ukraines-anti-drone-guns-down-russian-drones-recover-intelligence-2023-2?IR=T.

Steinhoff, J.K. (2023) The ethical dilemma of weaponizing artificial intelligence. *Small Wars Journal.* Available at: https://smallwarsjournal.com/jrnl/art/ethical-dilemma-weaponization-artificial-intelligence.

The Business Research Company (2023) Facial recognition global market report. *ReportLinker.* Available at: https://www.reportlinker.com/p06319890/Facial-Recognition-Global-Market-Report.html?utm_source=GNW.

The Economist (2023) How Ukraine's enemy is also learning lessons, albeit slowly. *The Economist.* Available at:

https://www.economist.com/special-report/2023/07/03/how-ukraines-enemy-is-also-learning-lessons-albeit-slowly.

Tiwari, S. (2022) Israel's vital intelligence contribution to Ukraine. *The Eurasian Times*. Available at: https://www.eurasiantimes.com/israel-is-providing-vital-intel-to-ukraines-russia/.

UAS Vision (2022) Ukrainian drone dropping rifle with a two-mile range. *UAS Vision*. Available at: https://www.uasvision.com/2022/06/30/ukrainian-drone-dropping-rifle-with-two-mile-range/.

Ukrainian World Congress (2023) *United24*. Available at: https://www.ukrainianworldcongress.org/united24/.

VANTAGE Market Research (2022) *Artificial intelligence in military market*. Available at: https://www.vantagemarketresearch.com/industry-report/artificial-intelligence-in-military-market-1446.

Vincent, J. (2017) *Putin's AI ambitions could reshape the world. The Verge*. Available at: https://www.theverge.com/2017/9/4/16251226/russia-ai-putin-rule-the-world.

Wired (2023) *Ukraine's tech startups are helping it in the war*. *Wired*. Available at: https://www.wired.co.uk/article/ukraine-runs-war-startup.

Wired (2023) *The use of facial recognition technology in the Ukraine conflict*. *Wired*. Available at: https://www.wired.com/story/russia-ukraine-facial-recognition-technology-death-military/.

Yarova, M. (2023) *How Clearview AI helps identify Russian war criminals*. *AIN CAPITAL*. Available at: https://ain.capital/2023/05/05/how-the-facial-recognition-service-clearview-ai-helps-to-identify-russian-war-criminals-in-ukraine/

Linguistic means of persuasion. A case study of strategic communication – Vladimir Putin's speech during the victory day parade in 2022

Jarosław Drygowski

Abstract

This chapter of the attached book analyzes the linguistic means of persuasion in strategic communication, using Vladimir Putin's speech during the 2022 Victory Day Parade as a case study. The chapter focuses on the importance of rhetorical tools like ethos, pathos, and logos in the context of Russia's war against Ukraine. The aim of this chapter is to explore how strategic communication, specifically public speeches, can be used as a form of propaganda to justify political actions and gain public support. The study includes a detailed analysis of syntactic, semantic, and lexical figures of speech, highlighting how such tools are employed to shape narratives, both domestically and internationally. The findings reveal that persuasive communication is central to Russia's hybrid warfare strategy, and the speech in question demonstrates a clear attempt to manipulate both Russian public opinion and the international perception of the conflict. The chapter concludes that strategic communication, especially in times of conflict, becomes a vital tool for political leaders, with the power to legitimize actions, influence narratives, and sway public opinion. This analysis contributes to the broader understanding of how propaganda and persuasive techniques in public speeches play an essential role in modern geopolitical conflicts.

Keywords: strategic communication, persuasion, Vladimir Putin, Ukraine, Russia, linguistic means

Introduction

The war in Ukraine broke out in February 2022. Since then, public opinion was flooded with reports about it created in Ukraine, Russia, European countries and the United States. It has quickly turned out that the Russian and Ukrainian narratives differ significantly due to the propaganda goals of the countries. The promotion of the Kremlin's narrative regarding the faults of the USA and the West, which had already begun in the mid-2000s, were intensified in 2014 after the annexation of Crimea. These faults concerned threats to the superiority of Russian values and intensions and the promotion of democracy through, for example, the protests and activities of non-governmental organizations. The official statements were disseminated not only by the Kremlin-controlled mass media but also by newly invented establishments, for instance 'troll farms', and their aim was to target the audience domestically and internationally (Gerber & Zavisca, 2016, p. 79). Therefore, the aims of the Russian narrative were to impact the national public opinion as follows:

> *Domestically, the arguments seek to legitimize the Putin regime, garner support for its policies, and demonize its critics. Internationally, they are part of a larger effort to project Russian 'soft power', sow doubts and uncertainty within the NATO alliance, weaken public support for policies countering Russian aggression in Ukraine, and solidify the allegiances of Russia's allies in former Soviet republics whom Russia considers part of its natural sphere of influence* (Gerber & Zavisca, 2016, p. 76).

Speeches delivered by heads of states can have dire consequences. Such consequences directly affect the security of neighbouring countries. Vladimir Putin's speech is an example of such rhetoric. The Russian head of state sends his message to the world immediately after the aggression against Ukraine, so such a message can be qualified in advance as an element of the aggressor's information war, in which a target for such a war should be expected.

The aim of the paper is to analyze one of the speeches of Vladimir Putin to find out the linguistic and semiotic means of expressing persuasively the role of the Russian Federation in Europe and justification for the conflict with Ukraine. The persuasiveness of the public speeches is one of the elements of strategic communication which in Russian–Ukrainian war has become astonishingly visible to the extent when the Russian and Ukrainian descriptions of events seem completely different.

The analysis of pertinent literature on strategic communication and its elements

Strategic communication encompasses a wide array of messages formulated for a variety of purposes. They may include orders which need to be clear, unambiguous, short and deprived of emotions. But they also include political speeches which have a completely different function which focuses on the persuasion and appeal. It happens so because

> *Strategic communication is a term that has become quite popular in communication science education in the second decade of the twenty-first century. Originally only used for a niche, that is, communication programs in the domain of national governments and the military (Farwell, 2012; Paul, 2011), it is now increasingly popular as an umbrella concept embracing various goal-directed communication activities usually covered by public relations, marketing and financial communications, health communications, public diplomacy, campaigning, and so forth (Holtzhausen & Zerfass, 2014, p. 3).*

Holtzhausen and Zerfass cite Hallahan et al. (2007, p. 4) who claim that the aim of strategic communication is the "purposeful use of communication by an organization to fulfill its mission". Additionally, the prerequisite for strategic communication is the purposefulness of the activity, that is to say the messages must be formulated with the aim of communicating efficiently.

It is pointed out that strategic communication is heavily grounded in the foundations laid down by Aristotle and his concept of rhetoric defined in the following manner:

> *Rhetoric may be defined as the faculty of observing in any given case the available means of persuasion. This is not a function of any other art. Every other art can instruct, or persuade about its own particular subject-matter; for instance, medicine about what is healthy and unhealthy, geometry about the properties of magnitudes, arithmetic about numbers, and the same is true of the other arts and*

sciences. But rhetoric we look upon as the power of observing the means of persuasion on almost any subject presented to us; and that is why we say that, in its technical character, it is not concerned with any special or definite class of subjects (Aristotle, (n.d.) p. 1-2).

Bearing that in mind, one cannot disagree with the opinion that:

Politics, at its core, is about persuasion. Various theories and explanations of persuasion have been suggested throughout the centuries. The roots of the study of persuasion can be traced in Ancient Greece. Greek philosophers were mainly concerned with the issues of ethical means of persuasion. Since Aristotle defined his principles of persuasion in his Rhetoric, there have been attempts at defining the principles of successful persuasion but for most of human history, persuasion has been studied as an art. In the early 1900s, research on (political) persuasion was carried out mostly as propaganda analysis and public opinion research. Studies of propaganda in the early part of the twentieth century can be regarded as the antecedents to the social scientific study of persuasion (Demirdöğen, 2010, p. 190).

Persuasive communication is an element of strategic communication which is especially frequently encountered in the so-called public speaking, which is the type of communication aiming at convincing someone to follow the speaker's point of view and to support the actions undertaken by him or her. According to Aristotle, a persuasive speech should be featured by ethos, pathos and logos. The aim of the rhetoric is to find out how to formulate the text so that it contains those free elements serving the purpose of affecting the perception of people and making them behave in a desired manner. Initially sociologists focused on the language of propaganda but

After World War II, researchers stopped referring to their subject of study as propaganda and started investigating various constructs of persuasion (Jowett & O'Donnell, 1992, p. 122).

Thus, nowadays we may assume that propaganda and persuasion are synonymous terms, and they may be used interchangeably. However, the term 'propaganda' is negatively pragmatically marked as it is associated with manipulation. Though persuasion is also a method of manipulation.

The research material and research methods

The research material was composed of the speech of the president of Russia, Vladimir Putin, delivered on 9 May 2022 during the Victory Parade on the Red Square. The President of Russia who also holds the office of the Supreme Commander-in-Chief of the Russian Federation Armed Forces attended a military parade marking the 77th anniversary of Victory in the 1941–1945 Great Patriotic War during which he delivered a highly persuasive speech with numerous references to Russian and Ukrainian military conflict. The speech is an example of the strategic communication addressed to the Russian nation in order to celebrate the anniversary and justify sending the troops to the territory of Ukraine. The speech is 1202 words long. The translation into English is the official version provided by the Kremlin authorities. The author has decided not to use other English language versions of the speech to describe the persuasive features as they were translated by Russian translators. It is due to the fact that such translation provided by the Kremlin may be assumed free from linguistic manipulation of international translators not sympathising with the Russian Federation and supporting Ukraine.

The research methods applied include the semiotic analysis of the language of persuasion, in the past called propaganda, in terms of Aristotle's tripartite division into ethos, pathos and logos. Within that structure the author distinguishes linguistic features of the speech serving the purpose of communicating in persuasive manner. Thus, the linguistic and semiotic analysis of the speech are also applied.

Ethos, pathos and logos in the speech of Vladimir Putin delivered on 9 May during the Victory Parade on Red Square

The speech delivered on 9 May 2022 in Moscow by Vladimir Putin is an example of strategic communication formulated on purpose in order to justify and fulfill the mission undertaken by the Russian government. The anniversary of the victory is used as a pretext to justify the invasion on Ukraine, which started in February 2022. The speech contains ethos, pathos and logos that are considered key elements of persuasiveness.

The first element of the persuasive speech is called ethos. It is strictly connected with the credibility of the speaker and his or her public image. In other words:

> *Ethos, was the first element in his theory of persuasion, which referred to the character the speaker wished to present. It could be defined as the charisma and the credibility of the speaker. As Aristotle had written in the 4th century B.C. (...) According to Aristotle, apart from the character, the artistic proofs a persuader used along with his/her reputation and image – all added up to create his/her charisma or ethos. Nonverbal messages like the speaker's physical appearance, as well as his reputation and the way he delivered his speech all contributed to ethos to some degree* (Demirdöğen, 2010, p. 191–192).

In order to find out the degree of ethos in the speeches of Vladimir Putin one needs to first briefly characterise him as a public figure present in the Russian and international political arena for a few decades.

The political career of Vladimir Vladimirovich Putin commences way before the day he took power as president of the Russian Federation after Boris Yeltsin. The connections with secret services and public authorities began in his student days. After graduation, Putin joins KGB for 16 years. In 1990, he begins a political career in Saint Petersburg. After 6 years, he moves to Kremlin to have a career at a larger scale. In his public and political activities, he successively held decision-making positions that made him a figure to be reckoned with. It should be admitted that the above-mentioned day of assuming the presidency is a breakthrough in both internal and external politics of Russia (Kurczab-Redlich, 2016). As Bieleń and Raś (2008, p.10) note:

> *The image of Yeltsin has been replaced with the image of a new leader – Vladimir Putin – resilient, decisive, calculating (which in politics is nothing negative), open to the world, bereft of complexes towards the West, and at the*

> *same time respecting tradition, even of the Soviet Union,*
> *capable of restoring to the Russians a sense of dignity and*
> *national pride.*

On this basis, it can be safely stated that he contributed to restoring Russia to its former glory. Therefore, he found the support of his compatriots, who dreamed of powerful *Матушка Россия* (literally: Mother Russia) ruled with a firm hand. Putin's charisma in the Russian Federation is undeniable as he even convinced his comrades to have the Constitution of the Russian Federation amended so that he could hold the office of the President of Russia more than twice.

The second element of persuasive or propaganda messages is pathos which aims at to the emotions of the audience and making it empathetic towards the speaker and his actions.

> *Pathos, was the mood or tone of the speech that appealed to*
> *the passions or the will of the audience. Aristotle's appeals*
> *to pathos were psychological appeals; they relied on the*
> *receiver's emotions. Before using these appeals, persuad-*
> *ers had to assess the emotional state of their audience – an*
> *ability or skill which might be called as empathy or emo-*
> *tional intelligence in contemporary terms. Aristotle cited*
> *some virtues like justice, generosity, courage, gentleness*
> *and wisdom as pathos or appeals to emotion. Many of*
> *these virtues were tied not only to emotional persuasion*
> *or pathos but to ethos as well* (Demirdöğen, 2010, p. 192).

The last element which is good logos is based on knowledge, commonly known facts, reason, logic and common sense.

> *Logos was the argument the speaker was advancing; that*
> *meant appeals to the intellect or to reason. It was depen-*
> *dent on the audience's ability to process information in*
> *logical ways; in order to appeal to the rational side of*
> *the audience, the persuader had to assess their informa-*
> *tion-processing patterns. Aristotle advised persuaders*
> *to use syllogistic arguments (enthymemes) in which the*
> *major premise was already believed by the audience*
> (Demirdöğen, 2010, p. 192).

Therefore, logos needs to refer to facts that are either well-known or verifiable. The linguistic tools used aim at creating the plausibility of the message.

Putin's speech is a skillful medley of pathos, ethos and logos combined together to create the sense of solidarity and patriotism, the conviction of the rightfulness of the Russian nation, which is portrayed as the saviour of the world, protector defending the country and counteracting the outbreak of the third world war.

Vladimir Putin in his speech refers to logos composed of well-known historical events, in general battles won by Russia e.g.

> *The defence of our Motherland when its destiny was at stake has always been sacred. It was the feeling of true patriotism that Minin and Pozharsky's militia stood up for the Fatherland, soldiers went on the offensive at the Borodino Field and fought the enemy outside Moscow and Leningrad, Kiev and Minsk, Stalingrad and Kursk, Sevastopol and Kharkov* (Putin, 2022).

First, special attention should be devoted to the symbolism of names of Minin and Pozharsky who represent the defenders of Russia in the Polish–Russian War of 1609–1618, also known as the Polish–Muscovite War or the Dimitriads. The conflict was waged between the Tsardom of Russia and the Polish–Lithuanian Commonwealth together with Zaporozhian Cossacks. Namely, some Polish and Lithuanian magnates tried to take advantage of Smuta (Russian: Смута) and intervened militarily in Russia to put their candidate on the throne (Brown, 1982). That historical event from 17th century is used to supports the Russian public media rhetoric of 2022 suggesting that Poland wants to annex the part of Ukraine into its territory.

Second, on September 5–7, 1812, the French army led by Napoleon Bonaparte clashed in the Battle of Borodino with the Tsar's army led by Mikhail Kutuzov. The latter withdrew his troops from the battlefield, allowing Bonaparte to take Moscow a few days later. However, the French commander did not achieve the planned goal of destroying the Russian army in direct confrontation, which soon resulted in his ignominious defeat (Zemstov, 2007, p. 90–112).

Third, president Putin mentions Moscow as one of turning points in the struggle of his people. As for the battles for this city, two clashes took place during this period, which raised the morale of the Russians. It is not known exactly which battle is meant, but it can be conjectured that the battle from the period of the Polish–Muscovite War is the one mentioned in the speech, because the anniversary of the victory and the expulsion of the Polish occupier from Moscow is a celebration of independence in the Russian Federation. Out of chronicler's duty, the author of this work will briefly describe these battles, as both ended in Russian success. Chronologically, the first event is the battle of 1612. In September of that year, two battles were fought in the suburbs of Moscow between the Polish–Lithuanian Commonwealth troops and the units of Russian levy. The Commonwealth troops tried unsuccessfully to reach their own troops besieged in Moscow, which, cut off from supplies, were losing their strength. Despite two battles fought on September 1 and 3, 1612, the Polish garrison in Moscow had to capitulate on November 7, 1612 (Gładysz, 2012, p. 32–52). The second event took place during the Second World War. According to Falin (2015, p. 7) the battle between Russian and German troops took place from October to December 1941. Its characteristic feature was that it was stretched over a 600 km section of the Eastern Front. The Wehrmacht attacked Moscow because it was a very important military and political target for the Axis forces. It is estimated that between 650,000 and 1 million victims could have died on the Soviet side alone.

Fourth, as Adeyeri and Akinola (2021) claim from September 8, 1941, to January 27, 1944, Leningrad (present-day Saint Petersburg) was surrounded by German and Finnish troops. History called these actions the Blockade of Leningrad. After 872 days, i.e. almost 2.5 years, this operation claimed 1.5 million victims on the Soviet side, military personnel of the Red Army and civilian residents of the city.

Fifth, the Battle of Kiev, as Read (2005, p. 731) delineates in his book, was fought during the Operation Barbarossa between the Soviet and Third Reich troops in 1941. As a result, the Wehrmacht completely encircled the city of Kiev, although this maneuver was not completely closed, and almost totally destroyed 43 Soviet divisions, so that this front virtually ceased to exist. Soviet losses were even more catastrophic than in the previous Battle of Minsk.

Sixth, as Sołonin (2007, p. 528–529) writes the Battle of Minsk brought the encirclement of Soviet troops around this city in late June and early July 1941. The Soviets failed to launch major counterattacks and were unable to break the German encirclement, which led to their defeat, resulting in the capture of more than 300,000 Red Army soldiers.

Jarosław Drygowski

Seventh, according to Lewis (2003) one of the most important engagements of World War II was the Battle of Stalingrad, fought by Axis forces against the Red Army. The battle was characterized by fierce fighting in the urban area making it one of the bloodiest battles in history and resulted in massive civilian casualties of up to 2 million inhabitants.

Eighth, as Simms (2003, p. 10) claims the Battle of Kursk commenced on July 5th, 1943, and ended almost two months later. The German offensive was halted there, and a battle was fought that went down in military history as the largest armored battle. From that moment on, the Red Army took the initiative until the victory in Berlin.

Ninth, according to Donnell (2016) upon an eight-month siege, the German and Romanian troops captured Sevastopol in July 1942. The Soviets troops fiercely and persistently defended the city, which was completely destroyed in the war.

Next, the First Battle of Kharkov was fought in October 1941. Kharkov was already an important industrial centre at that time; therefore, it was a substantial military target. The Red Army failed to hold the city in its own hands, so the entire technology park had to be evacuated or destroyed (Afanasenko, 2015). The Second Battle of Kharkov was fought in May 1942. The aim of the Red Army was to liberate Kharkov from Wehrmacht occupation and to increase the initiative of own troops in the southern section of the Eastern Front. German counterattacks, however, stopped the Soviet offensive, which was ruined by the tragic mistakes of Stalin and the staff of the Southwestern Front, which led to the counterattack the 6th Wehrmacht Army cutting off the attacking Red Army troops from the rest of the Front. Between February 21 and March 18, 1943, a series of battles took place, called by historians the Third Battle of Kharkov, as a result of which the Wehrmacht destroyed 52 divisions of the Red Army and recaptured the cities of Kharkov and Belgorod. (Tucker-Jones, 2016).

Vladimir Putin then finishes listing the city battles that took place in what is now Ukraine. Taking into account the fact that these battles are not mentioned either in terms of importance for the military effort of Soviet Russia, or in chronological terms, it should be assumed that this procedure is intended to emphasize that these territories are in the Russian sphere of influence. This can also be confirmed by the earlier mention of Minsk, which is the capital of today's Belarus.

These battles show the great successes and sacrifices of the Russians citizens, but also implicitly point to centuries-long enemies. The subliminal message is not to trust the enemy. All of the examples of battles were fought on Russian soil to show the interference of foreign countries in Russia's internal affairs. Russia only defended itself by paying a huge price. The enemies are present members of NATO: Poland, France, Germany.

That fragment of the speech in fact contains the typical elements of both logos and pathos. Pathos is expressed by nouns describing the homeland such as Motherland 'Родина' and Fatherland 'Отечество' (Putin, 2022, 2022). What is more, the pathos is strengthened by the usage of positive nouns such as patriotism with additional emphatic load added by the adjective 'true'. The verb phrases 'to be sacred', 'to stand up for', to go on the offensive', 'to fight the enemy' stress the pompousness of the speech. Something that is sacred is considered connected with the God, blessed by the God, important to such an extent that it should not be changed or amended in an away, questioned or criticized. In Putin's speech what is sacred is the defence of the country. Defending one's country has always been considered the duty of soldiers and an act of patriotism. In the first sentence patriotism is implicitly expressed but in the second sentence it is formulated explicitly: "It was the feeling of true patriotism that..." What is more, there is no reference to any act of aggression on the part of the Russian nation. Putin talks about going on the offensive and fighting the enemy which strengthens the associations with defensive actions, guarding the borders of the homeland and providing the security of the citizens. And the same rhetoric is continued in the next sentence referring directly to the Russian Ukrainian war which is portrayed as the defence of the Russian nation in the following manner:

> *Today, as in the past, you are fighting for our people in Donbass, for the security of our Motherland, for Russia* (Putin, 2022).

The military operations in Donbass are described as fighting for the security of Russia and its people. In Putin's rhetoric it is not an invasion but the rescue operation aiming at protecting the people and the homeland.

The next sentence, together with the opening line which is the exclamation ("I congratulate you on the Day of Great Victory!"), is the reference to the occasion on which the speech is delivered and without which the message conveyed would not be appropriate. It stresses the role of the Soviet Union in military operations and concluding the peace after the Second World War.

> *May 9, 1945, has been enshrined in world history forever as a triumph of the united Soviet people, its cohesion and spiritual power, an unparalleled feat on the front lines and on the home front* (Putin, 2022).

Putin (2022) builds ethos in his speech by presenting himself as a member and representative of the nation addressing the audience 'Comrades', 'Fellow Russian citizens', 'Comrade soldiers and seamen, sergeants and sergeant majors, midshipmen and warrant officers', 'Comrade officers, generals and admirals'. He does not consider himself a veteran but a military man, he creates himself as a fellow which is achieved by using first person plural pronouns such as 'we', 'us', 'our':

> *Victory Day is intimately dear to all of us. There is no family in Russia that was not burnt by the Great Patriotic War. Its memory never fades. On this day, children, grandchildren and great-grandchildren of the heroes march in an endless flow of the Immortal Regiment. They carry photos of their family members, the fallen soldiers who remained young forever, and the veterans who are already gone.*

> *We take pride in the unconquered courageous generation of the victors, we are proud of being their successors, and it is our duty to preserve the memory of those who defeated Nazism and entrusted us with being vigilant and doing everything to thwart the horror of another global war.*

The sense of solidarity is built by phrases such as:

- 'dear to all of us' expressing the sense of inclusion of all citizens into common experience and uniform feelings,

- 'there is no family ... that was not burnt by...' focusing on trauma and sacrifice experienced by all families forming the nation and unifying the nation through the torment and suffering,

- 'children, grandchildren and great-grandchildren of the heroes' expressing memory passed from generation to generation and the heroism inherited by future generations which is additionally enhanced by the phrase 'unconquered courageous generation of the victors' stressing the features of heroes such as courage and invincibility.

- 'our duty to preserve the memory of those who defeated Nazism' – it is a reference to the worst evil of the 20th-century carrying the pragmatic meaning of genocide and the greatest atrocities inflicted to innocent people only because of their ethnicity, race, sexuality, etc.

- 'successors ... entrusted us with being vigilant and doing everything to thwart the horror of another global war' – the reference to Nazism is juxtaposed with the heritage passed from generation to generation which is extremely important, it is a lofty ideal of being the guardian of the global peace. Vladimir Putin claims that it is the obligation of the Russian nation to prevent the third world war. Appealing to such ideals, to dreams of leading a happy and peaceful life is undeniably the strategy of appealing to the desires of common people, common good and the highest values propagated by idealists.

The logos of the speech is built by referring to the Victory Day and the Great Patriotic War. The Victory Day is a widely observed bank holiday in Europe, where it commemorates the end of World War II. In most countries of the continent in question, it is celebrated on May 8. However, in the former Soviet Union День Победы (literally: Victory Day) is celebrated a day later, on May 9. The latter date is also cultivated by the Russian Federation. This holiday is celebrated very solemnly, which is also attended by Vladimir Putin for propaganda reasons. As Kavaliauskas (2011, p. 325) accurately notices: "Today's Russia seems to be a conscious successor of the former Soviet Union, but not because of mere rationale choice, but because of cultural and mental sameness." The fact that the Victory Day is still celebrated a day later than in other parts of the world is a tradition stemming back to the times of the Soviet Union.

The second event mentioned to build logos and pathos of the speech is the already mentioned Great Patriotic War. Almost all over the world, the name "World War II" is commonly used, however, Russia has never followed this rule. Russians use the term "Great Patriotic War", which was coined decades ago by Soviets. This is Soviet propaganda term for the part of World War II covering the period from June 22, 1941 (beginning of the Operation

Barbarossa) to May 9, 1945 (capitulation of the III Reich). The term covers warfare in Europe excluding the Far East and focuses on the war effort of the Soviet Union. This terminology is used intentionally for two reasons. Firstly, the official entry of the USSR into the war. Secondly, the propaganda overtones of the wording "the great patriotic war", which emphasized the national character of the conflict and pointed to its universality, was intended to mobilize all citizens of this country to defend the homeland. (Tumarkin, 2003). Patriotism is a very positive behaviour of citizens. Thus, referring to patriotism, patriotic acts has served the purpose of constructing pathos ever since the term "the Great Patriotic War" was coined.

In the next fragment of the speech Vladimir Putin skillfully uses the strategy of dividing people living in the world into two groups: 'us and them'. That strategy serves the purpose of evoking a sense of unity and solidarity of people belonging to the category of 'us' and showing the differences between 'us and them'. That strategy is also well known in countries where genocide followed. Stanton (1996) calls that stage classification. Classification serves the purpose of showing people which a group they belong to and which a group they cannot belong to because of the profound differences in the system of values and ethics.

> *Therefore, despite all controversies in international relations, Russia has always advocated the establishment of an equal and indivisible security system which is critically needed for the entire international community.*

> *Last December we proposed signing a treaty on security guarantees. Russia urged the West to hold an honest dialogue in search for meaningful and compromising solutions, and to take account of each other's interests. All in vain. NATO countries did not want to heed us, which means they had totally different plans. And we saw it.*

> *Another punitive operation in Donbass, an invasion of our historic lands, including Crimea, was openly in the making. Kiev declared that it could attain nuclear weapons. The NATO bloc launched an active military build-up on the territories adjacent to us.*

> *Thus, an absolutely unacceptable threat to us was steadily being created right on our borders. There was every*

indication that a clash with neo-Nazis and Banderites backed by the United States and their minions was unavoidable" (Putin, 2022).

The next part of the speech is characterized by the same type of logos as one of the first fragments contains references to historical events and figures. This time, however, Putin compares the military operation in Donbass to the past victories, and soldiers fighting in the territory of Ukraine to the well-known Russian heroes:

Comrades,

Donbass militia alongside with the Russian Army are fighting on their land today, where princes Svyatoslav and Vladimir Monomakh's retainers, soldiers under the command of Rumyantsev and Potemkin, Suvorov and Brusilov crushed their enemies, where Great Patriotic War heroes Nikolai Vatutin, Sidor Kovpak and Lyudmila Pavlichenko stood to the end (Putin, 2022).

Apart from mentioning the heroes of the 17th-century war with Poland, Putin also enumerates other national heroes, such as Prince Svyatoslav, Grand Prince of Kiev, who is mainly known for his expeditions that led to the fall of two great powers: the First Bulgarian Empire and Khazaria; prince Vladimir Monomakh, is a saint in the Eastern Orthodox Church and was recognized ruler of the Kievan Rus (Lysenko, 2019); Peter Rumyantsev, was a military commander who became famous for his innovative art of war, efficiency and military reform (Knyazev *et. al.*, 2016); Grigory Potemkin, commander-in-chief in the war with Turkey (1787–1792) and favorite of Catharine the Great (Duran, 1969); Alexander Suvorov, the famous Russian commander Generalissimo who is said not to lose a single battle and commemorated for his numerous victories (Bakhov, Ryzhykov & Kolisnyk 2018),; Alexei Brusilov, known cavalryman and revolutionist, known for the so-called Brusilov Offensive in 1916 (Schindler, 2003); Nikolai Vatutin, was a Soviet military commander also in the battle of Kursk (Zamulin, 2012); Sidor Kovpak, was a Soviet partisan commander in Ukraine (Armstrong, 1963); Lyudmila Pavlichenko, was Ukrainian sniper fighting in the Red Army (Axell, 2011, p. 156). All heroes strengthen persuasion as they constitute logos of the speech.

The names are also frequently connected with Ukrainian territories and Ukrainian history. That strengthens the message of the common history, one multi-national country, one multi-national power. At the same time, the acts of heroism and sacrifice characterising mentioned princes, commanders, soldiers, freedom fighters serve the purpose of constructing the pathos of the speech. The names are well recognizable for Russian citizens. Each child at school knows the names of those national heroes.

The next fragment is an appeal to remember the past and counteract the atrocities that may happen again if nothing is done:

> *I am addressing our Armed Forces and Donbass militia. You are fighting for our Motherland, its future, so that nobody forgets the lessons of World War II, so that there is no place in the world for torturers, death squads and Nazis (Putin, 2022).*

Empathy and sympathy towards those who have suffered and those who lost their lives and loved ones is one of the leitmotivs of the speech. What is typical of the message conveyed, is that Russia is portrayed as the country who was frequently affected by invasions, Russian citizens were killed because of their citizenship or sense of nationality. Russia and its nation are the allegoric patriots fighting against their enemies.

> *Today, we bow our heads to the sacred memory of all those who lost their lives in the Great Patriotic War, the memories of the sons, daughters, fathers, mothers, grandfathers, husbands, wives, brothers, sisters, relatives and friends.*
>
> *We bow our heads to the memory of the Odessa martyrs who were burned alive in the House of Trade Unions in May 2014, to the memory of the old people, women and children of Donbass who were killed in atrocious and barbaric shelling by neo-Nazis. We bow our heads to our fighting comrades who died a brave death in the righteous battle – for Russia.*
>
> *I declare a minute of silence.*
>
> *(A minute of silence)* (Putin, 2022).

The phrase 'Odessa martyrs' refers to 42 people who lost their lives in riots between pro-Russian and pro-Ukrainian groups (International Advisory Panel Report 2015).

The next sentence expresses solidarity through empathy towards those who lost their dearest:

> *The loss of each officer and soldier is painful for all of us and an irretrievable loss for the families and friends* (Putin, 2022).

At the same time the President is extending a helpful hand – making a promise that those in need will receive an appropriate help from a variety of state bodies. It is supported by an action in the form of enacted piece of legislation ("The Presidential Executive Order to this effect was signed today"). That fragment also is building an element of ethos as Vladimir Putin portrays himself as a President who cares about the people of Russia and not only makes promises but also acts on his own to improve the well-being of his fellow citizens in hardship.

> *The government, regional authorities, enterprises and public organisations will do everything to wrap such families in care and help them. Special support will be given to the children of the killed and wounded comrades-in-arms. The Presidential Executive Order to this effect was signed today* (Putin, 2022).

The next two sentences are expressing empathy, showing concern and gratitude to the citizens of Russia holding specific functions that is to say soldiers, medics and paramedics:

> *I wish a speedy recovery to the wounded soldiers and officers, and I thank doctors, paramedics, nurses and staff of military hospitals for their selfless work. Our deepest gratitude goes to you for saving each life, oftentimes sparing no thought for yourselves under shelling on the frontlines* (Putin, 2022).

The next part of Vladimir Putin's speech is the appeal to higher values, that is ethnic tolerance. It is stressed that Russian soldiers are representatives of various ethnic and religious groups. What is more Russia is the country where tolerance is a daily practice. He claims that soldiers of different ethnic origin treat each other like brothers and are free of any racist feelings. But the countries of the West have made attempts at provoking ethnic conflicts and inciting racism in the territory of Russia to divide the people. Fortunately, the attempts were in vain as the power of Russia is in fact a deeply rooted in its multi-nationality or as Putin formulates it "a great invincible power of our united multi-ethnic nation". The whole fragment conveying the sublime message of the lack of racism in Russia and the harmonious multi-ethnic life of its people reads as follows:

> *Comrades,*
>
> *Soldiers and officers from many regions of our enormous Motherland, including those who arrived straight from Donbass, from the combat area, are standing now shoulder-to-shoulder here, on Red Square.*
>
> *We remember how Russia's enemies tried to use international terrorist gangs against us, how they tried to seed inter-ethnic and religious strife so as to weaken us from within and divide us. They failed completely.*
>
> *Today, our warriors of different ethnicities are fighting together, shielding each other from bullets and shrapnel like brothers.*
>
> *This is where the power of Russia lies, a great invincible power of our united multi-ethnic nation (Putin, 2022).*

The next fragment of the speech is the justification of the Ukrainian war which is conveyed both implicitly and explicitly as defending the country and its people:

> *You are defending today what your fathers, grandfathers and great-grandfathers fought for. The wellbeing and security of their Motherland was their top priority in life. Loyalty to our Fatherland is the main value and a reliable foundation of Russia's independence for us, their successors, too.*
>
> *Those who crushed Nazism during the Great Patriotic War showed us an example of heroism for all ages. This is the generation of victors, and we will always look up to them.*
>
> *Glory to our heroic Armed Forces!*
>
> *For Russia! For Victory!*
>
> *Hooray! (Putin, 2022).*

The pathos is structured by referring to well-being, security loyalty, independence, heroism – the highest values for each nation. The pompousness is enhanced by exclamations.

Figures of speech in the speech of Vladimir Putin delivered on 9 May during the Victory Parade on Red Square

Figures of speech may be divided into:

- Syntactic,
- Semantic,
- Lexical,
- Phonetic and
- Word-formation ones.

As the analysis is based on the translation of the speech from Russian into English the phonetic and word-formation figures of speech are not analysed. What is more, as far as syntactic elements are concerned only those not affected by the difference between the Russian and English sentence word order are taken into account.

There are the following syntactic figures of speech:

- Repetitions of the sentence content,
- Exclamations,
- Elliptic expressions,
- Comparisons.

The following repetitions of the sentence content have been identified:

- Victory Day is intimately dear to all of us. There is no family in Russia that was not burnt by the Great Patriotic War. Its memory never fades. On this day, children, grandchildren and great-grandchildren of the heroes, march in an endless flow of the Immortal Regiment. They carry photos of their family members, the fallen soldiers who remained young forever, and the veterans who are already gone.

- We take pride in the unconquered courageous generation of the victors, we are proud of being their successors, and it is our duty to preserve the memory of those who defeated Nazism and entrusted us with being vigilant and doing everything to thwart the horror of another global war.

- Today, we bow our heads to the sacred memory of all those who lost their lives in the Great Patriotic War, the memories of the sons, daughters, fathers, mothers, grandfathers, husbands, wives, brothers, sisters, relatives and friends.

- You are defending today what your fathers, grandfathers and great-grandfathers fought for. The wellbeing and security of their Motherland was their top priority in life. Loyalty to our Fatherland is the main value and a reliable foundation of Russia's independence for us, their successors, too.

The repetitions of the sentence content refer to Russian citizens being successors of generations of heroes who for centuries fought for Russia and its independence.

Exclamations are used for typical purposes in the speech. They are interjections used for expressing congratulations and cheering:

- I congratulate you on the day of great victory!

- Glory to our heroic Armed Forces!

- For Russia!

- For victory!

- Hooray!

Elliptical expressions are a type of expressions in which certain words have been omitted but the meaning is clear and the words missing may easily by inserted. Three exclamations nos. 2-4 may be classified also as elliptical expressions.

Comparisons in public speeches usually serve the purpose of presenting advantages and disadvantages, pros and cons. In the case of the speech by Putin, they are juxtapositions of the good country and evil countries:

Last December we proposed signing a treaty on security guarantees. Russia urged the West to hold an honest dialogue in search for meaningful and compromising solutions, and to take account of each other's interests. All in vain. NATO countries did not want to heed us, which means they had totally different plans. And we saw it (Putin, 2022).

Antithesis is the statement that contradicts the common perceptions. That figure is speech at the syntactic level is represented by the following statement:

> *But we are a different country. Russia has a different character. We will never give up our love for our Motherland, our faith and traditional values, our ancestors' customs and respect for all peoples and cultures* Putin, 2022).

The following semantic figures of speech may be found in the text:

- metonymy;
- allegory;
- comparisons,
- metaphors,
- euphemisms.

Metonymy is the figure of speech figure which replaces the name of some object or concept with a word closely related to the term in question. In the speech "Kiev" in reference to modern times means the government of Ukraine. "The Borodino Field" means the battle waged with Napoleon.

Allegory is the figure of speech used to express the symbolic meaning, typically hidden, frequently political. In that case the West is a symbol of evil powers, the enemies of Russia, Russophobic countries.

Semantic comparisons provide juxtapositions of associations. One of such comparisons includes the comparison of Russia to the savior of the world.

A metaphor is:

> *a rhetorical element that generally involves using a concrete word to express an abstract concept and which takes the form of elliptical comparison based on an analogy between two objects, two concepts, or two situations that possess a common characteristic (Delisle et al., 1999, pp. 157).*

The names of various cities, as described above, are given as the metaphors of the fight for independence with the invading country, 'young forever' is a metaphor meaning that soldiers died at the young age.

A euphemism is a word or expression which is:

considered offensive or hurtful, especially one concerned with religion, sex, death, or excreta. Some English euphemisms suggest royal or divine intervention, or even are borrowings from slang and colloquialism (Matulewska, 2007, p. 123).

The author has identified one euphemism 'the fallen soldiers' meaning soldiers who lost their lives in the battles fighting for the independence of the country. Instead of saying dead or deceased soldiers the euphemizing adjective has been used.

Lexical figures of speech:

- Repetitions,
- Elliptical expressions,
- Hyperboles,
- Polysemy,
- Archaization,
- Synonymy.

According to Rabab'ah and Abuseileek's (2012, p. 445) repetition "(...) is employed to perform a variety of language functions." These functions are:

(...) emphasis, clarity, emotions, highlight the obvious, be questionable, express annoyance, persuasion, express surprise, give instructions, ana as a filler in order to take time, when the speaker was searching for a paper for a proper word to say what would come next.

Lexical repetitions adding extra emphasis, increasing pathos through logos include wors such as: 'security', 'Kiev', 'Motherland', 'veteran', 'soldier' and 'defeat'. Their aim is in general to increase the persuasiveness of the speech.

Saint Isidore (Merchant, 2019) claim that "Ellipsis is an incompletion of speech, in which necessary words are missing.", or as Merchant (2019) adds: "in which words appear to be missing." Kempson *et al.* (2015, p. 114) broadens the above definition followingly: "Ellipsis is a phenomenon in which what is conveyed, in some sense to be explained, does not need to be fully verbally articulated." As already mentioned above when discussing the syntactic figures of speech, three exclamations nos. 2-4 (see above) may be classified also as elliptical expressions. But the names of cities where various battles were waged are also elliptical expressions serving the purpose of creating the atmosphere of the besieged nation that continually needs to defend its interests and borders.

As Snoeck Henkemans (2017, p. 269) defines it: "Hyperbole is rhetorical trope by means of which statements are made that are obviously exaggerated and thus untrue and unwarranted." Burgers *et al.* (2016, p. 415) are of the same opinion, claiming that: "Hyperbole involves extreme exaggeration by describing something (an 'ontological referent') as larger than it really is. For instance, if you are late for a meeting with a friend, and this friend tells you that they 'have been waiting *for ages*," this statement contains exaggeration of the waiting time." At the same time hyperboles are used to add extra emphasis, to increase the emotional load of the message and to communicate the feelings flooding the speaker, feelings that need to be spoken out. The hyperboles used by Putting include the phrase "atrocious and barbaric shelling" referring to the military operations that are heinous for civilians but in fact are something normal for troops no matter which side they are fighting for.

Finally, Matthews (2005, p. 285) claims that polysemy is "the case of a single word, having two or more related senses". Sometimes it is defined as "the association of two or more related senses with a single linguistic form". In general,

> The relation of polysemy binds terms belonging to the same part of speech, having the same spelling, the same pronunciation, the same etymology but more than one meaning where the meanings of the term are conceptually and historically related. In linguistics the distinction is made between polysemy and homonymy. The relation of homonymy binds two terms belonging to the same part of speech, having the same spelling, frequently the same or very similar pronunciation but differing in meaning and etymology. ... For the needs of this paper the term polysemy will be used in reference to the terms belonging to the same part of speech, having the same spelling, the same pronunciation but more than one meaning (Matulewska 2016, p. 73).

One of the most polysemous words in the speech is one of the proper names (a toponym), that is 'Kiev'. This toponym at the referential level designates a city in Ukraine. But in the speech, it is used to designate battles waged for this city, the government of Ukraine, and at the pragmatic layer it is used as a metaphor of the fight for independence and the geographical area traditionally constituting part of Russia.

Archaization may be briefly characterized by using archaic or obsolete words instead of their modern synonyms. The archaic word 'warrior' is used to designate 'soldiers'. The speech does not contain many archaisms as its aim is to be understandable and persuasive. The more frozen and archaic the language is, the less comprehensible the message is and consequently less persuasive.

As Matulewska (2016) claims:

> The relation of synonymy is a semantic relation and binds two terms with the same referential meaning – but not necessarily the same pragmatic meaning – which belong to the same part of speech and differ in spelling. In many publications, synonymy is perceived as a sort of semantic equivalence. However semantic equivalence should not be identified with translational equivalence due to the fact that the pragmatic aspects of meaning of lexical items may be vital for producing communicatively adequate messages in the target language. If one takes into consideration the conglomerate of meanings, which a given term may possess, and the fact that one may hardly find any terms with exactly the same conglomerate of meanings, it seems more appropriate to discuss quasi-synonymous terms rather than synonymous terms, especially in the context of specialised translation. To summarise, there are hardly any absolute synonyms, that is to say, terms that would have the same meanings and would be interchangeable in all communicative (situational) and syntactic contexts...

The following synonyms have been identified:

- 'Fatherland' and 'Motherland';
- 'Neo-Nazis' and 'enemy';
- 'comrades-in-arms', 'fellow soldiers', 'soldiers' and 'heroes'.

Synonyms in that case serve the purpose of making the speech stylistically varied, more attractive, plausible, and consequently also persuasive.

To sum up, all syntactic, semantic and lexical figures of speech serve the purpose of creating a persuasive speech falling into the category of strategic communication, appealing to the listeners and making them believe that the justice must be done and peace must be protected.

Conclusion

In conclusion, the logos of Vladimir Putin's speech is built around historical events such as: the Polish-Muscovite War of 1609–1618; the Battle of Borodino; the Battles of Moscow; the Siege of Leningrad; the Battle of Kiev; the Battle of Minsk; the Battle of Stalingrad; the Battle of Kursk; the Battle of Sevastopol; the Battles of Kharkov. Moreover is build around national heroes who are listed as anonymous citizens: 'the Immortal Regiment'; 'the fallen soldiers who remained young forever' (meaning who died young); soldiers under the command of ...'; the sons, daughters, fathers, mothers, grandfathers, husbands, wives, brothers, sisters, relatives and friends; Odessa martyrs, the old people, women and children of Donbass who were killed in atrocious and barbaric shelling by neo-Nazis; our fighting comrades who died a brave death in the righteous battle – for Russia and specific persons: Minin, Pozharsky, prince Svyatoslav, prince Vladimir Monomakh, Rumyantsev, Potemkin, Suvorov, Brusilov, Nikolai Vatutin, Sidor Kovpak, Lyudmila Pavlichenko.

The selected historical events are very symbolic. The Polish-Muscovite war of 1609–1618 serves the purpose of inciting fear in actions of the Polish society and government, clearly and obviously supporting Ukraine on the international level and local one, letting in and giving shelter to Ukrainian refugees. The Battle of Borodino in 1812 waged with Napoleon shows that there is historical evidence that France may be the enemy of Russia again. The Battle of Moscow with the Nazi Germany in 1941 and other battles fought against the Germans create the modern German nation a potential enemy of the Russian Federation as well.

The author of the speech has skillfully combined ethos of Vladimir Putin, logos and pathos to create the positive image of Russians. They are heroes defending their country, fighting for the peace and preventing the outbreak of the third world war. But the heroes are also of Ukrainian ethnic origin. The battles mentioned often took place in the Ukrainian territory. The message is that through the history Ukraine has been a part of the

Russian 'empire', 'Russian 'power', that Ukrainian fought hand in hand with Russians for the independence of one, unified country against multiple enemies. It significantly strengthens the message that Ukraine is a part of Russia and should be formally within its borders. The figures of speech used put extra emphasis and increase the persuasiveness of the speech. In general, the speech is a very good example of good rhetoric serving the purpose of strategic communication at the critical moment when important and controversial events are witnessed by citizens and need to be evaluated. What is more, politicians want such events to be evaluated in a manner most favourable for them.

Considering the security issues, one cannot deny the fact that the methods of spreading information and misinformation, including fake news are a part of hybrid warfare. Sometimes it is just the charismatic leader and properly structured rhetoric that wins the support of masses whether at the national or international level. The persuasiveness is a key element of many types of strategic communication.

References

Adeyeri, J. O. and Akinola, F. (2021) "Germen Occupation of Soviet Unioin during World War II: The Significance of the Libertion of Leningrad", *International Journal of History and Philosophical Research*, 9.1, p. 9–18. Available at: https://papers.ssrn.com/sol3/papers. cfm?abstract_id=3829082.

Afanasenko, V. I. (2015) "First Battle of Kharkov (7-26 October 1941)", *Военный сборник*, 8.2, p.72-83. doi: 10.13187/vs.2015.8.72.

Aristotle, (n.d.). *Rhetoric*. Available at http://etext.library.adelaide. edu.au/a/aristotle/ a8rh/book1.html.

Armstrong, J. A. (1963) *Ukrainian Nationalism.* Columbia University Press.

Axell, A. (2011) "Russia's Heroes 1941–45". *Journal of Military Studies*, 39.2, p. 152–159.

Bakhov, I., Ryzhykov, V. & Kolisnyk, O. (2018) "Leadership abilities of a Military Manager, Professionalism of a Commander as the Guarantee of the Practice of Effective Activity of a Military Organization", *International Journal of Engineering and Technology*, 7, p. 45-49. Available at: https://www.researchgate.net/

profile/Ivan-Bakhov/publication/33003 9098_Leadership_abili-
ties_of_a_military_manager_professionalismof_a_commander_
as_the_guarantee_of_the_practiceof_effective_activity_of_a_
military_organization/links/5dc9d08a458515143503bf2f/
Leadership-abilities-of-a-military-manager-professionalis-
mof-a-commander-as-the-guaranteeof-the-practiceof-effec-
tive-activity-of-a-military-organiza-tion. pdf.

Bieleń, S. & Raś, M. (2008) *Polityka zagraniczna Rosji.* Warszawa:
Difin.

Brown, P. B. (1982) 'Muscovy, Poland, and the Seventeenth Century
Crisis'. *The Polish Review,* vol. 27. Available at: https://www.jstor.
org/stable/25777894.

Burgers, C., Konijn, E. A. & Steen, G. J. (2016) "Figurative Framing:
Shaping Public Discourse through Metaphor, Hyperbole, and
Irony", *Communication Theory,* p. 410-430. doi: 10.1111/
comt.12096.

Delisle, J., Lee-Jahnke, H. & Cormier, M. C. (1999) *Translation Terminology.* John Benjamins Publishing Company.

Demirdöğen, Ü. D. (2010) "The roots of research in (political) persuasion: Ethos, pathos, logos and the Yale studies of persuasive
communications", *International Journal of Social Inquiry,* 3(1),
p. 189-201. Available at: https://dergipark.org.tr/en/download/
article-file/ 164133

Donnel, C. (2016) *The Defence of Sevastopol, 1941–1942: The Soviet
Perspective.* Barnsley: Pen and Sword Military.

Duran, J. A. (1969) "Catherine II, Potemkin, and colonization policy
in Southern Russia", *The Russian Review,* 28(1), 23-36.doi:
10.2307/126983.

Falin, V. M. (2015) "The Battle of Moscow – Turning Point of World
War II", Vestnik Rudin *International Relations,* 2, p. 7–13. Available at: https://journals.rudn.ru/ international-relations/article/
view/10731.

Farwell, J. P. (2012) *Persuasion and power: the art of strategic communication.* Washington, DC: Georgetown University Press.

Gerber, T. P. & Zavisca, J. (2016) "Does Russian Propaganda Work?",
The Washington Quarterly, p. 79-98.

Gładysz, A. (2012) „Niemcy – uczestnicy wojny moskiewskiej w wybra-
nych relacjach wyższych dowódców polskich (1609–1612)", *Teka
Komisji Historycznej, IX,* p. 32-52.

Hallahan, K. *at al* (2007) 'Defining strategic communication', *International Journal of Strategic Communication*, 1(1), p. 3–35. doi: 10.1080/15531180701285244.

Holtzhausen, D. & Zerfass, A. (2014) 'Strategic Communication Opportunities and Challenges of the Research Area' in: Holtzhausen, D. and Zerfass, A. (eds.) *The Routledge Handbook of Stategic Communication*. New York: Routledge.

International Advisory Panel Report. Council of Europe (2015). Available at: https://rm.coe.int/CoERMPublicCommonSearchServices/DisplayDCTMContent?documentId=090000168048851b.

Jowett, G. S. and O'Donnell, V. (1992) *Propaganda and Persuasion*. Newbury Park: Palgrave.

Kavaliauskaus, T. (2011) 'Different meanings of May 9th, Victory Day over Nazi Germany for Russia and the Baltic States', *Interdisciplinary Studies on Central and Eastern Europe*, p. 319-336.

Kempson, R. *et all* (2015) "Ellipsis", in Lappin, S. and Fox, C. *The Handbook of Contemporary Semantic Theory. New York City: John Wiley and Sonsp.*

Knyazev, V. M *et all* (2016) "Grand Generals of Russia in development of military physical training of soldiers and officers of Russian Army', *Theory and Practice of Physical Culture*.

Kurczab-Redlich, K. (2016) *Wowa, Wołodia, Władimir. Tajemnice Rosji Putina*. Warsaw: Wydawnictwo W.A.B.

Lewis, S.J. (2003) 'The Battle of Stalingrad', Block by Block: The Challenges of Urban Operations. Fort Leavenworth: U.S. Army Command and General Staff College Press.

Lysenko, P. F. (2019) "Turov Principality during the Grand Duke of Kiev Vladimir Monomakh (1113–1125)", *Proceedings of the National Academy of Sciences of Belarus, Humanitarian Series*, vol. 64, no. 4.

Matthews, P. (2005) *The Concise Oxford Dictionary of Linguistics*. Oxford: Oxford University Press.

Matulewska, A. (2007) *Lingua Legis in Translation*. Frankfurt am Main, Germany: Peter Lang Publishing House.

Matulewska, A. (2016) "Semantic Relations between Legal Terms. A Case Study of the Intralingual Relation of Synonymy", *Studies in logic, grammar and rhetoric,* vol. 45, no. 1.

Matulewska, A. (2016) "Walking on Thin Ice of Translation of Terminology in Legal Settings", *International Journal of Legal Discourse*.

Merchant, J. (2019) 'Ellipsis: A survey of analytical approaches', in Craenbroeck, J. v. and Temmerman, T. (eds.) A handbook of ellipsis.

Putin, V. (2022) Victory Parade on Red Square. Available at: http:// en.kremlin.ru/ events/president/news/68366.

Putin, V. (2022) Парад Победы на Красной площади. Available at: http://kremlin. ru/events/president/news/68366.

Rabab'ah, G. & Abuseileek, A. F. (2012) 'The Pragmatic Functions of Repetitions in TV Discourse', *Research in Language*, vol. 10, no. 4.

Read, A. (2005) *The Devil's Desciples: Hitler's Inner Circle*. New York: W.W. Norton & Company.

Schindler, J. (2003) "Steamrollered in Galicia: The Austro-Hungarian Army and the Brusilov Offensive 1916", *War in History*, vol. 10, no. 1.

Sołonin, M. S. (2007) *22 czerwca 1941 czyli jak zaczęła się Wielka Wojna Ojczyźniana*. Poznań: Dom Wydawniczy Rebis.

Stanton, G. (1996) *Ten Stages of Genocide*. Available at: https://www. genocidewatch.com/ tenstages.

Tucker-Jones, A. (2016) *The Battle for Kharkov, 1941–1943*. Barnsley: Pen and Sword.

Tumarkin, N. (2003) "The Great Patriotic War", *European Review*, vol. 10, no. 4.

Zamulin, V. (2012) "The Battle of Kursk: New Findings", *The Journal of Slavic Military Studies*, vol. 25, no. 3.

Zemstov, V. (2007) 'The battle of Borodino. The fall of the grand redoute'. *The Journal of Slavic Military Studies*, vol. 13, no. 1.

CHAPTER 5

Actions of Security Service of Ukraine in a period of defence of Kiev

Krzysztof Górecki

Abstract

This chapter focuses on the pivotal role of the Security Service of Ukraine (SSU) in fortifying state resilience during the Battle of Kiev in the early stages of the Russian invasion. This chapter first explores the fundamental concepts of intelligence and counterintelligence, elaborating on the evolution of the SSU and how governmental reforms transformed the agency from a reactive to a proactive posture. The analysis is based on open-source information provided by the SSU, highlighting key operations such as information warfare, detaining foreign agents, capturing collaborators, and neutralizing sabotage and reconnaissance groups. The study reveals that the SSU's primary focus was on conducting information operations, significantly contributing to Ukraine's overall defence strategy during this critical phase of the war. The findings demonstrate the importance of SSU's intelligence efforts in countering espionage and sabotage, further illustrating the SSU's role in bolstering national defence through strategic information operations

Keywords: SSU, battle of Kiev, counterintelligence, SBU, war in Ukraine

Introduction

Information is power. The significance of information in modern warfare is critical. The ongoing war in Ukraine proves that truth clearly. Those who know where the enemy is hiding and what his intentions are have an advantage. However, raw data is often not enough. It needs to be put in context and processed for decision-makers. Information is the domain of intelligence services. Their responsibility is gathering intelligence and protecting state secrets. To properly understand the idea of intelligence, first there is a need to define what intelligence is. There is an intellectual struggle among scientists in intelligence studies about how to give the right meaning to intelligence. However, one of the recent definitions seems to be one of the most interesting and, at the same time, the broadest. The Department of Defence, starting in 2021, set up the document "DOD Dictionary of Military and Associated Terms," where intelligence is defined as:

> *The product resulting from the collection, processing, integration, evaluation, analysis, and interpretation of available information concerning foreign nations, hostile or potentially hostile forces or elements, or areas of actual or potential operations. The activities that result in the product. The organizations engaged in such activities (DOD Dictionary of Military and Associated Terms, 2021, p. 107).*

The first thing that should be emphasized in this definition is that intelligence can be related to the internal and external activities of a state. The second thing that comes up from this definition are tangible parts of the intelligence cycle, which is an essential activity in every organization related to intelligence. As Lowenthal shows, the intelligence cycle is divided into seven steps, which are: identifying requirements; collection; processing and exploitation; analysis and production; dissemination; consumption; and feedback (Lowenthal, 2017, p. 73).

Thus, after it is known what intelligence is, it is reasonable from the perspective of a security state to answer how to oppose it. Because the state can secure only if their secrets are safe. That is the reason why it is necessary to focus on counterintelligence, which has a narrower conception than intelligence, even if both of them use similar tools. The aforementioned DOD Dictionary of Military and Associated Terms defines counterintelligence as:

> *Information gathered and activities conducted to identify, deceive, exploit, disrupt, or protect against espionage, other intelligence activities, sabotage, or assassinations conducted for or on behalf of foreign powers, organizations or persons or their agents, or international terrorist organizations or activities (DOD Dictionary of Military and Associated Terms, 2021, p. 51).*

Looking closely at this definition, it is clear that in the case of Ukraine, the institution that is fulfilling those kinds of activities is the SSU. The Security Service of Ukraine (SSU) is a civil counterintelligence service responsible for the protection of national sovereignty, territorial integrity, constitutional order, and the potential of Ukraine from the intelligence and subversion activities of foreign special services. SSU was raised on September 20, 1991, as the successor of the Ukrainian branch of the Soviet KGB (Larecki, 2017, p. 787).

A new reform of the SSU began in 2019 and brought a new bill for the Security Service of Ukraine. The main purpose of the reform was to make the SSU more effective at responding to modern threats, especially in the hybrid warfare domain. As a result, Bill 3196 on the reform of the Security Service of Ukraine was registered in the Parliament on March 10, 2020, which was prepared with expert consultations from NATO, the EU, and the USA. Bill 3196 regulates areas on which SSU is focused on:

- Protection of state secrets.
- Counterintelligence and counteractions to threats to state security.
- Protection of national statehood and territorial integrity.
- Cyber security.
- Protection of state secrets.

It needs to be emphasized that SSU is not dealing with economic crimes but, as an institution, is responsible for the protection of critical infrastructure. As it is in many countries in Europe, intelligence services have to counteract espionage and terrorist events that often target critical infrastructure. That said, it is necessary for SSU to provide modern protection to such facilities from physical and cyber threats.

Another matter that the new reform implicates is the number of staff. Reformed SSU significantly reduced the number of officers from 27 000 to 15 000 in time of peace. Because Ukraine is now at war, the number of servicemen today is over 27,000, which is an effect of the implemented mobilization plan. Lowering the number of staff has a purpose: to make the service more effective and flexible in responding to asymmetric threats used in hybrid warfare.

The aforementioned changes define the most important thing in the reformed Security Service of Ukraine, which is the approach. New assumptions of service enforced a change from a reactive approach to a proactive and risk-oriented approach. It means that SSU has chosen a path of offensive counterintelligence, which is more adjusted to hybrid actions conducted by Russia (Security Service of Ukraine, 2022).

The annexation of Crimea in 2014 was a complete failure for SSU as a counterintelligence service. It has shown weaknesses in the security state across the whole spectrum. This defeat forced SSU to reconsider their approach and intensify their efforts to better carry out their duties. Probably the Crimea failure was one of the main reasons that Ukrainian politics was forced to reform the SSU from an old-fashioned institution to a modern, tailored intelligence service in Eastern Europe.

Collaboration with western intelligence services had a major influence on improving the operation of SSU. Since beginning of Russian invasion United States government provide to Ukrainian services important support, in GOINT a specially in IMINT area. This kind of data had a significant influence on decision makers, which certainly contributed to the success of the first part of the war—the Battle of Kiev (U.S. Department of State, 2023).

The Security Service of Ukraine, as a special service, has a couple of tools that allow them to complete the tasks under their responsibility. To make this paper more understandable, I will separate the two main types of activities conducted by SSU: tradecraft and collation and information operations. The first of them is commonly recognizable, especially in terms of special services. One of the definitions of tradecraft is:

> *Specialized methods and equipment used in the organization and activity of intelligence organizations, especially techniques and method for handling communications with agents. 2. Operational practices and skills used in performance of intelligence- related duties* (Goldman & Meret, 2016, p. 578).

The second branch of activities related to SSU is the aforementioned collation and information operations. By the definition collation is *the process whereby information is assembled together and compared critically* (Goldman & Meret, 2016, p. 89). Information operations are defined as *employment of core capabilities of electronic warfare, computer network operation, in concert with specified supporting and related capabilities, to affect and defend information and information system and to influence decision making* (Goldman & Meret, 2016, p. 279).

Since the beginning of the war, there have been several important turning points. The first one was the battle of Kiev. Defence of the capitol had begun 25th of February and lasted to 2nd of April. That crucial time was extremely important to the moral strength of Ukrainian society and to their security services. In that time, SSU must double their endeavours in counteracting intense operations from Russian intelligence services and their cooperatives. Most of the successes announced by the Security Service of Ukraine on their website in that period were the culmination of long-term efforts. Because of that fact, it might be highly valuable to study those actions during that time.

The purpose of that paper is to show the reader the importance and significance of activities that security services should boldly perform as examples of SSU actions during war.

The author overlooked the daily news, which was shown on the official website of SSU. After that, all the information about actions was selected and divided into categories. Each incident was treated as one of a kind in its category, no matter how many, for example, persons were detained or how many subversive groups were neutralized. All collected data were shown with respect to type and quantity and analyzed by their significance.

During the research, the author reviewed literature and documents about counterintelligence to properly qualify events into certain categories that were chosen to better expose the meaning of collected data. What is more, there has been no research such as this conducted in an open-source scholar database yet. This is the reason why the author wants to fill this gap with this article.

To achieve the goal, the author will try to answer some important questions. First one is what kind of operations SSU conducted from the beginning of the war to 2nd of April? An answer to that will give us a spectrum in which SSU operate in times of war. The second question is, "How many of each kind of action were conducted? This answer will clarify where in the spectrum of operations conducted by SSU the centre of gravity is. The cause of the next question lies in the main effort on which SSU was focused. What was the significance of the operations conducted?

Types and quantity of actions taken by Security Service of Ukraine

During the Battle of Kiev, the SSU used several types of tactical actions, such as detaining agents of enemy secret services. On the 7th of March, SSU detained in Kiev a Russian agent who was cooperating with the GRU and who was the director of a defence company. This company from Dnipro delivered drones and software to them. Another example of this kind of operation, which is particularly interesting, was on the 8th of March, when Ukrainian counterintelligence detained the FSB's "sleeper agent," who had tried to join the local territorial defence unit. As SSU has revealed in the past, this agent served in the Berkut and was a security guard for a top official in Ukraine. In 2014, he fled to Russia. At the beginning of 2022, FSB handlers instructed the agent to come to Ukraine and lie low in Volyn. On February 23, the day before the invasion, he was told to get ready and wait for further instructions. From the beginning of the war in Ukraine until the 2nd of April, USS conducted 21 operations to detain agents of enemy secret services.

The next kind of SSU activity, which belongs to tradecraft, was capturing a collaborator. These kinds of actions are important because they are connected to the treason of citizens. On March 6, in Kiev, the SSU detained two brothers who sympathized with Russia. They propagated pro-Russian and pro-Belarusian points of view. Moreover, during the investigation, SSU proved the accused collaborated with the intelligence services of both aforementioned countries. The assignment set up by foreign services for the brothers was to destabilize the internal situation and ameliorate the picture of Russia and Belarus. Similar kinds of operations within the designated period of time were 35 (Security Service of Ukraine, 2022).

Another one of these tradecrafts that needs to be emphasized is the neutralization of sabotage and reconnaissance groups. Those kinds of groups are one of the crucial fundamentals of Russian hybrid warfare. That is why this particular activity of security services had tremendous meaning during this war. An example of that kind of counteraction against the enemy had taken place for the first time on the 27th of February since the war had started in the Mykolaiv region. SSU had eliminated the activity of sabotage and reconnaissance groups that tried to overtake strategic facilities in that part of the country. What is more, SSU informed us that in that region they had neutralized 15 of those groups earlier in time. The first sabotage group in Kiev was on March 3. The main purpose of that group was to gather information about military units that were in the capital. Over the course of the battle of Kiev, the SSU conducted eight operations of neutralizing sabotage and reconnaissance groups (Security Service of Ukraine, 2022).

> *One of the many operations conducted by SSU that also belongs to tradecraft is the detention of deserters. These kinds of actions also have significant importance, such as the detention of collaborators. On March 14, in the Vinnytsia region, SSU, in collaboration with the Border Guard Service, blocked an attempt by 10 men who were trying to illegally cross the border with Moldova. There were five similar detentions related to deserters during the discussion period* (Security Service of Ukraine, 2022).

> *Seizure of weapons warehouses is another kind of activity performed by security services. On March 4, in Vinnytsia region, SSU found a hidden warehouse in the forest where F1 grenades, 2 kg of TNT, 10 RGD, grenades for grenade launchers, and loaded magazines for automatic firearms were kept. This kind of action is rare, which proves that there were only two of them until April 4, since the beginning of the invasion* (Security Service of Ukraine, 2022).

However, the aforementioned examples of tradecraft seem interesting, but all of them need to end with investigative actions and the initiation of criminal proceedings to be effective in a democratic country. On March 4, SSU opened the first such proceedings against an LNR militant who cooperated with the Russian army and made himself the head of the civil-military administration; by doing so, he demanded full submission of the local authorities. What is interesting is that the official announcements of the SSU sparsely show information about legal actions because, during the Battle of Kiev, there were only four of that kind revealed (Security Service of Ukraine, 2022).

In modern warfare, information operations are equally important as tradecraft. Moreover, the results of those undertakings can sometimes have a more devastating effect than a missile attack. An example of these actions that need to be emphasized is the interception of radio and telephone conversations by Russian soldiers. The first of them since the beginning of the invasion took place on March 12. In that particular audiogram, SSU revealed that Russian soldiers received orders to kill everyone—civilians, children, whoever—to shoot everyone. However, in the same news report, there was also information that the situation of those Russian soldiers was dramatic because only a few of them survived and they were surrounded. Similar kinds of intelligence published on the SSU website in the designated period were 80 (Security Service of Ukraine, 2022).

Sometimes SSU includes in its daily posts attached videos with interviews of detained Russian soldiers. On March 4, the first message of that kind was published. What needs highlighting in this video is a former Ukrainian soldier who betrayed his country in 2014 and became a Russian soldier. His artillery division was ordered to attack Ukraine and marched towards Nova Kakhovka on February 24. Further in the video, this detained soldier said that they were told that everything had been set up and would be the same as in 2014, during the annexation of Crimea. Congruous videos were published in number 21 (Security Service of Ukraine, 2022).

The last activity that includes a wide spectrum of informational operations is operating in cyberspace. Modern warfare cannot be isolated from the cyber domain. Moreover, the Security Service of Ukraine did not forget about this aspect of war during the battle of Kiev. Already on February 27th, SSU posted that they were acting in cyberspace. But first, information about actions conducted in the cyber domain was shown on March 8. The operation was to contain large-scale cyber-attacks from Russia. These attacks were targeted to shut down telecommunication systems and critical infrastructure. What is important is that it revealed news that cyber sabotage had started before the invasion. Firstly at 13–14th of January, then 15–16th of February, and last one before full-scaled war on 23-24th of February. SSU posted 5 information about their cyber activity between 24th of February and 4th of April (Security Service of Ukraine, 2022).

Some operations, like the takeover of a destroyed enemy drone, are hard to qualify for any of the aforementioned types of actions. However, they were also published by SSU during the appointed period. That is why they need to be mentioned.

Significance of actions

The types and numbers of actions aforementioned are interesting, but as with all information, it needs to be given meaning. To understand them correctly, they need to be seen separately and as a whole. In this part of the paper, there will be some significance to each type and overall activity of the SSU during the Battle of Kiev. To make this paper more transparent, the activities of SSU were divided into two categories: first, tradecraft, and second, collation and information operations. In every one of those categories, there were subtypes to be distinguished. From the beginning, each of these categories and subtypes will be discussed.

Tradecraft activity is one of the most crucial and recognizable actions in intelligence services. In time, lots of legends grew up in this mysterious, covert area. However, ways are secret, but means are usually not. That is the reason why sometimes special services reveal their achievements. Because war is no longer a struggle between an army of opponents but a clash between entire nations, special services at that time need to adapt to that reality. To operate efficiently, they need to make connections with society. By that, it means that society knows that they are constantly working for results, and every citizen can help in that effort. To accomplish that goal, SSU is using their website and posting daily news. Sometimes three to five pieces of information are shown each day, starting on March 3, 2022. What needs to be emphasized is that the first news after the 24th of February that was posted on a website was related to tradecraft activity of SSU in lots of regions of the country. It should be understood as the first signal to society and to everyone who was reading this that the Security Service of Ukraine, as a whole state, has not broken down under enemy attack. Moreover, as part of their service, they doubled their efforts all over the country to win against invaders.

In that light should be seen information from 27th of February, the first one after invasion starts. Because SSU is a counterintelligence service, the first news was related to the detention of a group of Russian spies. On one hand, from a citizen's point of view, that message is important to create a sense of competence and quick reaction; on the other hand, from the Russian point of view, this is information that the whole group was exposed to, and their intelligence should be treated as a deception of the SSU even if it was not.

Similar activity from a counterintelligence perspective is capturing a collaborator. However, a collaborator is a citizen who openly supports hostile actions against his own country, unlike an agent who is cooperating with the enemy in a covert way. By revealing this kind of information, SSU probably first of all wants to deter collaboration with the enemy through inevitable punishment. However, the scale of collaboration might also be a problem. If the scale was too large, it might be shown by Russian propaganda that there was a lot of support from Ukrainian society for the Russian agenda. This may be a reason why SSU has not revealed precise data on how many people collaborated with Russians in official statements. One piece of information about the detention of collaborators was shown on the 15th of March, and it was related to some hackers who provided mobile communication for the enemy. Later in the same day, SSU announced that in the past 24 hours (March 14), they had captured over 60 collaborators all over Ukraine. The attitude adopted by Ukrainian servicemen in the first period of the war could be driven by the desire to prevent the breakdown of resistance and the strength of society.

As a military success, this should be treated as the neutralization of sabotage and reconnaissance groups. This kind of operation is rather connected to the activity of special forces. However, since February 24, SSU has declared its participation in all aspects of war, including actions on the battlefield. Nevertheless, this sort of information was more related to investigating those hostile groups and indicating the right units that neutralized them. In a broad perspective, this kind of news is important to create a vision in society of an SSU active posture during ongoing conflict. About this sort of activity, SSU informed the public in their first news after the outbreak of the war, which might be seen as proof of the thesis about the creation vision of an active attitude.

Detention of deserters in its character is like a matter of collaborators. On the one hand, it is important to inform citizens about failed attempts at desertion to prevent society from trying that. On the other hand, if the scale of this procedure was too large, it might be a problem in the informational dimension. The impact of large-scale issues related to desertion could break the will to fight in society. In that perspective, it is understandable why, during the Battle of Kiev, on the official website of the SSU, we could see only five cases connected to the detention of deserters.

Another example similar, from a functional perspective, to the neutralization of sabotage and reconnaissance groups is the seizure of weapons warehouses. Thus, this is more of a special forces' domain. However, by being a part of these operations, SSU is sending a signal to recipients that they are also operating within a wider spectrum of responsibility during wartime.

Hiram Johnson once said, "The first casualty when war comes is truth". That is the reason why, from an international perspective, the most important thing during the conflict, especially if some country finds itself as a democratic state, is investigative action and the initiation of criminal proceedings. Because during a war both struggling sides are usually willing to bend some rules, both of them will probably use lies to create their international image. But if a country is a democratic state, it needs to follow some rules even if the other side does not. Moreover, democratic states have to prove that they are following international law and documenting it. In this light, we should be seeing that kind of information being sent by SSU to the international environment. From an internal political point of view, this sort of news is not so popular. First of all, they are not as spectacular as the detention of spies. The second thing that needs to be emphasized is that there is a part of society that might be thinking that Russian soldiers do not deserve the western way of justice. Thus, that news might be provocative for them.

To strengthen the remittance SSU sometimes supports their daily news by revealing conversations of Russian soldiers which were intercepted. Moreover, to make those reports more reliable, SSU often included videos with interviews of detained Russian soldiers.

This kind of activity should be seen as creating better posture in Ukrainian soldiers, unlike Russians. Those intercepted conversations and video materials allow SSU to disclose the savagery and helplessness of enemy soldiers. This kind of information was definitely directed to Russians as well as to Ukrainians. In the first case, this message might be seen as a warning for any other Russian soldiers that if they want to survive, they should stay in their homeland. In the second case, this message should be seen as a manifestation of winning good over evil. That kind of broadcast certainly improved the nation's will to fight. What needs to be outlined is that this sort of action was the most common during the Battle of Kiev. Taking into consideration that the battle of Kiev was at the beginning of the invasion and that time was crucial to maintaining resistance and building up resilience, undoubtedly, those processes take time and money. To conduct the aforementioned operations, SSU does not have to spend a lot of financial resources because they are relatively cheap and have tangible effects.

The last one to notice was cyberspace. They are not spectacular, but their meaning in the modern world is only increasing. Russians used them as a preparation before invasion. During the Battle of Kiev, cyber-attacks were also used to create external chaos by disrupting communication systems. This is why prevention and countermeasures taken by SSU in cyberspace were so important. Furthermore, society needs to know that in that domain, Ukraine is also resisting, even if some of the attacks have succeeded.

Conclusions

In summary, the Security Service of Ukraine, as a counterintelligence institution, has played an important role against Russian invaders in the Battle of Kiev. To properly fulfill their task, this service was reformed to be more effective. The main change that allowed us to achieve our goal was a reorientation in our approach from a reactive to a proactive one. As a result of the aforementioned reforms, after the outbreak of war, Ukrainian society, along with the international community, has been witness to a great number of actions conducted by the SSU. From conducted analysis clearly results that a great part of all kinds of activity taken by the SSU during the battle of Kiev, was focused on information operations.

Although most of them were targeted to disrupt Russian war activity, news about those actions sent by Ukrainian counterintelligence reached two recipients. The first was Ukrainian society, which needed assurances about the strength of the state. This transparent approach to the activity of the intelligence service allows the SSU to create an internal environment for the development of bonds between citizens and state institutions based on the belief that citizens are responsible for state security. In effect, the activity of SSU contributes to establishing resilience in the country. Incidentally, another purpose of this undertaking was to counteract New Generation Warfare. The Russians' new doctrine puts pressure on the psychological domain, which is a key point to achieving dominance and, consequently, winning a confrontation with an opponent. To prevent psychological and behavioral advantage, SSU established special links between the service and society. As we can see, that kind of cooperation, which has built moral strength, was essential for Ukraine's victory during the battle of Kiev. On the other hand, the second receivers are foreign actors. First of all, the message was directed at the international community to inform them that Ukraine will not surrender and is determined to fight for its sovereignty. Although it might look unfortunate at first sight for Ukraine, their society will resist the invaders as long as they can, and if there will be support from Western countries, Ukraine will crave victory at all costs. It is necessary to include another recipient of SSU broadcasts: Russian soldiers, conscripts, and anyone who supports Russian perception. The message sent to them by the SSU is clear: there is no reason to take part in this war because the Russian army is weak, unless anyone dares try to confront the whole strength of the Ukrainian nation.

Thus, announcing information by the SSU on the website should also be seen as a psychological weapon used to disintegrate Russian spirit. However, the assessment of that overall effort is hard to evaluate. Nevertheless, the Security Service of Ukraine has had significant influence through active participation in warfare since the beginning of the Russian invasion, especially in terms of capital defence. As a state institution, it has fulfilled its tasks, not only through counterintelligence activity but also by holding up the spirit of the nation, which surely contributed to pushing back invaders from Kiev.

References

Goldman J, Meret S. (2016) *Intelligence and information policy for national security. Key terms and concepts.* Rowman & Littlefield

Larecki, J. H. (2017) *Wielki Leksykon Tajnych Służb Świata.* Kraków. Wydawnictwo RYTM.

Lowenthal, M. M. (2017) *Intelligence. From secrets to Policy, Washington, DC. DOD Dictionary of Military and Associated Terms.* Washington, DC.

Security Service of Ukraine (2022) Address of SSU Head Ivan Bakanov on occasion of SSU's 30th anniversary. Available at: https://ssu.gov.ua/en/novyny/zvernennia-holovy-sbu-ivana-bakanova-z-nahody-30richchia-stvorennia-sluzhby-bezpeky-ukrainy

Security Service of Ukraine (2022) Another belated 'insight' of Russian invader. Available at: https://ssu.gov.ua/en/novyny/shche-odne-zapiznile-prozrinnia-rosiiskoho-zaharbnyka

Security Service of Ukraine (2022) Another enemy's reconnaissance drone found in Poltava region. Available at: https://ssu.gov.ua/en/novyny/shche-odyn-vorozhyi-bezpilotny krozvidnyk-vyiavleno-na-poltavshchyni

Security Service of Ukraine (2022) Captive Russian tanker on 'Russia's success' in war with Ukraine (video). Available at: https://ssu.gov.ua/en/novyny/polonenyi-rosiiskyi-tankist-rozpoviv-pro-uspikhy-rf-na-viini-z-ukrainoiu-video

Security Service of Ukraine (2022) Dissatisfaction with Russian high command grows among Russian occupiers and riots are brewing (audio). Available at: https://ssu.gov.ua/en/ novyny/sered-rosiiskykh-okupantiv-zrostaie-nevdovolennia-vyshchym-komanduvan niam- rf-i-nazrivaiut-bunty-audio

Security Service of Ukraine (2022) Do you know how mobilization is carried out in places that Russia decided to 'protect'? (video). Available at: https://ssu.gov.ua/en/novyny/vy-znaiete-yak-prokhodyt-mobilizatsiia-na-terytoriiakh-yaki-vyrishyla-zakhyshchaty-rosiia-video

Security Service of Ukraine (2022) Every day SSU eliminates enemy agent networks, detects spies and saboteurs. Available at: https://ssu.gov.ua/en/novyny/sbu-shchodnia-zatrymuie-ta-likvidovuie-ahenturni-merezhi-voroha-vyiavliaie-shpyhuniv-i-dyversantiv

Security Service of Ukraine (2022) For Russian occupiers, Mykolaiv is scarier than Chechnya (audio). Available at:

https://ssu.gov.ua/en/novyny/for-russian-occupiers-mykolaiv-is-scarier-than-chechnya-audio

Security Service of Ukraine (2022) For Ukraine's victory, SSU exposes enemy agents and saboteurs. Available at: https://ssu.gov.ua/en/novyny/sbu-vykryvaie-vorozhykh-ahentiv-i-dyversantiv-dlia-peremohy-ukrainy

Security Service of Ukraine (2022) Former Russian law enforcement officer demonstratively tears up passport, veteran's and military IDs (video). Available at: https://ssu.gov.ua/en/ novyny/kolyshnii-pravookhoronets-rf-pokazovo-rozryvaie-svoi-pasport-posvidchennia-veterana-viiskovoi-sluzhby-i-viiskovyi-kvytok-video

Security Service of Ukraine (2022) In 30 years, SSU exposed almost 3,000 individuals who tried to undermine Ukrainian statehood. Available at: https://ssu.gov.ua/en/novyny/za-30-rokiv-sbu-vykryla-maizhe-try-tysiachi-osib-yaki-namahalysia-pidirvaty-ukrainsku-derzhavnist

Security Service of Ukraine (2022) Intercepted conversation on how things are going for Russian occupiers in Ukraine (audio). Available at: https://ssu.gov.ua/en/novyny/ perekhoplena-rozmova-sbu-pro-spravy-rosiiskykh-okupantiv-na-terytorii-ukraini-audio

Security Service of Ukraine (2022) Interrogation of another 'orc' from Russia who betrayed Ukrainian military in 2014 defecting to occupiers in Crimea (video). Available at: https://ssu.gov.ua/en/novyny/dopyt-cherhovoho-orka-z-rf-yakyi-naspravdi-vyiavyvsia-ukrainskym-viiskovymzradnykom-i-u-2014-rotsi-pereishov-na-bik-okupanta-v-krymu-video

Security Service of Ukraine (2022) Investigation of hacker attack on Ukrainian news websites. Available at: https://ssu.gov.ua/en/novyny/shchodo-rozsliduvannia-khakerskoi-ataky-na-novynni-saity-ukrainy

Security Service of Ukraine (2022) Lousy Russian soldiers, 'anti-retreat squads' and significant losses: how Kadyrov units actually fight in Ukraine (audio). Available at: https://ssu.gov.ua/en/novyny/lousy-russian-soldiers-antiretreat-squads-and-significant-losses-how-kadyrov-units-actually-fight-in-ukraine-audio

Security Service of Ukraine (2022) Lousy Russian soldiers, 'anti-retreat squads' and significant losses: how Kadyrov units actually fight in Ukraine (audio).

Security Service of Ukraine (2022) Manic desire to capture Ukraine in three days pushes Russia to send new conscripts and 'alternative servicemen' to battle (video). Available at: https://ssu.gov.ua/en/novyny/cherez-maniakalne-bazhannia-zakhopyty-ukrainu-za-try-dni-u-bii-kynuly-navit-novobrantsiv-ta-alternatyvnykiv-video

Security Service of Ukraine (2022) Militant of Russian PMC Wagner taken prisoner (video). Available at: https://ssu.gov.ua/en/novyny/u-polon-vziato-boiovyka-rosiiskoi-pryvat-noiviiskovoi-kompanii-vahner-video

Security Service of Ukraine (2022) Name Sumy causes fear and despair among enemy invaders (audio). Available at: https://ssu.gov.ua/en/novyny/u-vorozhykh-zaharbnykiv-nazva-mista-sumy-vyklykaie-strakh-i-rozpach-audio

Security Service of Ukraine (2022) New 'story' created for Russians: they want to hold 'victory parade' in Ukraine on May 9 (audio). Available at: https://ssu.gov.ua/en/novyny/dlia-rosiian-prydumaly-novu-baiku-9-travnia-khochut-provodyty-v-ukraini-parad-peremohy-audio

Security Service of Ukraine (2022) News from Russian occupiers' camp: commanders flee, soldiers with no food, weapons, money or medical care (audio). Available at: https://ssu.gov.ua/en/novyny/novyny-z-taboru-rosiiskykh-okupantiv-komandyry-tikaiut-soldaty-bez-yizhi-zbroi-hroshei-i-meddopomohy-audio

Security Service of Ukraine (2022) Occupiers are abandoning their own soldiers (video). Available at: https://ssu.gov.ua/en/novyny/occupiers-are-abandoning-their-own-soldiers-video

Security Service of Ukraine (2022) Occupiers are not ready to bear responsibility for their atrocities in Ukraine. Available at: https://ssu.gov.ua/en/novyny/vorozhi-okupanty-ne-hotovi-nesty-vidpovidalnist-za-svoi-bezchynstva-v-ukraini-video

Security Service of Ukraine (2022) Occupiers are preparing to stage rallies in Kherson for 'picture' in Russian media. Available at: https://ssu.gov.ua/en/novyny/okupanty-hotuiut-postanovochni-mitynhy-u-khersoni-dlia-kartynky-u-roszmi

Security Service of Ukraine (2022) Occupiers destroy their own military equipment and show it as 'destroyed Ukrainian equipment' (audio). Available at: https://ssu.gov.ua/en/ novyny/okupanty-nyshchat-vlasnu-boiovu-tekhniku-i-vydaiut-yii-za-pidbytu-ukrainsku-audio

Security Service of Ukraine (2022) Occupiers' equipment breaks massively together with their plans to capture Ukraine (audio).

Available at: https://ssu.gov.ua/en/novyny/tekhnika-okupantiv-ta-yikhni-plany-z-zakhoplennia-ukrainy-masovo-lamaiutsia-audio

Security Service of Ukraine (2022) Occupiers no longer believe in quick end to war in Ukraine. Available at: https://ssu.gov.ua/en/novyny/okupanty-vzhe-ne-viriat-u-shvydke-zavershennia-viiny-v-ukraini-audio

Security Service of Ukraine (2022) Occupiers no longer plan offensive operations and do not dream of victory (audio). Available at: https://ssu.gov.ua/en/novyny/okupanty-vzhe-ne-planuiut-nastupalnykh-operatsii-i-ne-mriiut-pro-peremohu-audio

Security Service of Ukraine (2022) Occupiers spread fakes to divert attention from their atrocities. Available at: https://ssu.gov.ua/en/novyny/okupanty-rozpovsiudzhuiut-feiky-shchob-vidvernuty-uvahu-vid-svoikh-zvirstv

Security Service of Ukraine (2022) One day of occupier's life costs USD 53, but not all will survive (audio). Available at: https://ssu.gov.ua/en/novyny/odyn-den-zhyttia-rosiiskoho-okupanta-koshtuie-53-ale-vyzhyvut-ne-vsi-audio

Security Service of Ukraine (2022) One of the best armies in the world is hiding in Ukrainian forests and villages (video). Available at: https://ssu.gov.ua/en/novyny/odna-z-krashchykh-armii-svitu-khovaietsia-v-ukrainskykh-lisakh-i-selakh-video

Security Service of Ukraine (2022) One of the strongest armies in the world turned out to be a bunch of looters and rapists (audio). Available at: https://ssu.gov.ua/en/novyny/odna-z-naisylnishykh-armii-svitu-vyiavylasia-zbihovyskom-maroderiv-i-gvaltivnykiv-audio

Security Service of Ukraine (2022) Putin does not believe in his army and resorts to Stalinist repressions (video). Available at: https://ssu.gov.ua/en/novyny/putin-ne-viryt-u-vlasnu-armiiu-i-vdaietsia-do-stalinskykh-represii-video

Security Service of Ukraine (2022) Putin's blitzkrieg in Ukraine fails, his army does not believe in victory (audio). Available at: https://ssu.gov.ua/en/novyny/blitskryh-putina-v-ukraini-provalyvsia-a-yoho-armiia-vzahali-perestala-viryty-v-svoiu-peremohu-audio

Security Service of Ukraine (2022) Putin's myth of 'denazification' of Ukraine is not accepted even by invaders (video). Available at: https://ssu.gov.ua/en/novyny/mif-putina-pro-denatsyfikatsiiu-ukrainy-ne-spryimaiut-navit-sami-rosiiski-zaharbnyky-video

Security Service of Ukraine (2022) Ruscist aggressors astonished by quality of life in Ukraine (audio). Available at: https://ssu.gov.

ua/en/novyny/u-rashystskykh-zaharbnykiv-rozryv-shablonu-vid-yakosti-zhyttia-v-ukraini-audio

Security Service of Ukraine (2022) Russia massively violates laws and customs of war in Ukraine (audio). Available at: https://ssu.gov.ua/en/novyny/russia-massively-violates-laws-and-customs-of-war-in-ukraine-audio

Security Service of Ukraine (2022) Russia sends troops to war in Ukraine but waives responsibility for their deaths (audio). Available at: https://ssu.gov.ua/en/novyny/rf-vidpravliaie-svoikh-viiskovykh-na-viinu-v-ukrainu-ale-znimaie-z-sebe-budiaku-vidpovidalnist-za-yikhniu-smert-audio

Security Service of Ukraine (2022) Russia's blitzkrieg fails: invaders understand that they can't capture Kyiv (audio). Available at: https://ssu.gov.ua/en/novyny/blitskryh-rf-provalyvsia-vorohy-rozumiiut-shcho-kyiv-yim-ne-vziaty-video

Security Service of Ukraine (2022) Russian army – drunkest in the world – one of Putin's occupiers about his 'colleagues' (video). Available at: https://ssu.gov.ua/en/ novyny/viiska-rf-naisynisha-armiia-svitu-tak-pro-svoikh-koleh-kazhe-odyn-iz-putinskykh-zaharbnykiv-video

Security Service of Ukraine (2022) Russian army has direct instruction to shoot civilians in Ukraine (video). Available at: https://ssu.gov.ua/en/novyny/armiia-rf-maie-priamu-vkazivku-rozstriliuvaty-tsyvilnykh-hromadian-v-ukraini-video

Security Service of Ukraine (2022) Russian contractor decides to surrender rather than be killed (video). Available at: https://ssu.gov.ua/en/novyny/russian-contractor-decides-to-surrender-rather-than-be-killed-video

Security Service of Ukraine (2022) Russian invaders in Ukraine don't have food or water, one combat ration has to be shared between two (audio). Available at: https://ssu.gov.ua/en/novyny/rosiiski-zaharbnyky-v-ukraini-ne-maiut-yizhi-ta-vody-a-sukhpaiok-vzhe-diliat-na-dvokh-audio

Security Service of Ukraine (2022) Russian invaders loot massively (audio). Available at: https://ssu.gov.ua/en/novyny/russian-invaders-loot-massively-audio

Security Service of Ukraine (2022) Russian invaders' dreams are shattered as quickly as myths about invincible 'liberators' army (audio). Available at: https://ssu.gov.ua/en/novyny/russian-invaders-dreams-are-shattered-as-quickly-as-myths-about-invincible-liberators-army-audio

Security Service of Ukraine (2022) Russian military no longer believe in equipment and weapons: to survive in Ukraine they turn to shamans and fortune tellers (video). Available at: https://ssu.gov. ua/en/novyny/rosiiski-viiskovi-vzhe-ne-viriat-u-svoi-tekhniku-ta-zbroiu-shchob-vyzhyty-zvertaiutsia-do-shamaniv-i-vorozhok-video

Security Service of Ukraine (2022) Russian occupier who betrayed Ukraine in 2014 interrogated by SSU (video). Available at: https:// ssu.gov.ua/en/novyny/na-dopyt-sbu-potrapyv-rosiiskyi-okupant-yakyi-zradyv-ukrainu-v-2014-video

Security Service of Ukraine (2022) Russian occupiers demoralized by heavy losses, poor logistics and embezzlement of funds by generals (video). Available at: https://ssu.gov.ua/en/novyny/rosiiski-okupanty-demoralizovani-velykymy-vtratamy-pohanym-tylovym-zabezpechenniam-i-rozkradanniam-koshtiv-heneralamy-video

Security Service of Ukraine (2022) Russian occupiers go to war as conscripts, but die as contractors (audio). Available at: https:// ssu.gov.ua/en/novyny/rosiiski-okupanty-ydut-na-viinu-strokovykamy-a-pomyraiut-kontraktnykamy-audio

Security Service of Ukraine (2022) Russian occupiers have to bury their 'comrades' at their own expense (audio). Available at: https:// ssu.gov.ua/en/novyny/rosiiski-okupanty-vymusheni-khoronyty-svoikh-tovaryshiv-vlasnym-koshtom-audioRussian occupiers looking for Ukrainian ammunition to shoot their legs and go to hospital (audio), Service of Ukraine (2022), https://ssu.gov.ua/en/novyny/another-conversation-intercepted-by-the-ssu-shows-how-much-demoralized-and-defeated-the-invaders-army-is

Security Service of Ukraine (2022) Russian occupiers see siege of Kyiv as opportunity to secure 'rich' life (audio). Available at: https:// ssu.gov.ua/en/novyny/rosiiski-okupanty-rozghliadaiut-oblohu-kyieva-yak-mozhlyvist-zabezpechyty-sobi-bezbidne-zhyttia-audio

Security Service of Ukraine (2022) Russian occupiers shelling residential areas cynically and without sentiment (video). Available at: https://ssu.gov.ua/en/novyny/rosiiski-okupanty-tsynichno-i-bez-sentymentiv-obstriliuiut-nashi-zhytlovi-budynky-video

Security Service of Ukraine (2022) Russian occupiers start massive looting in Ukraine (video). Available at: https://ssu.gov.ua/en/novyny/rosiiski-okupanty-rozpochaly-masove-maroderstvo-v-ukraini-video

Security Service of Ukraine (2022) Russian soldiers admit that war in Ukraine surpassed Chechnya in losses, while Ukrainian resistance surpassed Syrian (audio). Available at: https://ssu.gov.ua/en/novyny/rosiiski-voiaky-ziznaiutsia-ridnym-shcho-viina-v-ukraini-perevershyla-yikh-vtraty-v-chechni-a-za-rivnem-sprotyvu-syriiu-audio

Security Service of Ukraine (2022) Russian soldiers continue to mutilate themselves to evade battle (video). Available at: https://ssu.gov.ua/en/novyny/rosiiski-viiskovi-prodo-vzhuiut-sebe-kalichyty-aby-ne-voiuvaty-z-ukrainoiu-video

Security Service of Ukraine (2022) Russian tactics: less achievements on battlefield – more fakes and provocations in media (video). Available at: https://ssu.gov.ua/en/novyny/ taktyka-rf-chym-menshe-zdobutkiv-na-poli-boiu-tym-bilshe-feikiv-i-provokatsii-v-informprostori-video

Security Service of Ukraine (2022) Russian troops carry out provocation in Belarus. Available at: https://ssu.gov.ua/en/novyny/rosiiski-viiska-zdiisnyly-provokatsiiu-na-terytorii-bilorusii

Security Service of Ukraine (2022) Russians deceive their contractors to keep them on battlefield in Ukraine (audio). Available at: https://ssu.gov.ua/en/novyny/rosiiany-duriat-svoikh-kontraktnykiv-shchob-vtrymaty-na-viini-v-ukraini-audio

Security Service of Ukraine (2022) Russians run out of good news (audio). Available at: https://ssu.gov.ua/en/novyny/u-rosiian-zakinchylysia-khoroshi-novyny-audio

Security Service of Ukraine (2022) Since beginning of war, SSU detains over 350 members of sabotage and reconnaissance groups and disrupts international channels for recruiting mercenaries for occupying army (video). Available at: https://ssu.gov.ua/en/novyny/z-pochatku-viiny-sbu-zatrymala-ponad-350-uchasnykiv-drh-ta-likviduvala-mizhnarodni-kanaly-verbuvannia-naimantsiv-do-viiska-okupantiv-video

Security Service of Ukraine (2022) Since war started, SSU shuts down 5 enemy's bot farms with over 100,000 fake accounts. Available at: https://ssu.gov.ua/en/novyny/z-pochatku-viiny-sbu-likviduvala-5-vorozhykh-botoferm-potuzhnistiu-ponad-100-tys-feikovykh-akauntiv

Security Service of Ukraine (2022) Some occupiers 'open their eyes' in war in Ukraine and are trying to convey truth to 'zombie' relatives in Russia (audio). Available at: https://ssu.gov.ua/en/novyny/

deiaki-okupanty-prozrily-na-viini-v-ukraini-i-namahaiutsia-donesty-pravdu-do-zombovanykh-rodychiv-u-rf-audio

Security Service of Ukraine (2022) SSU collects facts on Russian war crimes for Hague through chatbots, hotlines, messenger apps and email. Available at: https://ssu.gov.ua/en/ novyny/ sbu-zbyraie-fakty-pro-voienni-zlochyny-rf-diiut-chatbot-hariachi-linii-mesedzhery-ta-poshtaSSU continues to detain Russian war criminals, traitors and collaborators who assist invaders, Service of Ukraine (2022), https://ssu.gov.ua/en/ novyny/sluzhba-bezpeky-ukrainy-prodovzhuie-vykryvaty-rosiiskykh-viiskovykh-zlochyntsiv-zradnykiv-i-kolaborantiv-yaki-dopomahaiut-vorohu

Security Service of Ukraine (2022) SSU detains 5 Russian collaborators and 'thief in law' (video). Available at: https://ssu.gov.ua/en/novyny/sbu-zatrymala-5-rosiiskykh-kolaborantiv-i-pidsanktsiinoho-zlodiia-v-zakoni-video

Security Service of Ukraine (2022) SSU detains 60 collaborators and eliminates 20 enemy sabotage and reconnaissance groups (video). Available at: https://ssu.gov.ua/en/novyny/ sbu-zatrymala-60-kolaborantiv-i-vykryla-20-vorozhykh-drh-video

Security Service of Ukraine (2022) SSU detains Belarusian spy and pro-Russian collaborators (video). Available at: https://ssu.gov.ua/en/ novyny/sbu-zatrymala-biloruskoho-shpyhuna-i-prorosiiskykh-kolaborantiv-video

Security Service of Ukraine (2022) SSU detains collaborator in Rivne region and Somalia terrorist group militant (video). Available at: https://ssu.gov.ua/en/novyny/sbu-zatrymala-kolaboranta-na-rivnenshchyni-i-boiovyka-z-terorystychnoho-uhrupovannia-somali-video

Security Service of Ukraine (2022) SSU detains Russian informants in Kharkiv, Odesa and Severodonetsk (video). Available at: https://ssu.gov.ua/en/novyny/sbu-zatrymala-informatoriv-rf-u-kharkovi-odesi-ta-sievierodonetsku-video

Security Service of Ukraine (2022) SSU detains Russian informants in Kyiv, Kharkiv and Poltava and exposes fraudsters who stole funds from volunteers (video). Available at: https://ssu.gov.ua/ en/novyny/sbu-zatrymala-rosiiskykh-informatoriv-u-kyieva-kharkovi-ta-poltavi-i-vykryla-shakhraiv-yaki-kraly-koshty-z-volonterskykh-rakhunkiv-video

Security Service of Ukraine (2022) SSU detains Russian spy who headed to Kyiv (video). Available at: https://ssu.gov.ua/en/novyny/sbu-skhopyla-rosiiskoho-rozvidnyka-yakyi-priamuvav-do-kyieva-video

Security Service of Ukraine (2022) SSU detains saboteurs, works for victory! Available at: https://ssu.gov.ua/en/novyny/ sbu-vykryvaiemo-dyversantiv-pratsiuiemo-dlia-peremohy

Security Service of Ukraine (2022) SSU detains traitor involved in missile strike on Kyiv TV tower. Available at: https://ssu.gov.ua/ en/novyny/sbu-zatrymala-zradnyka-prychetnoho-do-raketnoho-obstrilu-televezhi-u-kyievi

Security Service of Ukraine (2022) SSU detains traitor who 'surrendered' Lutsk military airfield to enemy (video). Available at: https://ssu. gov.ua/en/novyny/sbu-zatrymala-zradnyka-yakyi-zdav-vorohu-pid-obstril-lutskyi-viiskovyi-aerodrom

Security Service of Ukraine (2022) SSU detains two Russian informants in Donetsk region and interrogates 10 LNR militants. Available at: https://ssu.gov.ua/en/novyny/sbu-zatrymala-dvokh-rosiiskykh-informatoriv-na-donechchyni-dopytuie-shche-10-boiovykiv-lnr

Security Service of Ukraine (2022) SSU dismantles another agent network and neutralizes gang that attacked Territorial Defence Units (video). Available at: https://ssu.gov.ua/en/ novyny/sbu-likviduvala-novu-ahenturnu-merezhu-okupantiv-i-zneshkodyla-bandu-yaka-napadala-na-pidrozdily-teroborony-video

Security Service of Ukraine (2022) SSU dismantles large-scale network of Internet agents who called for support of Russian aggression. Available at: https://ssu.gov.ua/en/novyny/sbu-likviduvala-masshtabnu-merezhu-vorozhykh-internetahentiv-yaki-zaklykaly-pidtrymaty-rosiisku-ahresiiu

Security Service of Ukraine (2022) SSU exposes another bot farm in Kharkiv (video). Available at: https://ssu.gov.ua/en/novyny/ sbu-vykryla-novu-vorozhu-botofermu-u-kharkovi-video

Security Service of Ukraine (2022) SSU exposes coordinator of Russian sabotage groups in Kharkiv region and collaborator who wanted 'position' in occupying authorities in Dnipropetrovsk region (video). Available at: https://ssu.gov.ua/en/novyny/sbu-vykryla-koordynatora-dyversiinykh-hrup-rf-na-kharkivshchyni-i-kolaboranta-yakyi-khotiv-otrymaty-posadu-v-okupatsiinii-vladi-na-dnipropetrovshchyni-video

Security Service of Ukraine (2022) SSU exposes hacker who ensured mobile communication for occupiers in Ukraine. Available at: https://ssu.gov.ua/en/novyny/sbu-vykryla-khakera-yakyi-zabezpechuvav-okupantam-mobilnyi-zviazok-v-ukraini

Security Service of Ukraine (2022) SSU interception: Looting for

Russian occupiers is like going to supermarket (audio). Available at: https://ssu.gov.ua/en/novyny/ssu-interception-looting-for-russian-occupiers-is-like-going-to-supermarket-audio

Security Service of Ukraine (2022) SSU interception: Russian invaders flee from battle with Ukrainian military and consider themselves 'miserable rats' (audio). Available at: https://ssu.gov.ua/en/novyny/perekhoplennia-sbu-rosiiski-zaharbnyky-tikaiut-vid-zsu-i-vvazhaiut-sebe-pozornmy-krsamy-audio

Security Service of Ukraine (2022) SSU investigates forced deportation of Mariupol residents to Russia by Russian occupiers (video). Available at: https://ssu.gov.ua/en/novyny/sbu-rozsliduie-prymusove-vyvezennia-rosiiskymy-okupantamy-meshkantsiv-mariupolia-do-rf-video

Security Service of Ukraine (2022) SSU: On night of full-scale invasion, Russia aimed to destroy all cyber defence of Ukraine (video). Available at: https://ssu.gov.ua/en/novyny/u-nich-povnomasshtabnoho-vtorhnennia-rf-voroh-khotiv-znyshchyty-ves-kiberzakhyst-ukrainy-sbu-video

Security Service of Ukraine (2022) SSU: Ruscist son wanted to take his mother out of occupied city, but she refused (audio). Available at: https://ssu.gov.ua/en/novyny/sbu-synrashyst-khotiv-vyvezty-mamu-z-okupovanoho-mista-ale-ta-vidmovylas

Security Service of Ukraine (2022) SSU: Russian occupiers keep 'hitting bottom' every day (audio). Available at: https://ssu.gov.ua/en/novyny/ssu-russian-occupiers-keep-hitting-bottom-every-day-audio

Security Service of Ukraine (2022) SSU: Russian occupiers rape underage girls and eat dogs. Available at: https://ssu.gov.ua/en/novyny/ssu-russian-occupiers-rape-underage-girls-and-eat-dogs-audio

Security Service of Ukraine (2022) SSU: Russians screwed up in war with Ukraine (audio). Available at: https://ssu.gov.ua/en/novyny/sbu-rosiiany-vyznaiut-shcho-oblazhalysia-na-viini-z-ukrainoiu-audio

Security Service of Ukraine (2022) The SSU, the Armed Forces and other military units continue to destroy the enemy all over Ukraine. Available at: https://ssu.gov.ua/en/novyny/sbu-zbroini-syly-ta-inshi-viiskovi-pidrozdily-prodovzhuiut-znyshchuvaty-voroha-po-vsii-ukraini

Security Service of Ukraine (2022) Ukrainian captivity better than Russian army (video). Available at: https://ssu.gov.ua/en/novyny/ukrainian-captivity-better-than-russian-army-video

Service of Ukraine (2022) Putin's army ready to flee: Kremlin invents new 'promises' to keep it in Ukraine (audio). Available at: https://ssu.gov.ua/en/novyny/

armiia-putina-hotova-vtekty-z-ukrainy-shchob-yii-vtrymaty-kreml-prydumuie-novi-obitsianky-audioSecurityServiceofUkraine (2022) 'Fairy tale' life begins in Russia (audio). Available at: https://ssu.gov.ua/en/novyny/v-rosii-pochalosia-kazkove-zhyttia-audio

Service of Ukraine (2022) SSU has plenty of evidence of massive looting by occupiers (audio). Available at: https://ssu.gov.ua/en/novyny/ssu-has-plenty-of-evidence-of-massive-looting-by-occupiers-audio

Service of Ukraine (2022) SSU interception about whining occupiers (audio). Available at: https://ssu.gov.ua/en/novyny/perekhoplennia-sbu-pro-nyiuchykh-okupantiv-audio

Service of Ukraine (2022) SSU interception: relatives of Russian invaders recognize that situation in Russia is miserable (audio). Available at: https://ssu.gov.ua/en/ novyny/perekhoplennia-sbu-rodychi-rosiiskykh-zaharbnykiv-vyznaiut-plachevnist-sytuatsii-v-rf-audio

Service of Ukraine (2022) SSU intercepts more conversations of Russian invaders looting in Sumy region (audio). Available at: https://ssu.gov.ua/en/novyny/sbu-perekhopliuie-novi-rozmovy-rosiiskykh-zaharbnykiv-yaki-maroderstvuiut-na-sumshchyni-audio

Service of Ukraine (2022) SSU intercepts more information on Russian invaders' 'secret tactics' (video). Available at: https://ssu.gov.ua/en/novyny/sbu-perekhopyla-informat siiu-pro-cherhovu-sekretnu-taktyku-rosiiskykh-zaharbnykiv-video

Service of Ukraine (2022) SSU intercepts occupiers' conversations: they are ordered to fire at civilians in Kharkiv (audio). Available at: https://ssu.gov.ua/en/novyny/sbu-perekho   pyla-rozmovy-okupantiv-u-kharkovi-yim-daly-komandu-striliaty-v-tsyvilnykh-audio

Service of Ukraine (2022) SSU investigates criminal proceedings against Russian propagandists (video). Available at: https://ssu.gov.ua/en/novyny/slidchi-sbu-rozslidu iut- kryminalne-provadzhennia-shchodo-rosiiskykh-propahandystiv-video

Service of Ukraine (2022) SSU massively detains traitors returning to Ukraine with Russian troops (video). Available at: https://ssu.gov.ua/en/novyny/sbu-masovo-zatrymuie-zradnykiv-yaki-zaraz-povernulysia-v-ukrainu-u-skladi-rosiiskykh-viisk-video

Service of Ukraine (2022) SSU obtains more evidence that Russia does not value its soldiers and sends conscripts, who are 'not there', to war in Ukraine (audio). Available at: https:// ssu.gov.ua/en/novyny/sbu-otrymala-cherhovi-dokazy-shcho-rf-ne-tsinuie-svoikh-viisko vykh-a-znachna-chastyna-yikhnoi-armii-v-ukraini-strokovyky-yakykh-tam-niet-audio

Service of Ukraine (2022) SSU relentlessly detects and neutralizes sabotage groups and Russian agents in Ukraine. Available at: https://ssu.gov.ua/en/novyny/sbu-bezperervno-vyiavliaie-ta-zneshkodzhuie-dyversiini-hrupy-ta-ahentiv-rosiiskykh-spetssluzhb-v-ukraini

Service of Ukraine (2022) SSU shuts down bot farm, dismantles organized criminal group and detains pseudo-volunteer (video). Available at: https://ssu.gov.ua/en/novyny/sbu-likviduvala-botofermu-neitralizuvala-ozu-i-zatrymala-psevdovolontera-video

Service of Ukraine (2022) SSU steps up cyber defence of strategic facilities and creates emergency email. Available at: https://ssu.gov.ua/en/novyny/sbu-posyliuie-kiberzakhyst-stratehichnykh-obiektiv-i-stvoriuie-dlia-tsoho-hariachu-elektronnu-adresu

Service of Ukraine (2022) SSU thwarts Kremlin's plans for new 'people's republics' in Western Ukraine. Available at: https://ssu.gov.ua/en/novyny/sbu-zirvala-plany-kremlia-shchodo-novykh-narodnykh-respublik-na-zakhidnii-ukraini

Service of Ukraine (2022) SSU: Russian special services try to infiltrate Ukrainian Territorial Defence (video). Available at: https://ssu.gov.ua/en/novyny/sbu-rosiiski-spetssluzhby-namahaiutsia-intehruvaty-svoikh-ahentiv-v-pidrozdily-ukrainskoi-terytorialnoi-oborony

Service of Ukraine (2022) SSU's official statement on collaboration of Ukrainians with enemy. Available at: https://ssu.gov.ua/en/novyny/ofitsiina-zaiava-sbu-shchodo-spivpratsi-ukraintsiv-z-vorohom

Service of Ukraine (2022) To effectively defend Ukraine, SSU uses experience gained over 30 years – Ivan Bakanov. Available at: https://ssu.gov.ua/en/novyny/dlia-efektyvnoho-zakhystu-krainy-sbu-zastosovuie-ves-svii-dosvid-nabutyi-za-30-rokiv-ivan-bakanov

Service of Ukraine (2022) What scares is not the killing, but cheating us out of money – Russian occupier (audio). Available at: https://ssu.gov.ua/en/novyny/strashno-ne-to-chto-nas-ubyvaiut-a-to-chto-kydaiut-na-babky

U.S. Department of State (2023) Available at: https://www.state.gov/u-s-security-coope-ration-with-ukraine/Security Service of Ukraine (2022). Available at: https://ssu.gov.ua/ en/reforma-ssu

CHAPTER 6

The implications of the 2022 midterm elections for NATO and Ukraine

Maciej Grunt

Abstract

This chapter analyzes the geopolitical implications of the 2022 U.S. midterm elections on NATO's strategic posture and the ongoing conflict in Ukraine. The chapter explores how shifts in U.S. domestic politics, particularly changes in Congressional leadership, impact the future of transatlantic defence cooperation and the provision of military and economic aid to Ukraine. The study delves into the dynamics between the U.S. and its NATO allies, assessing the potential effects of a more divided or unified Congress on the Alliance's unified response to Russian aggression. It also examines the evolving U.S. foreign policy stance towards Ukraine and NATO in light of internal political shifts. Through this analysis, the chapter concludes that while the midterm elections may introduce uncertainties in the U.S.'s international commitments, the foundational strength of NATO's collective defence and solidarity towards Ukraine remains resilient. The findings suggest that while political shifts in the U.S. could influence future policy directions, the existing frameworks of cooperation within NATO and U.S.-Ukraine relations are expected to withstand these changes.

Keywords: U.S. foreign policy, 2022 midterm elections, war in Ukraine, international diplomacy, NATO

Introduction

The 2022 United States midterm elections marked a crucial turning point in the nation's political landscape, redefining the power dynamics within the federal government and, subsequently, the potential change of its foreign policy direction. This dissertation offers an in-depth analysis of how these elections specifically influenced U.S. foreign policy towards NATO and European partners, focusing on the critical policy areas and strategic alliances that might experience significant shifts.

As a leading global actor, the United States has consistently been at the forefront of shaping international relations and security dynamics. Its foreign policy, particularly towards its European partners and NATO, is deeply intertwined with the domestic political environment. The 2022 midterm elections, characterized by increasing polarization and a call for change, may lead to reevaluation of the U.S. approach to its transatlantic relationships.

In this dissertation, the primary factors driving the changes in U.S. foreign policy following the 2022 midterm elections will be investigated. What is more, a deep analysis concerning the role of domestic politics, vital legislative decisions and positions taken by various political actors will be conducted. The article focuses on the implications of these changes for NATO and European partners, assessing how the evolving American stance has influenced the strategic landscape, defence priorities, and cooperation mechanisms within the alliance.

By examining the U.S. political system and the 2022 midterm elections with their influence on U.S. foreign policy, this research aims to provide a nuanced understanding of the factors shaping the trajectory of transatlantic relations in the contemporary era. Furthermore, this study intends to contribute to the broader discourse on the interconnectedness of domestic politics and foreign policy as well as on the implications of political shifts for international alliances and strategic partnerships.

The U.S. Political System

The political system of the United States of America is a complex and dynamic federal system with a presidential democracy that has evolved throughout the nation's history. The system is comprised of three distinct branches of government – legislative, executive, and judicial – each with its unique powers and responsibilities as enshrined in the U.S. Constitution (Ritchie, 2010).

The legislative branch is responsible for crafting and enacting laws, and it is composed of two separate chambers: the House of Representatives and the Senate. The House of Representatives is composed of 435 members, with each member serving a two-year term, while the Senate is composed of 100 members, with each senator serving a six-year term (Hrebenar & Scott, 2015). Together, these two chambers can pass and approve legislation, declare war, and control the nation's budget.

The executive branch is responsible for enforcing the laws and is headed by the President, whom the people elect for a four-year term. The President is assisted by a Cabinet composed of various federal departments and agency heads. The executive branch can veto legislation passed by Congress, negotiate treaties, and take military action as Commander-in-Chief of the armed forces (Ritchie, 2010).

The judicial branch is responsible for interpreting the laws. It is composed of the Supreme Court and various lower federal courts (Jillson & Robertson, 2010). The Supreme Court is the highest in the land, composed of nine justices appointed by the President and confirmed by the Senate. The Supreme Court can interpret the Constitution and federal law as well as declare laws or executive actions unconstitutional.

Midterm elections are held every two years, allowing the American people to elect members of the House of Represen-tatives and one-third of the Senate. While the main focus of midterm elections is on Congressional races, they also have sig-nificant implications for the balance of power within the federal government (Moran, 2011). If the President's party loses control of one or both chambers of Congress, it becomes more difficult for the President to pass legislation and implement policy.

U.S. congress and the president in the international affairs

Regarding budgetary issues, the distribution of responsibility for financing military involvement within NATO and other transatlantic partners is a shared responsibility between the executive and legislative branches of the U.S. government. The President has the authority to negotiate and enter into agreements with other countries, including agreements related to military operations and funding (Ritchie, 2010). However, any funding for military operations must be approved by the Congress, which has the power of the purse.

The distribution of responsibility for foreign policy and budgetary issues in the U.S. political system is outlined in the U.S. Constitution and has been shaped over time through legal precedent and political practice (Tushnet, Graber & Levinson, 2015).

According to Article II, Section 2 of the U.S. Constitution, the President "shall have Power, by and with the Advice and Consent of the Senate, to make Treaties, provided two-thirds of the Senators" (Vile, 2016). This power gives the President significant authority in foreign policy decision-making process, including negotiating treaties and conducting diplomatic relations with other countries.

At the same time, the Constitution grants Congress significant power in foreign policy and national security matters. Article I, Section 8 gives Congress the power to "declare War, grant Letters of Marque and Reprisal, and make Rules concerning Captures on Land and Water" and to "raise and support Armies," among other powers related to national defence. Congress also has the power of the purse, meaning it controls the federal budget and can allocate funds for military operations, foreign aid, and other foreign policy initiatives (Tushnet, Graber & Levinson, 2015).

In practice, the distribution of responsibility for foreign policy and budgetary issues can be complex and involves a range of actors and interests. The President may negotiate treaties and agreements with other countries, but Congress must approve any funds associated with those agreements. Similarly, the President may direct military operations, but Congress may impose limits on those operations or refuse to fund them (Rosenbloom, 2016).

In recent years, debates over the appropriate level of funding for military operations in NATO and other transatlantic partners have been a topic of political discussion and negotiation between the President and Congress. In 2019, for example, the Trump Administration proposed a significant reduction in U.S. contributions to NATO, which sparked criticism from some members of Congress who argued that the alliance was vital to U.S. national security (Sullivan, 2018). Ultimately, Congress approved a budget that maintained U.S. funding for NATO at previous levels.

House of representatives and U.S. Foreign Policy

Considering the results of the 2022 elections and the fact that the Republican Party took over the House of Representatives, it is reasonable to analyze the influence of the House of Representatives on the United States foreign policy. How can Republicans influence foreign policy, including transatlantic relations, with only a narrow majority in the House of Representatives?

The United States House of Representatives has significant influence over shaping U.S. foreign policy, particularly regarding the country's activities within NATO and military support for Ukraine. This influence is derived from the House's power of the purse, which enables it to influence budgetary decisions that allocate funds for foreign aid and military involvement in NATO operations. Additionally, the House has the authority to hold hearings and conduct investigations into foreign policy decisions made by the executive branch, making it a key player in the U.S. political system.

One example of the House's impact on U.S. foreign policy towards NATO came in 2018 when the House passed a resolution reaffirming the country's commitment to the NATO alliance and urging the Trump administration to work with allies to strengthen the alliance (Durbin, 2018). The resolution also called for increased funding for the European Deterrence Initiative, which provides military aid to Ukraine and supports U.S. military operations in Europe. This demonstrates the House's support for maintaining strong relationships with NATO allies and its willingness to take action to ensure this.

Furthermore, the House played a significant role in providing military support for Ukraine in its conflict with Russia. In 2019 the House passed the Ukraine Security Assistance Initiative which provided $250 million in military aid to Ukraine (Risch, 2020). This support was crucial in helping Ukraine defend itself against Russian aggression and reflected the House's commitment to upholding U.S. foreign policy commitments.

The House's influence is not limited to budgetary decisions; it also has the power to hold hearings and conduct investigations into foreign policy matters. In 2019, the House held hearings on the Trump administration's decision to withhold military aid to Ukraine, which was seen as a violation of U.S.

foreign policy commitments to Ukraine and NATO (Committee on the Judiciary, 2019). This highlights the House's oversight role making the executive branch follow established foreign policy principles.

The House of Representatives is critical in shaping U.S. foreign policy towards NATO and Ukraine. Through its power of the purse, its ability to hold hearings and conduct investigations, and its ability to pass resolutions and legislation, the House is vital in promoting U.S. national security interests both in Europe and globally.

Impact of the midterm elections results on NATO

The results of the midterm elections have always been influencing U.S. administration and its strategic decisions concerning cooperation inside NATO and military involvement in Europe. Taking a closer look at the administrations of George W. Bush, Barack Obama, Donald Trump, Joe Biden and their foreign policies it can be undoubtedly stated that they have always been shaped by domestic political considerations and shifting international context.

During the George W. Bush administration, the 2006 midterm elections became a turning point for U.S. foreign policy. The Democrats won control of the House of Representatives and the Senate, marking a shift in public opinion against the Iraq War and military intervention abroad. It also changed the Bush administration's approach to foreign policy, including greater emphasis on diplomacy and multilateralism in dealing with international issues. Concerning NATO, the Bush administration sought to strengthen its role in promoting stability in Europe and increased U.S. military presence in Europe to counter the Russian threat (Trachtenberg, 2010).

In the Obama administration, the 2010 midterm elections saw the Republicans win control of the House of Representatives while the Democrats retained control of the Senate. This divided government made it more challenging for the Obama administration to pursue a coherent foreign policy, including cooperation in NATO and military involvement in Europe. Despite these challenges, Obama remained committed to strengthening NATO and continued supporting European allies through increased military presence, military aid, and diplomatic efforts (Goldberg, 2016).

After the 2014 midterm elections there were several significant changes in the approach of the Obama administration towards NATO and its European partners. One of the primary changes was the renewed focus on reassurance measures in Europe aimed at deterring Russian aggression. This included deploying additional troops, equipment, and military exercises in NATO's eastern flank countries, such as Poland and the Baltics. The administration also increased funding for the European Reassurance Initiative, supporting NATO allies in Eastern Europe.

Moreover, the midterm elections impacted the Obama administration's ability to work with Congress on foreign policy issues. With the Republicans taking control of the House and the Senate, the administration faced increased opposition and pressure from Congress on its foreign policy decisions. This resulted in a more cautious approach toward NATO enlargement. The administration was more hesitant to support the membership aspirations of Ukraine and Georgia for fear of antagonizing Russia and further inflaming tensions in the region (Frum, 2014).

Furthermore, the changing global landscape influenced the Obama administration's approach towards NATO and Europe. With the rise of China as a global power, the administration shifted its focus towards the Asia-Pacific region, which led to a reduction in resources and attention being paid to NATO and Europe (Frum, 2014).

The election of Donald Trump as President in 2016 marked a significant shift in U.S. foreign policy, including its approach to NATO and military involvement in Europe. Trump's "America First" foreign policy signaled a retreat from international engagement and alliances, including NATO. Trump called NATO "obsolete" and repeatedly criticized European allies for not contributing enough to their defence (James, 2017).

Trump's criticism of the alliance and his threats to withdraw U.S. troops from Europe and cut funding for U.S. military operations in the region were met with significant resistance from Democrats and Republicans in Congress. As a result, Trump could not follow through on his promises to weaken the alliance and reduce U.S. involvement in Europe.

The election of Joe Biden in 2020 marked a return to a more

traditional foreign policy approach, including a commitment to NATO and military involvement in Europe. Biden has sought to strengthen NATO by reaffirming the U.S. commitment to collective defence and promoting closer cooperation with European allies. Biden has also increased U.S. military presence in Europe and provided military aid to Ukraine, which is facing aggression from Russia.

The results of the former midterm elections have played a crucial role in shaping the strategic decisions of U.S. administrations concerning cooperation in NATO and military involvement in Europe. While the Bush and the Obama administrations sought to strengthen NATO and increase U.S. military presence in Europe, the Trump administration signaled a retreat from international engagement. The Biden administration is working to reaffirm U.S. commitment to NATO and promote closer cooperation with European allies. These shifts in U.S. foreign policy reflect the changing political climate and shifting international context over the past two decades.

Midterm 2022 elections

The U.S. 2022 midterm elections took place in a highly polarized political environment, with control of both the Senate and the House of Representatives hanging in the balance. The outcomes of these elections carry significant implications for the direction of American politics and policy as well as for the prospects of the two major parties. This article analyzes the election results, exploring their implications for party dynamics, legislative priorities, and policy-making at the federal level.

The Democrats managed to maintain control of the Senate, securing a slim majority with 51 seats compared to the Republicans' 49 seats. This outcome was primarily driven by crucial Democratic victories in several closely contested races, including Arizona, Pennsylvania, and Wisconsin. With this majority, the Democrats now have increased leverage in confirming presidential appointments, including judicial nominations, as well as advancing their legislative agenda (Jacobson, 2023). In contrast, the Republicans succeeded in regaining control of the House of Representatives. The final seat distribution resulted in 222

Republicans and 213 Democrats, reflecting the highly competitive nature of many House races nationwide.

The results have several implications for party dynamics within the U.S. Congress. For the Republicans, regaining control of the House provides them a platform to challenge the Democratic agenda and shape policy debates on key issues, such as immigration, healthcare, and fiscal policy. The GOP victory in the House also underscores the continued resonance of conservative messaging and policy priorities among a significant portion of the electorate (Doherty, 2023).

On the other hand, the Democrats continued control of the Senate allows them to advance their policy priorities and maintain a degree of influence in shaping the legislative landscape. However, their narrow majority in the Senate means they must navigate internal divisions and build consensus on key issues to achieve legislative successes (Sei, 2022).

The divided control of Congress following the 2022 midterms has significant implications for the policy-making process at the federal level. With the Republicans in control of the House and the Democrats maintaining their majority in the Senate, both parties must negotiate and compromise to pass legislation. This dynamic could result in more moderate policy outcomes as both parties work to find common ground on key issues. Alternatively, the divided Congress could lead to legislative gridlock, with both parties struggling to advance their respective agendas.

The 2022 U.S. midterm elections have reshaped the political landscape in the United States, with the Republicans regaining control of the House of Representatives and the Democrats maintaining their majority in the Senate. The divided control of Congress carries significant implications for party dynamics and the policymaking process at the federal level. As the country moves forward, it will be crucial for scholars, policymakers, and observers to closely monitor the legislative activity and policy debates that emerge from this new political configuration.

Historically, the party holding the White House tends to lose seats in the midterm elections. This pattern was partially evident in 2022, as the Democrats faced losses in the House but managed to regain control of the Senate (Jacobson, 2023). The nation's ongoing economic recovery from the COVID-19 pandemic played a significant role in shaping voter preferences. With inflation and labor market issues persisting, many voters sought a change in political leadership to address these challenges (*World Economic Forum*, 2023).

The redrawing of congressional districts following the 2020 Census impacted electoral outcomes, with some districts becoming more competitive while others solidified their partisan leanings (*Voter-Demographics-and-Redistricting*, 2023). Both parties invested heavily in voter outreach and engagement efforts, leading to increased voter turnout compared to previous midterm elections. These efforts likely contributed to the mixed results in both chambers of Congress (Schwarz, 2022).

117 and 118 congresses – NATO and Ukraine aid

The 117th (2021-2023) and 118th (2023-2025) (Masters, 2023) Congresses have witnessed considerable legislative activity related to NATO and Ukraine aid, reflecting the United States' commitment to its European partners and its ongoing efforts to counter Russian aggression. It is crucial to highlight the most important legislative measures enacted by the 117th and 118th Congresses, focusing on their implications for U.S. foreign policy and the broader strategic landscape in the region. Those measures are as followed:

- The NATO Support Act (117th Congress, 2021; Keating, 2022) reaffirmed the United States' commitment to the NATO alliance and sought to prevent the withdrawal of the U.S. from the organization without Congressional approval. The Act emphasized the importance of NATO as a cornerstone of U.S. national security and aimed to ensure the continued stability of the transatlantic partnership.

- The Ukraine Security Partnership Act (117th Congress, 2021; Risch, 2021) authorized $300 million in annual foreign military financing to Ukraine, including lethal and non-lethal aid, to help the country defend itself against Russian aggression. The Act underscored the United States' commitment to Ukraine's sovereignty and territorial integrity and provided a robust response to Russia's destabilizing actions in the region.

- The European Deterrence Initiative (EDI) (117th and 118th Congresses) (*EUROPEAN DETERRENCE INITIATIVE Department of Defence Budget Fiscal Year (FY) 2022, 2021*) is a U.S. Department of Defence funding mechanism designed to enhance the deterrence posture of NATO and reassure European allies of the U.S. commitment to their security. Both the 117th and 118th Congresses have consistently allocated resources to the EDI, demonstrating the United States' ongoing efforts to strengthen NATO's eastern flank and deter potential adversaries.

- The Eastern European Security Act (118th Congress, 2022; Smith, 2022) aimed to strengthen U.S. engagement with NATO allies in Eastern Europe and bolster their defence capabilities. The Act authorized funding for joint military exercises, infrastructure improvements, and the deployment of additional U.S. forces to the region, signaling a renewed focus on the strategic importance of Eastern Europe in countering Russian influence.

- The Comprehensive Assistance to Ukraine Act (118th Congress, 2023; Craig, 2022) expanded U.S. support to Ukraine beyond military aid, incorporating measures to bolster Ukraine's democratic institutions, civil society, and economic resilience. The Act demonstrated the United States' commitment to Ukraine's long-term stability and its efforts to integrate more closely with the European and transatlantic community.

- The Countering America's Adversaries Through Sanctions Act (CAATSA) (Royce, 2017) was initially enacted in 2017 to impose sanctions on Iran, Russia, and North Korea. Amendments to CAATSA during the 117th Congress sought to strengthen sanctions against Russia, especially in response to its aggression towards Ukraine. These amendments aimed to pressure Russia further to adhere to international norms and cease destabilizing activities in the region.

- The Black Sea Defence and Partnership Act (117th Congress, 2022) (*S.4509 – 117th Congress (2021-2022): Black Sea Security Act of 2022 | Congress.gov | Library of Congress*, 2022) aimed to enhance cooperation between the United States, NATO, and Black Sea countries. This legislation provided for increased maritime security assistance and established a NATO Center of Excellence for Black Sea Security in Romania. The Act underscored the strategic importance of the Black Sea region and sought to reinforce NATO's presence and influence in the area.

- The Transatlantic Telecommunications Security Act (117th Congress, 2022; Kaptur, 2022) addressed cybersecurity threats to NATO and European partners, particularly those from Chinese telecommunications companies such as Huawei and ZTE. The Act established a framework for coordinating cybersecurity efforts with NATO and the European Union, authorized funding for research and development in secure telecommunications technologies and promoted the adoption of trusted vendors in critical infrastructure projects.

- The Baltic Security and Defence Cooperation Enhancement Act (118th Congress, 2023) sought to deepen U.S. defence cooperation with Estonia, Latvia, and Lithuania, three NATO member states in the Baltic region. The Act authorized military assistance, including training and equipment, to bolster the Baltic states' defence capabilities against potential threats. This legislation reaffirmed the United States' commitment to the security of its Baltic allies and the broader NATO alliance.

The legislative measures enacted by the 117th and 118th Congresses on NATO and Ukraine aid have reaffirmed the United States' dedication to its European partners and its determination to counter Russian aggression. By providing financial, military, and diplomatic support to NATO and Ukraine, the United States has sought to uphold the rules-based international order and preserve the stability of the transatlantic alliance. As geopolitical tensions persist, policymakers must continue monitoring the evolving situation and ensure the effective implementation of these legislative measures in pursuing U.S. foreign policy objectives.

In conclusion, the United States has played a pivotal role in supporting Ukraine during the Russian invasion, providing comprehensive military aid, financial support, and diplomatic engagement. Providing lethal and non-lethal military equipment, training, and advisory support has significantly bolstered Ukraine's defence capabilities. Financial aid, including military financing, economic assistance, and humanitarian aid, has helped to stabilize Ukraine's economy and address the humanitarian crisis resulting from the conflict.

Diplomatically, the United States has spearheaded efforts to impose sanctions on Russia and build a coalition of international partners supporting Ukraine. These actions demonstrate the United States' commitment to Ukraine's sovereignty and territorial integrity, as well as the broader stability of the region. As the situation continues to evolve, it remains essential for the U.S. to maintain and adapt its support to Ukraine in order to counteract ongoing threats. One should also observe the behavior of the extreme factions of the Republican Party, which are already directly opposing further assistance to Ukraine and involvement in NATO's eastern flank (Knox, 2023).

GOP Far-Right Shift and Overseas Partnerships

In recent years, the Republican Party in the United States has undergone significant changes that have shaped its political identity and policy positions. These changes have been driven by various factors, including the rise of populist and nationalist sentiments, shifts in the party's demographic base, and the influence of conservative media outlets.

Historically, the Republican Party has been known for its conservative and pro-business stance on taxes, regulation, and free trade. However, in recent years, the party has moved away from this traditional conservatism towards a more populist agenda. This shift has been primarily driven by the rise of Donald Trump, who has been able to tap into the anger and frustration of many working-class Americans who feel left behind by globalization and economic change (Doherty, 2023).

One significant change in the Republican Party has been its increasing embrace of populist and nationalist rhetoric and policy positions. This trend can be seen in the party's support for stricter immigration policies, trade protectionism, and a more isolationist foreign policy (Kupchan, 2020). This shift has been partly fueled by the electoral success of populist candidates such as Donald Trump, who won the party's presidential nomination in 2016 by appealing to disaffected working-class voters with promises to "make America great again" (Stokes, 2018; Azari, 2016).

Another notable change in the Republican Party has been its growing appeal to specific demographic groups, such as white working-class voters and evangelical Christians. This shift has been accompanied by a move towards more socially conservative policies, including opposition to abortion and same-sex marriage. At the same time, the party has faced challenges in attracting younger and more diverse voters, who tend to have more liberal views on social issues and a more globalist perspective on foreign policy (Doherty, 2023).

The influence of conservative media outlets has also significantly shaped the Republican Party's policy positions and political strategy. Conservative media, such as Fox News and Breitbart News, have become increasingly influential in Republican circles, promoting a conservative agenda and shaping the party's messaging and public image. This has led to a more polarized political environment, with the Republican Party often espousing views that are sharply at odds with those of the Democratic Party and other liberal groups.

Another area where the GOP has shifted is on the issue of trade. The party once strongly advocated free trade and globalization, but it has become more protectionist and isolationist (Baker & Bader, 2022). This shift can be seen in the party's opposition to the Trans-Pacific Partnership (TPP) and its support for renegotiating the North American Free Trade Agreement (NAFTA).

Finally, the GOP has also shifted on the issue of foreign policy. Whereas the party was once known for its hawkish stance on foreign policy and its support for international alliances such as NATO, it has become more skeptical of these alliances and more isolationist in its approach to foreign policy (Skocpol & Hertel-Fernandez, 2016).

These changes in the Republican Party have had significant implications for U.S. foreign policy, particularly in the domain of activity within NATO and military support for Ukraine. The party's increasing isolationist tendencies and skepticism of international alliances have created tensions with traditional U.S. allies in Europe, including NATO members who rely on U.S. military support and leadership. Similarly, the party's support for a more confrontational stance towards Russia has often been at odds with the Trump administration's conciliatory approach.

GOP House of representatives' decisions on NATO and Ukraine

The Freedom Caucus is a group of conservative United States House of Representatives members founded in 2015. The group is known for its strong commitment to fiscal conservatism, limited government and individual liberties (Edwards, 2019). The caucus has grown in influence in recent years, particularly within the Republican Party, and has become a significant force in shaping policy decisions.

The Freedom Caucus was created by a group of conservative members of Congress who were frustrated with what they saw as the lack of commitment to conservative principles by the Republican Party leadership. One of the primary areas of focus for the Freedom Caucus has been fiscal conservatism. The group has strongly advocated reducing government spending, cutting taxes, and balancing the budget. The caucus has also been critical of government programs that it sees as wasteful or unnecessary (DeSilver, 2015).

In addition to fiscal conservatism, the Freedom Caucus has also been a vocal proponent of limited government and individual liberties. The group has strongly advocated for reducing the size and scope of government and has opposed efforts to expand government control over various aspects of American life.

One area in which the Freedom Caucus has been particularly influential is in its approach to foreign policy, particularly concerning NATO. The caucus has been critical of what it sees as the United States' over-reliance on international alliances, including NATO, and has called for a more restrained foreign policy approach (Theriault & Jones, 2017). The caucus has been particularly critical of NATO's expansion into Eastern Europe, which it sees as unnecessarily provocative towards Russia. Some caucus members have even called for the United States to withdraw from NATO, arguing that the alliance is no longer necessary and should focus on its interests instead (Homan & Lantis, 2020).

Despite these criticisms, the Freedom Caucus has also supported a strong military and national defence. The group has been a vocal advocate for increasing defence spending and has opposed efforts to reduce military size.

Overall, the growing importance of the Freedom Caucus within the Republican Party has significantly impacted the party's approach to policy issues, particularly regarding fiscal conservatism, limited government, and individual liberties (Green, 2019).

Before the official start of the 118th Congress, the House Freedom Caucus began exerting influence. Nearly all the approximately 20 House Republicans who threatened to disrupt Kevin McCarthy's bid for speaker are Freedom Caucus members or closely aligned with the group. Finally, McCarthy won the speaker position on the fifteenth ballot, but only after agreeing to increase Freedom Caucus representation on the influential Rules Committee and other crucial panels. McCarthy also consented to several rule changes that the Freedom Caucus had long pursued, many of which intended to transfer power from the speaker's office to committee chairs and rank-and-file members (Foran, 2023).

Isolationist GOP members from Freedom Caucus can exert influence on the House Speaker and the rest of the GOP through various means, including:

- Coalition Building: By forming alliances with like-minded members within the GOP and beyond, isolationist lawmakers can increase their leverage on the House Speaker and their party by presenting a united front on specific policy issues.

- Committee Positions: By securing key positions on influential committees, such as the House Foreign Affairs Committee or the House Armed Services Committee, isolationist GOP members can shape the legislative agenda, debate, and oversight of U.S. foreign policy initiatives.

- Public Advocacy: Isolationist GOP members can use their platforms to rally public support for their positions, applying pressure on the House Speaker and the GOP to adopt more restrained foreign policy stances.

The influence of isolationist GOP members on the House Speaker and the rest of the GOP may lead to shifts in U.S. foreign policy that affect overseas partnerships, including:

- NATO Commitments: Isolationist members may push for reduced U.S. military presence in Europe and increased burden-sharing among NATO allies, potentially straining alliance cohesion and impacting NATO's deterrence capabilities on its eastern flank.

- Bilateral Relations: Isolationist tendencies could result in a more transactional approach to U.S. foreign policy, focusing on bilateral trade and defence agreements prioritizing direct American interests, potentially sidelining broader strategic partnerships.

The presence of isolationist GOP members within the United States' political landscape has the potential to significantly impact American foreign policy, particularly regarding U.S. aid to Ukraine. This influence manifests itself in multiple ways, spanning from financial assistance and military aid to diplomatic support. Isolationist GOP members may also impact U.S. aid to Ukraine in several ways:

- Financial Aid: They may scrutinize financial assistance to Ukraine, pushing for aid reductions or stricter conditions to ensure that funds are used effectively and in line with U.S. interests. Isolationist GOP members are likely to closely scrutinize financial aid packages designated for Ukraine. Their scrutiny may extend to demanding more transparency about how the funds are utilized by the Ukrainian government and pushing for measures that ensure the funds are used in a manner consistent with U.S. national interests. This could involve advocating for stricter conditions attached to financial assistance or even pushing for a reduction in the overall aid allocated to Ukraine. Such a position could be framed under the broader goal of fiscal responsibility or national priorities, arguing that American resources should be focused on domestic issues.

- Military Aid: Another significant area of impact could be military aid to Ukraine. Isolationist GOP members may challenge the strategic wisdom of providing military assistance, raising concerns that such actions risk entangling the United States in a conflict with Russia, which could have broader geopolitical implications. These legislators may argue that the focus should be on national security matters that more directly affect the U.S., and thus, may push for either reducing or altogether halting military aid to Ukraine.

- Diplomatic Support: A third aspect of U.S. aid to Ukraine that could be influenced by isolationist GOP members is the country's diplomatic posture. Isolationists might argue that the U.S. should adopt a more restrained role in international affairs, including the ongoing conflict between Ukraine and Russia. Such a stance could diminish American involvement in diplomatic efforts aimed at resolving the conflict, potentially undermining international peace negotiations and weakening international support for Ukraine's sovereignty and territorial integrity.

One of the most critical manifestations of activity in foreign policy by the far-right faction of the Republican party in the House of Representatives of the 118th Congress was the submission of the Ukraine Fatigue Act resolution (Cappabianca, 2023). This resolution called for an immediate cessation of aid to Ukraine and called on both sides of the conflict to start peace talks. The resolution was signed by 10 Republicans, all being members of the Freedom Caucus.

House Resolutions differ from bills and joint resolutions in that they do not have the force of law and do not require the approval of the Senate or the President. Instead, they are used primarily for expressing the opinions, sentiments, or beliefs of the House on various issues or for governing the House's internal procedures and operations. They serve as a means for the House to communicate its stance or express its collective views without enacting legislation or involving other branches of government.

Once a House Resolution is introduced, it is typically referred to the appropriate committee for consideration. The committee may then report the resolution to the House, where it can be debated and voted upon. If a majority of the House members vote in favor of the resolution, it is considered "passed" or "adopted" by the House. However, as mentioned earlier, House Resolutions are not legally binding and do not carry the force of law.

Of course, as quoted above, the resolution does not constitute a law within the meaning of the American Constitution. Nevertheless, the mere fact of its appearance in the discourse of Congress is very symptomatic and revealing. It is likely that, taking advantage of the weak position of the speaker of the House of Representatives, the isolationist factions of the Republican party will introduce further issues to the political agenda that may result in a reduction or significantly hinder the provision of aid to Ukraine. It can also limit the financing of the U.S. military involvement on NATO's eastern flank.

On the other hand, having in mind that today the most prominent Senators and Members of the House of Representatives, have been defending and supporting Ukraine aid and further military involvement in NATO's eastern flank, one should be aware that the presidential campaign for the elections in 2024 will gain momentum. Depending on the results of the polls, the dynamics of the primary elections and the political agendas of the Republican Party candidates it is possible that the topic of aid to Ukraine may be reduced or pushed to the background. The same applies to the permanent military presence of U.S. troops on NATO's eastern flank.

In the short term, one should not expect sudden movements. However, observing the fundamental shifting changes of the Republican Party and the growing importance of extreme populist movements in its ranks, one can expect increasingly heated discussions about the sense and necessity of American support for Ukraine and Europe as a whole.

The far-right groups of the Republican Party in Congress have never been so strong, and we do not know whether they will eventually become the main new establishment of the GOP. This would entail a high risk for the North Atlantic Alliance and transatlantic relations with European partners. Above all, it would increase the likelihood of lowering the defence potential of NATO's eastern flank. It would probably end military support for Ukraine, forcing it de facto to start negotiations from an unfavorable initial position.

Conclusions

The isolationist wing of the GOP in the House of Representatives has the potential to significantly impact U.S. foreign policy, particularly regarding overseas partnerships and aid to Ukraine. By leveraging their influence on the House Speaker and the rest of the GOP, isolationist members may push for a more restrained and transactional approach to American engagement in Europe and beyond.

In the next two years, it is probable to hear a great deal more about and from House Freedom Caucus members due to the slim margin of Republican control of the House. The isolationist perspective underscores a belief in prioritizing national interests and avoiding entanglements in foreign conflicts. This shift could manifest in various ways, including a more cautious approach to military alliances, a reconsideration of overseas aid distribution, and a renewed emphasis on bilateral agreements that directly benefit U.S. interests.

The Freedom Caucus, driven by its core principles of limited government, fiscal responsibility, and adherence to the Constitution, can shape U.S. foreign policy on NATO's eastern flank and Ukraine aid in 2023 and beyond. As the geopolitical landscape continues to evolve, understanding the Freedom Caucus's position on these critical issues becomes increasingly important. Their influence within the broader U.S. policymaking landscape could significantly alter the direction of American foreign policy. As such, monitoring the Freedom Caucus's actions and statements on foreign engagement will be crucial for anticipating the future trajectory of American involvement in Europe and other regions.

Moreover, the Freedom Caucus's stance on these issues will likely invite responses, both supportive and critical, from other factions within the Republican Party as well as from Democrats. This interplay could lead to intense Congressional debates, possibly triggering wider public discourse about the fundamentals of U.S. foreign policy. Given the Caucus's ability to influence or even block key legislation, understanding its priorities can provide crucial context for upcoming Congressional votes on aid packages, defence budgets, and international agreements.

International stakeholders will also be keenly interested in the Freedom Caucus's positions. American allies and partners, especially those in Europe, may need to reevaluate their own strategies and commitments based on the potential shifts in U.S. policy influenced by the Caucus. This recalibration could extend to NATO planning, European defence budgets, and diplomatic strategies aimed at resolving the Ukraine-Russia conflict. On the flip side, nations adversarial to U.S. interests might perceive the Caucus's isolationist tendencies as an opportunity to expand their own influence in regions like Eastern Europe.

In terms of longer-term implications, the Freedom Caucus's views could also affect the career trajectories of emerging political leaders within the Republican Party. Those aligning with the Caucus's principles might find increased support and endorsement opportunities, whereas those opposing could face internal party conflicts, impacting their political futures.

Therefore, as we look ahead to a rapidly evolving geopolitical landscape, the Freedom Caucus stands as a pivotal player whose influence may extend well beyond the immediate realm of U.S. foreign policy. As such, ongoing monitoring and analysis of this group's actions, statements, and policy proposals will be vital for a comprehensive understanding of America's role in the world in the years to come.

The coming years will likely see the Freedom Caucus and the broader isolationist wing of the GOP play a central role in discussions and decisions concerning U.S. foreign policy. Their influence could potentially reorient the U.S. approach towards international engagements, marking a shift from the country's traditionally more interventionist stance. This potential shift emphasizes the importance of closely following the evolving political dynamics within the GOP and understanding their potential implications for U.S. foreign policy.

References

Azari, J.R. (2016) 'How the News Media Helped to Nominate Trump'.

Bacon, D. (2023) 'H.R.2922 – 118th Congress (2023-2024): Baltic Security Initiative Act'. Available at: http://www.congress.gov/ .

Baker, J.O. & Bader, C.D. (2022) 'Xenophobia, Partisanship, and Support for Donald Trump and the Republican Party', *Race and Social Problems*, 14(1), pp. 69–83. doi: 10.1007/S12552-021-09337-0.

Cappabianca, C. (2023) 'Florida Rep. Gaetz introduces 'Ukraine Fatigue' resolution'. Available at: https://www.ny1.com/nyc/all-boroughs/politics/2023/02/23/florida-rep--matt-gatez-introduces--ukraine-fatigue--bill-to-cut-country-s-aid .

Committee on the Judiciary (2019) *H. Rept. 116-346 – Impeachment Of Donald J. Trump President Of The United States.* Available at: http://www.congress.gov/.

Craig, A.(2022) 'H.R.6833 – 117th Congress (2021-2022): Continuing Appropriations and Ukraine Supplemental Appropriations Act, 2023'. Available at: http://www.congress.gov/.

DeSilver, D. (2015) 'What is the House Freedom Caucus, and Who's in it?'. Available at: https://policycommons.net/artifacts/618803/what-is-the-house-freedom-caucus-and-whos-in-it/1599803/.

Doherty, C. (2023) 'How Republicans view their party, key issues as 118th Congress begins'. *Pew Research Center.* Available at: https://www.pewresearch.org/short-reads/2023/01/19/how-republicans-view-their-party-and-key-issues-facing-the-country-as-the-118th-congress-begins/.

Durbin, R.J. (2018) *S.Res.535 – 115th Congress (2017-2018): A resolution reaffirming the United States commitment to the North Atlantic Treaty Organization.* Available at: http://www.congress.gov/.

Edwards, C. (2019) 'Freedom Caucus and Spending Cuts'. Available at: https://policycommons.net/artifacts/1318680/freedom-caucus-and-spending-cuts/1921971/.

Foran, C. (2023) 'House speaker vote: McCarthy elected House speaker after days of painstaking negotiations and failed votes'. *CNN Politics.* Available at: https://edition.cnn.com/2023/01/06/politics/mccarthy-speaker-fight-friday/index.html.

Frum, D. (2014) 'Obama at West Point: A Foreign Policy of False Choices'. *The Atlantic.* Available at: https://www.theatlantic.com/international/archive/2014/05/obama-at-west-point-a-foreign-policy-of-false-choices/371748/.

Frum, D. (2014) 'Obama Just Made the Ultimate Commitment to Eastern Europe'. *The Atlantic.* Available at: https://www.theatlantic.com/international/archive/2014/09/obama-commitment-eastern-europe-russia-nato/379581/.

Goldberg, J. (2016) 'President Obama's Interview With Jeffrey Goldberg on Syria and Foreign Policy'. *The Atlantic.* Available at: https://www.theatlantic.com/magazine/archive/2016/04/the-obama-doctrine/471525/.

Green, M. (2019) 'Legislative Hardball: The House Freedom Caucus and the Power of Threat-Making in Congress'. Available at: https://www.cambridge.org/core/elements/legislative-hardball/37488C1E94117DFBFF924E5B67188E07.

Homan, P. & Lantis, J.S. (2020) 'The Freedom Caucus and Factionalism in the Trump Era', in *The Battle for U.S. Foreign Policy*, pp. 151–186. doi: 10.1007/978-3-030-30171-2_6.

Hrebenar, R.J. & Scott, R.K. (2015) *Interest Group Politics in America*. Routledge. doi: 10.4324/9781315703381.

Jacobson, G.C. (2023) 'The 2022 Elections: A Test of Democracy's Resilience and the Referendum Theory of Midterms', *Political Science Quarterly*, 138(1), pp. 1–22. doi: 10.1093/psquar/qqad002.

James W. (2017) Trump Says NATO Is Obsolete but Still 'Very Important to Me'. *Reuters*. Available at: https://www.reuters.com/article/us-usa-trump-nato-obsolete-idUSKBN14Z0YO.

Jillson, C.C. & Robertson, D.B. (2010) 'Perspectives on American Government: Readings in Political Development and Institutional Change'. Available at: https://cir.nii.ac.jp/crid/1130282270985698560.

Kaptur, M. (2022) 'H.R.3344 – 117th Congress (2021-2022): Transatlantic Telecommunications Security Act'. Available at: http://www.congress.gov/

Keating, W.R. (2022) *H.Res.1130 – 117th Congress (2021-2022): Expressing support for the sovereign decision of Finland and Sweden to apply to join the North Atlantic Treaty Organization (NATO) as well as calling on all members of NATO to ratify the protocols of accession swiftly*. Available at: http://www.congress.gov/.

Knox, O. (2023) 'A New Congress Gets Its First Ukraine Test'. *The Washington Post*. Available at: https://www.washingtonpost.com/politics/2023/01/11/new-congress-gets-its-first-ukraine-test/.

Kupchan, C. (2020) *Isolationism: A History of America's Efforts to Shield Itself from the World*. Available at: https://books.google.com/books/about/Isolationism.html?hl=pl&id=lpj5DwAAQBAJ.

Masters, J. (2023) 'How Much Aid Has the U.S. Sent Ukraine'. *Council on Foreign Relations*. Available at: https://www.cfr.org/article/how-much-aid-has-us-sent-ukraine-here-are-six-charts.

Moran, A. (2011) 'The Oxford Handbook of American Elections and Political Behaviour', *Democratization*, 18(6), pp. 1294–1296. doi: 10.1080/13510347.2011.640081.

Risch, J.E. (2020) *S.4392 – 116th Congress (2019-2020): Ukraine Security Partnership Act.* Available at: http://www.congress.gov/.

Risch, J.E. (2021) *S.814 – 117th Congress (2021-2022): Ukraine Security Partnership Act of 2021.* Available at: http://www.congress.gov/.

Ritchie, D.A. (2010) *The U.S. Congress: A Very Short Introduction.*

Rosenbloom, D.H. (2016) 'The Handbook of Federal Government Leadership and Administration', *The Handbook of Federal Government Leadership and Administration.* doi: 10.4324/9781315439242/handbook-federal-government-leadership-administration-david-rosenbloom-patrick-malone-bill-valdez.

Royce, E.R. (2017) 'H.R.3364 – 115th Congress (2017-2018): Countering America's Adversaries Through Sanctions Act'. Available at: http://www.congress.gov/.

S.4509 – 117th Congress (2021-2022): Black Sea Security Act of 2022 (2022). Available at: https://www.congress.gov/bill/117th-congress/senate-bill/4509/text.

Schwarz, B. (2022) '2022 midterm election spending set to break record'. Available at: https://www.cnbc.com/2022/11/03/2022-midterm-election-spending-set-to-break-record.html.

Sei, J. (2022) 'Senate Committee on Foreign Relations: Hearing on Ukraine Assistance'. Available at: http://www.congress.gov/.

Skocpol, T. & Hertel-Fernandez, A. (2016) 'The Koch Network and Republican Party Extremism', *Perspectives on Politics*, 14(3), pp. 681–699. doi: 10.1017/S1537592716001122.

Smith, A. [D-W.-9] (2022) 'H.R.4350 – 117th Congress (2021-2022): National Defence Authorization Act for Fiscal Year 2022'. Available at: http://www.congress.gov.

Stokes, D. (2018) 'Trump, American Hegemony and the Future of the Liberal International Order', *International Affairs*, 94(1), p. 137. doi: 10.1093/ia/iix238.

Sullivan, E. (2018) 'Trump Questions the Core of NATO: Mutual Defence, Including Montenegro'. *The New York Times.* Available at: https://www.nytimes.com/2018/07/18/world/europe/trump-nato-self-defence-montenegro.html.

The US Economy Is Back on Track After COVID-19 Dip (2023). *World Economic Forum.* Available at: https://www.weforum.org/agenda/2023/02/us-economy-covid19-inflation/.

Theriault, S.M. & Jones, B.D. (2017) 'Keeping Your Friends Close: How the House Freedom Caucus Organized for Survival'. Available at: https://repositories.lib.utexas.edu/handle/2152/63755.

Trachtenberg, D. (2010) 'Comparative Strategy Finding the Forest Among the Trees: The Bush Administration's National Security Policy Successes'. doi: 10.1080/01495930490274481.

Tushnet, M., Graber, M.A. & Levinson, S. (2015) *The Oxford Handbook of the U.S. Constitution.*

Vile, J.R. (2016) *A Companion to the United States Constitution and Its Amendments.*

Voter-Demographics-and-Redistricting (2023).

CHAPTER 7

The role of hybrid warfare in the conflict between Russia and Ukraine prior to the 2022 Russian invasion

Dawid Kufel

Abstract

This chapter focuses on the complex interplay of hybrid warfare tactics employed by the Russian Federation. This study examines how Russia utilized a combination of traditional and unconventional methods, such as propaganda, disinformation, cyberattacks, and special operations, to destabilize Ukraine before the full-scale invasion in 2022. It critically evaluates the effectiveness of Ukrainian countermeasures, which, while partially effective, struggled to fully mitigate the impact of these hybrid tactics. The chapter uses a classical realism approach and draws on secondary sources to explore the influence of hybrid warfare on local and regional stability. It highlights key historical events, demonstrating how hybrid warfare has been used globally as a strategic tool. The research findings underscore the necessity for robust counter-propaganda and cyber defence measures to combat hybrid warfare. Ultimately, this chapter contributes to the broader discourse on security and defence, offering valuable insights for policymakers and researchers working to address the growing threat of hybrid conflicts in modern warfare.

Keywords: hybrid warfare, Russia, Ukraine, cyberwarfare, disinformation, special operations

Introduction

The war between Russia and Ukraine prior to the 2022 Russian invasion was characterised by extensive use of hybrid warfare tactics by the Russian Federation. Hybrid warfare encompasses a combination of both traditional and unconventional methods, such as propaganda, disinformation, cyberattacks, and special operations, used to achieve strategic goals in present-day conflicts (Danyk, Maliarchuk & Briggs, 2017). The first well-documented example of using these tactics in 21th century was the 2006 war between Israel and Hezbollah, a Lebanese non-state political party sponsored by Iran, where decentralised cells comprising regular troops and guerrillas effectively managed to fight against a modern and well-equipped Israeli army (Berti & Schweitzer, 2014).

The objective of this study is to investigate the role of hybrid warfare in Eastern Europe between 2014 and 2022 and to assess the effectiveness of the countermeasures and responses employed by Ukraine. The importance of this research stems from the fact that the conflict between Russia and Ukraine has been posing a substantial threat to global security and stability. The practice of hybrid warfare methods by the Russian Federation proved the efficacy of such techniques in accomplishing strategic goals, while also highlighting the problems faced by Ukraine and other inter-national players in countering those tactics. This study intends to provide a deeper knowledge of the role of hybrid conflict within the war and to evaluate strategies for countering such methods. A review of existing literature reveals a research gap in the assessing the effectiveness of Ukrainian countermeasures and responses to hybrid warfare. Therefore, there is a dire need for a comprehen-sive analysis to bridge the gap and provide further knowledge of the subject.

In light of those findings, this study seeks to answer the sub-sequent research question: "How did hybrid warfare contribute to the conflict between Russia and Ukraine before the 2022 Russian invasion, and what was the effectiveness of the countermeasures and responses employed by Ukraine?". This study aims to address the research query with the ambition to contribute to a deeper understanding of the role of hybrid warfare in modern conflicts and to identify effective strategies for countering such tactics in the future.

A historical look at the implications of hybrid warfare on security around the world

Hybrid conflict is a complicated and multifaced phenomenon that has had some devastating results throughout history. The 2006 Israel-Hezbollah war serves as a prime example of the way this form of warfare can be waged with deadly effectiveness. Hezbollah applied a combination of guerrilla techniques, rocket assaults, and media manipulation to achieve strategic and political targets, demonstrating the destructive potential of such approaches (Kalb, 2012). Diving further into history, the Gulf War in 1990–1991 provides some other examples of how hybrid methods may be employed. Iraq used propaganda, psychological operations, and unconventional techniques, altogether with the practise of using human shields, to demoralise coalition forces and decrease worldwide support for the conflict (The White House, n.d.).

The efforts of Argentina to assert control of the Falkland Islands during the 1980s serves as another example. The Argentinian authorities started propaganda and disinformation campaigns to undermine British claims for the islands, alongside they utilized special forces assaults and other unconventional strategies to infiltrate and sabotage the British military (Coli & Arend, 1985). In South Africa, the apartheid government used hybrid tactics to suppress opposition and maintain power. This included the use of propaganda and disinformation campaigns, as well as the establishment of covert unique operations units that engaged in targeted assassinations and sabotage (Baines, 2019). In the early 2000s, Palestinian militant groups, which included Hamas, used hybrid strategies to withstand Israeli forces and achieve political goals. This involved the usage of suicide bombings, rocket attacks, and propaganda campaigns to gain support among Arab states and undermine the legitimacy of the Israeli authorities (Schweitzer, 2010).

The Tamil Tigers in Sri Lanka used a combination of conventional and unconventional methods, including suicide bombings, targeted assassinations, and media manipulation, to wage a long and bloody insurgency against the Sri Lankan authorities (Horowitz, 2015). The Rwandan genocide of 1994 is perhaps one of the most tragic examples of the usage of hybrid warfare approaches. The Hutu government used propaganda and hate speech as part of a deliberate strategy to incite violence against the Tutsi minority, leading to a devastating genocide that claimed the lives of over 800,000 individuals (Uvin, 2001). Similarly, in Colombia, armed groups and drug cartels have used hybrid methods for decades to resist authorities and pursue political and criminal objectives. Those groups have applied guerrilla tactics, including targeted assassinations, and the infiltration of political establishments and law enforcement agencies, as means to achieve their goals (Taylor & Saab, 2009).

Such examples illustrate the dangers of hybrid warfare and the need for effective strategies to counter its use. Policymakers and stakeholders ought to be vigilant and collaborate in order to develop powerful responses to this ever-evolving threat ensuring the preservation of global security and stability.

The USE of hybrid warfare by Russia in Ukraine

Hybrid warfare may be broadly described as a series of carefully conducted actions encompassing military, diplomatic, economic, and informational domains, all aimed at achieving strategic targets (Wither, 2016). Its components can also include conventional and non-conventional threats, terrorism, and subversive activities, regularly leveraging cutting-edge non-conventional technologies to counterbalance the adversary's military superiority. The standard hybrid warfare campaign composes of three stages: preparatory, active, and final (Zhyhlei, Legenchyk & Syvak, 2020). The conflict in Ukraine during the preparatory phase (2000-2013) was characterised by several significant events. These include the reinforcement of Russian influence over Ukrainian leaders, Ukraine's government decision not to pursue European Union and NATO membership after the failed Orange Revolution protests in 2004, an increase in societal divides between pro-Western and pro-Russian factions, attempts to reduce financial and economic ties with Russia, and the use of energy supplies as a coercive control tool against Ukraine (Zhyhlei, Legenchyk & Syvak, 2020). During the active stage, several pivotal events occurred, including the annexation of Crimea, the deployment of Russian troops to the peninsula, the destabilisation of eastern and southern Ukrainian regions, the concentration of troops near Ukrainian borders and occupied areas, and a large-scale propaganda campaign aimed at discrediting Ukraine (Janjevic, 2017). The final phase, which started in October 2014, witnessed various developments, such as the provision of assistance by the Russian Federation to the newly-established authorities in the occupied territories, the legitimization of self-proclaimed governments in cases in which the aggressor state failed to acknowledge its involvement in the conflict, and the establishment of conditions to maintain the presence of the aggressor's army on Ukrainian soil (Zhyhlei, Legenchyk & Syvak, 2020).

During the preparatory phase (2000–2013), the Russian media were successful in creating favourable conditions for further military and political interventions in Ukraine, leading to the annexation of Crimea and the Donbas conflict. Within a relatively short period, pro-Russian authorities sponsored by Russian secret services, established voluntary battalions that supported the offensive operations of unmarked Russian troops. These troops were referred to as "friendly men" or "little green men" in Russian media, and subsequently the term became widely known worldwide. Additionally, the Russian media played a crucial role in orchestrating the 2014 referendum. This resulted in Crimea allegedly seceding from Ukraine and joining the Russian Federation. It's worth noting that these actions occurred during a time of general disorder in Ukrainian government institutions. The whole country was affected by the absence of the president, who fled to Russia, the lack of the prime minister, who abandoned his post, the shortage of commanders in the General Staff, and the considerable demoralisation of the armed and police forces (Hajduk & Stępniewski, 2016).

Russia implemented a similar strategy in the eastern regions of Ukraine, where Pro-Russian organisations in these regions supported Russian secret services. With the assistance of Russian media broadcasts and pro-Russia regional media, anti-government demonstrations were organized, leading to clashes with police and pro-western supporters. Attempts were made to take control of public authority buildings. Paramilitary units, consisting of pro-Russia residents and Russian volunteers, were formed, and a significant number of police force, security services, and military joined these units (Hajduk & Stępniewski, 2016). Local authority representatives aligned themselves with the separatists out of fear of being held accountable for illegal activities. As a result, provisional authorities were appointed, led by individuals under the influence of Russian secret services. These activities were accompanied by a propaganda campaign that exploited the fears and memories of the Second Patriotic War, portraying the "voluntary battalions" as fighting against evil and fascist Ukrainian forces (Hajduk & Stępniewski, 2016). To further destabilise the situation, the Kremlin and Russian media organised humanitarian convoys that, reportedly transported weapons used for fighting against Ukraine. Russian media widely covered these convoys and presenting them as material assistance for the unrecognized republics, as well evidence of Russia's significant and friendly support to the region's residents (Walker, 2014). The Russian media also targeted regular Russian citizens to convince them of the legitimacy of Russia's operations against its enemies. Unlike Ukrainian or international media, Russian media referred to the territories in question as people's republics, legitimizing the operations in public opinion (Hajduk & Stępniewski, 2016).

In terms of cyberwarfare, although Russia did not extensively deploy it during the initial stages of the Crimean operation, there were several instances of cyberinfrastructure attacks. One example occurred in February 2015, Ukrtelecom, the Ukrainian countrywide Telecommunications Operator, reported that unidentified criminals broken into their Simferopol city office and physically cut the cables that supplied communication links between the peninsula and mainland Ukraine. Multiple sources confirmed that Ukrtelecom's offices had been temporarily taken over and that fibre-optic cables were damaged in early March of 2014 (Rusnáková, 2017). Additionally, Ukrainian military communications were jammed, as reported by Valentyn Nalyvaichenki, the Chief of the Security Service of Ukraine. These attacks, directed at Ukrainian state representatives, were carried out from Crimea, which had been previously seized by Russian forces (Rusnáková, 2017).

Ukrainian countermeasures and responses to hybrid warfare

Ukraine responded to Russian separatist movements by employing a combination of methods that could be classified as hybrid as well.

Those included political propaganda, embargoes, and disrupting energy supplies to Crimea and occupied territories (Kostanyan, Remizov & Mundus, 2017). Ukraine also carried out police and intelligence operations. Thereafter, Ukraine shifted its main focus towards media and political diplomacy to delegitimise the occupiers and gain global support for their cause. Given Russia's military dominance, attempting to resolve the hybrid conflict through military means was no longer an option for Ukraine. As a result, Ukraine's countermeasures were revolved around political and diplomatic actions, including media campaigns and gaining international support (Schmid, 2019). For instance, Ukraine sought to strengthen its economic and political stability by deepening its integration within the European Union. It also implemented laws aimed at reducing corruption and strengthening its democratic institutions to minimise vulnerabilities to subversion and disinformation campaigns. Furthermore, Ukraine invested in independent media outlets and fact-checking groups to counter Russian propaganda (Schmid, 2019).

One crucial countermeasure was the development of a comprehensive media campaign. Despite facing military defeats, the Ukraine's authorities demonstrated that society was not entirely vulnerable to subversion and disinformation campaigns. Its efforts to integrate with the European Union and strengthen democratic institutions demonstrated a commitment to building a more resilient society (Schmid, 2019). The Ukrainian government sought to counter propaganda by increasing its own messaging and media presence, both domestically and internationally. This included the creation of new media outlets and additional funding to existing ones, as well as training of journalists and bloggers to promote Ukraine's perspective. Consequently in 2014, they formed a Ministry of Information Policy to regulate the media and protect citizens from manipulative information. Ukrainian President Petro Poroshenko stated that the main function of the ministry was to stop "the spreading of biased information about Ukraine" (Vikhrov, 2014). The comprehensive media campaign implemented by the Ukrainian government, which included increasing their own messaging and media presence, training journalists, and regulating the media, which proved to be effective in countering propaganda and disinformation campaigns. This strategic approach demonstrated Ukraine's commitment to building a more resilient society, and enabling the country to maintain its independence and sovereignty despite facing military defeats.

Another important aspect of Ukraine's response was its efforts to strengthen its military capabilities. This included modernizing its armed forces and increasing its defence spending. In August 2015, Ukraine initiated a major military reform to strengthen its armed forces, which were in a state of complete degradation following the collapse of the Soviet Union. The reform was aimed at transforming the Soviet military system into a modernized force, but Ukraine faced numerous challenges such as poor management, corruption, and a lack of adequate funding (Kiryukhin, 2018). However, the military reform was still in progress, and Ukraine's military potential remained significantly inferior to that of its primary adversary, Russia. Ukraine's previous military goals were focused on resisting terrorist threats, participating in international humanitarian and peacekeeping operations, for instance in Iraq (Foliente, 2008). Ukraine successfully developed rapid reaction and special operations forces, but its main defence forces were in a deplorable state. By 2013, the Ukrainian military had downsized compared to its Soviet predecessor, comprising only 184,000 soldiers, 700 tanks, 170 combat aircraft, and 22 warships (Kiryukhin, 2018). Despite these challenges, the country made significant progress in rebuilding its military capabilities with support from foreign states. By 2018, Ukraine had achieved its highest fighting capabilities since its independence in 1991 (Kiryukhin, 2018).

In 2014, Ukraine substantially increased funding for its military, resulting in a 36% rise in military personnel to 250,000 by 2018. This development is significant because the Ukrainian army moved to a contract service model, abandoning its unpopular draft system. The Ukrainian military conducted numerous exercises with foreign support to enhance the level of combat training of personnel. In 2016 alone, nearly 900 exercises took place, some involving international participation (Kiryukhin, 2018). Ukraine's military potential was further boosted by its combat experience and the technologies and experience of military personnel from NATO countries. Although Ukraine's security problems persisted due to its inferior military potential compared to Russia, the country's success in implementing military reform provided a foundation for the future of its armed forces (Kiryukhin, 2018).

Taking it all into consideration, Ukraine's efforts to strengthen its military capabilities through modernisation have increased defence spending, and a major military reform have yielded significant results in rebuilding its armed forces and achieving its highest fighting capabilities since independence. However, the country still faced challenges such as poor management, corruption, and a lack of adequate funding, and its military potential remained vastly inferior to that of its primary adversary, Russia. Therefore, this countermeasure turned out to be partially effective.

Nevertheless, once the attack phase of hybrid war begins, it's usually too late for the assaulted state to regain control through military means. Ukraine experienced this first-hand as it lost control over certain areas of its territory. This scenario was anticipated by Russian researchers and analysts who were acquainted with this new kind of conflict (Rácz, 2015). As it was anticipated by them, the attacker was militarily stronger and was able to limit the effectiveness of countermeasures. In the case of Ukraine, the government was unable to take decisive action against the Russian forces disguised as the „little green man" as they had been deterred by the chance of a large traditional attack from the tens of thousands of regular Russian troops placed along the border during military exercises, such as the ZAPAD joint strategic exercise (Rácz, 2015).

The Ukrainian government recognized the importance of improving economic resilience in the face of Russian aggression. This involved diversifying its economy and reducing its dependence on Russian energy sources. Ukraine also sought to strengthen its trade relationships with other countries, particularly those in Europe, to lessen its reliance on Russia (Iwański, 2016). Ukraine successfully reduced its dependence on Russian gas imports through effective action to increase opportunities to import gas via reverse connections with EU member states, mainly Slovakia. This was facilitated by favourable conditions in the European gas market, a decline in gas consumption in Ukraine, and milder winters. In 2015, the EU imported 10.3 billion cubic meters of gas, while Russia exported 6.1 billion cubic meters to Ukraine, reversing the previous year's levels (Iwański, 2016). Ukraine was successful in diversifying its gas supply pipelines due to several factors: first, it increased gas purchases from the West through reverse connections, second, they reduced consumption, third, the financial cooperation with the West, and lastly decreased gas purchases from Russia. In 2015, Ukraine's gas consumption fell by about 22%, and it passed a law on the natural gas market aimed at depoliticizing Naftogaz, Ukraine's largest state-owned oil and gas company, to make it transparent and profitable. To support its gas purchases, in 2016 Ukraine received international loans and signed contracts to buy 1.7 bcm of gas from EU neighbours. (Iwański, 2016). These efforts helped Ukraine by reducing its dependence on Russian energy sources and increased trade with other countries, especially European ones. However, further measures were needed to ensure long-term sustainability.

In addition to these actions, Ukraine also strived to counter Russian hybrid warfare through diplomatic channels. This involved working actively with international organizations and allies to draw attention to Russian actions and build support for Ukraine's position. Kyiv took legal action against Russia, including filing a lawsuit with the International Court of Justice (ICJ). Before 2022, Ukraine had filed a lawsuit against Russia over its 2014 aggression. Most complaints were lodged with the European Court of Human Rights (ECtHR). Ukraine filed a total of nine lawsuits for human rights violations in Crimea and eastern Ukraine (Zaręba, 2022). The incidents included the kidnapping of a child, the downing of flight MH-17, and ultimately the detention of a Ukrainian sailor in the 2018 Kerch Strait Incident. Kyiv also accepted the jurisdiction of the International Criminal Court (ICC) to prosecute war crimes committed on Ukrainian territory since 2014. Before the start of Russia's aggression in 2022, legal action had limited effect. The ICJ ordered Russia to stop discriminating against Ukrainians and Tatars in Crimea, although the lawsuit did not improve the situation on the peninsula. A preliminary review by the ICC was hampered by financial constraints. In one of the cases in the Black Sea, an arbitral tribunal concluded that most of Ukraine's claims on the issue of sovereignty over Crimea lacked jurisdiction. In 2019, legal action allowed Ukraine to release sailors captured in the Kerch Strait Incident as part of a wider prisoner-of-war exchange, while Russia released a captured warship, albeit in a non-serviceable state, which was returned to Ukraine (Zaręba, 2022).

The effectiveness of Ukraine's diplomatic efforts to counter

Russian hybrid warfare through legal action was mixed. While it allowed Ukraine to secure the release of some prisoners of war, and draw attention to Russia's actions, it did not lead to a significant improvement in the overall situation in Crimea and eastern Ukraine prior to the start of Russia's aggression in 2022.

Conclusion

In conclusion, this comprehensive study extensively examined the effects of hybrid warfare on the ongoing Russia-Ukraine conflict, specifically prior to the 2022 Russian invasion. The conflict in Ukraine has been characterized by the deliberate implementation of hybrid tactics, encompassing propaganda, disinformation, cyberattacks, and special operations, which have significantly impacted the security and stability of the region. The findings of this research affirm the remarkable success of Russia's hybrid warfare strategy in achieving its strategic objectives. By exploiting vulnerabilities and sowing discord through multifaceted tactics, Russia has effectively employed hybrid warfare. Conversely, Ukraine's responses and countermeasures have yielded mixed results in mitigating the consequences of Russian actions. Nonetheless, it is noteworthy to consider the potential applicability of these countermeasures in other ongoing or future conflicts.

Diplomatic efforts have played a pivotal role in Ukraine's response to the conflict, and this approach holds promise for other nations facing hybrid threats. Ukraine has actively engaged with international partners, including the European Union, NATO, and the United States, seeking alliances and support to confront Russian aggression. By effectively utilizing diplomatic channels, raising awareness about hybrid tactics, and exerting diplomatic pressure, countries grappling hybrid warfare can foster international collaboration and garner assistance to bolster their defence capabilities. Furthermore, the emphasis on economic resilience demonstrated by Ukraine provides valuable insights for other nations confronting hybrid conflicts. Recognising Russia's economic leverage, Ukraine has undertaken measures to diversify its energy sources, reduce its dependence on Russian supplies, and cultivate stronger trade relationships with other countries. This approach can be emulated by other nations to enhance their economic stability and reduce vulnerability to economic coercion in the face of hybrid warfare.

In terms of military capabilities, Ukraine's reforms hold relevance for other nations engaged in similar conflicts. Recognizing the hybrid nature of the conflict, Ukraine has prioritised improving the interoperability of its armed forces, modernising military equipment, and enhancing training programs. By adopting these reforms, other nations can bolster their defence capabilities and effectively address the hybrid threats. Moreover, Ukraine's use of political propaganda as a means to counter Russian disinformation provides insights applicable to other conflict scenarios. By exposing aggression, debunking disinformation campaigns, and promoting their own narratives, nations engaged in hybrid conflicts can counter the psychological impact of such tactics and maintain domestic and international support.

The implications of these findings extend beyond the Russia-Ukraine conflict, offering valuable lessons for policymakers worldwide grappling with hybrid threats. The study highlights the significance of adopting a comprehensive and coordinated approach, encompassing diplomatic engagement, economic resilience, military reforms, and strategic communication. By implementing these countermeasures, nations can effectively address hybrid threats and safeguard their security and stability.

To conclude, this study sheds light on the far-reaching effects of hybrid warfare in the Russia-Ukraine conflict and emphasizes the potential applicability of countermeasures in other ongoing or future conflicts. Diplomatic efforts, economic resilience, military reforms, and strategic communication offer promising avenues for nations grappling with hybrid threats. By adopting these approaches and promoting international collaboration, policymakers can effectively mitigate the impact of hybrid warfare and ensure security and stability in the face of complex conflicts.

References

Baines, G. (2019) 'Legacies of South Africa's Apartheid Wars', *Oxford Research Encyclopedia of African History*.

Berti, B. & Schweitzer, Y. (2014) 'Hizbollah and the Next War with Israel: Experience from Syria and Gaza', *Strategic Assessment*,

17(3). Available at: https://www.inss.org.il/wp-content/uploads/ sites/2/systemfiles/SystemFiles/adkan17_3ENG%20(3)_Berti-Schweitzer.pdf.

Coli, A. & Arend, A. (1985) *The Falklands Crisis and the Laws of War.* Available at: https://digital-commons.usnwc.edu/cgi/ viewcontent.cgi?article=1490&context=ils.

Danyk, Y., Maliarchuk, T. & Briggs, C. (2017) 'Hybrid War: High-tech, Information and Cyber Conflicts', *Connections: The Quarterly Journal*, vol. 16, no. 2.

Foliente, R. (2008) Ukrainians complete mission in Iraq. Available at: https://www.army.mil/article/15056/ ukrainians_complete_mission_in_iraq.

Hajduk, J. & Stępniewski, T. (2016) 'Russia's Hybrid War with Ukraine: Determinants, Instruments, Accomplishments and Challenges', *Studia Europejskie-Studies in European Affairs*, 2, Available at: http://cejsh.icm.edu.pl/cejsh/element/bwmeta1.element. desklight-2ac92738-4d5a-40b3-a48d-d3175455bc0b.

Horowitz, M. C. (2015) 'The Rise and Spread of Suicide Bombing', *Annual Review of Political Science*, vol. 18, no. 1.

Iwański, T. (2016) *Ukraine: successful diversification of gas supply, OSW Centre for Eastern Studies.* Available at: https:// www.osw.waw.pl/en/publikacje/analyses/2016-02-03/ ukraine-successful-diversification-of-gas-supply.

Janjevic, D. (2017) What are Russia's Zapad war games? DW. Available at: https://www.dw.com/en/what-are-russias-zapad-war-games/a-39702331.

Kalb, M. (2012) 'The Israeli-Hezbollah War of 2006: The Media as a Weapon in Asymmetrical Conflict', *SSRN Electronic Journal*.

Kiryukhin, D. (2018) *The Ukrainian Military: From Degradation to Renewal, Foreign Policy Research Institute.* Available at: https:// www.fpri.org/article/2018/08/the-ukrainian-military-from-degradation-to-renewal/.

Kostanyan, H., Remizov, A. & Mundus, E. (2017) *The Donbas Blockade: Another blow to the Minsk peace process.* CEPS Working Document No 2017/08. Available at: http://aei.pitt.edu/87772/.

Rácz, A. (2015) *Russia's Hybrid War in Ukraine: Breaking the Enemy's Ability to Resist.* Finnish Institute of International Affairs. Available at: https://books.google.pl/ books/about/Russia_s_ Hybrid_War_in_Ukraine.html?id=lMnijwEACAAJ&redir_esc=y.

Rusnáková, S. (2017) 'Russian New Art of Hybrid Warfare in Ukraine', *Slovak Journal of Political Sciences*, vol. 17, no. 3-4.

Schmid, J. (2019) 'Hybrid warfare on the Ukrainian battlefield: developing theory based on empirical evidence', *Journal on Baltic Security*, vol. 5, no. 1.

Schweitzer, Y. (2010) *The Rise and Fall of Suicide Bombings in the Second Intifada.* Available at: https://www.inss.org.il/wp-content/uploads/sites/2/systemfiles/(FILE)12898966 44.pdf .

Taylor, A. & Saab, B. (2009) *Criminality and Armed Groups: A Comparative Study of FARC and Paramilitary Groups in Colombia, Brookings.* Available at: https://www.brookings.edu/articles/criminality-and-armed-groups-a-comparative-study-of-farc-and-paramilitary-groups-in-colombia/.

The White House (n.d.) *Apparatus of Lies.* Available at: https://georgewbush-whitehouse.archives.gov/ogc/apparatus/printer.html.

Uvin, P. (2001) 'Reading the Rwandan Genocide', *International Studies Review*, vol. 3, no. 3. Available at: https://www.jstor.org/stable/3186243.

Vikhrov, M. (2014) *Ukraine forms 'ministry of truth' to regulate the media, The Guardian.* Available at: https://www.theguardian.com/world/2014/dec/19/-sp-ukraine-new-ministry-truth-undermines-battle-for-democracy.

Walker, S. (2014) 'Aid convoy stops short of border as Russian military vehicles enter Ukraine', *The Guardian.* Available at: https://www.theguardian.com/world/2014/aug/14/russian-military-vehicles-enter-ukraine-aid-convoy-stops-short-border.

Wither, J. K. (2016) 'Making Sense of Hybrid Warfare', *Connections: The Quarterly Journal*, vol. 15, no. 2.

Zaręba, S. (2022) "The Fight for Justice: Ukraine's Legal Steps in Its Defence Against Russian Aggression" *PISM.* Available at: https://pism.pl/publications/the-fight-for-justice-ukraines-legal-steps-in-its-defence-against-russian-aggression .

Zhyhlei, I., Legenchyk, S. & Syvak, O. (2020) 'Hybrid war as a form of modern international conflicts and its influence on accounting development', *Przegląd Wschodnioeuropejski*, vol. 11, no. 1.

CHAPTER 8

The Black Sea the competition and rivalry ground for Turkey and Russia

Jarosław Łęski

Abstract

This chapter focuses on the geopolitical competition and rivalry between Turkey and Russia in the Black Sea Region (BSR), which has influenced the course of the war in Ukraine. The study delves into how the BSR has been a historically strategic region for both countries, impacting their relations and broader regional dynamics. The main aim is to analyze the importance of the Black Sea for both Turkey and Russia in terms of military, economic, and political influence. The study further explores how the interplay of rivalry and cooperation between these two key actors shapes security, energy, and international relations within the region. The findings highlight that while Turkey and Russia have historically had fluctuating relations, their mutual strategic interests in the Black Sea continue to drive both cooperation and competition. The chapter concludes that maintaining a delicate balance between rivalry and cooperation will be key to ensuring stability in the region. Additionally, the chapter underscores the role of external actors, such as NATO and the European Union, which also have a vested interest in the Black Sea, further complicating the geopolitical landscape. Key points discussed include the military presence of both countries, control over strategic points such as the Bosporus and Dardanelles straits, and the importance of the BSR in terms of energy security and economic trade routes.

Keywords: Turkey, Russia, Ukraine, The Black Sea, NATO-EU, competition and rivalry

Introduction

The Black Sea region is the highest importance both in the regional and global context. Russia and Türkiye compete for the most significant influence in the Black Sea region. The geopolitical location of the Black Sea has a significant impact on the relationship and the current situation between the two countries. Unlike Western politics, Russia seeks to destabilize post-Soviet countries aspiring to join Western organizations through its aggressive policy and military force (Transnistria, South Ossetia, Abkhazia, Karabakh Mountains and Ukraine).

Turkey, currently having the most significant influence in the region due to complete control of the straits, which are the only access to the sea, has a two-way policy. On the one hand, as a member of NATO, which strives for Western influence and cares about its internal security, fearing Russia's dangerous policy, it conducts its foreign policy against a dangerous rival, which Russia undoubtedly is in this region. Undoubtedly, external players in which the region is interested are NATO, the European Union, China, and the countries of the Caucasus in the global and regional context, i.e. Turkey, Russia, Romania, Bulgaria, Georgia, Ukraine, Moldova, Azerbaijan and Armenia. Therefore, the current complicated geopolitical situation of the region was a stimulus to study, based on the available information and litera-ture, the relationship in Turkish-Russian relations in the context of the Black Sea Region.

The article's primary purpose was to describe the importance of the Black Sea region for relations between Russia and Turkey in the context of rivalry and cooperation. The main question is to find how similarities and differences influence cooperation between the countries and the areas that affect their rivalry and what factors influence the current security situation in the region.

To provide an answer, the author thoroughly examined and synthesized data from various sources such as scientific literature, professional publications, online resources, official speeches, and documentaries. Due to the intricate nature of the information, the author opted to present only the most crucial data, which necessi-tated a subjective evaluation.

The role of the Black Sea region

The Black Sea (BSR) region (Figure 8.1) is one of the critical areas where constant competition exists between countries for the most significant influence. The region's importance can be described as a ruthless crossroads between Asia Minor to the south, the Caucasus to the east, the East European Plain to the north and the Balkan Peninsula to the west. It is connected to the Mediterranean Sea by the Bosporus and Dardanelles straits, a sea route of international importance. The Kerch Strait connects them with the Sea of Azov (Polegkyi *et al.*, 2021).

The civilizational and cultural diversity of the countries in the BSR certainly directly impacts the relations that have taken place in the history of the basin and those that are currently ongoing. In addition, the policy of the coastal countries and the common need to maintain the security of the sea region and the economy have always been vital factors influencing the situation of the BSR. Respective actors are:

- Ukraine, which is moving towards the West and European integrity, has always been in terms of the economic influence of states on Russia. Today, Ukraine is under war with Russia since 24th February 2022.

- Russia, which together with Turkey is now considered the power of the BSR, undoubtedly wants to have the most significant influence in the region under their state goals. Nowadays, the country conducts an aggressive policy against the West using the argument of force (Moldova, Abkhazia and South Ossetia, Syria, and Libia). Due to historical differences, Russia perceives the West as a potential threat.

- Georgia is the only BS coastal state in the South Caucasus, which, like Ukraine, by joining the partnerships for a program, declared its political position concerning aggressive Russia, thus wanting to strive for clashes and Western influence.

- Turkey, which currently politically occupies most of the maritime outskirts, including the only access to the sea through the two straits of the Bosphorus and the Dardanelles, also represents a NATO entity but also pursues its policy towards Russia.

Figure 8.1. Map of the Black Sea Region

Source: Wikipedia, *Blac Sea, n. d.* https://en.wikipedia.org/wiki/Black_Sea#/
media/ File:Black_Sea_map.png.

The Black Sea Region (BSR) extends beyond countries with direct access to the basin. In his publication "The Wider Black Sea Region in the 21st Century" (WBSR), Daniel Hamilton highlights the significance of entities in the region from economic and security perspectives. Due to the geostrategic importance of the Black Sea, the Russian Federation may argue that the correct term for the BSR encompasses the area in and around the Black Sea, extending beyond the easternmost areas of the Carpathians to the South Caucasus and including the dynamics of the Baltic Sea region and the Caspian Sea moving towards the East. Therefore, the Western policy towards the WBSR should be based on the same statement as the Russian Federation, but with consideration for their interests and beliefs (Hamilton *et al.,* 2008).

Like many such points of intersection, it is often a friction point. This is the case in the current geopolitical environment of growing confrontation between Russia and the West. Any friction there will almost certainly involve NATO nations and the Alliance's interests, with three NATO states on the BS and several NATO partners on the BSR (Horrell, 2016).

Without a doubt, Turkey and Russia are the primary regional players in the BSR. With six countries in the BSR belonging to the EU and NATO, it has become a crucial aspect of security and business strategies. As a result, it is believed that a combination of cooperation and competition is necessary to gain complete control over the area. History shows the region's importance, especially the competition and rivalry between the Ottoman and Russian Empires. Both would struggle for supremacy over the benefits the region could bring the respective entities economically and security-wise. After the collapse of both empires, the 1923 Treaty of Lausanne would set the base for the Republic of Turkey, and the 1936 Montreux Convention would generate a fragile balance in the region (Ozbay *et al.*, 2011). Following WWII, such delicate harmony would be tested in the 1946 Turkish Straits crisis, when the Soviet Union pressed Turkey to renegotiate the Montreux Convention. Following the dissolution of the Soviet Union in 1991, the region did not have the same importance in Western eyes. However, the opposite was observed in Russia, as evidenced by Russia's activities in Georgia, Ukraine, and Nagorno-Karabakh in 2008, 2014, and 2020, respectively. Thus, it can be argued that the BS has been the primary field of operations for demonstrating Russia's resurgence into the geopolitical big picture in defiance of Western pressure (Carneiro *et.al.*, 2021).

Currently, the BSR is seen as the region's most economical region. However, at the regional level, landlocked countries tend to focus on the regional security aspect. According to the observations of Ben HODGES, described in detail in the article "Militarization of the Black Sea by Russia", the military potential and spheres of influence of the coastal states were described. Apart from militarization, the most critical fact has always been trade, namely trade routes. Therefore, the most significant for the region is the Turkish Straits, which Turkey fully controls in accordance with the signed Montreux Convention, which established:

established Turkish control over the straits and guaranteed free passage of warships belonging to Black Sea states not at war with Turkey. Non-Black Sea powers were restricted in sending their military vessels to the Black Sea (they must be under 15,000 tons per vessel, 45,000 in aggregate, and could only stay in the Black Sea for 21 days.

Another meaning is that Don and Kuban's rivers connect Russia with the Sea of Azov, located between the Crimean Peninsula and Russia, along with the Kerch Strait bordering the Black Sea. For Russia, complete control of these regions is essential, given the highest priority for Russia's security (Carneiro *et.al.*, 2021). Crimea has been at the centre of several news outlets in recent years, given the Russian annexation in 2014 from Ukraine. Considering the map and the (referred) naturally Russian assets in the region, it is clear that Crimea holds the key to all of the Federation's properties, making it the most important Russian asset in the Black Sea. From Moscow's perspective, because Crimea sits in the middle of the Sea, allowing crucial access to Ukrainian and Russian plains, no other power must be able to hold the Peninsula, as Russia would have to devote significantly more resources to safeguarding its security concerns, as well as foreign policy objectives such as power projection – such is the strategic importance of Sevastopol.

The Dnieper, Dniester, and Danube Rivers (Figure 8.2) are essential assets because they represent historic trade routes. The first divide is Ukraine, one of the few geographical features of the flat European Plain. Meanwhile, the second is the longest river on Ukrainian territory and serves as Moldova's "main water artery". Furthermore, it is a natural dividing line between Slavic-speaking and Latin-based nations. Finally, the Danube flows from the Swiss Alps to Constanța, Romania, where NATO has established an air base, albeit a limited one, to represent American presence in the region without relying on Turkey (Carneiro *et.al.*, 2021).

It is currently believed that the Black Sea has significant hydrocarbon resources and is the most convenient region for implementing projects for constructing gas pipelines connecting Asian producers and European consumers (Flagan et al., 2019; Ozel et al., 2019).

The Black Sea Basin

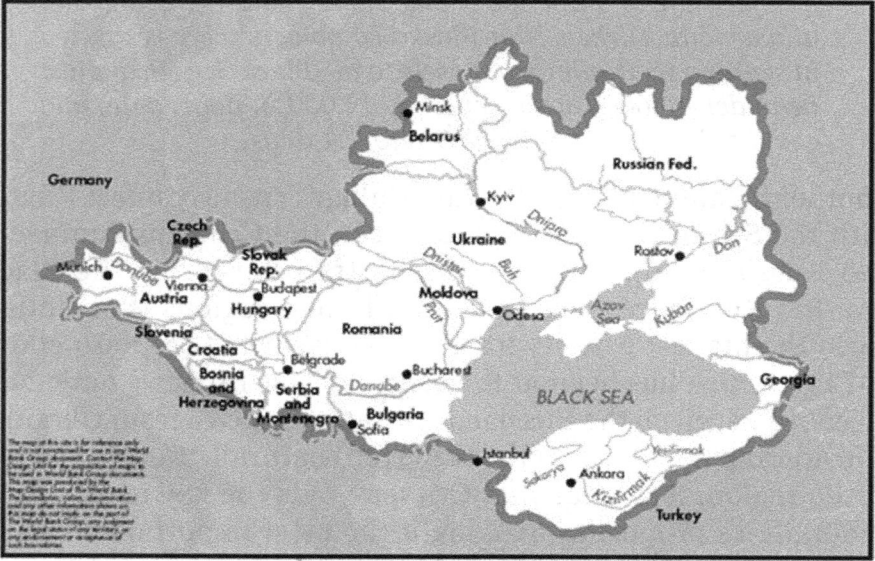

Figure 8.2. Black Sea River tributaries

Source: UN Atlas of the Oceans, https://www.oceansatlas.org/subtopic/en/c/922/.

To conclude, the BSR is a historically documented region of rivalry (battlefields) between the West and Russia (Asia and Europe) makes it particularly important, not only locally. In addition, the fact that the post-Soviet states want to break free from the hands and influence of the Russian Federation and thus increase Euro-Atlantic influence makes this region a particular flashpoint on the world security map. In addition, the commercial aspect of the region is essential, which has always been an important economic factor in coastal countries. China has recently been particularly interested in the Black Sea regarding trade.

Turkish-Russian Interactions

In order to understand the importance of the essence of relations between Turkey and Russia, it is necessary to describe the relations between the countries not only in historical meaning. Therefore, essential aspects of creating relations and rivalry between the two countries are, among others, dependencies such as geopolitical, economic, security, international relations, way of thinking, strategic and domestic goals, foreign affairs etc. Therefore, in the following chapter, the author focuses on the commonalities and differences between the two countries in the light of the abovementioned aspects.

Due to the extensive Turkish-Russian history and many detailed studies, the author will focus on general information about the historical ties between Turkey and Russia. Since the time of the great Ottoman Empire, relations with Russia have been based on an alliance against a common enemy rather than a common goal. According to a report by the Center for Space Studies of the post-Soviet War Studies University, between the reign of Ivan the Terrible and the treaty of March 1918, the two empires fought twelve wars, fighting for supremacy in the Black Sea basin, the Balkans and the South Caucasus. The beginnings of cooperation arose right after the end of the First World War. The first step of the joint dialogue was the signing of the Lausanne-Montreux Convention of 1936, regulating access to the Black Sea for merchant ships and warships.

According to prof. Fatih ÖZBAY, the prosperity of coop-eration lasted only in the interwar period when both regimes supported the common interest of both countries. Although Turkey and the Soviet Union became adversaries as members of two opposing blocs after World War II, the geopolitical balance established in the Black Sea by their cooperation survived the Cold War. In the aftermath of World War II, these countries became enemies again and remained so for much of the Cold War. Turkey turned to the West when it joined NATO in 1952. There were multiple reasons for Anka-ra's decision, including U.S. support for Turkey's financial system and the emergence of a multiparty system in Turkish politics (Ozbay, 2011).

Shortly after the collapse of the Soviet Union in 1991, the geopolitical situation changed, and the two countries resumed dialogue and, thus, cooperation. The first step in diplomacy was the creation of the Friendship Principles Treaty on 25 May 1992. the first step in diplomacy was the creation of the Treaty of Friendship on May 25, 1992. The war in Chechnya also caused ambiguous political dysfunctions between the countries

	Immediate post-Cold War era to the late 1990s	Later phase of the post-Cold War era: late 1990s and beyond
Nature of the relationship	Cooperation with significant elements of conflict	Deepening of cooperation in spite of differences in political orientations and geopolitical rivalry States continue to be the key actors; the role of private sector interests increases in parallel to the growth and diversification of the two economies Dynamic region with weak institutionalism; nation-states and national business associations continue to be the dominant actors; the importance and increasing frequency of bilateral summits involving heads of states. Erdogan and Putin play important roles in promoting bilateral relations; Gül and Davutoglu are also key actors on the Turkish side
Key driving forces	State-driven cooperation with private sector backing; regional agreements such as BSEC provide a facilitating but secondary role BSEC provides a loose framework for cooperation; weakly institutionalized regionalism in the absence of common norms and political orientations of the member states	
Regional context for cooperation		
Role of leadership	Özel is the crucial figure in pushing for cooperation on the Turkish side, as the architect of the BSEC Project. There is no direct counterpart on the Russian side. Deep conflicts; Russia resents Turkey's quest to play a leadership role with respect to Central Asian Republics; the two states interfere in each other's minority conflicts, with Russia indirectly supporting the PKK and Turkey indirectly supporting Chechen insurgents	Degree of conflict significantly reduced by the pragmatic turn in Turkish foreign policy; Turkey largely refraining from an active regional role in areas considered to be in Russia's sphere of influence

Table 8.1. Two phases of Russian–Turkish relations in the post-Cold War era

Source: Onis & Yilmaz, "Turkey and Russia in a shifting global order: cooperation, conflict and asymmetric interdependence in a turbulent region", *Third World Quarterly* (2015) https://www.tandfonline.com/doi/abs /10.1080/01436597.2015.1086638.

in 1996–1999. The most potent terrorist attack on September 11, 2001, despite their differences, brought the countries closer by declaring a standard anti-terrorist policy. However, the improvement and significant return to action lasted until the start of the Russo-Georgian war in 2008, when Turkey began to see

Russia as a rival and distanced itself. The annexation of Crimea in 2014 altered the region's standard policy. The Turkish-Russian dispute over Syria, which triggered a severe crisis between the two countries in late 2015, has also significantly hampered Ankara-Moscow regional dialogue. Indeed, the reason for the deterioration was both countries' policies and, to a large extent, Turkey's response to the Russian Su-24 aircraft violating airspace, which was successfully shot down by Turkish armed forces. Russia's immediate reaction, which included sanctions on Turkish services and raw materials, emphasized its dissatisfaction with the situation in Syria. To soften the image, Turkey's president apologized for the accident and promised financial assistance to the families of the deceased pilots. Despite Western opposition, economic and military cooperation was resumed, as evidenced by the purchase of anti-access/area denial (A2/AD) systems. As a result of the purchase, Turkey-US-NATO relations deteriorated, and Turkey was barred from participating in the F35 build and development program (Flanagan, 2020).

E. Hamilton believes the durability of the rapprochement will be tested, especially since we see similar characteristics in the new semi-relationship. They are, once again, based on a pragmatic approach and compartmentalization: While Moscow and Ankara have formed a pragmatic partnership in Syria, they disagree on the fate of Bashar al-Assad and the role of Kurds in the post-war Syrian state. They, too, found themselves on opposing sides of Libya's escalating civil war and the recent military clash between Armenia and Azerbaijan. As previous statements demonstrate, the fact that both countries have a complicated relationship with the West provides an incentive for cooperation but may not provide a foundation for it. In light of the above facts, describing Russian-Turkish relations in two phases before and after the Cold War is justified. Table 8.1 shows the phases of relations between the two countries.

The economy tie in the Black Sea region

When analyzing the economics of both countries, this fact should be seen in the broader context of the maritime trade of goods and the energy market—garding the first, because the Balkans,

Eastern Europe, Anatolia, and the Caucasus are shared regions, several commercial ports are capable of hosting large commercial vessels capable of carrying raw materials, grain, cargo containers, and petroleum. As one would expect, the main trading routes are concentrated in the Turkish Straits (Figure 8.3), given that it is the only natural passage to the Mediterranean Sea and global maritime trade. Ports such as Trabzon, Samsun, and Istanbul in Turkey, Varna in Bulgaria, Constanta in Romania, Odessa in Ukraine, Novorossiysk and Sochi in Russia, and Batumi in Georgia. The BSR is, as argued by Prof. Burak Seker (Seker, 2019; Ozel *et al.*, 2019):

> *a poker table in which new dimensions of European energy security are emerging, with transition countries, producing countries and leading stakeholders. More specifically, the Black Sea is one of the main energy transit routes from the Caspian Sea and Russia to the EU markets. Despite this apparent interdependency, harmonized cooperation is not a guarantee. Energy has become a controversial issue in the region rather than unifying. Whether they like it or not, all countries in the region have to participate in energy policies. Oil and gas production and transport in the wider Black Sea region have a direct impact on the formation of regional energy alliances, but are subject to regional and international geopolitical developments.*

> *The two long-term trends that have characterized the Black Sea are the "increased reliance of EU countries on non-EU hydrocarbon imports and increased oil and gas export capacity on the supply side of Russia and Caspian countries." As a result, European energy security is one of, if not the primary drivers of, the region's importance, along with the willingness and readiness of non-EU actors such as Russia, Turkey, and Caspian countries to capitalize on the situation. As a result, "many actors, including China, have turned to the goal of developing strategic partnerships in the BSR in response to rising energy demand (Seker, 2019).*

Following the dissolution of the Soviet Union, both Georgia and Azerbaijan pursued independent energy-supply plans, sparking the development of regional transportation infrastructure. In the meantime, Western interest in Caspian energy resources was growing.

Figure 8.3. Russia-Turkey gas pipeline plans

Source: Agency France-Presse via European Data News Hub (2018).

At the same time, Russia and Ukraine inherited a shared energy infrastructure from the Soviet era that put Moscow at the centre, allowing energy to be used as a "key instrument of control with which to assert its own economic and political interests among its fellow post-Soviet states." Similarly, Turkish leaders would see the recent independence of former Soviet Central Asian states as an opportunity to capitalize on Turkey's strategic location to develop opportunities for the Turkish economy.

Armenia's actions were limited due to complex relations with its neighbours (except Russia), making Azerbaijan the key regional actor in this context; the Baku-Tbilisi-Ceyhan oil pipeline (BTC) was established in 2005, is a testament to such regional development. On the European side, the EU would work to improve energy security by diversifying its sources and supply routes. Nowadays, projects such as the Southern Gas Corridor (SGC) and TurkStream are indicative of the different energy alliances in the Black Sea as currently, in 2021, both projects have been completed (Carneiro *et al.*, 2021; Ozel *et al.*, 2019).

On the one hand, the SGC is a success in Europe because it allows the EU to bypass Russia, on which it is heavily reliant, via pipelines that primarily run through Ukraine. The SGC focuses on transporting Azeri gas to Italy, further establishing Azerbaijan,

Georgia, and Turkey as essential players in Europe's economy and vice versa (Carneiro *et al.,* 2021; Ozel *et al.,* 2019).

Considering trade in the Region, historical and current importance in terms of security and economic importance, one can argue that the BS is a body of water that ranks near the top of the world's most significant hotspots, such as South China or the Horn of Africa. As a result, Non Black Sea actors are expected to have a stake in the Region.

Commonalities and differences

Although both countries have positive and negative relations, the following aspects should be considered regarding their similarities and differences. According to Stanislav Secrieru, Dimitar Bechev, and Sinikukka Saari in their recent paper for the European Union for Security Studies (EUISS), namely Fire and Ice: The Russian-Turkish Partnership (2021), as well as E.Carnairo, F.Garcia in their paper named "How Influential is black Sea in Russo-Turkish Relations – Lisbon 2021" the similarities between Turkey and Russia should be considered in the context of the political system, economic order, standard foreign policy and their geopolitical perception of each other:

- Politics. Both countries exercise their decision-making power through informal and formal influences. Importantly, it concentrated in the hands of two people. Both regimes are focused mainly on their interests in being in power.

- Economy. Economically, A. Carnrio argues that resources such as subsidies or public contracts are "allocated based on proximity to the leader and the party in power, rather than in an open bidding system", making way for corruption and clientelism (Carneiro *et al.,* 2021).

- Identity politics. Anti-Western – both governments use widespread anti-Western nationalist rhetoric and scapegoating in the US and, to a lesser extent, in Europe to mobilize public support. Through state propaganda and subordinated and strictly controlled media, Putin and Erdoğan present themselves as the fathers of their nations and guarantors of aspirations for socioeconomic modernization and a higher status in the international arena (Daley, 2022).

- Strategic culture and foreign policy. Regarding the latter, and further to the previous argument, both Ankara and Moscow see themselves as "sovereign centres of gravity in international relations." This involves a standard policy of striving for autonomy and independence, especially from the West. Therefore, the turn towards the Eurasian powers is essential to cooperation in pursuing independence. Both countries know they are a trade bridge between Europe and Asia. Moreover, Russia and Turkey see themselves as emerging powers in the international arena and "see their rising status as confirmation of an emerging multipolar world where the West is falling and the 'rest' is rising." The statement about "civilization poles with unique history and culture" mixes religion with a rich historical culture in its foreign policy, which can be confirmed by the location of military bases in allied countries, including military development in various fields. In terms of foreign policy, the two presidents maintain close diplomatic relations. President Putin and President Erdogan, coincidentally or not, both believe in realpolitik and the balance of power as pillars in the international arena, which means that assertive diplomacy is to be expected, as well as tit-for-tat and divide-and-conquer tactics (Carneiro *et al.*, 2021).

However, differences regarding political dynamics (both domestic and international), the economic realm, national ideologies, foreign policies and relations with the West and China are just as influential as what makes both countries resemble each other in such a way that demonstrates the complex nature of Russo-Turkish relations (Carneiro *et al.*, 2021):

- Politics. First of all, Türkiye has a more robust democratic heritage than Russia. Turkey's government systems were multi-party in character from the 1960s until the AKP came to power; they were a coalition. Conversely, Russia represented only a communist system, a dominant society with a brief episode of pluralism lasting only a few years. The second difference concerns the role of the executive and the balance between it and other branches of government. After the reforms of the 2020 constitution, Russia confirmed the president's strong position. After changing its legislative laws, Turkey established an authoritarian presidency (Secrieru *et al.* 2021).

- Economy. Russia's and Turkey's economies differ in many ways. The Russian economy heavily relies on natural resource exports, whereas Turkey relies on industrial goods and services exports, domestic consumption and public investment. State corporations dominate the Russian economy, whereas in Turkey, despite large, influential corporations, the small and medium-sized enterprise (SME) sector is the primary employer, exporter, and contributor to GDP. In terms of economic freedom, Turkey trails Russia; in terms of currency reserves, Russia far outnumbers Turkey. Overall, the Russian economy is less open but more stable than the Turkish economy, which is more open but more vulnerable to external shocks and foreign investment reversals.

- Identity politics. Another distinctive feature worth highlighting is national ideology. The presence of large non-Russian communities and Islam's position as a *de facto* second state religion leads to a framing of Russian nationalism in the state (*rossiyskiy*) rather than strictly ethnonational (*russkiy*) terms. This conception is essential to Moscow's claim to primacy in the post-Soviet region where populations still speak the Russian language and are exposed to Russian culture. The Republic of Turkey, by contrast, has been conceived and constructed as an insular national state surrounded by hostile neighbours. Turkishness was defined in strictly ethnolinguistic terms, and minority identities suppressed until recently. Though in the 1990s Ankara sought to propagate the idea of Turkishness in the post-Soviet region, later, this approach was deprioritised, albeit not discarded. The AKP's shift of focus to Sunni Islam and the legacy of the Ottoman empire allows for a more inclusive definition which has yet to prove its potency (Flanagan, 2020).

- Strategic culture and foreign policy. Links with the West are a significant contrast for both countries. Turkey was approaching cooperation with the West and the United States, joining the European Economic Community (EEC), and has also implemented many domestic reforms to become a member of the EU. Despite disagreements, Türkiye still considers the EU a key trading partner. Conversely, Russia sees NATO as an enemy and tends to maintain a controlled trade relationship with the EU. In foreign policy, Ankara and Moscow see themselves as sovereign centres of gravity in international relations. An example is Russia having natural resources, the right of veto in the UN or nuclear weapons. Turkey, on the other hand, has an ideal country location between Asia and Europe. Moreover, it participates in the essential G20 forums. At the same time, population growth and military potential play key factors here (Carnerio *et al.*, 2021).

Thus, Russia's self-esteem and ambitions are much more global than Turkey's. Both countries have directed their potential towards cooperation with China; however, this Russian-Beijing partnership has deeper roots and considerable stability due to earlier cooperation. Areas of cooperation range from trade to military exercises, exchange of authoritarian best practices, cooperation at the UN on global issues, and joint efforts to create standards at the international level (Secrieru *et al.* 2021).

Table 8.2. Russia and Turkey: commonalities and differences

	COMMONALITIES	DIFFERENCES
Politics	• Personalization and over-concentration of political power • Weak institutions and powerful informal networks	• Consolidated autocracy vs competitive authoritarianism • Short-lived pluralism vs strong democratic legacy
Economy	• Economic clientelism and widespread corruption	• Resource-based economy vs value added manufacturing and services • Dominance of state companies vs prevalence of SMEs • Serni-closed economy vs open economy
Identity politics	• Anti-Western nationalism	• State nationalism vs ethno/religious nationalism
Strategic culture/ foreign policy	• Sovereign centers of gravity • State-civilization • Autonomy from the West • Pivot to China • Bridge between Europe and Asia • Privileged olein former imperial space • Tit-for-tat logic	• Global vs regional power • Multidirnensional partnership with Chine vs booming trade with China • Asymmetric alliances ves symmetric Alliance • More autonomy vs iess autonomy from West

Source: Author's elaboration.

Alliances remain essential in both Moscow's and Ankara's toolboxes, but their nature and application differ. The Kremlin regards formalized alliances as a sign of great power. The asymmetric alliances to which Russia belongs provide Russia with a platform to claim regional primacy, speak for allies on the international stage, and avoid feeling isolated on the international stage. On the other hand, Turkey is a member of NATO, a club that it does not dominate but has clout in.

Despite frequently defying other members, Ankara relies on the Atlantic Alliance's security guarantees. Although Turkey is not a member of the EU, it maintains close economic ties. As a result, Turkey is attempting to strike a delicate balance between aspirations to become a lone power and the imperatives of maintaining NATO membership and EU ties, both of which are critical to its security and economic development (Secrieru *et al.,* 2021). Tu sum up the relationship, below is a tabular overview (Table 8.2) of the similarities and differences between Turkey and Russia.

Contemporary issues. The Russia-Ukraine war and the security of the Black Sea region

Ukraine's Black Sea policy is among the most important factors influencing its security and development. Ukraine has consistently sought to strengthen its relations with the region's countries and maintain stability in this strategic area over the last few decades. Ukraine borders the Black Sea for over 1,300 kilometers and has important seaports, including the Black Sea's largest port, Odessa. As a result, the BSR is critical to Ukraine's economy, which relies heavily on commercial and industrial activity there. At the same time, the Black Sea is a strategic area for Ukraine in terms of security and defence due to the countries surrounding it and the threats there exist. Ukraine is attempting to shape three critical goals in its BSR policy: security, economic development, and integration with Europe and NATO. To achieve these objectives, Ukraine undertakes several actions, including (Hodges, 2021; Kuczyński, 2019):

- developing relations with BSR countries by initiating and participating in various political and economic initiatives, such as the Eastern Partnership or the Black Sea Synergy;
- developing of port and industrial infrastructure in the region, including modernization of seaports and increased transport capacity;
- developing of the armed forces, including the construction of neo-conservative forces.
- carrying out diplomatic and political activities to ensure regional stability and peaceful conflict resolution, including in relations with Russia.

In particular, Ukraine seeks to strengthen cooperation with the region's countries in the security field. To this end, it undertakes some initiatives, such as increasing its military presence in the region, organizing military exercises and training the armed forces of the region's states. At the same time, Ukraine is engaged in dialogue and cooperation with NATO in the security field, including within the Partnership for Peace program framework and the action plan within the NATO-Ukraine Association (Biscosi, 2019). This cooperation aims to increase Ukraine's defence readiness and improve coordination with NATO forces in regional security. It is also worth emphasizing that Ukraine's policy towards the BSR has a solid historical and cultural foundation. Ukraine considers the Black Sea an essential element of its national and cultural identity and distinguishes it in the region. In this context, Ukraine is also taking several measures to protect the marine and cultural environment of the Black Sea, including improving water quality and protecting cultural heritage (Stercul, 2023).

However, it should be noted that Ukraine's policy towards the Black Sea is complicated and affected by many challenges. First, Ukraine faces Russia's aggressive actions in the Black Sea, including the annexation of Crimea and support for the separatists in the Donbas. Russia is also blocking the Kerch Strait, which prevents Ukraine from having free access to the Sea of Azov. By limiting sea access, Ukraine's economy and security zone will undoubtedly be weakened (Gladysz, 2019; Kuczyński, 2019).

The war in Ukraine is one of the most enormous and tragic armed conflicts of the 21st century. This conflict began in 2014, after the outbreak of the Euromaidan protests and the overthrow of President Viktor Yanukovych. Russia annexed Crimea in March of the same year, and fighting between Ukrainian government forces and Russian-backed separatists soon began in the country's East. After eight years, Russia has now violated Ukraine on 24 February 22. The causes of the war in Ukraine are complex and multifaceted. Firstly, this conflict results from long-term tensions between Ukraine and Russia, which have their roots in the history and culture of both nations. Secondly, Russia wants to maintain its influence in Ukraine and prevent it from moving closer to the West, which would threaten Russia's interests (Khylko, 2022). The third cause of the war is the lack of unity in Ukraine. The country is politically and culturally divided between the West and the East, which leads to disputes and conflicts. Some residents of eastern Ukraine feel less connected to the country and more to Russia, which separatists supported by Russia use. Fourth, the legacy of post-imperial Russia is one of the critical cultural and historical elements that influenced the development of Russia as a state. Russian patriotism is one of the elements of the post-imperial heritage that Putin refers to. Under tsarism, this ideology was fundamental, and now Putin continues this theme in his policy. Strong leaders have always led Russia; Putin is trying to continue that tradition.

Putin often speaks of Russia as an empire that needs to regain its influence and establish its interests in the international arena. This ideology is driven by the desire to restore Russia to the position of one of the most critical players in the world. The legacy of post-imperial Russia also influences Putin's foreign policy. As an imperial power, Russia has always had significant influence in regions such as Central Asia and the Middle East. Putin is using this tradition to strengthen Russia's position in the region and gain importance in international relations. Unfortunately, despite numerous attempts to resolve the conflict through diplomacy, such as the Minsk agreement, the situation in Ukraine remains complicated. The conflict is still ongoing, and from time to time, there is an increase in violence and tensions between Ukraine and Russia.

To conclude, Ukraine's policy towards the BSR is essential for stability and security in the region and for the country's development. Ukraine strives to strengthen cooperation with the region's countries in security and economic development while engaging in dialogue and cooperation with NATO. However, Ukraine's policy towards the Black Sea faces serious challenges, such as Russian aggression and rivalry between other countries.

NATO and EU interest in the Black Sea Region

NATO and the European Union's policy toward the BSR is critical to ensuring stability, security, and peace in this strategic region for Europe and Asia. Both organizations support the development and security of the region's countries and prevent conflicts and crises that could affect the entire region. The organization's mutual support is the goal of the standard policy, consultations, information exchange, and resource exchange (Horrell, 2016; Polegkyi, 2021).

EU policy towards the BSR focuses on three main areas: supporting democracy, the rule of law and economic reforms, strengthening energy security and supporting stability and good unneighborly relations. The EU is active in the region through the Eastern Partnership Program, which aims to strengthen relations with the EU's eastern neighbors, including the Black Sea countries (Eastern Partnership, 2022). NATO's policy towards the BSR focuses on ensuring defence and security, fostering partnership and cooperation with the countries of the region, as well as building stability and promoting democratic values (Secrieru *et al.*, 2021; Oleksiejuk, 2012).

However, EU-NATO cooperation in the BSR has its challenges. One of the main challenges is the need to consider both organizations' separate interests and goals and coordinate activities to avoid duplication of activities and increase the effectiveness of their initiatives. In addition, developing conflicts and tensions in the region, such as the crisis in Ukraine or aggressive actions by Russia, require the EU and NATO to react quickly and effectively (Khylko, 2022; Romanyshyn, 2023). Therefore, cooperation between the EU and NATO in the BSR is crucial to ensuring stability, security and peace in this strategic region for Europe and Asia. However, it requires constant dialogue, coordination of activities, flexibility, and readiness to react quickly to the region's changing political and security conditions (Lutzkanova, 2017).

Caspian and Mediterranean Sea

The Caspian Sea is one of the world's largest enclosed bodies of water, lying on the border of five countries: Russia, Kazakhstan, Turkey, Iran and Azerbaijan. Due to its strategic location and natural resources, the Caspian Sea plays a vital role in the context of security in the region and on a broader scale (Bartsch *et al.*, 2020).

The first factor that makes the Caspian Sea of excellent security importance is its natural wealth. The bay has large deposits of crude oil and natural gas, making it an essential energy resource source for the entire region (Malcolm, 2017). With the intensive development of the energy sector, however, there are threats such as the risk of industrial accidents, terrorism, piracy or sabotage, which may affect the stability and security of the entire region. The second factor contributing to the security importance of the Caspian Sea is its role in trade and transit. The Gulf is an important transport corridor for Russia, Iran and Kazakhstan, which use it to export goods and energy resources. There are also plans to build new pipelines and gas pipelines, which could change the political and economic landscape of the entire region. However, with the growing importance of trade and transit, new threats are also emerging, such as smuggling, organized crime and terrorism (Hodges, 2021; Oral, 2022). The third important factor that contributes to the security importance of the Caspian Sea is its strategic location. The Gulf is located at the junction of regions such as the Middle East, Eastern Europe and Central Asia, which makes it an area where the interests and influences of various countries and organizations intersect. Therefore, any event taking place in the Caspian Sea may affect the political situation and security of the entire region, as well as international relations (Malcolm, 2017).

In this context, the United Nations and the Organization for Security and Cooperation in Europe are important in monitoring the situation and taking action for peace and stability in the region. Cooperation between the region's countries, including through regional organizations such as the Organization for Economic Cooperation, can also contribute to greater regional security and stability. All countries should cooperate to ensure stability and security in the Caspian region, protect economic and political interests, and ensure regional and global security and stability (Bartsch *et al.*, 2020).

In conclusion, the Caspian Sea is a vital area for security on many levels, including its natural resources, role in trade and transit, and strategic location. The stability and security of the Caspian Sea are essential for the stability and security of the entire region and impact global energy markets. Conflicts, tensions and misunderstandings related to the Caspian Sea can destabilize the region, increase the risk of armed conflicts, disrupt trade and transit, and affect the prices of energy resources worldwide.

The Mediterranean Sea and the Black Sea are linked by the Bosphorus Strait and the Dardanelles Strait, making them mutually influential regarding security. The Mediterranean Sea is a strategically important region for Europe's security due to its geographical location and economic, political and military importance. This sea is an important trade route, and its shores are inhabited by hundreds of millions of people. In addition, the region is strategically important to many countries, including the Middle East, North Africa and Russia. The Black Sea, on the other hand, as the inner sea of Europe, is strategically important for the security of the entire continent due to its location and economic, political and military importance (Hodges, 2022). Many countries, including Russia, Turkey, Ukraine and Romania, have access to the Black Sea and use it for commercial and military purposes. The importance of the Mediterranean for the security of the Black Sea stems from the fact that some Mediterranean countries, including Russia, use it to deliver their goods to the Middle East and other countries in the region, including Syria and Iran. In addition, the Mediterranean Sea is where the military fleets of many countries, including Russia and NATO, can operate, which may affect the region's stability. In the event of a conflict in the BSR, Mediterranean countries can influence its course and outcome by providing humanitarian and military aid and putting pressure on the parties to the conflict to reach a peaceful solution (Senen, 2018).

In conclusion, the Mediterranean and the Black Sea are interconnected regarding security due to their geographical location and economic, political and military importance. Therefore, stability in one of these regions affects the stability of the other, and states and international organizations must act to ensure security and stability in both regions.

Conclusion

The Black Sea Region is questionably strategic importance for the global level of security due to the deep interests of global players in Russia, Turkey, NATO, the EU and China, given its geopolitical location described in the literature as the crossroads of Europe and Asia. Therefore, for the common security of the region, dialogue and diplomacy of all interested parties play a crucial role. The superpowers can achieve this through joint cooperation in all areas (economy, energy security, trade, etc.).

Turkish-Russian relations historically wealthy and, at the same time, complex in the entire instrument of power. Despite many areas of cooperation, Ankara and Moscow also have numerous areas of rivalry. In the era of cooperation Turkish-Russian relations are common economic interests, including the energy sector, which shows a significant increase in GBD year after year on both sides of the stock market index. Moreover, both countries cooperate in strategic security (Syria, the Balkans, and Central Asia). There is no doubt that both countries share a similar perception of the relationship between Asia and Europe, indicating their position as a country. In addition, the total system of power builds mutual trust between the two leaders very strongly. Another issue of both countries' dependence on the West brings them closer mentally.

The negative aspects of relations point to Turkey's relations with the West, including NATO membership and aspirations for EU membership. The flash point is complete control of access to the Black Sea. Russia's actions in the Nagorno-Karabakh region, the annexation of Crimea, the seizure of Abkhazia, South Ossetia and the ongoing war in Ukraine significantly worsen relations between the two countries. The incident of shooting down Russian planes on the border with Syria immediately showed an adverse reaction towards the partner.

In order to consider the importance of BSR security, the Caspian and Mediterranean regions should be taken into account, the maintenance of which affects the security of the Black Sea due to their geographical location and their natural sea and trade routes, the richness of natural deposits, which may consequently be hot spots in relations between countries dividing these seas. The most challenging factor to check in Turkish-Russian relations is their joint dialogue and exchange of information, which is caused by the authoritarian rule of both leaders and limited access to reliable information due to complete control of the media. Therefore, the information instrument would be a further field of study to supplement the article's content.

References

Bartsch, et al. (2020) *Antagonisms in the EU's neighbourhood: Geopolitical Ambitions in the Black Sea and Caspian Region.* Bertelsmann Stiftung

Biscosi, G. (2019) 'Ukraine And Black Sea: A Russian Geopolitical Problem'. Available at: https://www.researchgate.net/publication/358738950.

Carnerio, et al. (2021) *How Influential Is The Black Sea In Russo-Turkish Relations?* Catholic University of Portugal. Available at: http://hdl.handle.net/10400.14/37960 .

Dalay, G. (2022) 'Deciphering Turkey's Geopolitical Balancing and Anti-Westernism in Its Relations with Russia', *SWP Comment 2022/C 35*, 20 May.

Eastern Partnership (2022) *The Eastern Partnership (EaP) is a joint initiative involving the EU, its Member States and six Eastern European Partner countries: Armenia, Azerbaijan, Belarus, Georgia, the Republic of Moldova and Ukraine.* Available at: https://www.eeas.europa.eu/eeas/eastern-partnership_en.

Flanagan, S., et al. (2019) *Russia, NATO, and Black Sea Security Strategy: Regional Perspectives from a 2019 Workshop.* Rand National Defence Research Institute, Santa Monica, CA. Available at: https://apps.dtic.mil/sti/citations/AD1096677 .

Flanagan, S. (2020) *Russia, NATO, and Black Sea Security: Complex Political and Security Dynamics in the Black Sea Region.* Rand. Available at: https://www.rand.org/ pubs/research_reports/ RRA357-1.html.

Gladysz, M. (2019) 'Baltic-Black Sea Region in the European Security System: Ukraine's and Russia's Interests'. Ivan Franko National University of Lviv. ISSN 2450-3576.

Hamilton, D. *et al.* (2008) *The Wider Black Sea Region in the 21st Century: Strategic, Economic and Energy Perspectives.* Centre for Transatlantic Relations.

Hodges, B. (2021) *The Black Sea … Or a Black Hole?* Center for European Policy Analysis. Available at: https://cepa.org/article/the-black-sea-or-a-black-hole/.

Hodges, B., et al. (2022) *Russia's Militarization of the Black Sea: Implications for the United States and NATO.* Available at: https://cepa.org/comprehensive-reports/russias-militarization-of-the-black-sea-implications-for-the-united-states-and-nato/.

Horrell, S. (2016) 'A NATO Strategy for Security in the Black Sea Region', *Atlantic Council – Brent Scowcroft Center On International Security*, 10. Available at: https://www.jstor.org/stable/resrep03475.

Khylko, H. (2022) *Security in the Black Sea Region after the Russian Invasion of Ukraine*. Available at: https://neweasterneurope.eu/2022/09/29/security-black-sea-ukraine/.

Kuczyński, G. (2019) *Rosja na Morzu Czarnym. Strategia „MARE NOSTRUM"*. Warsaw Institute. Raport Specjalny.

Lutzkanova, S. (2017) 'NATO and EU Strategies for the Black Sea Region: The Challenge of Power Balance in New Security Environment', *Journal of Shipping and Ocean Engineering*, 7, pp. 210–215.

Malcolm, C. (2017) *The History of the Caspian Sea in the Region*. New York: Delta Press .

Oleksiejuk, D. (2021) 'Rosnące napięcia na Morzu Czarnym – wnioski dla NATO'.

Oral, F. (2022) 'Role of the Caspian Region within the Context of Energy Security'. Available at: https://dergipark.org.tr/en/download/article-file/2783773 .

Ozbay, F. (2011) 'The Relations between Turkey and Russia in the 2000s', *Perception*, XVI(3). Available at: https://www.researchgate.net/publication/289088222_The_relations_between_Turkey_and_Russia_in_the_2000s.

Ozel, S., et al. (2019) 'The Economics of Turkey-Russia Relations', *Foreign Policy & Security*.

Polegkyi, O., et al. (2021) *Security Dilemma in the Black Sea Region in Light of the Russian-Ukrainian Conflict*. Institute of Central Europe. Available at: https://ies.lublin.pl/wp-content/uploads/2021/11/ies_policy_papers_no_2021-005.pdf.

Romanyshyn, I. (2023) *Ukraine, NATO and the Black Sea*. NATO Defence College, Research Division.

Secrieru, S., et al. (2021) *Fire and ICE: The Russian-Turkish Partnership*. European Union Institute for Security Studies. Available at: https://www.iss.europa.eu/content/fire-and-ice.

Seker, B. (2019) *The Black Sea Energy Routes and Their Effects on Maritime Transport*. Maritime Security Centre of Excellence (MARSECCOE). Available at: https://www.marseccoe.org/marsec/upload/files/202010/5f7d870946de8-1602062089.pdf.

Senen, F. (2018) 'The New Mediterranean Geopolitical Framework from the EU Perspective'. Available at: https://www.iemed.org/publication/the-new-mediterranean-geopolitical-framework-from-the-eu-perspective/.

Stercul, N. (2023) 'Security and Synergies – The Importance of the Black Sea Region and Russia's War on Ukraine'. Available at: https://libmod.de/en/security-and-synergies-the-importance-of-the-black-sea-region-and-russias-war-on-ukraine/ .

Wikipedia (n.d.) Black Sea map. Available at: https://en.wikipedia.org/wiki/Black_ Sea#/media/File:Black_Sea_map.png.

CHAPTER 9

The role of NATO strategic communications in the war in Ukraine and its conceptual dilemmas

Agata Mazurek

Abstract

This chapter examines the dynamic and evolving strategies of NATO strategic communications (StratCom) in the context of the ongoing war in Ukraine. It explores the five pillars of NATO's strategic communications—public diplomacy, social communication, military and non-military public affairs, and information and psychological operations—and how they have been tested and adapted since the Russian aggression against Ukraine. The study analyzes how NATO's StratCom has responded to the altered security environment, focusing on the conceptual and definitional dilemmas that have emerged. By studying the narrative shift in Allied communications and the impact of this shift on the military, diplomatic, and political landscapes, the chapter provides a detailed assessment of how NATO's communication strategies have not only supported Ukraine but also exposed Russian hostile actions. The findings indicate that NATO's StratCom has evolved into a robust, warfare-driven communication model that reflects consistency, coherence, and effective responses to disinformation and cyber threats from Russia. The chapter concludes by offering recommendations for enhancing NATO's communications coherence, engagement with civil societies, and strengthening cyber capabilities to protect both NATO and Ukraine from ongoing threats.

Keywords: NATO, strategic communications, NATO StratCom COE, war in Ukraine, security, hybrid warfare

Introduction

The North Atlantic Treaty Organization (NATO) is a peaceful political and military alliance of 31 countries of North America and Europe which commit themselves to the pursuit of peace and security, as well as engagement in common defence.[1] Within time, together with NATO's development, also its strategic communications has developed, constituting "an integral part of the efforts to achieve the Alliance's political and military objectives" (NATO StratCom COE, 2021). In 2014, international recognition of the importance of this scope of actions led to its institutionalization by establishing the NATO Strategic Communications Centre of Excellence[2] – which operates apart from other existing bodies-responsible for the creation, dissemination and direct engagement in key communications with the public.

Before the war in Ukraine broke out, the Euro-Atlantic Alliance had focused predominantly on *a soft security* approach, along with political liability and political engagement in collective security. Afterwards, NATO modified its character – or rather went back to its original roots – and returned to a *hard security* approach, increasing military engagement in Allied deterrence, defence and resilience capacities (Rynning, 2022).

With the outbreak of this armed conflict, distinct changes in the strategy and narrative of the Organization could be observed. This evolution must have given an adequate reflection in adapting Allied strategic communications to the new geopolitical situation. In spite of the indisputable relevance of NATO strategic communications in the contemporary (dis)information age, the existing literature lacks comprehensive analyses thereof. Consequently, the objective of this research is to analyse, compare and identify

---

1. The principles, values and vision of the Organization are stipulated in the *Preamble to the North Atlantic Treaty* (1949), a document constituting the legal basis of the Alliance:

   The Parties to this Treaty reaffirm their faith in the purposes and principles of the Charter of the United Nations and their desire to live in peace with all peoples and all governments. They are determined to safeguard the freedom, common heritage and civilisation of their peoples, founded on the principles of democracy, individual liberty and the rule of law. They seek to promote stability and well-being in the North Atlantic area. They are resolved to unite their efforts for collective defence and for the preservation of peace and security. (NATO, 1949)

2. It is a multinational military organization established in 2014, located in Riga, having NATO accreditation and being independent of NATO units (thus, the NATO StratCom COE cannot act as the official voice of NATO). It is composed of both military and non-military experts who do the research, conduct workshops and prepare analyses. The organization's budget is provided by its founding states and other parties.

the shifts in NATO StratCom in order to describe and assess its present role in the war as well as point to conceptual and definitional ambiguities.

NATO strategic communications is based on 5 pillars – categories of communication activities: *public diplomacy, public affairs, military public affairs, information operations* and *psychological operations.* Due to the abundance of data connected with strategic communications concerning the contemporary conflict in Ukraine, a variety of actors engaged and, simultaneously, in order to conduct an in-depth analysis, the subject matter of this article has been narrowed down. Thus, the author examines solely the selected types of materials and strategic communications activities. However, what needs to be taken into consideration is the fact that the activities considered within the particular pillars are often multifaceted and tend to fall into more than one category.

The author used framework analysis in coalescence with applied qualitative research, where comparative analysis is based on an inductive approach; and both primary and secondary research has been conducted. Source literature embraces selected key authentic NATO documents, texts and video recordings published or broadcast on its website and online platforms; publications of the NATO Strategic Communications Centre of Excellence (NATO StratCom COE); as well as NATO-related media coverage and interviews with the NATO Secretary General exemplifying certain tendencies and phenomena referring to the war in Ukraine.

It should be noted that the analysis of the effectiveness and extent to which strategic communications has influenced international audiences as well as the Ukrainian and Russian parties to the conflict cannot be estimated by the author using the quantitative research method due to the lack of available tools and statistics. Therefore, qualitative research was applied to gather and analyse meaningful data, taking into account the current socio-political discourse and the evolving security environment.

In pursuit of the aforementioned objective of this research, the author is going to answer the following questions:

- What are the ambiguities concerning the main NATO strategic communications terms and their semantic scopes within the context of Russian aggression in Ukraine?

- How has the narrative of NATO strategic communications changed since the outbreak of the war in Ukraine?

- What are the roles of the individual means of Allied communication in the war in Ukraine?

- How can the roles and activities of NATO StratCom in the war in Ukraine be assessed?

In the final part, the conclusion of the article is accompanied by the author's recommendations and future research propositions, which reflect the conceptual dilemmas concerning the abovementioned issues. It is to be marked that the undertaken study investigates the subject which is ongoing, complex and not yet sufficiently elaborated in the scientific literature. Hence, the article is of exiguous character.

Russian aggression in Ukraine – introductory aspects

The background regarding Russian aggression in Ukraine is necessary to introduce the title issues. On 24 February 2022, Russia invaded Ukraine without declaring war, and this state of affairs has remained until today. Diverse publications and also media sources refer to it as *(international) armed conflict, war* or *warfare*, whereas Russian authorities themselves call it a *special military operation*. Therefore, to understand why the word war was chosen in the title of this article, the differences among the abovementioned terms and their usage require explanation.

In international humanitarian law, *armed conflict* is described as "the logical outcome of an attempt of one group to protect or increase its political, social and economic welfare at the expense of another group" (Bernard, 2015). Although *armed conflict* has more general meaning than war, and the term *war* signifies "an intense armed conflict (...) characterized by extreme violence", these days there is a tendency to use both notions interchange-ably or use the word *armed conflict* instead of *war,* which in turn has become somewhat obsolete in the modern relatively peaceful world (Greenwood, 1987). In addition, with the advent of artifi-cial intelligence and the information technology era, the concepts of *war* and *warfare* have evolved to an unprecedented extent. Contemporarily, attacks and hostile actions occur not only in traditional domains (ground, air, sea) but also in space and cyber domains. In fact, "all domains are warfighting domains because all domains are simply a continuation of our world that can be contested for control of resources" (Crimm, 2022).

Waging a modern war means a variety of operations in different environments and discourses, yet mutually interconnected in terms of their common pursuit of attaining the established purpose. More and more often war(fare) embraces both conventional and unconventional styles; and a combination of tactics, including actions on the threshold of war. Moreover, the state of war may remain unspoken or even denied, making the legal status difficult to ascribe. These characteristics come under the umbrella term *hybrid warfare* (Bernard, 2015; Bachmann & Gunneriusson, 2015).

Hybrid warfare still does not have a concrete official definition as it is an ongoing process. However, security experts – *i.a.* J. Schmid[3] (2022) and S. Marahrens[4] (2022) are consentaneous, claiming that the Russian attack in conjunction with other hostile activities epitomizes hybrid warfare, because it was prepared and planned subversively, in a hidden manner, with the use of traditional and non-traditional means of war (attacking critical infrastructure and cyber domain, including information operations, etc.).

It needs to be reiterated that the Russian Federation is the only country which uses the term "special military operation" or "special operation" instead of *war* or *war of aggression* in relation to the current situation in Ukraine. Russian Foreign Minister Sergey Lavrov claims that Russia was made to conduct "the special operation" due to "the inability of Western countries to negotiate; and the Ukrainian government's war against its own people"; and in order to "protect Russians living in Ukraine's Donetsk and Luhansk regions, and eliminate threats to Russian security (...) that the EU and United States-led NATO military alliance had consistently created in the territory since (...) 2014" (UN News, 2022). Russia has claimed that Article 51 of the United Nations Charter, which allows a nation to use self-defence, authorizes its military activities in Ukraine. Actually, Russia officially used it as an alleged measure to prevent the genocide of the Russian minority and, ultimately, an official pretext to start the conflict.

---

3. Johann Schmid, PhD, is the former Community of Interest Strategy and Defence Director at The European Centre of Excellence for Countering Hybrid Threats in Helsinki, Finland.

4. Col. Sönke Marahrens is the Community of Interest Strategy and Defence Director at The European Centre of Excellence for Countering Hybrid Threats in Helsinki, Finland.

Ambiguities concerning the main NATO strategic communications terms and their semantic scopes within the context of Russian aggression in Ukraine

Referring to the topic of this dissertation, the key elements included in the title are objects of conceptual dilemmas. Therefore, to fully comprehend the given notions and avoid prospective misunderstandings, it is inevitable to consider their definitions and semantic scopes.

Strategic communication(s) is a broad concept "used to denote the higher-level concerns behind communicative efforts by organizations [and governments] to advance organizational mission. It embraces a number of "activities of disciplines including public relations, management communication, and advertising." Simultaneously, it is also more and more often regarded "as a developing subfield within communication" (Thorson, 2013). According to Hallahan *et al.* (2007, pp. 3) strategic communication is "the purposeful use of communication by an organization to fulfill its mission". Regardless of the source, the common features of various definitions of strategic communication are: *interdisciplinarity, deliberate* activities in pursuit of some fixed *goals*, drawing main attention to *strategy* (not particular tactics), and *a holistic* approach to communications (Hallahan *et al.*, 2007; Thorson, 2013; NATO StratCom COE, 2020).

From the perspective of security and defence science, strategic communications is a synthesis of the information activities of a strategic entity (a state, alliance or coalition), aimed primarily at creating views and decisions of other entities from the strategic environment (subordinate, cooperating, neutral, competing or hostile entities) in a manner which is satisfactory and desirable for its own strategic interests. Thus, strategic communications is determined by public diplomacy, social communication, as well as information and psychological operations (Gawęcka, 2021).

In the Euro-Atlantic framework, the definition of strategic communications formulated by the NATO StratCom COE acts as a model description of the concept for all allies and partners. For example, in the Polish legal system there is no clear, explicit official definition of the term in question. The sole act of law which indirectly relates to strategic communications is *the Decision No. 284/MON of the Minister of National Defence of 8 July 2014 on the appointment of a team for the development and implementation of the strategic communications system in the Ministry of National Defence.* In the document, there is only an assurance that the strategic communications system being created will be based on the rules and procedures appropriate for NATO.

Therefore, for the purpose of the analysis included in this dissertation, the definition presented by NATO has been applied. NATO perceives strategic communications[5] as a sub-area of communication, which is holistic in nature, "based on values and interests, that encompasses everything an actor does to achieve objectives, in a contested environment". It requires swiftness and developing "long-term, complex solutions, and effective ways of influencing big, important discourses in a very competitive environment". Specifically, *NATO-related strategic communications*, as defined by NATO StratCom COE, is "the coordinated and appropriate use of NATO communications activities and capabilities in support of Alliance policies, operations and activities, and in order to advance NATO's aims" (NATO StratCom COE, 2020).

There are three main objectives of NATO strategic communications, namely:

- Participating "in achieving the successful implementation of NATO operations, missions, and activities" (since StratCom planning is included in "all operational and policy planning");

- Creating "public awareness, understanding, and support for specific NATO policies, operations, and other activities in all relevant audiences" (it is to be done in the form of cooperation with allied members); as well as

- Engaging in public diplomacy by increasing "general public awareness and understanding of NATO".

Thus, the communication-based actions being taken embrace five pillars:

- *Public diplomacy* (or *people's diplomacy*), namely a range of official methods and means used by the organization and its member governments across NATO and in the respective countries "aimed at communicating directly with foreign publics" so that they support the strategic objectives of the Alliance (Munro & Rodriguez, 2022);

---

5. In some sources the term *strategic communications* is presented as a singular form, and in other sources – as a plural form. Thus, *communications* may collocate with verbs either in singular or plural forms. In this dissertation, singular verbs have been used since this is the most commonly appearing form in NATO-related literature.

- *Non-military public affairs* (*i.e.* informative and supportive actions using the media);

- *Military public affairs* (which means advocating military operations and goals);[6]

- *Information operations*[7] (*i.e.* a campaign including military counsel or integration of a variety of influence, cyber and cognitive actions to affect the opponent);[8] and

- *Psychological operations* – utilising *i.a.* means of communication to influence the emotions, perception, approach and conduct of the target recipient, while striving to achieve political and/or military aims (NATO StratCom COE, 2020).

It ought to be highlighted that the practical dimension of the abovementioned pillars includes a number of agencies, means/channels of communication and activities contributing to the support for Ukraine:

- the work of Public Diplomacy Division at NATO Headquarters; publishing informative brochures and other materials about the Russian invasion; organizing tailor-made programmes (e.g. on Russian disinformation) for universities, politicians and prospective leaders; establishing *Allied contact point embassies*[9] (Lithuanian Embassy in Kyiv will be serving this function in the years 2023-2024); maintaining NATO and NATO StratCom COE websites and their profiles on social media platforms: *Facebook, Instagram, Twitter*[10] and a video-sharing platform *YouTube* (they are open to the general public and there are shared: images, podcasts and information regarding all aspects of the war in Ukraine; along with the coverage of high-level meetings, conducted research and recent or upcoming events discussing both military and civil means of aid for Ukraine and stopping Russian aggression);

- informing the public, companies and governments in the media (also online) about the findings; warning and giving recommendations in the context of security and defence, artificial intelligence (AI), media and

---

6. It involves planning and engagement in external communications (media relations and outreach activities), internal communications as well as community relations (*NATO Military Public Affairs Policy*, 2011).

7. Which denote "the integrated employment, during military operations, of information-related capabilities (...) to influence, disrupt, corrupt, or usurp the decision-making of adversaries and potential adversaries while protecting our own" (Fecteau, 2022).

8. They may also be called "a campaign that is dedicated to obtaining a decisive advantage in the information environment".

9. They are situated on the territories of partner countries, helping to interact with local communities (NATO, 2022) and aiming at enhancing quicker integration between Ukraine and NATO.

10. NATO has its accounts also on *LinkedIn* (a social networking platform specializing in professional and business contacts) and *Flickr* (an online service for hosting and sharing photographs).

social media activities – e.g. revealing the cases of Russian hybrid tactics in Ukraine and its neighbouring states;

- publishing or broadcasting the statements of military representatives and defence ministers of allied and partner countries, presenting them in the media/social media coverages to support the activities of NATO and NATO StratCom COE to the benefit of Ukraine;

- conducting research and cyber simulations with the help of AI – and often also the military staff – to trace, predict and influence the adversary's actions;

- depicting a consistent view of NATO and NATO StratCom COE as reliable goodwill organizations, building trust within Ukrainians, promising further Euro-Atlantic integration and contrasting this picture with Russian disinformation, breach of law, dishonesty and various forms of aggression.

The abovementioned dimensions of activities influence the changes in NATO strategic communications.

NATO strategic communications changes since the outbreak of the war in Ukraine

Since the outbreak of the war in Ukraine, the nature of NATO strategic communications has changed and the warfare narrative has appeared, focusing mostly on the discourse of hostile Russian activities, its information campaigns, the ways to defend against it and the need to support Ukraine. For example, in the new *NATO Strategic Concept 2022* and numerous press conferences, the NATO Secretary General[11] and the heads of state and government of the NATO Allies have officially called the Russian invasion of Ukraine "the war of aggression" (NATO, 2022; CNN, 2023). These channels of communication clearly epitomise the StratCom pillar of public diplomacy, but also military and non-military public affairs. Moreover, it has been explicitly stated that international security architecture has been violated, "the Euro-Atlantic area is not at peace", and

---

11. this person, apart from being "responsible for steering the process of consultation and decision-making in the Alliance and ensuring that decisions are implemented" and the "head of the International Staff", also acts as NATO's "principal spokesperson" who represents it publicly (...) in international organisations and in the media (NATO, 2022).

Russia has been named "the most significant threat to Allied security" (NATO, 2022).

In June 2022, the leaders of NATO member states adopted and issued to the public a new *Strategic Concept,* which is a key document defining "the Alliance's priorities, core tasks and approaches"; it "describes the security environment facing the Alliance, reaffirms our [Euro-Atlantic] values, and spells out NATO's key purpose of ensuring our collective defence" (NATO, 2022). The document also presents three principal tasks of the Organization: "deterrence and defence; crisis prevention and management; and cooperative security", simultaneously including several novel break-through ideas:

- The Russian Federation is officially and explicitly deemed to be "the most significant and direct threat to Allies' security and to peace and stability in the Euro-Atlantic area", striving "to establish spheres of influence and direct control through coercion, subversion, aggression and annexation", resorting to "conventional, cyber and hybrid means" against NATO and its partners; and whose "military posture, rhetoric and proven willingness to use force to pursue its political goals undermine the rules-based international order";

- China is depicted as a challenge to Euro-Atlantic interests and security due to its coercive policies, use of various "political, economic and military tools to (...) project power", as well as "malicious hybrid and cyber operations (...) and disinformation [that] target Allies and harm Alliance security";

- the proliferation of the Russian-Chinese strategic partnership, along with "their mutually reinforcing attempts to undercut the rules-based international order", as well as Russian "military integration with Belarus" are presented as serious causes for NATO concern;

- even greater increase in Allied deterrence, defence and resilience capacities is supposed to be the current necessity to the Organization's key purpose;

- several references to Article 5 of the North Atlantic Treaty – in the context of: (1) Allied commitment to defend each other; (2) hybrid operations, which are treated as equivalent to armed aggression: "Hybrid operations against Allies could reach the level of armed attack and could lead (...) to invoke Article 5".

Following Putin's invasion of Ukraine, Allied member states decided to update their deterrence and defence, and adapt them to new circumstances. Due to the fact that doctrines and concepts tend to shift and develop gradually, at a low pace, and administrative issues usually slow down the implementation of new ideas and equipment; and in order to enhance the appropriate measures, "NATO is maintaining a broad definition of security and is focusing on vital domains such as resilience and countering hybrid threats (...) and human security" (NATO, 2022). Definitely, this will equip the Organization with a wide range of tools and measures, so that we will have a variety of choices (i.e. various types of responses) to choose from in the future.

By repetitive mention of Russian and Chinese hostile, unlawful actions and authoritarian ambitions as well as the implementation of hybrid tactics (different domains, types and sources), *NATO 2022 Strategic Concept* communicates a change and precarious state of the Euro-Atlantic security environment, which constitutes a serious threat to regional and – in the long term – also global security architecture. In such context the accompanying assertion that "a strong, independent Ukraine is vital for the stability of the Euro-Atlantic area" gains a geopolitical dimension and becomes more meaningful to the international audience.

The first and foremost shift regards NATO's clear focus on hard power, which is reflected in the expanded role of its strategic communications. The earlier *coverage-style narrative* – mostly restricted to conveying important messages in the media – having faced a new situational context, evolved to the narrative of power. Consequently, in addition to its informative function, Allied communication assumed also an overtly impressive, advisory and persuasive function, influencing international public opinion as well as non-military and military authorities of NATO member and partner countries. This tendency is noticeable in the accumulation of specific language and rhetoric tools accompanied by military vocabulary.

Currently, the strong and steady leadership of NATO Secretary General Jens Stoltenberg can be observed. In the present warfare discourse, in media interviews and at international forums NATO Secretary General has a serious yet calm facial expression, appears to be confident and uses predominantly the active voice to be transparent and to reveal the actor (i.e. the subject of an action). Mentioning the adversary, he is direct – he uses sharp terms, such as "war", to specify the situation and proper names (e.g. Russia, President Putin) in order to indicate a concrete country, person, etc. The NATO Secretary General acts as an ultimate authority figure and expert in security and defence sectors, and the function of his speeches has become more persuasive. To exemplify, he indicates our joint obligations by means of repetitive usage of modal verbs "have to" (e.g. "we have to remember [...] this is the war of aggression" (CNN, 2023)) and "must" (e.g. "we must do even more, even faster" (NATO News, 2023), "we must continue to provide Ukraine with the weapons it needs", "we must continue to strengthen our deterrence and defence" (NATO News, 2023)), and also counsels, expresses necessity or strongly recommends certain actions, using a modal auxiliary verb "need to" (e.g. "we need to give them more armour, more heavy and modern weapons" (CNN, 2023), "we need to ensure that all the systems and all they [Ukrainians] have worked as they should" (MSNBC, 2023)).

Additionally, the Secretary General reiterates a collective pronoun – *inclusive "we"*, referring to the Allies, partners and general publics of western democratic countries; thus, this rhetorical device creates a sense of community and speaker-audience relation. He also appraises specific actions (what is important, threatening, etc.) and his performances may be categorized as appraisal speeches or comments. In this spirit, he highlights the legitimacy of Allied initiatives and the unity of NATO, contrasting them with the unlawful, aggressive conduct of Russia – i.a. Ukraine is depicted as a "sovereign, independent nation" which has been invaded by Russia; it "has the right for self-defence"; and "we have the right to support them in upholding that right" (CNN, 2023). Through the zero conditional (e.g. "If President Putin wins, [...] it is dangerous for us") he presents the Soviet threat as a real, actual situation and authoritarian implications as a general truth.

The roles of the individual means of Allied strategic communications

In media interviews and at international forums, NATO Secretary General Jens Stoltenberg along with military and non-military authorities of some Allied member states (including Poland) encourage – or rather summon – all Allies and partners to help Ukraine militarily. In justification, it is consistently reiterated that this is our common interest, and it constitutes the only way to counter the adversary and guarantee the restoration of peace and international security.

Given the discourse and objectives of the democratic leaders' speeches, it might be assumed that the abovementioned are part of psychological operations aimed at the wider publics of both Allied and partner states. Official assurances of support, declarations of cooperation and unity in association with warnings about the threat of future wide-scale armed attacks and enumeration of concrete types of armaments (either launched by the aggressive adversary or provided to Ukraine by various peaceable nations) are supposed to raise awareness and understanding of common people, pointing to the seriousness of the situation, and serve as arguments to convince public opinion to support NATO strategic objectives and currently recommended immediate actions. Thus, it is an example of a specific kind of public diplomacy, namely *political advocacy campaigns* (Munro & Rodriguez, 2022), where the authorities urge to convince the target audience (herein: the citizens of Allied countries) rapidly in order to achieve immediate results: acceptance of expensive military aid and NATO's hard power approach.

Public statements and press conferences held by the official representatives of NATO along with the EU and the USA – the greatest superpowers able to block the Russian offensive – might also perform the function of shuttle diplomacy. It is symptomatic that, when asked about his message to Russia, the NATO Secretary General neither addresses President Putin nor Russian military command. Conversely, he directs his speech to Allied nations and, apparently, also to the global community (e.g. "We have to remember [...] it is in our security interest to support the Ukrainians" (CNN, 2023)).

On numerous occasions, NATO and Allied leaders have repeated that the Russian President has shown no signs of openness to conciliation, and diplomatic activities have been fruitless, "One year since the launch of Russia's invasion, President Putin is not preparing for peace. On the contrary, he is preparing for more war," Jens Stoltenberg alarms (NATO, 2023). Thus, solely the arguments of power accompanied by consistency in conduct and acute consequences speak to the authoritarian ruler Vladimir Putin. To clarify, David Petraeus, a renowned US general, a former CIA director, a former commander of the multinational forces in Iraq and Afghanistan, claims that aggression in Ukraine will come to an end when Russia's leaders realize their failures and realize that they cannot sustain the war, which is waged both on the Ukrainian battlefield and – indirectly (economically) – against their own homeland (Hebermann, 2023). In this context, international military and non-military authorities highlighting the unshakeable Euro-Atlantic unity and unprecedented NATO-EU cooperation in confronting Russian invasion, as well as warning about the perspective of imposing even more severe sanctions against Russia, and expounding on Putin's miscalculations and failures might dissuade President Vladimir Putin from further acts of aggression.

NATO makes use of every opportunity to communicate its unity and international collaboration in supporting Ukraine, which is confirmed individually and in multinational formats both by the Secretary General and the heads of Allied states. To exemplify, recently Jens Stoltenberg has met the EU leaders on several occasions, has participated in consultations and has presented joint statements concerning the Russian issue. Besides, he acts as a special guest of various security forums, summits and conferences, *e.g.* in February 2023, at Munich Security Conference; and also, together with US President Joe Biden, he attended the Extraordinary Summit of the Bucharest Nine (B9) in Warsaw.

During the former event, the NATO Secretary General proclaimed that—due to the Russia-Ukraine war—"our security environment has changed for the long term", and President Putin "wants a different Europe, where Russia controls neighbours." The Euro-Atlantic response to such an oppressive and expansionist approach is even more important when juxtaposing it with Chinese aspirations and interests. Namely, the People's Republic of China is observing whether the Russian Federation will fail and be punished for its military aggression or it will win and enjoy benefits. The Secretary General thereby pointed out that "the war in Ukraine demonstrates that security is global, rather than regional" (NATO, 2023).

During the latter meeting, the NATO Secretary General reassured that "NATO Allies have never been more united," and "we will protect and defend every inch of Allied territory, based on our Article 5 commitment to defend each other" (NATO, 2023). The North Atlantic Alliance continues its open-door policy, however, at an increased speed. The 2022 applications of Finland and Sweden for membership in NATO followed the quickest ratification process faced by the Organization, to which all current members had to agree unanimously. In his statement Mr Stoltenberg convinces the audience that the progressing integration has positively affected the level of security in both countries, and their accession will further enhance it, simultaneously "mak[ing] our Alliance stronger and safer (...) at a critical time for our security" (NATO, 2023). The speech includes tangible examples of the benefits which each party already enjoys and those which they will enjoy upon NATO enlargement.

Furthermore, the Secretary General's utterances and his messages to the wider public are backed up and confirmed by other prominent figures, such as General Christopher G. Cavoli, Supreme Allied Commander Europe (SACEUR)[12]; or heads of state and governments of Allied member and partner states. For example, in January 2023, at the annual Society and Defence Conference in Sweden – among the representatives of the government, youth, media, business, trade unions and non-government organizations (NGOs) – Gen. Cavoli spoke about the Russian invasion on the territory of Europe as the most serious situation regarding security policy after the Second World War. Subsequently, he explained and justified the need for the updated strategic plans of NATO in the military dimension (Folkoch Försvar, 2023).

As regards the NATO Strategic Communications Centre of Excellence, an analysis of the range of its activities indicates the Centre's holistic approach to strategic communications, thereby dealing with all five pillars of NATO StratCom (public diplomacy; public affairs; military public affairs; information operations; and psychological operations). It definitely performs a number of functions in all dimensions and stages of the strategic communications process, contributing to both military and civilian dimensions of NATO StratCom. The Centre serves as a scientific hub; informal

---

12. SACEUR "is one of NATO's two strategic commanders and is at the head of Allied Command Operations (ACO) (...) responsible to NATO's highest military authority – the Military Committee (MC) – for the conduct of all NATO military operations" (NATO, 2022).

Allied advisory body contributing to the development of strategic communications doctrine; education and training centre; as well as a whistle-blower warning or alarming the Euro-Atlantic Alliance – and the global community in general – about threats and violations in the information environment.

In the context of the war in Ukraine, the experts from the NATO StratCom COE do the research and simulations, conduct projects and workshops, teach delegates from Allied member states and Ukrainian (along with other) partners, as well as prepare analyses largely regarding cyberspace and Russian information warfare. *Information warfare* is another key term in this article which lacks a precise official definition. According to NATO[13], it denotes "an operation conducted in order to gain an information advantage over the opponent. It consists in controlling one's own information space, protecting access to one's own information, while acquiring and using the opponent's information, destroying their information systems and disrupting the information flow" (NATO Defence Education Enhancement Programme, 2020).

Information warfare is closely related to the Russian concept of *reflexive management*[14] (developed already in the 1960s) and part of Russian hybrid warfare. It embraces wide-ranging hostile information operations, psychological operations and a combination of both. In practice, it comes down to attacks within the information environment – especially cyber-attacks on IT infrastructure and mass attacks in conventional media and social media, using various forms of manipulation. The former may denote breaking into, disrupting or damaging information systems of adversaries, including public institutions and private sectors of critical infrastructure, as well as leaks and misuse of the given information; while the latter – dissemination of propaganda and disinformation (trolls, bots, fake news, deepfakes, etc.). The ultimate goals of applying these means of influence are the following: distorting the perception of reality, polarisation of views, disintegration of society, creating distrust towards the government and the state apparatus, and finally – destabilisation of a foreign state or other entity.

The NATO StratCom COE detects and reveals such hostile

---

13. Although the detailed understanding of this term differs even among the Allies, NATO has developed a general definition including general common elements.

14. Its meaning is similar to the American concept of *perception management*.

actions of the Russian Federation within the information environment of Ukraine and western countries[15], whereas a large amount of the effects of its work (unclassified information) is presented publicly online, proving that Russia intends not only to destabilise democratic societies in Ukraine but also within the EU and NATO, and strives to disintegrate and prevent them from helping Ukraine. On its website the Centre regularly publishes journals, articles and reports; and on its profile in social media, it uploads *e.g.* podcasts and interviews with specialists expounding on the abovementioned phenomena related to Russian aggression against Ukraine, its neighbouring states, members of the EU and NATO. The Allied StratCom COE not only informs international public opinion about the threats or incidents of Kremlin's information warfare, but also warns, gives recommendations and protects by developing appropriate counter-measures (such as AI tools). The Centre indicates the current trends, shows vulnerabilities, *i.a.* of traditional and online media in various countries (including the Russian Federation); develops programmes resolving media- or cyber-related issues; and helps NATO to identify both the existing and prospective threats, as well as to adapt new Allied doctrines and adjust to the changing cyber and information domains.

Moreover, it is evident that the current NATO strategic communications activities position the parties to the conflict on the basis of opposites and unambiguity. Through audio-visual and textual materials included on the NATO and NATO StratCom COE websites as well as their profiles on social media platforms, the audience receives a clear, consistent message in which the Russians appear as illegitimate invaders and barbarians, while Ukrainians as martyrs for the freedom of their country and all Europe. Most likely, this is intended to evoke among recipients the right attitude, along with sympathy and antipathy towards respective parties. Undoubtedly, in particular, the widespread media coverage of Russia's atrocities and images of brutally killed Ukrainian civilian population (exemplified by genocide in Bucha) are the releases which will be printed in people's memory. This is supposed to make the general public aware of the situation in Ukraine, provide the public with information/facts and their interpretation, and also to

---

15. The Russian state uses propaganda and disinformation also in relation to its own society, but with a different aim – to present the reality in a way which is favourable to the authoritarian regime, and to gain the support of Russian citizens *i.a.* for the Russian "special operation" in Ukraine.

increase the likelihood of its steadfast approval for the Ukrainian side and NATO's defence plans in this regard.

Although in the media and online communications channels NATO representatives openly declare NATO support for Ukraine and encourage the leaders of Allied states to aid Ukrainian armed forces, simultaneously they communicate strategically NATO's[16] detachment from military engagement in the ongoing war to avoid escalation of the conflict. Therefore, the Alliance provides assistance by means of non-lethal measures and advises the most desirable conduct to help Ukraine win, but also treats the concrete military support (weapons and equipment) as an individual decision reserved for the government of each member state. The aforementioned approach, official Allied recognition of Ukrainian authorities and borders, condemnation of Russian invasion, calling on Russia to cease fire and engage in peace talks, warning President Putin against the implementation of his nuclear threats or further military actions, invocation of Article 5 of the North Atlantic Treaty, enlargement policy along with a military build-up on the eastern flank of NATO – they all serve several purposes. They fulfil the primary role of the Organization as a defensive alliance, confirm the unity and joint obligations, strengthen the Alliance, and are supposed to deter the adversary.

Numerous materials on the NATO website and its profiles on social media platforms are devoted to the reinforcement of deterrence and defence as well as positive depiction of both Ukrainian and Allied national and joint armed forces. The events such as the implementation of the rapid reinforcement model, increasing the number and size of multinational battlegroups, as well as deployment of warfare vehicles and equipment which strengthen NATO's eastern border always receive much publicity and are proudly proclaimed all over the world.[17] Online videos, photo albums, reports, interviews with military representatives and ordinary soldiers, together with articles containing snapshots referring to joint military exercises, presentation of new weapons, delivery of necessary equipment to Ukraine, etc. are regularly uploaded, posted and published for global audiences.

---

16. Understood collectively as the whole organization.

17. NATO's military presence in the east of the Alliance.

Thanks to these, NATO and its member states communicate the transparency of their military activities; recipients have almost tangible contact with Allied soldiers, receive messages full of positive emotions and associations, and get used to the growing military activity of the Organization. Moreover, as a consequence, prospective Russian adversaries (on all levels of the military and non-military ladder of actors) are facing NATO's psychological pre-emptive actions.

Assessment of NATO strategic communications roles and activities

The author made the assessment of NATO strategic communications efforts on the basis of key *principles of strategic communication* framework applied by the U.S. Department of Defence, which distinguishes 9 attributes of prototypical strategic communications:

- *Leadership-driven* (leaders largely contribute to and direct the application of strategic communications),

- *Credible* (reliability, accountability and honesty of communication),

- *Understanding* (awareness of socio-cultural differences and various approaches),

- *Dialogue* (a wide spectrum of possibilities to have two-sided/multi-sided communication in order to enhance understanding, create links and bonds between the participating entities),

- *Pervasive* (conveying the intended meaning through all available means – deeds, texts, speeches, photographs, videos, etc.),

- *Unity of effort* (efforts in all dimensions and stages of strategic communications shall be amalgamated and synchronised),

- *Results-based* (the activities taken are supposed to reach some predetermined level/results in order to reach the ultimate goal(s)),

- *Responsive* (reacting quickly; and also using an appropriate communicate to a proper group of target recipients),

- *Continuous* – i.e. development and implementation of strategic communications are accompanied by constant studies, examination, assessment and lessons learned (Murphy, 2011).

Taking into account the given attributes as criteria for evaluation and juxtaposing them with the author's research and critical analysis of the wide spectrum of sources, it is legitimate to state that the present NATO StratCom efforts within the context of the Russian war in Ukraine are complete, mature and well adjusted. Indeed, all nine necessary qualities have been implemented and they bring visible results, and also NATO strategic communications still serves three long-term purposes. As exemplified by key public documents and performances (speeches, interviews, etc.) of principal representatives of the Organization, it fulfils the given roles as well as describes and evaluates the current state of both regional and global security, confirming the unchanged Euro-Atlantic values and superior goal of NATO.

However, apart from these, we can observe some significant changes: within the Allied narrative, position (or self-positioning) and short-term goals. Firstly, there has been a shift from an informational *coverage-style narrative* to a more persuasive *warfare narrative*, including the accumulation of military vocabulary and direct reference to the ongoing war in Ukraine, in Europe. Secondly, the way primary NATO figures (especially the Secretary General) position themselves communicates the power and leadership of the Organization in security and defence areas; and now guidance and strong advice are frequently conveyed through strategic communications channels.

Besides, the regular reiteration of messages concerning a dramatic situation in Ukraine, unlawful Russian invasion, atrocities, violation of international and humanitarian laws, imperialistic motivation and rejection of available diplomatic and conciliatory solutions as well as preparations for further full-fledged war—in addition to informing the international audience—serves an impressive function. The NATO Secretary General assures the Euro-Atlantic community that it is our right and our interest to support Ukraine constantly. Otherwise, not only Russian attacks may spread in our region, but also Chinese authorities – encouraged by the lack of acute consequences for the aggressor – may decide to do the same. This assurance of regional and global security threats, together with the aforementioned messages, are part of a political advocacy campaign aimed at evoking prompt public acceptance of current NATO's priorities (particularly: costly individual and joint military ventures of member and partner states) and its new hard power approach.

Conclusions

The role and influence of NATO strategic communications has evolved along with the evolution of the security environment caused by Russia's aggression in Ukraine. Nonetheless, despite the existing ambiguities concerning the main Allied terms and their semantic scopes within the context of the Russia-Ukraine war, its communicative and strategic relevance cannot be overestimated. NATO StratCom decidedly performs a number of functions in all dimensions and stages of the Organization's strategic communications process, contributing to both military and civilian dimensions of NATO. Allied strategic communications is still responsible for informing, explaining and increasing the acceptance of the broader public for all plans and activities of the Alliance so that it contributes to the realization of Euro-Atlantic defensive aims. However, its functions have expanded along with the advent of the Russian war of aggression, entailing violation of the established borders and attacking militarily Ukraine – a democratic sovereign state; breaching international law and order, in coalescence with the level of brutality unprecedented in Europe since World War II. These events have shown the picture of a new (real) face of unchanged Russian imperialist ambitions, thereby signifying a direct threat also to other European countries, especially to those in the eastern flank of NATO, and posing a serious global threat because—if not condemned, sanctioned and won over by unified democratic countries—the unlawful armed attacks could encourage other authoritarian regimes (such as China) to follow these footsteps.

Consequently, NATO has undertaken a fundamental conversion of its strategy from soft power to hard power, which in turn has been mirrored in the functioning of Allied strategic communications. The narrative of NATO strategic communications has altered from the *coverage-style* to *warfare narrative*. It means that currently, it not only focuses on conveying important information in the media, but also – or predominantly – on recommending, strongly persuading, guiding and coordinating certain decisions and the conduct of non-military and military leaders of NATO member and partner states. Another key narrative change regards the self-positioning of primary NATO figures (especially the Secretary General) communicating in the media and other

StratCom channels the power and leadership of the Organization. Currently, they expose their new overtly impressive, advisory and persuasive functions, influencing international public opinion as well as non-military and military authorities of NATO member and partner countries, aiming at the sustained common Allied support for the oppressed Ukraine and the protection of Allied security.

Since in democratic countries the high-level decisions regarding national and international security, defence and crisis management require social consent, it is of utmost importance to communicate to the wider public a convincing narrative in an effective way. NATO StratCom efforts—characterised by a holistic approach, operating in various communication channels, stages and dimensions (public diplomacy; public affairs; military public affairs; information operations; and psychological operations) as well as possessing all attributes of prototypical strategic communications—significantly contribute to both military and civilian dimensions of NATO. Allied strategic communications within the context of the war in Ukraine is concurrently related to global and regional security; and it mirrors the Organization's conduct, vision, and defence strategy, including NATO values, interests, long-term and short-term goals. Moreover, NATO StratCom is well organized, adjusted to the given discourse and target audience, and preserves a consistent narrative. Therefore, the author of this article is positive that Allied communication efforts are a success and should be positively evaluated. In this spirit, the Secretary General as well as other civil and military representatives publicly highlight the necessity of providing Ukraine with constant tangible support in the military area, including weapons, equipment, training, logistics, maintenance and exchange of intelligence data, seeking approval of western societies and authorities.

Based on the extensive research and critical analysis of the given resources, specific recommendations might be put forward. Namely, to sustain the wide-ranging activities in the area of NATO strategic communications, while placing emphasis on several issues. These include: (1) the unification of NATO strategic communications terms and their semantic scopes within the context of Russian aggression in Ukraine by adopting the agreed official definitions; (2) the development and strengthening of Allied information operations, especially cyber capabilities (both defensive and offensive) to protect Ukraine and NATO from Russian disinformation and cyber attacks, expose sinister intentions of the Kremlin and enable counter actions; (3) coherence and openness of political communication among various Allied countries; as well as (4) engagement with civil societies accompanied by extensive educational programmes on information and media literacy.

Last but not least, the research and analysis conducted for the purpose of this dissertation have helped the author to identify the relevant areas requiring future research. The areas being proposed embrace:

- the investigation of semantic scopes and the way(s) in which individual Allied member states understand and judge the meaning of specific NATO terms (in particular, the concepts related to the war in Ukraine shall be treated as a priority). It could be a significant step towards the unification of definitions and terminology;

- the detailed evaluation of the influence of specific NATO StratCom means and channels on particular types/groups of audiences; as well as

- the analysis of the prospective possibilities to implement the new emerging technologies for the benefit of strategic communications.

The abovementioned pieces of research could contribute to strengthening and advancing strategic communications of the whole Organization and also its members and partner states, including Ukraine.

Reference

Bachmann, S.D. and Gunneriusson, H. (2015) 'Hybrid Wars: The 21st-Century's New Threats to Global Peace and Security', *Scientia Militaria, South African Journal of Military Studies*, vol. 43, no. 1. Available at: https://ssrn.com/ abstract=2506063.

Bernard, V. (2015) 'Editorial – Tactics, techniques, tragedies: A humanitarian perspective on the changing face of war, The evolution of warfare', *International Review of the Red Cross*, vol. 97, no. 900. Available at: https://international-review. icrc.org/sites/ default/ files/irc_97_900-1.pdf.CNN (2023) *Hear NATO chief's message to Russia following tank shipment announcement*. Available at: https://www.youtube.com/watch? v=sTmm9 KyiQz0.

Crimm, M. (2022) 'Can we please stop talking about domains?', *Defence News: Commentary*. Available at: https://www.

defencenews.com/opinion/commentary/2022/02/18/ can-we-please-stop-talking-about-domains/.

Fecteau, M.J. (2022) 'Understanding Information Operations & Information Warfare: The Muddled Meaning of IO (and IW)', *Global Security Review: Defence & Security*, 22 June. Available at: https://globalsecurityreview.com/ understanding-information-operations-information-warfare/.

Folkoch Försvar (2023) "Hard power is a reality" – Christopher G. Cavoli, Supreme Allied Commander Europe (SACEUR),. Available at: https://www.youtube.com/ watch?v=IFIhlAHnRbg.

Gawęcka, J.A. (2021) 'Komunikacja strategiczna', in Wasiuta, O. and Wasiuta, S. (eds.) *Encyklopedia bezpieczeństwa*, vol. 2. Kraków: Libron.[Accessed: 11 September 2024].

Greenwood, C. (1987) 'The Concept of War in Modern International Law', *The International and Comparative Law Quarterly*, vol. 36, no. 2. Available at: http://www.jstor.org/ stable/759997.

Hallahan, K., et al. (2007) 'Defining strategic communication', *International Journal of Strategic Communication*, pp. 3–35.

Hebermann, J.D. (2023) 'Strafmaßnahmen gegen Russland müssen noch verschärft werden [Punitive measures against Russia have to be tightened]'. RedaktionsNetzwerk Deutschland. Available at: https://www.rnd.de/politik/ex-cia-chef-david-petraeus-warnt-in-interview-vor-putin-UOCU4SL5G5H5DHALYCJZPGTPZQ.html.

Marahrens, S. (2022) *Strategic Game: Hybrid Warfare* [Lecture to postgraduate students Global Affairs and Diplomacy]. Akademia Sztuki Wojennej [War Studies University].

MSNBC (2023) *Ukraine needs more weapons, says NATO secretary general.* Available at: https://www.youtube.com/ watch?v=yBo81moC6QY.

Munro, A. & Rodriguez, E. (2022) 'Public diplomacy', *Encyclopædia Britannica*. Encyclopædia Britannica, Inc. Available at: https:// www.britannica.com/topic/public-diplomacy.

Murphy, D.M. (2011) *Information Operations Primer: Fundamentals of Information Operations*, U.S. Army War College Dept. of Military Strategy, Planning, and Operations & Center for Strategic Leadership, AY12. Available at: https://apps.dtic.mil/sti/pdfs/ ADA555809.pdf.

NATO (1949) *The North Atlantic Treaty.* Available at: https://www. nato.int/cps/en/natolive/ official_texts_17120.htm.

NATO (2011) NATO Military Public Affairs Policy. Available at: https://www.nato.int/ims/ docu/ mil-pol- pub-affairs-en.pdf.

NATO (2022) *Communications and public diplomacy.* Available at: https://www.nato.int/ cps/en/natohq/topics_69275.htm.

NATO (2022) *NATO Secretary General.* Available at: https://www.nato.int/cps/ en/natohq/topics_50094.htm.

NATO (2022) *NATO Strategic Concept 2022.* Available at: https://www.nato.int/strategic-concept/.

NATO (2022) *Strategic Concepts.* Available at: https://www.nato.int/ cps/ en/natohq/ topics_56626.htm.

NATO (2022) *Supreme Allied Commander Europe (SACEUR).* Available at: https://www.nato.int/cps/en/natohq/topics_50110. htm.

NATO (2023) *NATO Secretary General in Munich: give Ukraine what they need to win.* Available at: https://www.nato.int/cps/en/ natohq/news_212044.htm.

NATO (2023) *NATO Secretary General thanks US and B9 leaders for their strong support for NATO and Ukraine.* Available at: https://www.nato.int/cps/en/ natohq/ news_212160.htm.

NATO (2023) *Opening remarks by NATO Secretary General Jens Stoltenberg at the Plenary Session of the B9 Summit in Poland.* Available at: https://www.nato.int/cps/en/ natohq/ opinions_212158.htm.

NATO (2023) *Statement by Secretary General Jens Stoltenberg on Finland and Sweden's NATO membership.* Available at: https://www.nato.int/cps/en/natohq/ opinions_ 212882.htm.

NATO Defence Education Enhancement Programme (2020) *Information warfare: Media – (dis)information – security.* Available at: https://www.nato.int/nato_static_fl2014/ assets/ pdf/2020/5/pdf/2005-deepportal4-information-warfare.pdf.

NATO News (2023) *NATO Secretary General with the President of the European Commission Ursula von der Leyen,* 11 January. Available at: https://www.youtube.com/watch? v=K3oJkJczeaA.

NATO News (2023) *NATO Secretary General with the US Secretary of State Antony J. Blinken,* 8 February. Available at: https://www.youtube.com/watch?v=r8eYgGrhkFY.

NATO Strategic Communications Centre of Excellence (2020) *About Strategic Communications.* Available at: https://stratcomcoe.org/ about_us/about-strategic-communications/1.

NATO Strategic Communications Centre of Excellence (2021) *About NATO StratCom COE*. Available at: https://stratcomcoe.org/about_us/about-nato-stratcom-coe/5.

Rynning, S. (2022) *'NATO and the Transatlantic Link'* [PowerPoint presentation]. Available at: https://shorturl.at/GerXQ.

Schmid, J. (2022) *The Challenge of Hybrid Warfare* [Lecture to postgraduate students Global Affairs and Diplomacy]. Akademia Sztuki Wojennej [War Studies University], Warsaw.

Thorson, K. (2013) 'Strategic Communication', *Oxford Bibliographies*, Oxford University Press.

UN News (2022) *Russia had 'no choice' but to launch 'special military operation' in Ukraine, Lavrov tells UN*. United Nations. Available at: https://news.un.org/en/story/ 2022/09/1127881.

CHAPTER 10

Development of strategic alliances – is Russia ready to undermine U.S. supremacy?

Tomasz Mączka

Abstract

This chapter explores the evolving geopolitical dynamics concerning strategic alliances formed by Russia and their potential to challenge U.S. global supremacy. This chapter delves into Russia's foreign policy strategies, focusing on its growing partnerships with countries such as China, India, and Iran, and the increasing cooperation within multilateral frameworks like BRICS and the Shanghai Cooperation Organisation (SCO). Through analyzing Russia's military, economic, and diplomatic maneuvers, the chapter assesses whether these alliances signify a coherent strategy aimed at undermining U.S. dominance in global affairs. Key findings highlight Russia's efforts to foster a multipolar world order, while also addressing the internal and external challenges it faces, including economic sanctions, technological gaps, and strained relations with the West. The chapter concludes that while Russia's alliances represent significant geopolitical shifts, they are not yet robust enough to fundamentally challenge U.S. supremacy without deeper structural changes and stronger economic ties.

Keywords: U.S., China, Russia, BRICS, new world order

Introduction

The armed conflict ignited by the Russian Federation on 24 February 2022 in Ukraine has become a catalyst for geopolitical changes on the global stage. From the economic turmoil in global markets to the formation of political alliances and the reorientation of the existing economic order. Although the Russian aggression against a sovereign European country is not an isolated military incident in the modern history of the world, the moment in which it occurred may change the present political world order forever. The two World Wars in Europe at the beginning of the twentieth century shaped the geopolitical world order for many decades to come. From the rubble of the European continent emerged two new military world powers of the time – the Soviet Union and the United States of America. Both of these states quickly became adversaries, around which two economic and political blocs were formed. Over the years, the newly emerged powers clashed on many levels, eventually leading to the degradation of one of them – the communist bloc united under the leadership of the Soviet Union. However, despite the disintegration of the USSR and the transition of many states under American influence, the newly-established Russia still represented both military and political capabilities. In the following article, I will show how, as a result of many isolated factors, the political significance of the Russian Federation in the future remains as uncertain as ever. Economically, the discussed realignment of the main players has already taken place long ago, and Russia's natural successor on the superpowers' podium seems to be the People's Republic of China.

Despite the obvious disproportions in the economic potential, during the ongoing conflict in Ukraine, Russia is attempting to challenge the hegemony of the United States. They are using arguments based on creating a competitive alliance of states. An alliance that could oppose the economic power of the West and would become a counterweight to the existing political order. In the long perspective, this would establish the foundations for a multipolar world – without the U.S. hegemony in terms of shaping the political order in other parts of the world. However, the fundamental question remains: is Russia ready to challenge the military and economic might of the U.S. while being weakened by a non-successful war?

Shaping a new world order

The world today has been divided into two very distinct political blocs with regard to the ongoing war in Ukraine. On the one side of the barricade, we have countries strongly condemning Russian aggression and openly supporting Ukrainian defence efforts, while on the other side, there are countries for whom current events are the simple outcome of certain geopolitical factors. According to the latter, there is a common vision that the conflict should not be the cause of such extensive economic sanctions imposed on the parties involved in the dispute. This attitude is probably related to geographical distance and a less emotional attitude toward the conflict itself. In the Western world, the memory of World War II and the *Détente* policy pursued towards Nazi Germany before the war. In fact, we can say that the history lesson has been well studied by Western politicians. Nevertheless, the arguments of the Western leaders, completely fail to reach the audience of the global south. For them, this is just a local conflict that should not be a reason to terminate a prosperous and profitable economic relationship.

While analysing the Russia-Ukraine war and its impact on shaping political decisions by world leaders, the Western world also forgets the differences in the perception of the current conflict by countries from outside our cultural sphere. After World War II, as the two major powers of the time began to compete, several major armed conflicts took place across the world. Just to mention the most important of these – in 1950-53 the Korean War and in 1955-75 the Vietnam War. These absorbed far more human and material resources than the current conflict in Ukraine. Moreover, they resulted in huge numbers of military and civilian casualties. Thus, contrary to common media rhetoric, the current war is not the biggest geopolitical disaster after 1945. Of course, there is an accumulation of certain economic factors that may distort public perception. Today's world, affected by post-pandemic problems such as broken supply chains or global inflation, seems to link such facts with the ongoing war. Furthermore, in Western society, we seem to forget what role the military actions taken by the Western powers in previous centuries have done in shaping the current political order. The question of brutal colonial policy or territorial conquests carried out during the state-building process is also completely ignored here. The failure to take these factors into account in the discussion of international relations leads to a complete failure to understand the intentions of states outside our cultural circle. Currently, this is the case in African and Asian countries (Nair, 2022).

During the examination of the ongoing polarisation between the Western world and the rest of the international community, it is worth mentioning the words of Samuel Huntington: "The West won the world not by the superiority of its ideas or values or religion [...] but rather by its superiority in applying organized violence. Westerners often forget this fact; non-Westerners never do" (Huntington, 2011). This argument fits perfectly into the Russian narrative regarding the legitimacy of its actions towards the Ukrainian state. According to Moscow's rhetoric, the annexation of further Ukrainian territories is merely a rectification of historical mistakes or an attempt to protect the Russian sphere of influence from NATO expansion in the region. Speaking of historical mistakes, the Russians have in mind, for example, the decision of Nikita Khrushchev in 1954, who incorporated the Crimean Peninsula into the then Ukrainian Soviet Socialist Republic for administrative reasons. By the way, his wife was of Ukrainian descent and he himself grew up in the Donbas region (Grigas, 2016).

The Russian position was very clearly articulated in the autumn of 2014, shortly after the annexation of Crimea and the destabilization of the eastern regions of Ukraine, by the secretary of the Russian Security Council at the time. Nikolai Patrushev, in a rather detailed tone, described the reasons behind the collapse of the Soviet Union. According to his words, the policies pursued by the US during the Cold War directly led to this event. Furthermore, he stated that Russia, as a result of the collapse of the USSR, "...unilaterally surrendered its assets on the world stage without being compensated at all" (Egarov & Patrushev, 2014). Such a fact, combined with their lack of response, caused that "Washington planned to extend its sphere of direct influence to the Black Sea, Caucasus and Caspian regions" (Egarov & Patrushev, 2014). All the measures taken to annex Crimea and then subjugate the whole of Ukraine were therefore the result of a natural restitution of lost territories. This attitude is being propagated to the world and has apparently found its audience.

Lost empire

Unfortunately, the Russian political elite, in their attempt to position themselves as a world power, completely forget that with the collapse of the USSR, the entire communist ideology also went bankrupt. The political tool designed to give Russia leadership within the Socialist world proved to be a complete economical failure. This made the world announce overnight the unilateral victory of democracy and the Western paradigm in fundamental matters (Bala, 2018). With every following decade and another economic crisis, Russia became a diminishing actor in the global world. The country, with its declining economy, was not able to stretch its commitments in different corners of the world as the U.S. and China are doing for example. This has made Russia an even less important player on the political stage with each passing year. Of course, this does not change the fact that Russia was still eager to play a significant role in its closest sphere of influence. The best example is Belarus, a country that is so strongly dependent in economic terms on Russia that it is practically incapable of functioning without the financial support of its gestor. However, if we consider the scale of this support and the fact that Belarus has a population of less than 10 million and an economy in terms of GDP per capita that ranks 91st in the world, it is obvious where Russia can position itself (CIA, 2021).

However, while Russia managed to subjugate Belarus politically and economically, it was becoming gradually impossible to maintain a similar status for the nation of Ukraine. Following the annexation of the Crimean Peninsula and the destabilization of the eastern regions of Ukraine, a joint future for the two states was deemed impossible. The Ukrainian drift towards the West seemed unstoppable, and the political decisions taken by the Ukrainian side did not allow Moscow to calmly tolerate such a state of affairs. This is in line with the views of Alexander Dugin, a man who has undoubtedly had a huge influence on the ideological shaping of the current generation of Russian politicians and military officers. In his visions of a Eurasian empire renewed on the ruins of the Soviet Union, Ukraine holds a key role there. With its demographic and industrial potential, it is a vital geopolitical element, in order to counterbalance the growing American influence in the region. According to Dugin's predictions, Ukraine, tempted to join NATO and the EU, will be forced to disintegrate as a result of internal splits

(Siudak, 2014). In one of his television interviews, Dugin quite accurately diagnosed the dynamics of the political developments shaping the country at the time of the Orange Revolution and the economic crisis which followed in 2009. As a result of contradictory geopolitical national movements in Ukraine, he assessed that sooner or later there had to be an internal upheaval manifesting itself in a crisis of statehood. The outcome of this was to be the formation of two types of Ukrainian nationhood – one oriented towards the Western World and opposed to Russia, and the other in the East under its influence. Of course, at that time there was still no discussion about any military action, but he had already mentioned the inevitability of a territorial division of Ukraine and the absorption of the industrialised eastern part of the country by Russia. In his mind, this conflict was inevitable and the process of drawing new borders was to be painful because it was going to take place in the hearts and souls of the citizens (Dugin, 2009).

From a Russian perspective, an armed attack and taking control of the Ukrainian state was strategically a profitable idea. It is no secret that Russia has viewed Ukraine and Belarus as exclusive spheres of influence since the collapse of the Soviet Union. The cultural proximity and economic ties inherited from the Soviet Union, to a large extent, made these countries dependent on each other in certain spheres. This can clearly be seen in the area of the arms industry, which under the USSR was, for obvious reasons, the wheels of the economy at the time. For decades, military production, centrally planned from Moscow, relied on products from factories in various parts of the Soviet Empire. In the field of advanced technology, the Ukrainian Soviet Socialist Republic had a lot to offer. It is enough to mention industrial giants such as *Motor-Sich*, which was responsible for the development and production of a large number of aircraft and helicopter engines that powered the USSR's aviation, and *Zorya-Mashproekt*, which produced gas turbines for naval vessels. After the occupation of Crimea in 2014, Ukraine decided to cut off Russian contractors from its key military technologies. This caused huge problems for the Russian military and forced the arms industry to develop proprietary designs based on its own production capacity. In 2015, Russian Deputy Prime Minister Dmitry Rogozin in front of the parliament admitted that Ukrainian components were used in the production of 186 types of Russian military equipment (Aksenov, 2015). It is likely that the

Russians have not completely resolved the shortage of Ukrainian components to this day, as evidenced by reports coming from *Ukraine's Secret Service (SBU)* of illegally supplying military goods to the Russian military industry. Ukrainian authorities suggested that involved criminals established transnational channels for the illegal supply of wholesale batches of Ukrainian aircraft engines to Russia via countries in Europe, West and East Asia to avoid existing trade restrictions (Culverwell, 2022).

Another key argument for the Russian invasion was the industrial areas with all their raw material inventory, located within the borders of present-day Ukraine. For such a rickety Russian economy, they were and still are extremely valuable. Zbigniew Brzezinski in the early 1990s, in one of his publications for Foreign Affairs magazine, emphasised that "it cannot be stressed enough that without Ukraine, Russia ceases to be an empire, but with Ukraine suborned and then subordinated, Russia automatically becomes an empire" (Brzezinski, 1994).

Although the war in Ukraine is still going on and it is not possible to decide its final outcome, it is quite obvious that Russia has not achieved its goals. Taking into account the material and human costs incurred so far, any balance of profits and losses at the moment speaks against the aggressor. If we add to this the lost markets for Russian oil and gas in Europe, declining budget revenues, ubiquitous economic sanctions, further pauperization of Russian society and marginalization of Russia's position in the international arena are on the horizon. The image losses suffered by this country during this war are also indisputably huge, and the loss of benefits related to this will last for years to come.

Building a new alliance

In today's world, Russia has little to offer its economic partners. Apart from the aspect of energy resources, which Moscow frequently deploys as a form of blackmail, the country is incapable of building any serious international alliances. After the invasion of Ukraine in early 2022, Russia, completely isolated from Western economies, attempted to build a new political bloc in opposition to the USA. They anchored its major diplomatic effort around the BRICS group of countries, including Brazil, Russia, India, China

and South Africa. It must be admitted that Moscow has hit the favourable ground for its rhetoric. This is particularly true in view of the current economic turbulence and the ongoing trade war between the US and China.

Russia's diplomatic efforts on the international stage are mostly focused on trying to undermine the dollar's dominance in the global monetary system. The fact is that this rhetoric is perfectly in line with global social trends, which, after years of the Federal Reserve Board's loose fiscal policy, are focusing on the search for a more stable alternative as a new foundation in a dynamically changing world. However, to precisely understand the genesis of this problem we need to go back to Breton Woods of 1944, where the foundation for the current monetary system was laid. The *United Nations Monetary and Financial Conference* established international relations in the sphere of managing the world's monetary systems. The result of this meeting was also the establishment of the *World Bank* and the *International Monetary Fund (IMF)*, which its creators intended to be a tool for regulating the established monetary system.

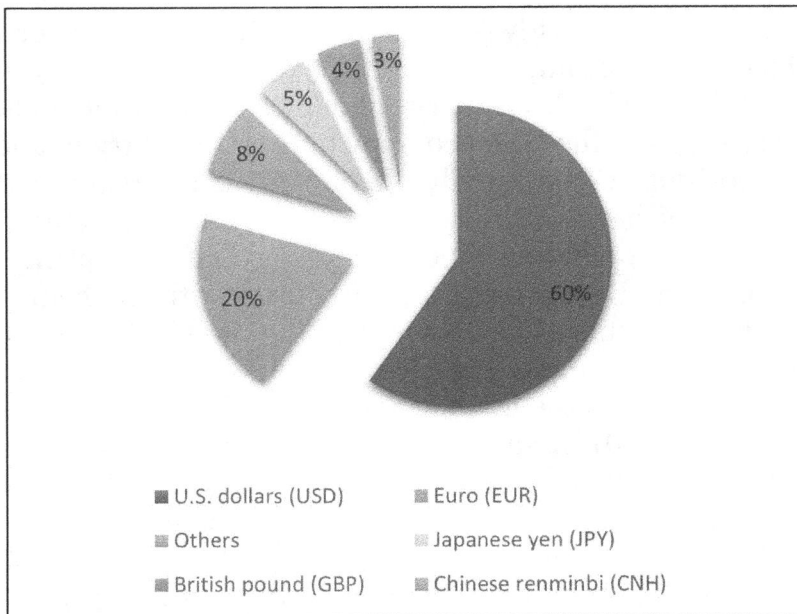

Figure 10.1. Currency composition of official foreign exchange reserves for 2022/3

Source: https://data.imf.org/?sk=e6a5f467-c14b-4aa8-9f6d-5a09ec4e62a4.

The new economic order consequently led to the global dominance of the U.S. dollar, which was rigidly pegged to the established value of gold. The entire financial world has since been correlated to the U.S. economy, and the growing demand for the dollar allowed the Fed to increase the money supply by monetizing its debts. As a result of the Bretton Woods agreements, the U.S. dollar became the world's reserve currency, which has since provided political stability during the successive financial crises sweeping through the global economy. Today, the U.S. dollar is responsible for nearly 60% of the world's foreign exchange reserves, which is still the overwhelming majority. If we additionally consider the ratio of all currencies in the basket of G7 countries, we have the picture of the total financial dominance of the Western Hemisphere over the rest of the world before us. It is remarkable, that the ratio of foreign exchange reserves held in U.S. dollars has been on a downward trend since the beginning of this century. According to IMF analysts, this trend partly reflects the decreasing role of the U.S. currency in the global economy, especially when it comes to competition from other currencies broadly used by central banks for their international transactions. However, that huge decline in statistics has been mostly seen since the EURO was introduced in 1999 (Arslanalp & Simpson-Bell, 2021).

Confidence in U.S. Treasury bonds and the widespread belief in the strength of the USA economy puts this country in a fairly strong position. Consequently, this allows it to create its debt unlimitedly as long as there is demand for the U.S. currency. This fosters a policy of financial incentives for countries that support its actions. The USA carries out these tasks with the help of its subsidiary institutions like the *IMF* and the *World Bank*. So, when there is financial diplomacy or the imposition of economic sanctions, it is clear why the U.S. has such a powerful tool in its hands (Greenwald, 2020). It should be remembered that the USA has for decades pursued a sanctions policy against countries hostile to its interests. Suffice it here to mention the example of Cuba and Venezuela, whose economies, under the onslaught of U.S. trade restrictions and economic sanctions, have been in a permanent economic crisis for years. Major financial institutions, fearing secondary sanctions, do not attempt to circumvent them, and the fear of losing access to the U.S. financial market effectively blocks any temptation to do so. According to an article by Peter Goodman in the New York Times, "...banks cannot risk jeopardizing their access to the plumbing of the dollar-based global financial network [and] they have taken pains to steer clear of nations and companies deemed pariahs in Washington" (Goodman, 2019).

Scenarios for abandoning dollar settlements in the oil trade and replacing this currency with, for example, the Chinese yuan, are already being considered out loud. Such a move basically erodes the US dollar's decades-old dominance in international trade and finance. This sudden change is probably happening because of the US sanctions imposed on Russia after the outbreak of war in Ukraine. However, the most important factor from the point of view of these countries is probably Moscow's successful economic response to these restrictions. In the first weeks of the war, the Russians forced buyers of their oil and gas products to pay in rubles (Cohen, 2022). The simple idea was to help prop up their domestic currency and together with several other steps imposed by the Russian Central Bank, they succeeded. The message for the rest of the world was obvious.

Changing the flow

The current economic order and distribution of power in the global economy, in which the U.S. still invariably plays a major role, is to the distaste of many aspiring countries. Furthermore, a number of economic analytics today notice that the current voting policy in the *World Bank* and the *IMF* gives gross over-representation to the USA and the rest of the richest countries from the G7 group (Grenville, 2021). This is clearly an issue for the less fortunate partners who seek greater social justice in the international arena and the ability to protect their interests in the absence of a common vision for crisis management. The main goal here is not only identifying this anomaly but persuading the over-represented to give up their privileges. Big and successful nations like China for long have been expressing frustration that Bretton Woods institutions such as the *International Monetary Fund* and the *World Bank* do not recognize their rising national power. During the Chinese president's extremely important visit to Moscow in March 2023, his closing message touched on this worldview. During a goodbye handshake, he said to his Russian counterpart: "Together, we should push forward these changes that have not happened for 100 years. Take care" (Al Jazeera, 2023). This message can be clearly read as a challenge to the Western world.

It remains an open question whether the countries united in the BRICS alliance will manage to challenge the economic dominance of the Western world in the coming period with such a problematic partner like Russia as a leader. In addition, despite the still declared readiness of many countries to join the new alliance, it should not be forgotten that among the participants themselves, there is often a rather powerful conflict of interest. Suffice it to say that there are huge political tensions between the most important members of the group, which are China and India. The creator of the acronym himself more than two decades after its introduction, in a critical article for the Financial Times, summed up the BRICS activities with the statement that „...they have done very little policy co-ordination to foster their own collective economic effort. [...] China is the only BRIC country to have surpassed its growth projections, and India is not too far off from meeting its estimates. But due to dismal second decades, neither Brazil nor Russia have seen their nominal U.S. dollar shares of GDP grow any bigger than they were back in 2001" (O'Neill, 2021).

Despite the internal and structural problems that define the BRICS, Moscow, together with Beijing, is not relenting in its attempts to turn this bloc into an anti-US alliance. Obviously, this is the goal of both countries, but in the longer term, this behaviour could enhance China in shaping its political agenda over a wider part of the globe. Their common success in attracting new members cannot be denied either. Since the outbreak of the war in Ukraine, several countries – including Iran, Argentina and Algeria, have announced their desire to join the group. Thus, renaming the organisation unofficially as BRICS+, as the statutes of this entity have still not been formally established. The biggest benefactors of this expansion are, of course, Russia and China, who, against the current deepening tensions with the West, are vigorously seeking allies in the fight against US influence in the region – each, of course, with its own associated agenda. Despite widespread criticism about the potential of this organisation, these countries are pursuing their respective goals with stoic calm. One of these is the New Development Bank, whose creation is an attempt to replace Western funding of economic projects in the countries of the region, thereby creating an alternative to institutions such as the World Bank and IMF.

The common factor that unites all the member states is a shared ambition to recognise their potential on the international level. Moreover, most of them are united by their historical experience and the memory of the aggressive colonial policies of Western states. Of course, Russia does not fit completely into this group in this context, given its imperialist past. However, luckily for Moscow, their territorial ambitions have never in history reached their current allies. Another thing that unites the common interests of the BRICS+ countries is their aversion to the sanctions policy pursued by the West, with the United States in the lead. The most outspoken opponents of these measures are naturally China and Russia, which are currently the victims of this practice. According to the article by Jacob Mardell, a research specialist at the *Mercator Institute of China Studies (MERICS)* in Berlin: „The West has for a long time underestimated the importance of the Global South to China's struggle for supremacy against the United States. As China-U.S. relations further deteriorate, developing countries will become increasingly important to Beijing as trade partners, sources of legitimacy on the global stage, and as battlegrounds to set international standards for emerging technologies" (Mardell, 2022). China's main objective in the coming decades will be to further expand this alliance and thus deepen the economic dependence between its members. Naturally, China, as the largest economy in this group, will in time impose its leadership over the rest, effectively sealing the political marginalisation of the rest. The question is which country will be the first to withdraw from this arrangement.

It is significant that Saudi Arabia may also join the new alliance, which could consequently shake up the current map of political influence. A victim of this geopolitical turn would probably be the current US-based international security architecture. BRICS with new partners such as Iran and Saudi Arabia would become a powerful organisation. Bringing together three of the world's key oil producers could open the way for accession by the rest of the countries belonging to OPEC. This would mean a huge threat to the price stability of this key global commodity. As a consequence, it could lead to a supply imbalance if the newly formed BRICS+ group decides to sell oil exclusively to its members. For the West, this would mean a war in the field of energy resources, which, in the time of global competition for the rare earth elements market, does not seem to be any sort of futuristic scenario. The organisation is growing with the intention of being a counterweight to Western influence and an attempt to break its dependence on the United States. In reality, it could become a tool for China to control Central Asia and the Middle East.

Scenarios for abandoning dollar settlements in the oil trade and replacing this currency with, for example, the Chinese yuan, are already being considered out loud. Such a move basically erodes the US dollar's decades-old dominance in international trade and finance. This sudden change is probably happening because of the US sanctions imposed on Russia after the outbreak of war in Ukraine. However, the most important factor from the point of view of these countries is probably Moscow's successful economic response to these restrictions. In the first weeks of the war, the Russians forced buyers of their oil and gas products to pay in rubles (Cohen, 2022). The simple idea was to help prop up their domestic currency and together with several other steps imposed by the Russian Central Bank, they succeeded. The message for the rest of the world was obvious.

Rising dragon

Ironically, after the outbreak of war in Ukraine, the entire eyes of the Western world were turned towards China. Partly in anticipation of their response and position, but also out of fear of a possible accelerated invasion of Taiwan. After the full-scale Russian offensive in Ukraine, something that seemed unlikely a few years earlier made the world realise how determined authoritarian leaders can be in implementing their nationalist declarations. Moreover, China, in its demands for the restitution of the island of Taiwan and the One China policy it has been proclaiming for decades, has a more legal and historical basis for this step than the Russians. However, as always in such disputes, no one takes into account the voice of the community concerned. In the case of Ukraine, however, this local voice would not necessarily favour only one side of the conflict.

In terms of international law, a military solution to the conflict over Taiwan would be quite a puzzle for the international community. Ben Saul, in a recent discussion published in *The Interpreter*, questioned whether a war against China in defence of Taiwan would be legal at all. In his conclusion about Taiwan's self-determination, he stated that: „All of these pro-Taiwan arguments are uncertain and controversial. They are based on contested assessments of state practice, sometimes wishful thinking, and limited case law or UN resolutions. A betting person might be tempted to back the more conventional legal answers favouring China" (Saul, 2021). Of course, all of this may be just an academic dispute, because when it comes to real life and politics: "The shifting balance of power can also affect the legal views of states and whom they side with" (Saul, 2021). Nowadays, we see that the "rules-based international order" is really a question of will, because it stays anarchic if there is no one ready to enforce these rules. Regarding the Taiwan issue, we see a huge political will to defend it at all costs, but whether this argument will be enough for China's rising power to give up its core political objective remains a rather rhetorical question.

As a threat from China has been growing in popularity among Western society for a relatively short time, this adversary has been prominent in the military doctrines of the U.S. military for long time. Moreover, the threat of conflict in the Gulf of Taiwan has never been as tangible in history as it is now, with Chinese President Xi Jinping setting specific targets in his speeches to the nation: "We must comprehensively strengthen military training and preparation, and improve the army's ability to win, [...] The complete unification of the motherland must be realized, and it will be realized" (Gale, 2022).

From a purely military point of view, China's growing Navy is the only one in the world that will be able to stand up to the military might of the U.S. Navy in the near future. It already has more ships than the American one, and the pace of building new vessels is alarmingly impressive. Although technologically the Chinese Army still stands behind its main rival on the international stage, the determination to build up its military capabilities rightly inspires respect among Western military experts. According to the Chinese Army White Papers[18], they are planning to

---

18. A Defence White Paper is a key policy document which provides the Government's vision for defence. It is a public document which outlines the broad strategic policy framework for defence planning, with a medium-term outlook.

comprehensively advance the modernization of military theory, organizational structure, military personnel, weaponry and equipment in step with the modernization of the country. Basically, they are willing to complete the modernization of national defence and the military by 2035. By doing so, China wants to fully transform the People's Armed Forces into a world-class Army by the mid-21st century (Ministry of National Defence The People's Republic of China, 2019).

Conclusion

This chapter has aimed to describe the diminishing role and international position of Russia in today's dynamically changing world. With the collapse of the Soviet Union and the inability to unleash its economic potential, Russian politicians have attempted historical revisionism aimed at the territorial reconstruction of the lost empire. With the brutal invasion of neighbouring Ukraine, which was intended to establish the foundations for Russia's return to the international stage, all the economic relations with the West, which had been carefully developed over decades, lay in ruins. Thus, Russia's chances of successfully building its military and political power were most likely doomed. On the Ukrainian steppes, along with the burned-out wreckage of Russian tanks, the country's economic future is also fading. In an era of broken relations with its Western partners and loss of markets for Russian energy resources, the country is likely to be pushed into the arms of the rising Asian dragon. China by making its partner economically dependent will, in the long term, further marginalise Russia's position on the international stage. Therefore, Russian attempts to build an anti-US coalition will, at most, accelerate the global split into two political blocs – Chinese and American. Russia's efforts to undermine the current position of the United States are nothing more than a reflection of China's growing ambitions and are an illustration of the challenges the USA will face in the near future. However, Russia's role in this process is likely to be reduced to that of a secondary actor.

Moreover, the potential of the US and its determination to maintain its leading position as a global power cannot be underestimated. Washington has a wide range of measures at its disposal to preserve its role on the global stage, and will certainly not hesitate to deploy them in the event of a direct threat to its core global interests. What will be the character of their response to the challenging behaviour of the BRICS is a question of time. The U.S. interests are being threatened and this is particularly evident in the case of their currency. Diversification of foreign exchange reserves is an ongoing process that will gain momentum in the face of current political tensions. This will particularly affect the countries from the so-called global south, to whom dependency on the USA is often seen as a threat. It is significant that by breaking their ties with the West they are most likely to find themselves in the orbit of Chinese influence. However, given the current level of foreign exchange reserves, it is unlikely that the U.S. dollar will lose its status as the world's most important reserve currency in the near future. The U.S. currency has unquestionable credibility and liquidity. The fundamentals of a strong dollar are the US economy and the size of its capital market, which is now the largest in the world. In addition, the country provides a stable and trustworthy legislative system that attracts investors from all over the globe. Although China is most likely to become the world's largest economy, its currency will probably not meet the conditions necessary to dethrone the U.S. dollar. Mainly because of political reasons and the lack of transparency within their country.

In essence, the present international position of the United States will most likely erode at some point and the country will lose its superpower status. This process is inseparable from the rise and fall of all empires in the history of mankind and will certainly not spare the United States of America. However, given the factors currently in place, its dominant role will remain for a long time and the only factor capable of sudden disruption could only be a direct military conflict with its biggest rival – The People's Republic of China. Of course, it would first have to result in a victory over the USA and its allies, but we are not going to receive a simple answer to this question in the foreseeable future.

References

Aksenov, P. (2015) "Ukraine crisis: Why a lack of parts has hamstrung Russia's military", *BBC*. Available at: https://www.bbc.com/news/world-europe-33822821 .

Al Jazeera (2023) 'Xi tells Putin of "changes not seen for 100 years"' (2023) Russia: Al Jazeera Newsfeed. Available at: https://www.youtube.com/watch?v=bEpTRr7QcWg&t=28s.

Arslanalp, S. & Simpson-Bell, C. (2021) "US Dollar Share of Global Foreign Exchange Reserves Drops to 25-Year Low", *International Monetary Fund Blog*. Available at: https://www. imf.org/en/Blogs/Articles/2021/05/05/blog-us-dollar-share-of-global-foreign-exchange-reserves-drops-to-25-year-low.

Bala, M. (2018) „Wizja Europy Środkowowschodniej w projektach geopolitycznych ideologa eurazjatyzmu, Aleksandra Dugina", *Kultury Wschodniosłowiańskie – Oblicza i Dialog*, vol. 4.

Brzezinski, Z. (1994) "The Premature Partnership", *Foreign Affairs*, vol. 73, no. 2.

CIA (2021) *Country Comparisons – Real GDP per capita, The World Factbook*. Available at: https://www.cia.gov/the-world-factbook/field/real-gdp-per-capita/country-comparison.

Cohen, P. (2022) "Putin says "unfriendly countries" must buy Russian oil and gas in rubles.", *New York Times*. Available at: https://www.nytimes.com/2022/03/23/business/putin-russian-oil-gas-rubles.html.

Culverwell, D. (2022) "Ukrainian secret service detains Motor Sich president over Russian collaboration accusations", *Bussines News Europe*. Available at: https://www. intellinews.com/ukrainian-secret-service-detains-motor-sich-president-over-russian-collaboration-accusations-260262/.

Dugin, A. (2009) „Rozpad Ukrainy jest nieunikniony". Russia: YouTube. Available at: https://www.youtube.com/watch?v=1PPuRlC9fok.

Egarov, I. & Patrushev, N. (2014) "Ukraine crisis – the view from Russia". Moscow: Rossiyskaya Gazeta. Available at: https://www.theguardian.com/world/2014/oct/24/ sp-ukraine-russia-cold-war.

Gale, A. (2022) "China's Military Is Catching Up to the U.S. Is It Ready for Battle?", *Wall Street Journal*. Available at: https://www.wsj.com/articles/china-military-us-taiwan-xi-11666268994.

Goodman, P. S. (2019) "The Dollar Is Still King. How (in the World) Did That Happen?", *New York Times*.

Greenwald, M. (2020) *The future of the United States Dollar: Weaponizing the US Financial System*. Available at: https://www. atlanticcouncil.org/wp-content/uploads/2020/12/ The-Future-of-the-US-Dollar-Report-web-v3.pdf.

Grenville, S. (2021) "Twenty years of BRICS", *The Interpreter*. Available at: https://www. lowyinstitute.org/the-interpreter/ twenty-years-brics.

Grigas, A. (2016) *Beyond Crimea: The New Russian Empire*.

Huntington, S. (2011) *The Clash of Civilizations and the Remaking of World Order*.

Mardell, J. (2022) "Can China Achieve Its BRICS Ambitions?", *The Diplomat*. Available at: https://thediplomat.com/2022/07/ can-china-achieve-its-brics-ambitions/.

Ministry of National Defence The People's Republic of China (2019) *China's National Defence in the New Era*. Available at: http://eng. mod.gov.cn/xb/Publications/WhitePapers/ 4846452.html.

Nair, C. (2022) "The Emerging World Order is Post-Western and Pre-Plural". Available at: https://www.institutmontaigne.org/en/ analysis/emerging-world-order-post-western-and-pre-plural.

O'Neill, J. (2021) "Twenty years on, the Brics have disappointed", *Financial Times*. Available at: https://www.ft.com/content/ 034ba0e7-7518-437e-854c-7c0dd5d74e34.

Saul, B. (2021) "Would a war over Taiwan be legal?", *The Interpreter*. Available at: https://www.lowyinstitute.org/the-interpreter/ would-war-over-taiwan-be-legal.

Siudak, M. (2014) „Rosja, Europa i świat w opinii Aleksandra Dugina". Available at: https://geopolityka.net/rosja-europa-i-swiat-w-opinii-aleksandra-dugina/.

CHAPTER 11

The war in Ukraine in the context of global and regional security within the historical perspective

Rafał Olender

Abstract

This chapter analyzes the ongoing conflict in Ukraine by placing it within a broader historical and geopolitical context. It examines how the war has reshaped global and regional security dynamics, particularly with respect to the balance of power in Europe. The chapter delves into the historical relationships between Ukraine, Russia, and the Western world, shedding light on past conflicts and tensions that have contributed to the current situation. Key themes include the role of NATO, the European Union, and other international organizations in responding to the conflict, as well as the shifting alliances and strategies of global powers. By providing a historical perspective, the chapter underscores how the war in Ukraine is not an isolated event but a continuation of longstanding geopolitical rivalries. The findings highlight the implications of the conflict for future European security architecture and global diplomatic relations.

Keywords: NATO, Russian invasion of Ukraine, NATO-Russia relations, NATO expansion, global security, European security

Introduction

Russia and Ukraine emerged as independent states after Soviet Union dissolution in 1991 and this political event may be considered as beginning of modern era for both. Modern Russia and Ukraine were shaped by series of political, economic and military events happening in 90s and early 00s. Those events finally led to conflict as both states took separate ways[19].

At 5.00 local time 24th of February 2022 Russian military forces grouped at territories of Belarus, Russian Federation, Donetsk People Republic, Luhansk People Republic and Russian occupied Crimea crossed Ukrainian borders beginning Russian invasion of Ukraine. Ukrainian border service stated that Russian Armed Forces begun attacks in Luhansk, Sumy, Kharkiv, Cherni-hiv and Zhytomyr regions – located in eastern and northern Ukraine (Yeung *et al.*, 2022). Russian forces were estimated few days before conflict started by United States officials at about 150,000 troops (New York Times, 2022).

Russian invasion was deemed as illegal and violating inter-national law. Actions took by Russian officials and military commanders directly violated United Nations Charter 2(4), which obliges members of UN to refrain from using "force against the territorial integrity or political independence of any state". Russian President Vladimir Putin stated that Russia used justi-fied force citing Article 51 of the United Nations Charter, which provides that "nothing in the present charter shall impair the inherent right of individual or collective self-defence if an armed attack occurs against a member of the United Nations". However it has been not proven that Ukraine committed or threatened to commit any military attacks against Russia or any other members of UN. Even though Russia could point Ukrainian hostile plans for Donetsk and Luhansk Peoples Republics Article 51 of UN Char-ter is void regarding those entities since they aren't UN member states. Vladimir Putin stated as well that Ukraine was committing genocide about separatist republics of Donetsk and Luhansk (Bellinger III, 2022). Mentioned regions broke away from Ukraine in 2014 and for almost 8 years weren't widely recognized by any state member of UN. Russian President recognized both entities as independent on 21st of February 2022, 3 days before Russian invasion on Ukraine (Deutsche Welle, 2022).

Before starting war Russian Federation officials in January of 2022 formulated their demands regarding not only Ukraine but aimed as well at revamping security structures in Europe. Their

---

19. Origins for current conflict in Ukraine can be traced up even 1000 years back to Kievan Rus' founding. Both states involved in war are linking their historical roots to that political entity and pointing at Rus' heritage as important to their culture.

demands were directed not only to Kyiv officials as well to U.S. and NATO counterparts. They have demanded guarantees on Ukrainian neutrality and barring Ukraine from being admitted to NATO. They have pointed as well at need of implementing autonomy for eastern Ukrainian regions according to 2015 Minsk agreements. Demands regarding NATO policies were formulated in form of proposals on security. Russians pointed that NATO forces deployed after 1997 in Central and Eastern Europe should be withdrawn. They wanted as well to implement new ban on deploying intermediate-range missiles in Europe. NATO and United States officials pointed that withdrawing forces to lines from 1997 is unrealistic, however they pointed that there is possible compromise on implementing new treaty on intermediate-range missiles (Maynes, 2022).

Russian invasion caused tremendous deaths on both sides. In the middle of November 2022 Russian loses been estimated by US officials at between 70,000 to 80,000 Russians killed or wounded. Chairman of the Joint Chiefs of Staff, Gen. Mark Milley pointed that Russian causalities may be higher than 100,000 in dead and wounded combined. Milley assessed Ukrainian causalities as comparable to Russian (Matthews, 2022). Russian Ministry of Defence however stated in September of 2022 that they have lost 5,937 troops killed (Tlis, 2002).

War initiated the biggest refugee crisis in Europe since World War II with 7,996,573 Ukrainians recorded as refugees and 4,952,938 registered for Temporary Protection or similar national protection schemes in Europe as for 24th of January 2023 according to United Nations High Commissioner for Refugees (UNHCR, 2023). Russian invasion caused as well civilian causalities with at least 6,919 killed and 11,075 injured according to Office of the High Commissioner for Human Rights of United Nations as for period from 24th February 2022 to 2nd January 2023 (OHCHR, 2023). Moreover, it has been proven that Russian forces conducted war crimes and crimes against humanity with the most famous Bucha massacre happening in March 2022 with targeted killing civilians tolled over 400 dead (Al-Hlou *et al.*, 2022).

Russian invasion on Ukraine had also high economic impact on both Russian and Ukrainian economies. Global economy was affected as well, especially when comes to energy sources prices and availability. As for October of 2022 above 700,000 Russian citizens left Russia to avoid being mobilised and sent to war in Ukraine (Novaya Gazeta Europe, 2022). Moreover, at the end of 2022 at least additional 300,000 men were drafted into Russian military forces Estimates in spring of 2022 were predicting recession in Russia – loss of GDP was ranging between 8–10%. Those estimates were however adjusted with GDP loss between 3-4% (Prokopenko, 2022). Ukrainian GDP loss is estimated to be around 19,1% in the first quarter of 2022 and by 37,2% in the second quarter. Overall, from January to September of 2022 Ukrainian GDP fell by around 30%. The National Bank of Ukraine forecasted that GDP decline will be at 37,5% in the fourth quarter of 2022 (Matuszczak, 2022).

Many developing nations are as reliant on Russian and Ukrainian wheat imports. Chief Economist of the Food and Agriculture Organization of the United Nations (FAO) pointed that around 1,72 billion people may have serious problems with having access to food in 2022 (Whiting, 2022). War in Ukraine affected as well global energy crisis. At the end of 2022 barrel of oil was worth almost 140$, which was close to all-time record. Economic sanctions put on Russia are resifting global energy supply chains and sources (Gaffen, 2022).

Russian incursion into Ukraine was met with international reactions, both from countries and international organisations. The United Nations General Assembly adopted on 2nd of March 2022 resolution deploring Russian aggression on Ukraine with 141 votes in favour, 5 against and 35 abstentions (UNRIC, 2022). Both NATO (NATO, 2022) and European Union (European Council, 2022) are condemning Russian actions in Ukraine. Moreover, many countries implemented economic sanctions against Russia (Brookings, 2022).

As shown above, the chapter contains research methods from political science including historical, systemic and institutional analysis as well as comparative studies, illustrated with empirical facts and examples.

Concerning the important but changing role of NATO as regional security factor in Eastern and Central Europe, within the historical perspective allow to deal with a question about finding out why Russia is perceiving NATO expansion eastwards as a threat to state existence. Crucial for the answer is to provide brief description of diplomatic games between Russian and NATO officials between implementation Partnership for Peace Agenda and NATO expansion to first former Warsaw Pact states;

Finally, it is fundamental to assess the NATO role in the war in Ukraine as well as Russian reactions on it. Pointing at NATO reactions on Russian war preparations from autumn 2021 to winter 2022 and situation after invasion has begun. This contains as well strategic communication between NATO, its members, Russia, Ukraine and other countries. It's worth to mention as well that war in Ukraine swayed Swedish and Finnish societies and politicians when comes to NATO membership. This issue includes as well providing Western equipment deliveries and aid to Ukraine. It's also very important to show NATO shifting its strategic policies from regional to global in this case.

When discussing the abovementioned questioning topics, the perspective of the transformation of the level and dimension of the conflicts caused by Russia (from local – regional level, as in Georgia to wider – regional – European as in Ukraine) must be of the core of the consideration. Their characteristics translate into perception of the meaning of mainly regional but also global security and stability, including military and non-military aspects of it, such as political and economic in particular; any of these destabilisations can have a negative impact on worldwide security.

Political and historical background for war in Ukraine

Process of USSR dissolution began with Mikhail Gorbachev being elected by Politburo General Secretary of the Communist Party of the Soviet Union on 11th of March 1985. During election at age of 54 he was the youngest member of the Politburo. Gorbachev was convinced that country needs deep reforms and those cannot be achieved by applying proved Soviet-style solutions. During his first year of reign General Secretary was trying to learn actual scale of issues troubling USSR and building his political base (Kort, 2008, p. 220). Reforms pushed by Gorbachev were labelled as *perestroika* (restructuring). It was a program of political and economic reforms aimed at improving dynamic of Soviet economy (Gorokhovska, 2021, p. 11). *Perestroika* included few new policies, with some expanding beyond pure economic reform like policies of glasnost, *democratizatsia* and *novoe myshlenia*. Glasnost (openness) was referring to reducing of censorship, providing freer circulation of information and creating environment for public debates. The main goal of Gorbachev was reducing of paranoid secrecy and ending of cover-ups happening all the time in Soviet Union. *Democratizatsia* (democratisation) was aimed at expanding political spectrum represented during party and state elections. Goal was meant to be achieved by allowing more potential candidates during elections. Democratisation however wasn't about evolving Soviet political system into Western style democracy. *Novoe myshlenie* (new thinking) was set of foreign policy ideas, especially when comes to establishing and improving peaceful relations with Western countries (Kort, 2008, p. 222-224).

Then a catastrophic event on a scale not known to Soviet history happened. On 26th of April 1986 explosion destroyed reactor of Chernobyl Nuclear Power Plant in Ukraine. Blast sent huge amounts of radioactive elements and particles into atmosphere and affected thousands of Soviet citizens from many countries (e. g. from Poland, Finland, Sweden, Germany, Czech Republic). Big areas of Ukrainian Soviet Socialist Republic and Byelorussian Soviet Socialist Republic were contaminated. Accident was caused by flawed reactor design, inadequate safety measures and paranoid secrecy. Contrary to policy of glasnost authorities tried to limit circulation of information. First rumours about accident came from Soviet citizens listening to Western radio. State run media reported the accident for the first time on 28th of April (Suny, 2006, p. 574-575).

Policies pushed by Gorbachev and Politburo resulted in growing national consciousness amongst non-Russian minority groups. Some minorities like inhabiting Caucasus Armenians and Azerbaijanis clashed with each other. Baltic nations started demanding in 1987 autonomy or even independence (Kort, 2008, p. 225-226). Internal issues forced Soviet authorities to shift their foreign policy goals. It resulted in starting withdrawal troops from Afghanistan which was finished at 15th of February 1989. Loosening Soviet grip on Warsaw Pact countries resulted in falling communist regimes in Central and Eastern Europe. The transition from a bipolar to a unipolar world, with the United States as the dominant power, had a significant influence on security architecture in the region where the Soviet Union collapsed, as well as on global security considerations. In the autumn of 1989 Berlin Wall fell providing World with one of the most important events marking end of the Cold War. Economy policies included in *perestroika* failed to improve Soviet economy. Initially in years 1985–1987 Gorbachev tried only to improve central planned economy without transforming it into market based one. The most famous economic error of early Gorbachev era was adopting anti-alcohol program which was based on idea of reducing production of alcohol at state owned distilleries. State monopoly provided in this case significant budget revenues. Soviet citizens filled the gap in this case by producing their own alcohol which deepened loss of state incomes (Kuznetsov *et al.*, 2012, pp. 164–169). Goals for economic acceleration were about to be achieved by decentralising state-run economy mostly with recognising forms of non-state enterprises. In November of 1986 Soviet Union legalised family-based and individual work like private tuition, taxi services or car repairs. However, the State Planning Committee (Gosplan) and ministries were still able to keep their power over newly created enterprises. Those entities were charging more than state run subjects while providing services on the same quality levels. Not implementing price liberalisation and fair competition doomed decentralisation concept. In 1990 Soviet social scientists opted mostly for market economy instead on central planned economy reforms based on decentralisation (Suny, 2006, p. 333-335).

Soviet Union survived falling of communist regimes in Central and Eastern Europe. Year 1990 wasn't easy though. Freshly elected Chairman of the Presidium of the Supreme Soviet of the Russian SFSR Boris Yeltsin started contesting Party and Gorbachev authorities. General Secretary of the Communist Party mistakenly believed in existing entity called *Soviet nation* ignoring raising nationalistic sympathies in Soviet republics. Politburo proceeded with project of the New Union Treaty which was about to save USSR as a state. At 11th of March 1990 Lithuania declared as independent state and announced that USSR constitution is invalid on its territory. Gorbachev who was elected as first President of the USSR called Lithuanian action as illegitimated and called declaration of independence as illegal. Other republic followed Lithuania in next months (Puchenkov, 2020). Issues with

Lithuania weren't solved through entire 1990. Soviet military was deployed on 11th of January in Vilnius. Troops were ordered to take control of key sites, which resulted assault on TV broadcast tower and TV station 2 days later. Lithuanian civilians gathered to stop Soviet military equipped with tanks. Soldiers drove into crowd and started shooting people resulting in 14 civilians being killed and around 700 wounded (Wesolowsky, 2021).

New Union Treaty draft was published in November of 1990. Document proposed reorganising USSR into federal state with ceding more power to federal republics (Suny, 2006, p. 513-514). On 17th of March 1991 referendum was held in the first time in Soviet history. Voters were asked question "do you consider necessary the preservation of the Union of Soviet Socialist Republics as a renewed federation of equal sovereign republics in which the rights and freedom of an individual of any ethnicity will be fully guaranteed?". 76,4% voters answered yes to this question. Referendum was boycotted by 6 of 15 republics[20]. New Union Treaty was proceeded by remaining republics in "9+1" formula (Puchenkov, 2020). Document was about to be signed on the 20th of August 1991. Meanwhile Mikhail Gorbachev was spending his holidays in his home at the Crimean coast. President of the USSR planned returning to Moscow day before signing New Union Treaty. However, him and his family and colleagues were put under house arrest at the 18th. In the morning of 19th state of emergency was declared in Moscow. State Committee for the State of Emergency was created. The main role in attempted power takeover took Soviet vice-president Gennady Yanaev[21]. Forces opposing Gorbachev tried arresting Yeltsin but failed achieving their goal. Chairman of the Presidium of the Supreme Soviet of the Russian SFSR resisted putsch in the Russian White House being surrounded by civilians supporting him. Some military forces backed up Yeltsin against plotters. Coup failed because of lacking civilian support. Attempted takeover was another blow to Gorbachev's popularity. In result of August events Lithuania, Latvia and Estonia declared independence[2]. Those declarations were recognised by Soviet Union on 6th of September. Armenia soon followed, meanwhile Georgia and Moldova were already

20. Baltic republics, Armenia, Georgia and Moldova.

21. He was assisted by Prime Minister, minister of Internal Affairs, chief of the KGB, minister of the Defence Council and leader of the Peasant's Union. ZMIENIĆ NUMERACJĘ NA 2 I 3

considering themselves as independent states[3] (Kuznetsov *et al.*, 2012, pp. 170–172).

Yeltsin being the main winner of August coup attempt stopped supporting New Union Treaty. Gorbachev tried saving project by switching from federation into loose confederation. Leaders of the three Slavic republics – Yeltsin, L. Kravchuk of Ukraine and S. Shushkevich of Belarus signed on 8th of December 1991 that USSR ceased to exist and they are forming Commonwealth of Independent States. Gorbachev on 25th addressed Soviet citizens in a televised broadcast stating that USSR is coming to an end and he is resigning as President of the USS (Suny, 2006, p. 349).

Ukraine organised independence referendum and first presidential elections on 1st of December 1991. Over 90% of voters supported Ukrainian independence and Kravchuk won elections with majority of 62% of votes. Independence was recognised by Poland and Hungary seeking Russia counterweight in the east. Canada with significant Ukrainian community followed. United States however was seeking preserving USSR worrying about Eurasian stability. Finally, Washington recognised Ukrainian independence at 25th. Boris Yeltsin seeing high support for independence recognised Ukraine. However, many Russians couldn't believe "losing" Ukraine. Around 11 million Russians were cut off in the Ukraine and issues about status of Crimean Peninsula, transferred in 1954 from Russia to Ukraine were voiced. Moreover, Russia great power status without Ukraine were put into danger and Russian attitudes to Ukrainians from "elder brother" positions were quite frequent in society (Subtelny, 2009, p. 583-585).

After Soviet Union dissolution Ukraine inherited third largest nuclear arsenal. Some politicians in Washington were keen on allowing Ukraine being nuclear state. However, US Secretary of State James Baker had vision on Russia being only nuclear state after USSR breakup. The main goal was not allowing for successor states becoming "Yugoslavia with nukes". The Joint Strategic Command was created in the end of December 1991 under the auspices of Commonwealth of Independent States. However, issues with Ukrainian nuclear stockpile arose quickly and those led to President of Ukraine taking administrative control over strategic armaments. Ukrainian parliament voted for resolution opting for denuclearisation in return for security guarantees. In the middle of 1992 Ukrainian Ministry of Foreign Affairs insisted to US that Russia should be involved in guaranteeing security of Ukraine. However Ukrainian-Russian relations worsened because of Russian support of Crimean separatism and division of the Soviet Black Sea Fleet. Russian support for separatists during conflict in Transnistria and resolution of Russian parliament voted on the 12th of May 1992 declaring Soviet decision of ceding Crimea to Ukraine illegal provided further deterioration of bilateral relations (Budjeryn, 2014).

In 1994 Ukraine after long negotiations with US and Russia decided to join NPT as non-nuclear state. This had a significant impact on global security since the decision of reducing one nuclear state has been taken; it opted to erase all of its nuclear capability, and it definitely had an impact on regional security by removing Ukraine off the list of nuclear holding countries. Ukrainian policy-makers were assured by United States that their state won't have to deal with potential Russian threat alone. Security guarantees were stated in a Memorandum on security assurances in connection with Ukraine's accession to the Treaty on the Non-Proliferation of nuclear weapons which was signed on 5th of December 1994 in Budapest. Multilateral document was signed by Ukraine on the one side and the Russian Federation, United Kingdom of Great Britain and Northern Ireland and United States of America on the other side (Umland *et. al.*, 2021).

Both Russia and Ukraine were negotiating in 90s status of Black Sea Fleet, specially regarding the economic implications of security. Talks were finalised in May 1997 with Ukrainian and Russian PMs Pavlo Lazernko and Victor Chernomyrdin signing the Black Sea Fleet Agreement for 20 years. Deal divided former Soviet Black Sea Fleet and allowed Russia for being present on Ukrainian territory for price of 98 million USD annually. Those payment were however used to cover Ukrainian 3 billion gas debt to Russia. The key points of agreement were: splitting Black Sea Fleet by 50% with Russia buying some of the most modern ships with cash payments, Russian leasing the ports around and in Sevastopol for 20 years, setting up Crimea and city of Sevastopol territorially a sovereign part of Ukrainian state. Besides the annual payment Russia credited Ukraine with 526 million USD for using part of Ukrainian fleet and with 200 million USD for transferring Ukrainian nuclear stockpile to Russia. It also worth mentioning that Ukrainian Constitution isn't allowing those kinds of agreement to be valid for more than 5-7 years and prohibiting presence of foreign troop on state territory. After Orange Revolution in 2004 relations between countries cooled off and some Ukrainian officials stated that Russia should be paying at least 1,8 billion dollars annually for using Sevastopol which is one of the biggest Russian naval bases (Volten *et. al.,* 2007, pp.129–130). Agreement was renewed in 2010 with date of expiration in 2042. Russia was allowed to station some forces at military bases located in Crimea[22]. Russian military forces were required to respect sovereignty of Ukraine, honouring Ukrainian law and precluding interference within internal affairs of Ukraine (Kimball, 2014).

Russian attempts to rebuild empire and political position of Ukraine

It might be said, that twenty-first century is designed by Russian aspirations to reconstruct the empire. They include numerous military and non-military components such as economic and political aspects. The changing position of Ukraine in the area as an unstable country has an impact on both regional and global security.

On 31th of December 1999 Boris Yeltsin addressed a televised speech to Russian nation. Yeltsin announced resignation from office and appointed Prime Minister Vladimir Putin as his successor. It worth mentioning that Putin was appointed as chief of government only few months before Yeltsin speech. However, Putin wasn't a political newcomer. He was former lieutenant of KGB and served as advisor to St. Petersburg mayor Anatoly Sobchak in 90s. In 1998 he was appointed by Yeltsin administration as head of the Federal Security Service (FSB), which is the successor of Soviet KGB (Ziegler, 2009, p. 182). Putin secured his position as President of Russian Federation by winning elections on 26th of Marth 2002 with 52.94 per cent of the vote. Communist candidate Gennady Zyuganov was second with 29.21 per cent of casted votes (White *et al.,* 2008).

Putin came into power during turbulent times. Russian economy suffered major blow in 1998. In late 90s state was struggling

---

22. Up to 25,000 troops, 132 armoured combat vehicles and 24 pieces of artillery.

with serious debt and was resulted with emitting billions of rubles worth short-term bonds. Economic situation forced Russian government to seek 22 billion USD load from the International Monetary Fund. In result of growing debt Russian government defaulted on its bonds thus declaring Russia bankrupt on 17th of August 1998. Russian ruble collapsed which resulted with millions of Russians losing their savings (Ziegler, 2009, p. 182).

Political instability was also deepened by violence from Caucasus spreading into Russia. In December 1994 Russian military war with Chechnya. Conflict ended up with signing in August of 1996 Khasavyurt agreement where republic was granted with a five-year interim period of self-rule. Chechnya drifted in the late 90s into instability with Muslim radicals gaining more power. Harsh elements of Sharia law were imposed in republic. In the summer of 1999 Chechen militias started incusing into Russian Dagestan (Sakwa, 2020). Between 4th and 16th of September 1999 four apartment building in Moscow, Buinaksk and Volgodonsk were blown. Over 300 people were killed. In city of Ryazan on 22th of September one of the flat apartment owners noticed white Lada parked in the front of building. Car had licence plates covered with paper imitating regional code for Ryazan. The owners daughter noticed man emerging from flat basement, checking his watch and then joining other two waiting in a car. Owner called for the police. Bomb was found and disarmed by local bomb squad. Explosives were seized later by the FSB. Agents however forgot to take detonator which was secured by local police and identified as military grade. Someone made a call from Ryazan to Moscow from public telephone. Operator was able to catch fragment of the conversation. Caller indicated that they cannot get out of city undetected. Voice on the other side advised caller to split up and go back on your way out. Number was later traced as belonging to FSB. 2 days later director of FSB Nikolai Patrushev after having meeting at Kremlin announced that security forces conducted successful training exercise in Ryazan. However, Chechens were blamed for conducting those acts of terrorism. Bombings provided support for Putin as Prime Minister and spurred social support for military intervention in Chechnya (Satter, 2016, p. 15-22). Former Russian spy Alexander Litvinienko residing in the United Kingdom also pointed ins his book 'Blowing up Russia: Terror from Within' that Russian FSB was responsible for blowing up residential buildings in 1999. Litvinenko was poisoned using polonium-210 and died at 23th or November 2006, three weeks after having tea with former Russian agents Andrei Lugovoi and Dmitri Kovtun in London. Russian authorities denied being involved in Litvinenko poisoning (BBC, 2016).

First Putin term was marked by few violent events. On 12th of August 2000 defective torpedo on the board of Kursk nuclear submarine exploded sinking the boat in the Barents Sea. British and Norwegians offered assistance in recovering submarine and saving underwater trapped sailors. Russian authorities rejected offer which ended up with losing all 118 crew members. On 23th of October 2002 Chechen militants seized above 850 hostages at a theatre in Moscow. Russian special forces used gas to over-power terrorists. In result at least 129 hostages lost their lives. On 1st of September 2004 terrorist attack happened in the town of Belsan in Northern Ossetia. Chechen militants took 1100 chil-dren, teachers and parents' hostage. After three days of siege and unsuccessful negotiations bomb exploded inside the building. Military and polices forces begun assault which resulted in chaotic fire exchange. At least 330 hostages, mostly children were killed. Putin denied state responsibility for poor responding at both act of terrorism. He also used both cases as excuse to consolidate his power (Ziegler, 2009, p. 185–189).

Putin secured his 2nd term winning elections held at 14th of March 2004. He won by getting 71.31 per cent of votes. Russian constitution however barred him from running for his 3rd term. He pointed at his protégée Dmitri Medvedev becoming next Pres-ident of Russia. Medvedev secured easy win at elections held at 2nd of March 2008 getting 70.28 per cent of votes. After elections Putin was nominated at 8th of May 2008 as next Russian Prime Minister (White *et. al.*, 2008).

In November of 2003 Rose Revolution happened in Georgia. Social unrest caused by electoral frauds, corruption and poor eco-nomic performance ended up with President of Georgia Eduard Shevardnadze resigning. Elections held in January of 2004 were won by pro-Western Rose Revolution leader Mikheil Saakashvili. One of the goals of new President was restoring Georgian territo-rial integrity with reintegrating two separatist states – Abkhazia and South Ossetia. Georgian foreign policy was also redirected. Relations with US, EU and NATO were deepened. Goals for

European integration and Georgian admission to NATO were set. Foreign policy shifting resulted in worsening relations with Russia and igniting conflicts with both separatist states (Max Planck Institute, 2009).

On 7th of August 2008 Georgian forces shelled South Ossetian capital of Tskhinvali. In response amassed near Georgian borders Russian forces responded with full scale invasion on 8th of August. War lasted 5 days and ended up with Russian victory. During conflict 170 servicemen 14 policemen, and 228 civilians from Georgia was killed and 1747 wounded. 67 Russian servicemen were killed and 283 were wounded. 365 South Ossetian servicemen and civilians were killed. Cease fire was signed by Mikheil Saakashvili on 15th of August. His Russian counterpart did the same day later. On 22nd of August Russia partially withdrew troops from Georgia meanwhile maintaining forces in both Abkhazia and South Ossetia. 4 days later Russia recognised independence of both separatist states. Decision was condemned by both US and EU. Study conducted by EU established mission found that conflict started because of on-going historical tensions and overreaction provided by both Russia and Georgia. Report pointed that Georgian attack on Tskhinvali was the starting point of conflict. However, it was pointed as well that escalation was the result of years of provocations, incidents and increasing tensions (CNN Editorial Research, 2023).

Ukrainian presidential elections of 2004 begun with the first round happening in October and continued with second round on 21th of November. Official results ended up with pro-Russian candidate and protégée of current president Leonid Kuchma Viktor Yanukovych winning against Western-oriented Viktor Yuschenko with 52 per cent of the vote. Yanukovych was inaugurated as Ukrainian president on 23th of January 2005. During those elections a clear divide between voters from Eastern regions of Ukraine sympathising with Russia bcaked Yanukovych and those from Western regions backing Yuschenko was noticed (White et. al., 2009). The protests begun at November of 2004 after independent election monitors pointing at mass election frauds and voter tampering. Ukrainian state agency – Central Election Commission reported voter turnout for eastern regions of Ukraine being similar to national average at 78-80 per cent. Commission after 4 hours of silence increased turnout in those regions greatly – for example at Yanukovych home base Donetsk region numbers went from 78 to 96,2 per cent overnight with support for Russian-leaning candidate at 97 per cent. At neighbouring Luhansk region numbers rose from 80 to 89,5 per cent during night with 92 per cent Yanukovych support. It's estimated that during night around 1.2 million new voters were virtually added with 90 per cent of them supporting Kuchma protégée. Those numbers provided enough for Yanukovych to secure winning by 800.000 vote margin (Karatnycky, 2005). However, election fraud was just the last straw. Ukrainian society was tired of Kuchma reign and poor economic performance. Moreover, Yushchenko was subject of constant harassment at state-controlled media. He was almost killed on 6th of September 2004 by mysterious illness which left permanent scars on his face. It was proven later that he was suffering from targeted dioxin poisoning (Bivings, 2022). Mass protests ended up with sieging few cabinets of ministers, office of the presidential administration and Kuchma residence at 27th of November. 6 days later Ukrainian Supreme Court annulled results of the second round and called for fresh elections. To avoid further unrest Speaker of Parliament Volodymyr Lytvyn backed by European Union's Foreign Affairs Commissioner Javier Solana, Polish President Aleksander Kwasniewski and Lithuanian President Valdas Adamkus who were visiting Kyiv during late stage of protests brokered a deal between both parties (Karatnycky, 2005).

The key point of agreement was amending Ukrainian Constitution to reduce powers of president. Ukraine was about to become parliamentary-presidential republic with president being responsible for conducting foreign policy, security and national defence with having veto power over the parliament. Those changes were about to enter into force in 2006. Yushchenko accepted agreement believing that one year is enough to deal with post-Kuchma legacies. Fresh elections happened on 26th of December with Yushchenko securing 52 per cent win over Yanukovych. Winning margin was around 2.2 million votes out of 28 million cast. Yushchenko won in 17 regions of western, central and north-eastern Ukraine and Yanukovych secured winning in 10 southern and eastern regions. Yushchenko made a speech next day and addressed nation saying: 'We are free. The old era is over. We are a new country now'(Karatnycky, 2005).

The next Ukrainian presidential elections were held at the beginning of 2010. First round took place on 17th of January with Viktor Yanukovych securing 35.32 per cent of per cent of the vote. His main opponent Yulia Tymoshenko got second place with 25.05 per cent of voters' support. In second round which took place on 7th of February Yanukovych won with 48.95 per cent of the votes against Tymoshenko's 45.47 per cent. Some 4.38 per cent of votes were casted "against all candidates". Turnout was 68.81 per cent with total 25,493,529 ballots filled. Around 1.2 of votes were declared invalid. OSCEs The Office for Democratic Institutions and Human Rights reported that elections were conducted in orderly and fair manner with only minor incidents happening. International Election Observation Mission visited 220 polling stations during elections and found only 8 polling stations during first round and 13 stations during second turn showing some transgressions (OSCE, 2010).

Yanukovych victory can be attributed to several factors. Ukrainian economy was struggling with outcomes of global economic crisis started in 2008-2009[23]. Ukrainian economy recovered in 2010 with 4.9 per cent GDP growth at first quarter. Recovery wasn't however caused by internal factors but by increasing demand for Ukrainian export commodities, mostly steel. Addressing those issues Yanukovych approached elections with bold economic postulates. His economic agenda called 'Ukraine is for the people' was however more populist than substantive. Yanukovych promised transforming Ukrainian economy, easing bureaucratic barriers for enterprises, implementing rural recovery program, increasing social benefits and implementing tax holidays for small enterprise (Kholod, 2012). Future Ukrainian President gained as well support of the wealthiest Ukrainian oligarch Rinat Akhmetov and natural-gas trader Dmytro Firtash. Both poured millions into his campaign. Yanukovych led Party of Regions was also positioning themselves as representation of Russian speaking voters from Eastern Ukraine. Main opponents from Orange Revolution camp were divided, politically ineffective and struggling with corruption accusations (Kudelia, 2014).

Yanukovych had also strong parliamentary background with 235 members of coalition called 'Reforms and Order'. On 11th

---

23. Ukraine's GDP fell in 2009 by 15 per cent. In January of 2009 compared to the same month of previous year national manufacturing output decreased by 42 per cent while construction fell by 58 per cent.

of March 2010, he appointed Mykola Azarov as Prime Minister. New government implemented during first 2 years few crucial economic reforms including tax and pension reforms. New social programs and benefits were also implemented. Yanukovych brokered new gas deal with Russia aimed to lower prices in return for extending leasing Black Sea fleet in Sevastopol up to 2042. Kharkiv Accords addressing those were signed on 21th of April 2010 (Kholod, 2012). Economic reforms were too shallow and couldn't transform into higher approval ratings for Yanukovych and at the end of 2011 only 26 per cent of Ukrainians supported him. Group of Yanukovych advisors led by Serhiy Liovochkin urged for signing EU Association Agreement since ideas of European integration were popular in Ukrainian society and Ukraine was under Western pressure when comes to democratic standards (Kudelia, 2014). On 30th of March 2012 Ukraine and EU initialled the Association Agreement aiming at strengthening relations and cooperation between parties. Chapter on Deep and Comprehensive Free Trade Area was initialled on 19th of July 2012. Deal was approved by the EU Council and passed for EU members states for ratification. Document was published on 9th of August at Ukrainian government website (Ukraine Government, 2017). The whole concept of aligning with EU backfired at Yanukovych and Ukrainian government. One of the key EU demands was releasing former Prime Minister Yulia Tymoshenko from prison and Yanukovych wasn't craving to fulfil those. In addition, talk with EU spurred Russian reaction. Russian officials threatened to end privileged treatment of Ukrainian companies and actually limited import from Ukraine by imposing tariffs. Yanukovych finally on 21st of November 2013 decided to suspend talks with EU (Kudelia, 2014).

Decision caused wave of protests which initially weren't treated by government as a threat. Yanukovych reacted with some minor repressions, promised conciliation and staged some counter demonstrations as well. However, after 9 days authorities decided to use violent force against protesting crowd. This shift was caused mostly by hardliners in government marginalising peace-making groups. In the mid of December 2013 government decided to use riot police to clear main square of Kyiv where protested set up their main camp (Kudelia, 2014). On 28th of January Azarov resigned and voiced his concerns about Ukrainian unity and integrity (Interfax, 2014). Violence raised in January and February 2014 with around 90 people being killed in Kyiv between 18th and 21st of February according to authorities. On 22nd of February Yanukovich was deposed and left Kyiv. Vladimir Putin denounced decision as coup d'état and stated that Russia will use any necessary means in response. On 24th Yanukovich fled to Russia (Houeix, 2022).

Yanukovich deposing caused pro-Russian unrest, mostly in eastern regions and Crimea. Those actions were supported and initiated by Russia. Both Russian and Ukrainian military forces went on alert on 20th of February during Maidan protests escalation. Russian army started their operations at Crimean Peninsula on 22nd and 23rd of February with battalions of Spetsnaz and airborne forces of VDV being deployed from their bases. Russia also airlifted troops to cut off Crimea from mainland Ukraine. On 24nd city council in Sevastopol elected Russian citizen as mayor. Russian forces also been deployed near city square violating agreements with Ukraine. Day later 200 Russian special forces been deployed from landing ship in Sevastopol. On 27th around 50 Russian special forces pretending to be local militia stormed Crimean Parliament and raised Russian flag over the building. The same day soldiers without markings surrounded Ukrainian Belbek Air Base. Day later Russian military took Simferopol airport allowing VDV airlift there. On 1st and 2nd of March more troops were disembarked from landing ships. Ukrainian fleet was blocked at port with their commander Denis Berezovsky defecting to Russia. Russian forces besieged Ukrainian bases on peninsula hoping for more defections. With those not happening both sides agreed not to rely on violence. Ukrainian army lost control over units trapped in Crimea. Communication at some area was as well jammed by Russians. The Crimean Parliament declared referendum regarding independence for 25th or May 2014. Voting was however moved twice – initially to 30th or March and then finally to 6th of March (Kofman *et. al.*, 2017). Officially referendum ended up with 96.77 per cent of 1.274.096 voters favouring independence. Crimean authorities asked to be admitted to Russian Federation which happened with signing accession treaty and incorporation Crimea by Russia on 21st of March 2014 (Marxsen, 2014). By 26th of March process of annexation was complete. Afterwards Russia returned seized military hardware to Ukraine.

From 18,000 of trapped Ukrainian soldiers only around 6,500 chose to leave for Ukraine (Kofman *et. al.,* 2017).

Ukraine was facing Russian backed protest in Eastern part of country as well. Traces are pointing that some Russian citizens been paid for crossing the border and participating in turmoil. There are also cases of Russians coming on their own to help the cause. However, most of protestors were Russian speaking Ukrainians, supporting Yanukovych and his party. On 1st of March regional administration building in Kharkiv were seized by protesters. Similar incident happened 8 days later in Luhansk where protesters demanded for referendum regarding annexation entire Luhansk Oblast to Russia. By the 10th of March Ukrainian police secured every captured administration building and quelled protests. Central government replaced governors appointing oligarchs to vacated posts. Unrest seemed to be under Kyiv control until Russian GRU operative Igor Strelkov and his comrade Igor Bezler stormed building of local administration in Donetsk and proclaimed its territories belonging to newly proclaimed Donetsk Republic on 7th of April. From 6th to 23rd of April separatists captured few administration buildings in key eastern cities. Ukrainian Interior Ministry deployed rapid-response forces at Luhansk on 11th of April and took city halls in Slovyansk, Kramatorsk, and Krasny Liman day later. Separatists however were able to seize around 300 assault rifles and 400 handguns at Donetsk security service building and started armed rebellion against government in Kiev. Ukrainian forces tried to recapture rebelling cities from 15th to 23rd of April but were halted in most cases at separatist outposts at outskirts. At that time Ukrainian army had around 6,000 combat ready troops and their commanders were mostly Russian speaking which resulted with them avoiding fighting with Russian speaking civilians in urbanised areas. Most of local police members defected to separatists or were intimidated. By August around 5,000 policemen and 3,000 servicemen defected from governmental forces (Kofman *et. al.,* 2017). On 11th of May referendums were held in Donetsk and Luhansk with crushing support for independence (Houeix, 2022).

Voting out Yanukovych from his office resulted in Ukrainian Parliament calling on 22nd of February 2014 for new Presidential elections scheduled for 25th of May. Those happened in tense political situation – Crimea was already lost, both Donetsk and Luhansk declared independence, separatists were resisting and military wasn't gaining any ground. There was also risk of elections being disrupted by on-going unrest. Petro Poroshenko won in the first round with 54.70 per cent of casted votes. Yulia Tymoshenko was second with only 12.82 per cent support (OSCE, 2014). On 6h of June French president François Hollande, German chancellor Angela Merkel, Russian president Vladimir Putin and Petro Poroshenko met in France's Normandy during seventieth anniversary D-Day. Sides agreed on forming *Normandy format* which included Russia, Ukraine, Germany and France. Group was aimed at resolving conflict in Ukraine. Poroshenko announced unilateral ceasefire on June 20 as well, which however failed at stopping hostilities (Houeix, 2022). From June up to the end of August Russia delivered mechanized equipment, tanks, advanced munitions and medium range air defence systems to separatist through the border. Russian aid resulted in Ukrainian Air Force losing tactical attack and transport planes (Kofman *et. al.,* 2017). On 17th of July Russian separatists armed with Russian provided BUK-M1 SAM system downed Malaysia Airlines flight MH17 near Donetsk killing all 298 passengers (including 80 children) and crew members (Miller, 2016).

Separatists` situation was dire in August. Ukrainian forces started regaining control over both breakaway republic territories. On 24th of August Russian forces switched to conventional operations and invaded Ukrainian territory with around 4,000 troops and defeated Ukrainian forces at Ilovaisk (Kofman *et. al.,* 2017).

On 5th of September both sides of conflict signed in Minsk agreement called 'Minsk protocol' or 'Minsk 1' regarding ending hostilities and solving both republics status. Agreement failed due to increasing hostilities. On 2nd of November both Donetsk and Luhansk held Presidential elections. Alexander Zakhartchenko was elected in Donetsk and Igor Plotniski won in Luhansk. Ukraine denounced those as violation of Minsk agreement. On 23rd of December Ukrainian parliament voted in favour of joining NATO. On 13th of January 2015 Russia begun 2nd offensive which resulted with Ukraine losing battle of Debaltseve. Ukrainians were forced to sign another Minsk agreement. 'Minsk 2' was highly favourable for Moscow and separatists. Treaty forced both sides to withdraw heavy weaponry, promised restoration of Ukraine's territorial integrity and withdrawing foreign troops. Kyiv was forced to recognise autonomy of both republics (Houeix, 2022).

According to Office of the United Nations High Commissioner for Human Rights 108 protestors and other individuals and 13 law enforcement officers were killed during Maidan protests in Kyiv and other cities from November 2013 to February 2014. Pro-Russian protests from 26th of February to 31th of August resulted with around 60 civilians being killed. Armed conflict from mid-April 2014 and 31th of May 2016 resulted in at least 9,404 people being killed, including around 2,000 civilians (OHCHR, 2016).

Conflict stalled from 2015 to 2018 with only minor skirmishes happening. On 25th of November 2018 Russian forces seized 3 Ukrainian ships trying to pass under newly built Crimean bridge and arrested 24 crew members. In response Petro Poroshenko enabled martial law for 30 days in Ukraine's Russian-speaking regions (Houeix, 2022). Next Ukrainian Presidential elections were held on 31st of March. First round ended up with Volodymyr Zelensky securing 30.24 per cent of votes and Poroshenko ending up with 15.95 per cent. In second round held on 21st of April Zelensky won by securing 73.22 per cent of votes against Poroshenko's 24.45 per cent (OSCE, 2019). Zelensky was a former actor and comedian who went to elections with campaign against corruption and been calling for détente with Moscow. French President Emmanuel Macron tried to broker agreement between sides. Russia released detained sailors on 7th of September and both sides met in Minsk under the aegis of the Organisation for Security and Cooperation in Europe on 1st of October to talk about organising elections in separatist republics. On 9th of December Zelensky and Putin met at summit in Paris. On 31st of December Ukrainians signed new 5-year deal for transiting Russian gas through Ukrainian territory (Houeix, 2022).

Relations however deteriorated. Kyiv at the end of 2018 tried to minimalize Russian impact on Ukrainian religious structures. The new Ukrainian Orthodox Church was formed and it was granted independence from Russian Orthodox Church on 5th of January 2019. Ecumenical Patriarch of Constantinople Bartholomew signed decreed granting Ukrainian Orthodox Church independence which was denounced by Russian church authorities (Paris, 2019). On 12th of June Ukraine was granted enhanced opportunities by NATO allowing both parties to cooperate without making any statements on Ukrainian alliance membership. Zelensky and his and his party which held most seats in Rada were however aligning themselves as pro-NATO. On 1st of April 2021 Ukrainian President accused Russians of massing troops near borders. Russian authorities stated that they have been only conducting routine exercises. 5 days later Zelensky declared that Ukraine admission to NATO would solve war in Donbas. He also declared his support for Ukraine's EU membership (Houeix, 2022). Hostilities in the east also continued[24] (OHCHR, 2022). US tried to convince Russian counterparts that Ukraine won't join NATO soon. Moscow however demanded formal declaration. In December 2021 US intelligence sources been reporting that Russians prepared 100,000 soldiers for invasion with prospect of increasing numbers up to 175,000 in January 2022 (Roth, 2021).

To sum up, Russian attempts to rebuild its power in twenty first century, have negative impact on regional (Georgia, Afganistan Chechenya) and even global security – when bearing in mind, especially the influence of war in Ukraine on European and even worldwide political and economic instability.

War in Ukraine regarding laws of armed conflicts

The military element of security explored various legal and armed conflict problems and even doubts; they should be specified. On 21st of February 2014 Vladimir Putin signed decrees recognizing both Donetsk People's Republic (DNR) and Luhansk People's Republics (LNR) as independent states and allowed for Russian military forces to conduct 'peacekeeping' operation on those areas. Day later Federation Council, the upper house of Russian parliament approved Putin decision for deploying military forces. Putin publicly stated on 22nd of 2022 that boundaries of both republics are extending to substantial areas of Luhansk and Donetsk oblasts, which were still partially *de facto* under Ukrainian control and *de jure* parts of sovereign state of Ukraine (Human Rights Watch, 2022). Russia will announce annexing those oblasts along with

---

24. Office of the United Nations High Commissioner for Human Rights pointed that during entire 2021 25 civilians in total been killed in eastern Ukraine – 7 in result of direct hostilities, 12 from mines and explosive remnants of war and 6 from other causes. In 2020 26 civilians perished in result of armed conflict – 8 from direct hostilities, 17 from mines and explosive remnants of war and 1 from other causes.

Kherson and Zaporizhzhia oblasts on 30rd of September. Russian forces weren't at any stage of conflict controlling 100 per cent of territories of mentioned oblasts. Vladimir Putin stated as well that these acts irreversible (Menkiszak *et. al.*, 2022). It's also worth mentioning that Kremlin isn't using term 'war' regarding conflict in Ukraine. Russian authorities coined term 'special military operation' to justify aggression on Ukraine and undermine its sovereignty (Gorobets, 2022).

Conflict happening in eastern Ukraine from February 2014 to February 2022 can be described as mixture of non-international armed conflict regarding clashes between Ukrainian government and separatist forces and international armed conflict when Russian direct involvement is taken into account. Full scale Russian aggression changed this conflict into full scale international armed conflict between two states. It's worth mentioning that for an international armed conflict to happen, there must have been operational usage of military forces from at least two states. Threshold for that type of conflict is very low and it does not require a certain duration or intensity. Moreover, and especially important regarding Russia calling it 'special military operation' international armed conflict is determined by the facts, not the subjective intent of parties involved (Rulac, 2023).

In this case laws of armed conflicts should be applied. Those can be divided into two types: those regarding if war is legal in term of international law (*jus ad bellum*) and those regarding how forces should be acting during war (*jus in bello*). States can justify conducting war in modern times using 3 main reasons: in self-defence, when being asked by another state to assist with sending troops (Russia sending troops to Syria is good example) and basing on Article 51 of the UN Chapter (Iraqi invasion of Kuwait resulted with authorisation granted by UN Security Council which allowed for multinational forces to repel aggression). In this case possible NATO and EU expansion towards east cannot serve as war justification for Russia. On the other hand, Ukraine is conducting war of self-defence and every invitation for external military assistance is legal in terms of international law. It's also worth mentioning that in this case UN Security Council cannot act since Russia is its permanent member with right to veto every resolution (Howard, 2022).

In case of law regarding conducting war, it can be referred

as international humanitarian law and applies to all involved parties. The main goal of *jus in bello* laws is to protect war victims and secure their fundamental rights, no matter their affiliations are. Four Geneva Conventions are regarded as main pillars of international humanitarian law. First convention was signed in 1864 defining protection for wounded, forbidding targeting medical facilities during fighting. Second convention extended rules of first one to shipwrecked military forces. Third convention obliged parties involved to treat prisoners of war in humanely manner with allowing for neutral countries or entities to inspect prison camps. Fourth convention was signed in 1949, allowing for UN members to punish member states committing crimes unlawful killing, torture, serious bodily injury or suffering, unlawful deportation (ethnic cleansing), unlawful confinement, and gender-based crimes such as rape and forced prostitution. This convention was expanded by three additional protocols, which extended protection of civilians during conflicts against racist regimes, during wars of self-determination and internal conflicts (Howard, 2022). Both Ukraine and Russia are parties to 1949 Geneva Conventions and Protocol I. States involved in war are as well parties of European Convention on Human Rights (ECHR), the International Covenant on Civil and Political Rights (ICCPR), and the Convention against Torture and Other Cruel, Inhuman or Degrading Treatment or Punishment (CAT) (Human Rights Watch, 2022).

Laws of armed conflicts are limiting attacks to 'military objects'. Those can be described as personnel and objects that are making an effective contribution to military action and whose destruction, capture, or neutralization offers a definite military advantage. This category of targets include: enemy combatants, weapons and ammunition, objects being used to conduct war including buildings and vehicles. Laws of armed conflicts indicates that some civilian causalities will occur during military conflicts. However, parties involved should be distinguishing between civilians and combatants, targeting only combatants and other military targets. Parties involved in conflict are forbidden from targeting homes, apartments and businesses, places of worship, hospitals, schools, and cultural monuments, unless those are being used for military purposes, thus considered as military targets (Human Rights Watch, 2022).

Third Geneva Convention is also stating that prisoners of war (POW) should be treated in orderly manner. Being POW applies not only to members of armed forces but as well to militia or even people accompanying military but not belonging to them and civilians taking up arms. Any mistreatment including killing, harming, torturing, causing suffering or injuries to body and health, depriving POWs from fair trial for war crimes is considered as war crime (Human Rights Watch, 2022).

After beginning conflict in Ukraine majority of members in the UN General Assembly pointed to Russia as the aggressor which caused war. During Security Council on 27th of September several states charged Russia with violations of laws of armed conflicts. Both International Criminal Court and the UN's Independent International Commission of Inquiry on Ukraine documented evidence of acts being war crimes including indiscriminate killings and sexual and gender-based violence against civilians. More than dozen countries submitted proofs for Russia committing genocide in Ukraine to International Court of Justice (Howard, 2022).

Russian forces committed numerous war crimes during their occupation of Ukrainian territories. Up to 400 civilians was executed in city of Bucha after being interrogated by Russian soldiers. Unarmed men of fighting age and people that crossed Russian soldier paths were the most common victims. Evidences of war crimes included satellite imagery, videos and other visual evidence (Al-Hlou *et. al.*, 2022). As for December of 2022 UN Human Rights Monitoring Mission in Ukraine proved that at least 73 civilians (54 men, 16 women, 2 boys and 1 girl) were killed in Bucha from 5th to 30th of March 2022. Another 105 alleged killings were being probed back then by Mission. Report presented by UN Human Rights Monitoring Mission in Ukraine pointed that for the first 6 weeks of Russian invasion at least 441 civilians (341 men, 72 women, 20 boys and 8 girls) in only 3 regions of Ukraine were victims of war crimes conducted by Russian military (OHCHR, 2022). In located north from Kyiv city of Irpien at least 290 civilian victims been found. Disproportionate number of victims were women (Bezpiatchuk, 2022). Mass civilian graves with signs of torture and mistreatment were found in liberated at September 2022 city of Izium. At least 436 bodies with 30 showing signs of torture were found. Only 21 of those were military bodies (Kesaieva *et. al.*, 2022).

Civilian infrastructure was also targeted. On 8th of April 2022 Russian ballistic missile with a cluster munition warhead dispersed over the train tracks and station at city of Kramatorsk. At least 58 civilians were killed with over 100 being injured. Russian government denied responsibility for attack (Human Rights Watch, 2023). During autumn and winter or 2022 and 2023 Russian forces begun attacking critical energy infrastructure using ballistic missiles and suicide drones. On 20th of October 2022 Ukrainian authorities announced power outage because Russian attack damaged around 40% of Ukrainian energy facilities. The sole purpose of those attack was to deprive civilians of heat, electricity and water as the winter was coming (Amnesty International, 2022).

Russian military was also responsible for war crimes regarding Ukrainian POWs. In July of 2022 video showing Ukrainian prisoner of war being castrated by Russian soldiers was published (Weiss *et. al.*, 2022). On 8th of April 2023 video was posted to a pro-Russian social media channel, depicting Wagner group mercenaries showing beheaded corpses of two Ukrainian soldiers. Victims appeared to have their hands cut off as well. Second video was posted on Twitter and showed Russian soldier during summer 2022 cutting off head of Ukrainian soldier. Voice at the beginning of video was suggesting that victim was still alive during attack (Cotovio *et. al.*, 2023).

On 17th of March International Criminal Court issued arrest warrant for President of the Russian Federation Vladimir Putin and Commissioner for Children's Rights in the Office of the President of the Russian Federation Maria Alekseyevna Lvova-Belova. Both were charged for the war crime of unlawful deportation of Ukrainian children (International Criminal Court, 2023). Ukrainian government pointed that up to March of 2023 at least 16,221 children were forcibly relocated to Russia. UNs Commission of Inquiry on Ukraine pointed at evidence of illegal children transfer happening with them being mistreated, abused and denied proper care (Gozzi, 2023).

Russian forces are using rockets with antipersonnel PFM mines, which are also called 'butterfly mines'. Using those is violating international laws of armed conflicts since this kind of weapon cannot discern between civilians and combatants.

It's also worth mentioning that Russia isn't party of 1997 Mine Ban Treaty (Human Rights Watch, 2023). While Ukraine as state-signatory of treaty is being probed by The President of the Anti-Personnel Mine Ban Convention because of allegations of using those kind of weaponry (Convention on the Prohibition of Use, Stockpiling, Production and Transfer of Anti-Personnel Mines and on Their Destruction, 2023). Both sides were documented as well for using cluster munitions. Russian forces been using those hundreds of times. Ukrainian forces used those types of munitions at least three times during conflict (Relfef Wev, 2022). Russian forces been also caught using incendiary ammunitions over populated areas. In September of 2022 video showed village of Ozerne in eastern Ukraine being attacked with those rounds (Simko-Bednarski, 2022).

NATO as regional security factor in Eastern and Central Europe

Relations between Soviet Union and Western powers quickly deteriorated after ending World War II. Western European governments were worried about rising influence of communist ideology and potential Soviet aggression. United States already provided Marshall Plan in 1947 but recipients of aid were aware that economic aid will fail if their countries won't be secured in political and military terms. And US seemed to be the only country who could guarantee security there. Secret meeting between British, Canadian and American representatives begun in March 1948. All parties involved acknowledged that some kind of security organization was necessary because United Nations or proposed Western Union consisting United Kingdom, France and the three Benelux states wasn't enough. US Truman administration was struggling with opposition voicing their concerns if UN Charter isn't enough to provide peace after World War II therefore new alliance between US and Western Europe isn't necessary. New treaty was proceeded using few UN Charter articles as basis. However, at the end only Article 51 – the right for individual and collective self-defence applied to new alliance basis with Article 5 of Washington Treaty. Another issue was the scope of new alliance. Initially NATO was to consist of the United States, Canada and signatories of the Brussels Treaty forming Western Union. Strategic reasons pushed parties to include other states into new alliance. Norway, Denmark and Iceland were included because of their importance to power projection on North Atlantic. The same case happened for Italy and Mediterranean Sea. Portugal was a dictatorship back then but Azores were really important when comes to providing transatlantic links (Kaplan, 2004, p. 1-3). The North Atlantic Treaty was finally signed on 4th of April 1949 by Belgium, Canada, Denmark, France, Iceland, Italy, Luxembourg, the Netherlands, Norway, Portugal, the United Kingdom, and the United States. In early 1952 the United States surprised members by stating that Greece and Turkey should be invited to alliance. Both were invited to join at NATO Lisbon meeting in February 1952 (Sayle, 2019, p. 17-22).

Including West Germany into Western security framework was the next big issues. From 1950 to 1954 French politicians been talking with their German counterparts about creating European Defence Community (EDC). Those plans however failed. In December 1953 leaders of UK, France and the United States met in Bermuda along with NATO General Secretary. Parties agreed that Germany should be included in defensive agreements in Western Europe. In September and October 1954 allies had few meetings regarding alliance reshaping and ending up occupation of West Germany. Former British, French and American occupation forces were maintained in the same numbers but those were from now on allied forces aimed at defending West Germany. To ease some worries about remilitarisation of Germany Chancellor Konrad Adenauer pledged to NATO members that Federal Republic of Germany won't be building atomic, biological and chemical weapons on German soil. West Germany was finally admitted to NATO in 1955 (Sayle, 2019, p. 25-27).

Consolidation of Western security structures was noticed in Moscow. Soviet Union and its satellite states signed on 14th of May 1955 in Warsaw treaty forming Warsaw Pact. New alliance included: Soviet Union, Poland, East Germany, Czechoslovakia, Hungary, Romania, Bulgaria and Albania. Chinese, North Korean and North Vietnamese representatives were also present in Warsaw during signing treaty. Warsaw Pact was initially viewed as 'cardboard castle' by Western officials (Mastny *et. al.*, 2005, pp. 2-3).

During 50s NATO adopted 'Massive Retaliation' doctrine based on using nuclear weapons as response for conventional Soviet Union attack on NATO members. It allowed allies to maintain smaller conventional forces and focus on developing civil economies. Alliance unity was shattered however by Suez Crisis in 1956 where US, UK and France failed with conducting political consultations. After Cuban crisis which almost spurred nuclear exchange tensions between West and East eased during period called détente. In 1966 France announced withdrawing from NATO's integrated military command structure and asked from removing allied headquarters from French soil. NATO HQ was moved from Paris to Brussels in October 1966. France however stayed in alliance and pledged to fulfil Washington Treaty in case of hostilities (NATO, 2023).

In 1968 Soviet Union with most of Warsaw Pact countries invaded Czechoslovakia. The main goal was to stop political liberalisation called Prague Spring. Soviet Union explained aggression using new coined strategy called Brezhnev Doctrine. It justified Soviet Union to intervene using military means when Moscow was losing grip on their satellite states. NATO and Warsaw Pact continued however détente through most of 70s. New tensions arose in 1979 because of Soviet Union invading Afghanistan. In 1982 the newly democratic Spain was admitted to NATO – it was first member joining since 1955 (NATO, 2023). Those tensions continued during early 80s and ended up with the second biggest nuclear 'close calls' after Cuban crisis in November 1983 during NATO's Able Archer 83 war games. Situation was tense already with Ronald Reagan announcing on 23rd of March plans for Strategic Defence Initiative and Soviets shooting down civilian airliner Korean Airlines 007 on 1st of September. Exercises were conducted in November 1983 and simulated escalating tensions with simulating US military declaring DEFCON 1 and conducting nuclear attack. KGB had already Operation RYAN on-going from 1981, aimed at detecting signs or Western preparations to execute sudden nuclear attack on Soviet Union. Exercises ended up without further escalation. Soviet Minister of Defence Ustinov wrote in *Pravda* afterwards that NATO's war games are becoming more and more difficult to distinguish from a real armed forces preparation for aggression (Uenuma, 2022).

Gorbachev taking the lead in 1985 allowed for diplomatic

talks and decreasing tensions. In 1987 Soviet Union and the United States signed Intermediate-Range Nuclear Forces (INF) Treaty, eliminating all nuclear cruise and ground ground-launched ballistic missiles with intermediate ranges. This event is marked as beginning of the Cold War end. In 1989 communist regimes begun transforming their political systems to democracies. Fall of Berlin Wall on 9th of November 1989 marked beginning of new era (NATO, 2023). Warsaw Pact counties agreed on 25th of February 1991 in Budapest to cease military cooperation. Alliance was dissolved during meeting in Prague on 1st of July 1991 (Czarnecka, 2015). During Warsaw Pact dissolution, Soviet troops been already leaving Central Europe. On June 16th 1990 last Soviet soldier left Hungary (Budapest Business Journal, 2020). Similar events happened in Czechoslovakia on 1st of July 1990 (Powers, 1990), Poland on 18th of September 1993 (Pomfret, 1993) and newly united Germany on 31st of August 1994 (Atkinson, 1994).

Soviet Union demise and Warsaw Pact dissolution left security void in Central and Eastern Europe. Entering area which was previously dominated by Moscow provided some challenges. Every subject trying providing political and military security in Central and Eastern Europe should be aware of Russian goals, which haven't changed since World War II. Firstly, Russia seeks to keep 'cordon sanitaire' along its borders to prevent encirclement by hostile powers. Secondly, Moscow considers keeping warm water ports such as Sevastopol, Kaliningrad and Vladivostok as strategic priority. Having non-freezing ports is important for naval power projection. Thirdly, Russia is avoiding destruction of its own territory. In the early 90s NATO had to address those issues on one hand meanwhile increasing cooperation with former Warsaw Pact countries on the other. Those goals were achieved by shifting focus from military to political approach (Thomas, 2022). In 1991 NATO established North Atlantic Cooperation Council (NACC) as a forum for cooperation and dialogue with former Warsaw Pact countries. The first meeting between NATO-members and former Warsaw Pact countries took place on 20th of December 1991. During summit Soviet ambassador announced that Soviet Union has dissolved and he's representing Russian Federation now. Day later the Alma-Ata Protocols were signed formally dissolving USSR and forming new Commonwealth of Independent States (CIS). All former Soviet Union republic were invited to join NACC. Azerbaijan and Georgia joined Council in 1992 along with Albania. Central Asian republic followed soon (NATO, 2022).

At the end of 1993 NATO started developing new security cooperation framework with former Warsaw Pact countries, including former Soviet Union republics. NATO created with Russian consent Partnership for Peace (PfP) Program, which served as 'waiting room' for countries which were aspiring to becoming NATO member. Alliance membership was open to every PfP participant, who met NATO standards, including real commitment to democracy and not having internal or neighbourly conflicts. Countries aspiring for NATO membership had to apply for Membership Action Plan and then been examined by NATO officials regarding country internal politics. Both Ukraine and Russia weren't admitted to PfP directly, instead of that NATO regarding size and strategic importance of both created NATO-Ukraine Council and NATO-Russia Council later. In both cases requirements for states were similar to regular PfP membership which meant participating in all but NATO's operational planning meetings (Thomas, 2022). Partnership for Peace was launched in 1994 and included 21 partner countries[25] (Ogunnoiki *et. al.*, 2019).

NATO focus in 90s wasn't however solely political. Alliance intervenes twice during Balkan wars – in 1995 in Bosnia-Herzegovina and in 1999 in Kosovo. During Bosnia-Herzegovina intervention NATO was assisting ground UN forces with airstrikes against Serbian forces which were committing ethnic cleansing in Bosnia. Kosovo case was more complicated. Bosnia-Herzegovina was one of the states consisting on Yugoslavian Federation. Kosovo was autonomous region within Serbia. Both cases however involved ethnic cleansing and on-going civil war which created humanitarian crisis. Russia opposed Kosovo intervention not only because Moscow had good relationship with Belgrade but also because of on-going war in Chechnya, region regarded by Russians as part of Russian Federation. NATO intervention wasn't backed as well by UN resolution – UNSCR 1244 allowing

---

25. Armenia, Austria, Azerbaijan, Belarus, Bosnia and Herzegovina, Finland, Georgia, Ireland, Kazakhstan, Kyrgyzstan, Malta, Moldova, North Macedonia, Russia, Serbia, Sweden, Switzerland, Tajikistan, Turkmenistan, Ukraine and Uzbekistan.

deploying military forces was adopted in June 1999 which was three months after NATO involvement (Thomas, 2022).

As for NATO expansion into Central Europe in 1994 Boris Yeltsin claimed that area of Commonwealth of Independent States is Russian sphere of influence. Russian Federation was intended to be responsible for ensuring peace and stability in territories of former Soviet Union (Goshko, 1994). Madrid summit in July 1997 confirmed that Czech Republic, Hungary and Poland will be invited to join NATO by 1999. During summit NATO officials announced that 3 states joining will be first wave of NATO admissions and membership will be offered to some other former Soviet-bloc states. Before Madrid Summit Russian President Boris Yeltsin signed together with NATO leaders the Founding Act of Mutual Relations, Cooperation and Security between NATO and the Russian Federation on 27th of May 1997. Yeltsin despite signing this agreement voiced his concerns about NATO expansion eastwards (Hanson, 1998). Both Russian nationalists and democrats felt that NATO expansion was happening despite agreements. US Secretary of State James Baker visited Moscow on 9th of February 1990 and during talks with Gorbachev took handwritten notes of his own remarks regarding not expanding NATO beyond unified Germany borders. Those were only proofs of such talks happening (Sarotte, 2014). Western leaders were also supposed to promise to Gorbachev and Shevardnadze during 'Open Skies' summit in Ottawa on 12th February 1990 to not expand NATO beyond unified Germany eastern borders. Both consultations haven't end up with singing formal bilateral treaties (Rybkina, 1998, p. 32-33).

During Washington Summit in 1999 Czech Republic, Hungary and Poland took their seats as full members of NATO. In 2002 NATO-Russia Council was established for cooperating between Russia and individual NATO members on equal terms. NATO expanded in few waves. In 2004 Bulgaria, Estonia, Latvia, Lithuania, Romania, Slovakia and Slovenia were admitted. In 2009 Albania and Croatia became full members. Montenegro joined in 2017, followed by North Macedonia in 2020 (NATO, 2022).

Admitting Baltic states to NATO was crucial from European geostrategic point of view. It worked in two ways – Russia lost ability to expand military and politically in Baltic Sea region. NATO was also able to build more military bases in countries sharing borders with Russia. Estonia, Latvia and Lithuania are located at Russian western border. Moreover, Lithuania and Latvia are sharing border with Belarus blocking Russian expansion through this state (Radcliffe, 2018). It's worth mentioning that city of Narva which is located in the north-eastern Estonia at border with Russian Federation is located only 120 kilometres from southern suburbs of 2nd biggest Russian city St Petersburg (Ben-Gad, 2014). Immediately after Lithuania, Latvia and Estonia joining NATO Russian authorities stated that alliance expansion was 'line in the sand'. NATO expansion was considered as serious threat to national security. In 2007 after removing Soviet-era statue commemorating fallen Soviet soldiers from centre of Tallinn Russia waged hybrid warfare against Estonia. Campaign included cyber-attacks aimed at online media, government websites and services, banking websites. Moreover, some misinformation tactics were used including redirecting web users to sites with fake news stories or spreading those through social media channels (Radcliffe, 2018).

NATO was present not only in Central and Eastern Europe but also got involved in Middle East at beginning of 21 century. After attacks conducted by Al-Qaeda at 9th of September 2001 for the first time in alliance history Article 5 of Washington Treaty was invoked. Perpetrators of attacks had their training camps and were protected by Taliban government of Afghanistan which was refusing to hand over Al-Qaeda's leader Osama Bin Laden and closing down terrorist training camps. On 7th of October 2021 NATO operation called Enduring Freedom begun with airstrikes against Taliban and Al-Qaeda targets. From August of 2003 NATO was leading UN-mandated International Security Assistance Force (ISAF) which was aimed at providing stability and support for new democratic Afghan government. ISAF forces withdrew from Afghanistan in 2014 transferring security responsibilities to Afghan forces. Small contingents of NATO forces stayed in Kabul up to summer of 2021 when Afghan government collapsed against Taliban offensive. In August 2021 NATO forces provided airlift helping 120,000 people leaving Afghanistan, including 2,000 Afghans who were cooperating with NATO forces (NATO, 2022).

On 20th of March 2003 United States led coalition including United Kingdom, Australia and Poland invaded Iraq. US

President George Bush claimed that Iraqi leader Saddam Hussein is manufacturing and stockpiling weapons of mass destruction. Military intervention was supported politically by total 30 countries. Invasion was opposed by big NATO countries like Germany, France and Turkey (BBC News, 2023). Moreover, Turkish government in February 2003 requested NATO assistance according to Article 4 of Washington Treaty. NATO provided military support including deploying three Dutch antiaircraft systems and redeploying AWACS planes from Germany. The main task of those forces was protecting Turkish territory and population from potential attacks with tactical ballistic missiles. US led coalition defeated Saddam Hussein's forces and ended his regime. Multinational Force (MNF) was created for securing and governing country. Polish government was tasked with preparing forces for leading one of the MNF's sectors. Warsaw requested NATO assistance in some supporting roles like communications, logistics, force generation and movements. North Atlantic Council agreed to provide help in those matters. NATO wasn't however directly military involved in Iraq. Poland formally assumed leadership of the Multinational Division Central South in Iraq on 3rd of September 2003. Polish troops were withdrawn from Iraq in October 2008 (NATO, 2022).

Relations between NATO and Russia worsened after poisoning Alexander Litvinienko in 2006 and Russo-Georgian war in August 2008. NATO Secretary General stated as follows on 11th of August 2008: 'The NATO Secretary General, Jaap de Hoop Scheffer, is seriously concerned about the events that are taking place in the Georgian region of South Ossetia and said that the Alliance is closely following the situation. The Secretary General calls on all sides for an immediate end of the armed clashes and direct talks between the parties' (NATO, 2008). This statement was followed by North Atlantic Council statement condemning Russian recognition of South Ossetia and Abkhazia regions of Georgia. Council pointed that Russian decision is violating many of UN Security Council resolutions regarding Georgian territorial integrity and its inconsistent with the fundamental OSCE principles. Council found as well Russian actions being in question to its commitment to peace and security in the Caucasus (NATO, 2008). Meetings using

NATO-Russia Council as a platform and cooperation in some areas were suspended. At the NATO Summit in Strasbourg and Kehl on 4th of April 2009 leaders of NATO acknowledged disagreements but decided to resume political and practical cooperation as well (NATO, 2020).

Relations worsened further in September 2009 because of US proposed missile defence system in Poland and Czech Republic. System intended to intercept Iranian or North Korean missiles was deemed by Russia as a threat to their security. Project was later cancelled by Barack Obama (BBC, 2009). 2011 NATO intervention in Libya was criticised by Russian officials. Vladimir Putin called UN resolution authorising NATO involvement resembling 'medieval calls for crusades' (The Times, 2011).

Russian annexation of Crimea in 2014 sparked strong NATO reaction. North Atlantic Council on 2nd of March 2014 condemned Russian military actions against Ukraine as a breach of international law and contravening the principles of the NATO-Russia Council and the Partnership for Peace. NAC called Russia for respecting its obligations under UN Charter and following OSCE principles. Council called as well for Russia to respect Budapest Memorandum of 1994, the Treaty on Friendship and Cooperation between Russia and Ukraine of 1997 and agreements between Ukraine and Russia regarding Black Sea Fleet status (NATO, 2014). In further response on 1st of April 2014 all practical cooperation with Russia been suspended. During Warsaw Summit in July 2016 NATO leaders declared that their approach towards Russia won't change without Moscow changing attitude towards its commitments and international law. Until then returning to 'business as usual' is impossible (NATO, 2020). During Warsaw Summit NATO decided as well to establish an enhanced forward presence in Estonia, Latvia, Lithuania and Poland to demonstrate solidarity, determination and ability to act by triggering response to any aggression. Canada, Germany, the United Kingdom and the United States offered serving as framework nations being deployed to Baltic States and Poland (NATO, 2016).

Russian authorities been warned numerous times at the end of 2021 by NATO leaders and NATO Secretary General Jens Stoltenberg regarding Russian military build-up near Ukrainian borders. On 30th of November 2021 NATO Secretary General warned that another Russian invasion of Ukraine would carry a 'high price' adding that 30 NATO members are representing more than 50 per cent of the global economy (Herszenhorn, 2021). He stated as well that Russia has not rights for establishing sphere of influence and that Ukraine is viewed as NATO's partner whom been provided training and other forms of military support. Stoltenberg added as well that it's only Ukraine and 30 NATO members that decide if and when Ukraine is ready to join NATO and Russia has not rights to veto that decision (Basu, 2021).

On 17th of December Russian Ministry of Foreign Affair published draft of New Treaty between The United States of America and the Russian Federation on security guarantees. Russian demands included: stopping eastward NATO expansion, ceasing and not concluding any military cooperation with former Soviet Union states (including countries in Eastern Europe, Southern Caucasus and Central Asia), withdrawing NATO forces to positions occupied in 1997 before admitting former Warsaw Pact and Soviet Union states, not deploying armed forces, heavy bombers, surface warships, or intermediate-range and shorter-range missiles outside of NATO territory (Russian Federation Ministry of Foreign Affairs, 2021). US diplomats responded that they will consider those demands but called as well some of those as 'unacceptable' (Basu, 2021). Last official meeting between Russian and NATO officials within Russia-NATO Council framework took place on 12th of January 2022 (Russian News Agency, 2022). On 24th of February 2022 Russia launched full-scale invasion of Ukraine.

NATO role in the war in Ukraine and Russian reactions

Russia invading Ukraine caused some anxiety in Finland and Sweden. Both countries been cooperating with NATO since mid of 90s within Partnership for Peace framework. Russian waging war on independent and sovereign state in Europe caused increased support for NATO members in Finnish and Swedish society[26] (Armstrong, 2023). Anticipating both countries potential

---

26. Polls conducted in October 2021 in Finland showed only 24% support for NATO membership; similar poll year later showed 85% support for the cause. In Sweden in Jannuary 2022 NATO membership support had 37% support; similar poll conducted in July 2022 noted 64% NATO support.

application for membership Vladimir Putin threatened to deploy hypersonic missiles and nuclear weapons in Kaliningrad in reaction to Finland and Sweden NATO admission (Faulconbridge, 2022). Both countries applied for member status on 18th of May 2022. Their talks were however blocked by Turkey. Ankara demanded extradition of 30 people accused of terrorism-related charges, most of them were Kurdish activists (Milne *et. al.*, 2022). Turkey's parliament voted to ratify accession Finland to NATO at the end of March 2023. Finland joined alliance as 31st member on 4th of April 2023 doubling Russian border with alliance twice as used to be. As for April 2023 Sweden accession to NATO was still stalled by Hungary and Turkey (John, 2023).

There is also political will in Moldova for joining bigger security alliance because of war in neighbouring Ukraine and small contingent of Russian soldiers stationing in Moldova's breakaway region Transnistria. Moldova been also subjected to Russian attempts of hybrid warfare during last months of 2022. President Maia Sandu stated in January 2023 that Moldova is eying on joining 'a larger alliance'. She wasn't however calling mentioned alliance by its name (Lynch, 2023).

After Russian invasion US gathered wide coalition including NATO, EU and allied countries from all over the World aimed for helping Ukraine both in terms of non-lethal and lethal material delivery. On 26th of April 2022 during meeting at Ramstein Air Base in Germany Ukraine Defence Contact Group was formed (Herszenhorn *et. al.*, 2022). As for 14th of February 2023 group is including 30 NATO member states and 24 other countries[27]. In addition, few countries[28] have confirmed providing military aid (both lethal and non-lethal) to Ukraine (Barros, 2023). During meeting held on 20th of January 2023 members supported decision to provide Ukraine with heavy offensive weaponry to support planned spring offensive. As for 24th February of 2023 parties promised providing or provided 31 M1 Abrams tanks (US) and 71 Leopard 2 tanks[29]. In addition, joint German-Dannish-Dutch initiative announced delivering from 100 to 178 Leopard 1A5 tanks (Marcus, 2023). It's also worth mentioning that NATO member states are the biggest

---

27. Australia, Austria, Bosnia and Herzegovina, Cyprus, Georgia, Ireland, Japan, Kenya, Kosovo, Liberia, Moldova, New Zealand, South Korea, Sweden, Tunisia.

28. Azerbaijan, Cambodia, Colombia, Israel, Morocco, Pakistan, Sudan and Taiwan.

29. Leopard 2 tanks deliveries were announced by Germany, Portugal, Sweden, Poland, Spain, Norway and Canada.

donors of aid for Ukraine[30] (Trebesch *et. al.*, 2023).

Russian President stated in October 2022 that he wasn't bluffing during his previous statements claiming that Russia may use nuclear weapons in defence. Those remarks were treated seriously by Western officials. Retired US General and former CIA chief David Petraeus said that US and its NATO would destroy Russian troops and equipment in Ukraine in retaliation of using nuclear weapons in Ukraine. Those attacks would be aimed as well at sinking entire Russian Black Sea Fleet (Faulconbridge, 2022). Former Russian President Dmitry Medvedev remarked few times at the end of 2022 that Russian defeat in Ukraine could trigger nuclear war. Those threats were met with NATO Secretary-General Jens Stoltenberg stating: 'The risk of using nuclear weapons is low. But Russian nuclear rhetoric is utterly irresponsible. It is dangerous. Russia should know that a nuclear war can never be won and therefore should never be fought' (Towfigh Nia, 2022).

United Western response and building wide coalition tasked with helping Ukraine, including delivery of tanks and infantry fighting vehicles sparked as well Russian reaction. On 25th of March 2023 Vladimir Putin announce deploying tactical nuclear weapons to Belarus. Russian President stated that NATO is already stationing nuclear weapons as a part of the alliance regarding NATO Nuclear Sharing agenda. NATO spokesperson Oana Lungescu day later criticised announcement as misleading. She also stated that NATO allies are fully respecting their international commitments unlike Russia. Lungescu also added that NATO is closely monitoring Russian moves regarding deploying tactical nuclear weapons to Belarus (Brzezinski, 2023).

Russian aggression of Ukraine caused as well resifting NATO strategic goals. From 28th to 30th June 2022 NATO members met during Madrid summit addressing new threats emerging. Russia was called the most significant and direct threat to NATO members security regarding Euro-Atlantic region. That statement was contrasting with 2010 summit concept where Russia was deemed as strategic partner for NATO. It's probably the strongest example of diplomatic language addressed by NATO

---

30. By 24th of February 2023 United States provided 43,2 billion euros worth military aid. United Kingdom delivered material worth 6,6 billion euros, Germany 3,6, Poland and Netherlands both 2,4, Canada 1,4 and Norway 1,4. Moreover eastern NATO members were popular destination for Ukrainian refugees with Poland housing around 1,563,000, Germany 1,000,000 and Czech Republic 490,000 as for February 2023.

towards Russia since 1991. NATO officials addressed China as well during meeting. Chinese policies were labelled as challenging to NATO's security, values and interests. It was the first time China was mentioned in NATO's strategic concept. Document warned about China's ability to conduct hybrid, cyber- and disinformation activities threatening NATO's interests. Concerns were raised about deepening strategic partnership between Russia and China as well. NATO members were described however as being open to constructive engagement with China. It's also worth mentioning that during Madrid summit Indo-Pacific partners including Australia, New Zealand, Japan and South Korea were invited to NATO meeting for the first time in alliance history (European Parliament, 2022).

NATO's Secretary General announced as well a 'fundamental shift' including three main goals in order to provide deterrence and defence. Firstly, NATO members decided to boost if necessary enhanced forward presence consisting of eight multi-national battle groups to brigade-levels. Those forces are currently deployed at NATO's eastern flank. United States announced increasing US troop deployment to some eastern European allies and creating permanent headquarters of the US Army's V Corps in Poland. Secondly forces are about to be boosted to high-readiness troops. NATO's Response Force will be increased to 300,000 troops. For the first time since Cold War ending those forces will be designated to defend specific member states. United Kingdom already decided to deploy additional 1,000 soldiers to defend Estonia. And thirdly members decided to increase their equipment deployment to Eastern flank. It included creating deploy stockpiles, facilities and redeploying military equipment. France already deployed a missile defence system to Romania (European Parliament, 2022).

Ukraine's NATO membership prospects changed as well during conflict. After Vladimir Putin declaration regarding annexing occupied territories Volodymyr Zelensky on 30rd of September 2022 announced that Ukraine is requesting 'accelerated' NATO membership. Zelensky stated 'De facto, we have already proven compatibility with alliance standards. They are real for Ukraine — real on the battlefield and in all aspects of our interaction' and 'We trust each other, we help each other, and we protect each other. This is the alliance'

(Times of Israel, 2022). Ukrainian membership prospects were addressed by NATO Secretary General Jens Stoltenberg on 21st of April 2023. He stated that 'All NATO allies have agreed that Ukraine will become a member' and 'President Zelensky has a very clear expectation, we discussed this. Both the issue of membership but also security guarantees, and of course Ukraine needs security. Because no one can tell when and how this war ends. But what we do know is that when the war ends, we need to ensure that history doesn't repeat itself'. Ukrainian President is about to attend NATO's annual summit happening in Vilinus in July 2023. Ukrainian officials are expecting as well for NATO to agree on roadmap to membership and they are pushing this as a condition for Zelensky's attendance (Sabbagh *et. al.*, 2023).

Conclusions

Political-historical perspective of analysis reflects the complexity and dynamics of the on-going full-scale Russian aggression against Ukraine and its implications for regional and global security. Countries regarded few decades ago as 'brotherly' are fighting because of Russian having no regards for international law and attempting to rebuild its former spheres of influence and trying to act as an actor of bipolar security system, similar to situation from 1945–1991. Russia in this case sees Ukraine as part of their own land. Russian officials and ordinary citizens are perceiving Ukraine as 'artificial state'. Moreover, since Orange Revolution Ukraine started drifting away from Russian orbit. This movement slowed down during Yanukovych Presidential term. Attitudes towards EU and NATO were however quite positive in Ukrainian society and those attitudes finally led to Euromaidan protests, resulting in Yanukovych fleeing to Russia. Those events were perceived by Moscow as major security threat. In response for Ukraine drifting towards EU and NATO Russia seized Crimea and begun supporting pro-Russian separatism in Eastern Ukraine which resulted in creating two separatist republics and conflict happening from 2014 to this day with Russian openly invading Ukraine in 2022 being last act of it.

Soviet Union collapse created security void with new threats and challenges. USSR demise caused serious concerns about nuclear proliferation. Those were however solved without any incidents happening and Russia became only one nuclear capable Soviet successor state. Ukraine was however granted with security guarantees in return for ceding nuclear stockpiles to Russia. New states emerged from Soviet Union collapse were struggling with political and economic instability unable filling security gaps in terms of regional stability.

Ending of the Cold War resulted in shifting world from bipolar to unipolar. NATO was perceived in Russia as a tool for US world dominance and biggest threat to strategic security. Former Warsaw Pact states and former Soviet Baltic republics were seeking for security guarantees perceiving Russia as big unknown and then finally as threat to their security. Those concerns were addressed by NATO expanding eastwards. However, NATO approaching Russian borders became the main threat to Russian interests in their former spheres of influence. Diplomatic games happening between implementing security frameworks such as Partnership for Peace, aimed at cooperating between former enemies and actual admitting new states are showing why Russia treats NATO as security issue. Russian officials are pointing that Western counterparts were promising not to expand their military presence eastwards. Even though those promises were supposedly been made in the early 90s both sides haven't agreed on such terms signing multilateral treaties. Russia is depicting its assertiveness against Western countries and Ukraine as defending its political, military and cultural zone. War in Ukraine is labelled as a 'special operation' with no declaration of war being in place. Moscow is justifying aggression by safeguarding Russian-speaking minority in Ukraine against fascists. All war crimes conducted by Russian military are blamed on Ukrainian side using propaganda and fake news. Defending 'Russian world' against Western threat is common theme in Russian history and NATO approaching Russian borders may be regarded by Russian policy-makers as another possible invasion threatening Russian existence.

NATO reactions for Russian military build-up near Ukrainian borders at the end of 2021 and military invasion were crucial. NATO was trying to solve potential war using diplomatic means but also provided intelligence data, delivered small arms and other equipment. Alliance even responded to Russian proposition for solving tensions regarding not only Ukraine but also NATO troops itself. After Russian invasion begun Western partners condemned Russian actions, implemented wide economic sanctions and provided more sophisticated military equipment. Russian invasion of Ukraine swayed Swedish and Finnish societies and politicians when comes to NATO membership. Those countries joining NATO will cause reshaping security framework in Europe. Ukrainian is aided by not only NATO members but also by countries from all over the world. Alliance is providing platform for cooperation with third parties such as Japan, South Korea, Australia or New Zealand. Those countries are also present at NATO summits which indicates alliance shifting its strategic policies from regional to global.

Because of the Russian onslaught, nations who were previously neutral (Finland and Sweden) felt endangered and opted to join NATO, where they were welcomed with open arms. This produced several complications for the Russians, including (expanding the boundary with the Alliance to cover the whole Finland border, thereby establishing the Baltic Sea as a NATO internal sea). Furthermore, the Alliance was reinforced as a result of this invasion. Many nations began to plan for additional military spending, as well conducting more joint military exercises.

Security gap in Central and Eastern Europe was initially filled with expanding NATO. Russia couldn't preserve Soviet spheres of influence which allowed for NATO to expand into all former satellite states and Warsaw Pact members and even to former Baltic Soviet republics. Russian economy benefiting on higher oil and natural gas prices improved however in the early years of 21st century allowing to pour more funding into military and take more assertive stance towards neighbouring states.

Assertive stance meant conducting hybrid warfare and waging kinetic wars against Chechnya, Georgia and Ukraine. Those wars were waged by Russian military and authorities having no regards for civilian and even their own troops lives. Russian troops been proved committing serious atrocities during on-going invasion of Ukraine with Bucha massacre being the most known.

Considering all those circumstances NATO seems to be stabilising factor in Central and Eastern Europe, despite Russian claims. NATO members are benefitting having security guarantees and weren't affected by direct Russian aggression since alliance expansion eastwards. Some security threats like cyber-attacks, aggressive covert operations or Russian propaganda has been addressed in NATO policymaking.

It's worth mentioning that NATO is acting in this case as global leader cooperating with states all over the globe trying to provide aid and increase stability. Wars in Chechnya and Georgia were local. However war of 2008 affected both NATO and European Union with some states being involved in supporting Georgia against Russia and France brokering cease fire. Those conflicts weren't affecting global economy and had small impact on global security in the long run. Ukraine is by far more populous and bigger thus on-going local conflict is affecting Europe, Middle East, Central Asia in terms of security aftershocks and global economy more than wars in Chechnya and Georgia When comes impact on global economy global food security and raising energy sources prices are great examples. Cases of those wars waged by Russia on its neighbours are showing that local bilateral conflicts may cause widespread regional and even global issues in terms of politics, economy and security.

Those factors are important when considering possible NATO evolution from regional alliance into global security force. Some indicators like military support from Pacific states or parties from all over the globe being involved in providing material help to Ukraine are pointing that may happen. Those actions are really important considering possible growing assertiveness of China, predictions of Ukraine's scenario happening in Taiwan and some states seeking their opportunities in destabilising or even breaking current global order. We must ask here if European NATO members will be eager to help Taiwan facing Chinese invasion considering that war may affect global economy even more than conflict in Ukraine, all because Taiwan is one of the leading semiconductor manufacturing countries.

Themes analysed in this article are showing not only intensity but as well impact of war in Ukraine for regional and global security. International law and international humanitarian law breaches are in this case not only indicators of sheer brutality but also are impacting international community with UN, NATO, OSCE and other parties being involved.

Current relations between NATO and Russia as by far the

worst since ending of Cold War. Unprovoked Russian aggression destabilised not only Euro-Atlantic region but it's also taking toll globally. NATO however is probably the most powerful military alliance in history of human kind considering military equipment, training but also economic power of member states. Providing only a small per cent of full capabilities of military equipment and know-how seems to be enough to provide peace to Ukraine and allow for Kyiv to sit at the peace-talks table against Russian counterparts on at least equal terms.

It's quite obvious that NATO learned its lessons from Russian annexation of Crimea and war in Donbas and Luhansk. Reaction towards Russian military build-up happening at the end of 2021 was mixture of de-escalatory tools using NATO-Russia Council while providing intelligence data, training and first big military equipment deliveries to Ukraine.

The war in Ukraine has a significant and pejorating impact on regional and global security. This invasion affects not just states in the region, but also countries in global term. Nevertheless, international politics are conducted in dynamic environment with a lot of unknown and unexpected factors affecting relations. War is consisting of violent and dynamic events. Therefore, is hard to predict perfectly results of Ukrainian and Russian operations happening right now.

NATO seems to be addressing those unknown forming strategy for new decades. Inviting Australia, New Zealand, Japan and South Korea to NATO Madrid Summit marks forming new strategy where Russia is the most important Euro-Atlantic threat right now with envisioning China as a possible great contester in coming years. Not only for US but as well for Western world.

It's also worth mentioning that US and China rivalry may bring some future divides between Western European NATO members seeking economic ties with Beijing and US backed by some Eastern European NATO allies.

As for today the main goal for NATO members should be definitely bringing peace to Ukraine and ending unnecessary war which is resulting in civilian suffering, committing war crimes, economic decline for both Ukraine and Russia, increasing security tension in other World regions with main concerns about situation on South China Sea and Taiwan and risking global recession in the long run.

References

Al-Hlou Y. *et al.*, (2022) "Caught on Camera, Traced by Phone: The Russian Military Unit That Killed Dozens in Bucha", *New York Times*. Available at: https://www.nytimes.com/ 2022/12/22/ video/russia-ukraine-bucha-massacre-takeaways.html.

Amnesty International (2022) Ukraine: Russian attacks on critical energy infrastructure amount to war crimes (2022), *Amnesty International*. Available at: https:// www.amnesty.org/en/latest/ news/2022/10/ukraine-russian-attacks-on-critical-energy-infrastructure-amount-to-war-crimes/.

Armstrong M. (2023) "How War in Ukraine Pushed Finland and Sweden Toward NATO", *Statista*. March 31 2023. Available at: https:// www.statista.com/chart/27422/public-support-joining-nato-finland-sweden/.

Atkinson R. (1994) "Russian troops leave Germany", *The Washington Post*. Available at: https://www.washingtonpost.com/archive/ politics/1994/09/01/ russian-troops-leave-germany/65e3176c-fbe6-47c4-979d-f5fdcb259f6c/.

Barros G. *et. al.* (2023) Russian Offensive Campaign Assessment, February 14, 2023, *Institute for the Study of War*. Available at: https://understandingwar.org/backgrounder/ russian-offensive-campaign-assessment-february-14-2023.

Basu Z. (2021) "NATO chief: "Russia has no right to establish a sphere of influence"", *Axios*. Available at: https://www.axios. com/2021/12/01/nato-russia-ukraine-invasion.

Basu Z. (2021) "U.S. to consider Russia's NATO proposal, but calls some demands "unacceptable"", *Axios*. Available at: https://www.axios. com/ 2021/12/17/russia-nato-ukraine-invasion.

BBC Newa (2016) Litvinenko A. Profile of murdered Russian spy', *BBC*. 21 January 2016. Available at: https://www.bbc.com/news/ uk-19647226.

BBC News (2023) Why did the US and allies invade Iraq, 20 years ago?, *BBC*. Available at: https://www.bbc.com/news/world-64980565.

BBC News UK (2009) Q&A: US missile defence, *BBC*.. Available at: http://news.bbc.co.uk/ 1/hi/world/europe/6720153.stm.

Bellinger III, J. B. (2022) "How Russia's Invasion of Ukraine Violates International Law", *International Institutions and Global Governance Program*. 28 February 2022. Available at: https://www.cfr.org/ article/how-russias-invasion-ukraine-violates-international-law.

Ben-Gad M. (2014) "The tiny Estonian town that could spell the end of NATO", *The Conversation*.. Available at: https://theconversation.com/the-tiny-estonian-town-that-could-spell-the-end-of-nato-24679.

Bezpiatchuk Z. (2022) "Irpin: Russia's reign of terror in a quiet neighbourhood near Kyiv". *BBC*.. Available at: https://www.bbc.com/news/world-europe-61667500.

Bivings L. (2022) "#Explaining Ukraine, Ukraine's Orange Revolution", *The Kyiv Independent*. Available at: https://kyivindependent.com/explaining-ukraine/ ukraines-orange-revolution.

Brookings (2022) Sanctions on Russia Over Ukraine, Session 20 of the Congressional Study Group, *Brookings*. Available at: https://www.brookings.edu/research/ sanctions-on-russia-over-ukraine/.

Brzezinski B. (2023) "Dangerous and irresponsible": NATO condemns Putin's nuclear-arms plan", *Politico*. Available at: https://www.politico.eu/article/dangerous-and-irresponsible-nato-condemns-vladimir-putin-nuclear-arms-plan-ukraine-belarus-war/.

Budapest Business Journal (2020) The end of the 'Temporary Stationing' of Soviet Troops In Hungary, *Budapest Business Journal*. Available at: https://bbj.hu/budapest/culture/ history/the-end-of-the-temporary-stationing-of-soviet-troops-in-hungary.

Budjeryn M. (2014) *Issue Brief #3: The Breach: Ukraine's Territorial Integrity and the Budapest Memorandum*. Available at: https://www.wilsoncenter.org/publication/issue-brief-3-the-breach-ukraines-territorial-integrity-and-the-budapest-memorandum

CNN Editorial Research (2023) "2008 Georgia Russia Conflict Fast Facts", *CNN*. Available at: https://edition.cnn.com/2014/03/13/world/europe/2008-georgia-russia-conflict/index.html.

Convention on the Prohibition of Use, Stockpiling, Production and Transfer of Anti-Personnel Mines and on Their Destruction (2023) Landmine treaty president to engage with Ukraine on alleged use of prohibited weapon, *Anti-Personnel Mine Ban Convention*.. Available at: https://www.apminebanconvention.org/en/newsroom/article/article/landmine-treaty-president-to-engage-with-ukraine-on-allegations-of-use-of-prohibited-weapon/.

Cotovio V. *et al.* (2023) "Zelensky slams 'beasts' who purportedly beheaded Ukrainian soldiers after video emerges", *CNN*. Available at: https://edition.cnn.com/2023/04/11/ europe/beheading-videos-ukraine-intl-hnk-ml/index.html.

Czarnecka D. (2015) "Dissolution of the Warsaw Pact – 1 July 1991", *ENRS*. Available at: https://enrs.eu/article/dissolution-of-the-warsaw-pact-1-july-1991.

Deutsche Welle (2022) Russia recognizes independence of Ukraine separatist regions', *Deutsche Welle*. Available at: https://www.dw.com/en/russia-recognizes-independence-of-ukraine-separatist-regions/a-60861963.

European Council (2023) EU response to Russia's invasion of Ukraine (2023), *European Council, Council of the European Union*. Available at: https://www.consilium.europa.eu/ en/policies/eu-response-ukraine-invasion/.

European Parliament (2022) Outcome of the Madrid NATO Summit, June 2022, *European Parliament Think Tank*. Available at: https://www.europarl.europa.eu/thinktank/ en/document/EPRS_ATA(2022)733604

Faulconbridge G. (2022) "Russia warns of nuclear, hypersonic deployment if Sweden and Finland join NATO", *Reuters*. Available at: https://www.reuters.com/ world/europe/russia-warns-baltic-nuclear-deployment-if-nato-admits-sweden-finland-2022-04-14/.

Faulconbridge G. (2022) "Will Russia use nuclear weapons? Putin's warnings explained", Reuters. Available at: https://www.reuters.com/world/europe/qa-will-russia-use-nuclear-weapons-putins-warnings-explained-2022-10-04/.

Gaffen D. (2022) "How the Russia-Ukraine war accelerated a global energy crisis", *Reuters*. Available at: https://www.reuters.com/business/energy/year-russia-turbocharged-global-energy-crisis-2022-12-13/.

Gorobets K. (2022) Russian "Special Military Operation" and the Language of Empire, *OpinioJuris*. Available at: https://opiniojuris.org/2022/05/24/russian-special-military-operation-and-the-language-of-empire/.

Gorokhovska, A. (2021) *Thirty Years Since Independence: Defining Ukraine's Strategic Culture* Available at: https://ssrn.com/abstract=4275620.

Goshko J. M. (1994) 'Yeltsin claims Russian sphere of influence', *The Washington Post*. Available at: https://www.washingtonpost.com/archive/politics/ 1994/09/27/yeltsin-claims-russian-sphere-of-influence/fe3fe83b-bef3-4c10-b9bf-4784 b4ec39c6/.

Gozzi L. (2023) "Deportation of Ukrainian children to Russia is war crime – UN", *BBC*. Available at: https://www.bbc.com/news/world-europe-64985009.

Hanson, M. (1998) Russia and NATO Expansion: The Uneasy Basis of the Founding Act, *European Security*, vol. 7, no. 2 (Summer 1998).

Herszenhorn D M. *et al.* (2022) "US rallies global allies to help Ukraine repel Russia", *Politico*. Available at: https://www.politico.eu/article/ukraine-war-russia-united-states-defence-consultative-group/.

Herszenhorn D.M. (2021) "NATO warns Russia of 'high price' for any attack on Ukraine", *Politico*. Available at: https://www.politico.eu/article/jens-stoltenberg-nato-otan-russia-ukraine-united-states/.

Houeix R. (2022) "From the Maidan protests to Russia's invasion: Eight years of conflict in Ukraine", *France 24*. Available at: https://www.france24.com/en/ europe/20220228-from-the-maidan-protests-to-russia-s-invasion-eight-years-of-conflict-in-ukraine.

Howard M. (2022) *"A Look at the Laws of War – and How Russia is Violating Them", United States Institute of Peace.* Available at: https:// www. usip.org/publications/ 2022/09/ look-laws-war-and-how-russia-violating-them.

Human Rights Watch (2022) Russia, Ukraine & International Law: On Occupation, Armed Conflict and Human Rights, *Human Rights Watch*. Available at: https://www.hrw.org/news/ 2022/02/23/ russia-ukraine-international-law-occupation-armed-conflict-and-human-rights.

Human Rights Watch (2023) Death at the Station, Russian Cluster Munition Attack in Kramatorsk, *Human Rights Watch*. Available at: https://www.hrw.org/video-photos/interactive/2023/02/21/death-at-the-station/russian-cluster-munition-attack-in-kramatorsk.

Human Rights Watch (2023) Ukraine: Banned Landmines Harm Civilians, *Human Rights Watch*. Available at: https://www.hrw.org/news/2023/01/31/ukraine-banned-landmines-harm-civilians.

Interfax (2014) Ukrainian Prime Minister Azarov resigns, *Interfax-Ukraine*. Available at: https://en.interfax.com.ua/news/general/187663.html.

International Criminal Court (2023) Situation in Ukraine: ICC judges issue arrest warrants against Vladimir Vladimirovich Putin and Maria Alekseyevna Lvova-Belova, *International Criminal Court*. Available at: https://www.icc-cpi.int/news/situation-ukraine-icc-judges-issue-arrest-warrants-against-vladimir-vladimirovich-putin-and.

John T. (2023) "Finland joins NATO, doubling military alliance's border with Russia in a blow for Putin", *CNN*. Available at: https://edition.cnn.com/2023/04/04/europe/finland-joins-nato-intl/index.html.

Kaplan L. S. (2004) NATO Divided, NATO United: The Evolution of an Alliance. Praeger Westport, Connecticut, London.

Karatnycky A. (2005) Ukraine's Orange Revolution, *Foreign Affairs vol. 84, no. 2* .

Kesaieva Y. *et al.* (2022) "Signs of torture, mutilation on bodies at Izium mass burial site: Ukraine officials", *CNN*. Available at: https://edition.cnn.com/2022/09/23/ europe/ukraine-izium-mass-burial-bodies-recovered-torture-intl-hnk/ index.html.

Kholod N. (2012) *Reforming the Ukrainian Economy under Yanukovych: The First Two Years*. Available at: https://www.academia.edu/1454464/ The_Political_Economy_ of_ Reforms_ in_Ukraine_under_President_Yanukovych.

Kimball S. (2014) "Bound by treaty", *Deutsche Welle.*. Available at: https://www.dw.com/en/bound-by-treaty-russia-ukraine-and-crimea/a-17487632.

Kofman M. *et al.* (2017) Lessons from Russia's Operations in Crimea and Eastern Ukraine. Available at: https://www.rand.org/pubs/research_reports/RR1498.html.

Kort, M. (2008) A brief history of Russia. Boston University.

Kudelia, S. (2014) "The house that Yanukovych built", *Journal of Democracy,* no. 3. Available at: https://muse.jhu.edu/article/549493.

Kuznetsov I. S. *et al.* (2012) *Modern Russian History: A Textbook*. Chonnam National University Press.

Lynch S. (2023) "Time to join NATO? Moldova eyes joining 'a larger alliance", *Politico*. Available at: https://www.politico.eu/article/maia-sandu-moldova-nato-alliance-joining-ukraine-war-russia-invasion/.

Marxsen Ch. (2014) The Crimea Crisis – An International Law Perspective. *Kyiv-Mohyla Law and Politics Journal,* vol. 2, no. 2.

Mastny V. *et al.* (2005) A Cardboard Castle? An Inside History of the Warsaw Pact, 1955-1991. Central European University Press.

Matthews A. L. (2022) "The Ukraine War in data: More than 100,000 Russian casualties — and almost as many on the Ukrainian side", *GRID*. Available at: https://www.grid.news/story/global/2022/11/17/the-ukraine-war-in-data-more-than-100000-russian-casualties-and-almost-as-many-on-the-ukrainian-side/.

Matuszczak S. (2022) "A struggle to survive. Ukraine's economy in wartime". *Centre for Eastern Studies.* Available at: https://www.osw.waw.pl/en/publikacje/osw-commentary/2022-10-18/a-struggle-to-survive-ukraines-economy-wartime.

Max Planck Institute (2009) Independent International Fact-Finding Mission on the Conflict in Georgia, *Report Volume I.* Available at: http://www.mpil.de/en/pub/publications/ archive/independent_international_fact.cfm.

Maynes Ch. (2022) "4 things Russia wants right now", *National Public Radio.* Available at: https://www.npr.org/2022/01/12/1072413634/russia-nato-ukraine.

Menkiszak M. *et al.* (2022) "Russia announces the annexation of four regions of Ukraine", *Centre for Eastern Studies.* Available at: https://www.osw.waw.pl/en/publikacje/ analyses/2022-10-03/russia-announces-annexation-four-regions-ukraine.

Miller N. (2016) "Malaysia Airlines flight MH17 was shot down from pro-Russian rebel controlled territory, investigation finds", *The Sydney Morning Herald.* Available at: https://www.smh.com.au/world/malaysia-airlines-flight-mh17-was-shot-down-from-prorussian-rebel-controlled-territory-investigation-finds-20160928-grqter.html.

Milne R. *et al.* (2022) "Erdoğan blocks N|TO accession talks with Sweden and Finland", *Financial Times.* Available at: https://www.ft.com/content/3d1ab5d0-19a6-41bd-83a4-7c7b9e2be141.

NATO (2008) Statement by the North Atlantic Cooperation Council on the Russian recognition of South Ossetia and Abkhazia regions of Georgia, *NATO.* Available at: https://www.nato.int/docu/pr/2008/p08-108e.html

NATO (2008) Statement by the Secretary General of NATO on the Russian recognition of Abkhazia and South Ossetia, *NATO.* Available at: https://www.nato.int/docu/pr/ 2008/p08-107e.html

NATO (2014) North Atlantic Council statement on the situation in Ukraine, *NATO.* Available at: https://www.nato.int/cps/en/natolive/official_texts_107681.htm

NATO (2016) Warsaw Summit Communiqué, *NATO.* Available at: https:// www.nato.int/ cps/en/natohq/official_texts_133169.htm.

NATO (2022) A short story of NATO, *NATO.* Available at: https://www.nato.int/ cps/en/natohq/declassified_139339.htm.

NATO (2022) NATO and Afghanistan, *NATO.* Available at: https:// www.nato.int/ cps/en/natohq/topics_8189.htm.

NATO (2022) NATO and the 2003 campaign against Iraq, *NATO*. Available at: https://www.nato.int/cps/en/natohq/topics_51977.htm.

NATO (2022) North Atlantic Cooperation Council (1991–1997), *NATO*. Available at: https://www.nato.int/cps/en/natohq/topics_69344.htm.

NATO (2023) NATO's response to Russia's invasion of Ukraine', *NATO*. Available at: https://www.nato.int/cps/en/natohq/topics_192648.htm.

New York Times (2022) Live Updates: Biden to Confer With Allies As Ukraine Tensions Rise', *New York Times*. Available at: www.nytimes.com/live/2022/02/18/world/ukraine-russia-news.

Nova Gazeta Europe (2022) Forbes: about 700,000 people leave Russia since mobilisation started. Available at: https://novayagazeta.eu/articles/2022/10/04/forbes-about-700000-people-leave-russia-since-mobilisation-started-news.

Ogunnoiki *et al.* (2019) NATO at 70: The History, Successes and Challenges of the Transatlantic Alliance In The Post-Cold War Era, *African Journal of Social Sciences and Humanities Research,* vol. 2, no. 2.

OHCHR(2016)*Accountability for killings in Ukraine from January 2014 to May 2016.* Available at: https://www.ohchr.org/ en/documents/country-reports/accountability-killings-ukraine-january-2014-may-2016.

OHCHR (2022) United Nations Human Rights Office of the High Commissioner . Available at: https://www.ohchr.org/en/press-releases/2022/12/un-report-details-summary-executions-civilians-russian-troops-northern.

OHCHR (2023) United Nations Human Rights Office of the High Commissioner. Available at: https://www.ohchr.org/en/news/2023/01/ukraine-civilian-casualty-update-3-january-2023.

OSCE (2019) *Ukraine presidential election 31 March and 21 April 2019 Final Report.* Available at: https://www.osce.org/odihr/elections/ukraine/439631.

OSCE (2014) *Ukraine early presidential election 25 may 2014 final Report.* Available at: https://www.osce.org/odihr/elections/ukraine/120549.

OSCE (2010) *Ukraine presidential election 17 January and 7 February 2010 Final Report.* Available at: https://www.osce.org/odihr/elections/ukraine/67844.

Paris F. (2019) "Ukrainian Orthodox Church Officially Gains Independence From Russian Church", *NPR*. Available at: https://www.npr.org/2019/01/05/ 682504351/ukrainian-orthodox-church-officially-gains-independence-from-russian-church,

Pomfret J. (1993) "last Russian troops leave Poland", *The Washington Post*. Available at: https://www.washingtonpost.com/archive/politics/ 1993/09/19/last-russian-troops-leave-poland/09b43e47-1ee7-494d-a37a-7d65f06ad 6 d1/.

Powers Ch. T. (1990) "Soviet Troops Begin Czech Pullout; All to Leave by '91", *Los Angeles Times*. Available at: https://www.latimes.com/archives/la-xpm-1990-02-27-mn-1311-story.html.

Prokopenko A. (2022) "The Cost of War: Russian Economy Faces a Decade of Regress", *Carnegie Endowment for International Peace*. Available at: https:// carnegieendowment.org/politika/88664.

Puchenkov A. S. (2020) Ethnic Disintegration and the Dissolution of the USSR. *Vestnik of Saint Petersburg University. History,* vol. 65, no. 3. https:// doi.org/10.21638/ 11701/spbu02.2020.308.

Radcliffe C. M. (2018) NATO Enlargement: Poland, The Baltics, Ukraine and Georgia. University of Central Florida, Orlando.

Relfef Wev (2022) Zelensky visit to U.S. | Cluster munitions have no place in war, United Nations Office for the Coordination of Humanitarian Affairs. Available at: https:// reliefweb.int/report/ukraine/zelensky-visit-us-cluster-munitions-have-no-place-war.

Roth A. (2021) "Russia edges closer to war as new arms arrive on Ukraine's border", *The Guardian*. Available at: https://www.theguardian.com/world/2021/dec/12/russia-closer-to-war-ukraine-border-putin-buk-missiles.

Rulac Geneva Academy (2023) International armed conflict in Ukraine, *RULAC*. Available at: https://www.rulac.org/browse/conflicts/international-armed-conflict-in-ukraine.

Russian Federation Ministry of Foreign Affairs (2021) Treaty between The United States of America and the Russian Federation on security guarantees, *Russian Federation Ministry of Foreign Affairs..* Available at: https://mid.ru/ru/foreign_policy/rso/nato/1790818/ ?lang=en.

Russian News Agency (2022) Russia-NATO Council ends Brussels meeting that lasted four hours, *TASS..* Available at: https://tass.com/politics/1386919.

Rybkina L. (1998) Facing new dangers: A young view. Mezhdunar. Otnosheniia.

Sabbagh D. *et al.* (2023) "All NATO members have agreed Ukraine will eventually join, says Stoltenberg", *The Guardian.*. Available at: https://www.theguardian.com/ world/2023/apr/21/all-nato-members-have-agreed-ukraine-will-eventually-join-says-stoltenberg.

Sakwa, R. (2020) "The Putin Paradox" *I.B. Tauris*. Available at: https:// kar.kent.ac.uk/ 80013/.

Sarotte M. E. (2014) "A Broken Promise? What the West Really Told Moscow About NATO Expansion". *Foreign Affairs vol. 93, no. 5.*

Satter, D. (2016) The less you know, the better you sleep – Russia's road to terror and dictatorship under Yeltsin and Putin. Yale University Press / New Haven & London.

Sayle T. A. (2019) Enduring Alliance: A History of NATO and the Postwar Global Order. Cornell University Press.

Simko-Bednarski E. (2022) "Chilling video shows incendiary ammo falling on Ukrainian town", *New York Post.*. Available at: https:// nypost.com/2022/09/20/chilling-video-shows-incendiary-ammo-falling-on-ukrainian-town/.

Subtelny, O. (2009). Ukraine: A History. University of Toronto Press.

Suny, R. G. (2006) The Cambridge History of Russia. Cambridge University Press.

The Times (2011) West in "medieval crusade" on Gaddafi: Putin, *The Times*. Available at: http://www.timeslive.co.za/world/ article979191.ece/West-in-mediaeval-crusade-on-Gaddafi--Putin.

Thomas M. (2022) US&NATO Strategic Errors, Not NATO Expansion, Led to War in Ukraine, *The Ukrainian Quarterly, no. 1.*

Time of Israel (2022) Ukraine pushes for 'accelerated' NATO membership after Putin annexes regions, *The Times of Israel.* Available at: https://www.timesofisrael.com/ ukraine-pushes-for-accelerated-nato-membership-after-putin-annexes-regions/.

Tlis F. (2023) "VOA Interview: What to Know About Russia's Manipulated War Statistics", VOA. Available at: https://www.voanews.com/a/ voa-interview-what-to-know-about-russia-s-manipulated-war-statistics/6913900.html.

Towfigh Nia O. (2022) "NATO chief slams Russian nuclear threats", Anadolu Ajansı. Available at: https://www.aa.com.tr/en/politics/ nato-chief-slams-russian-nuclear-threats/2796 719.

Trebesch Ch. *et al.* (2023) "The Ukraine Support Tracker: Which countries help Ukraine and how?", *Kiel Working Paper*, no. 2218.

Uenuma F. (2022) 'The 1983 Military Drill That Nearly Sparked Nuclear War With the Soviets', *Smithsonian Magazine.* 27 April 2022. Available at: https://www.smithsonianmag.com/ history/ the-1983-military-drill-that-nearly-sparked-nuclear-war-with-the-soviets-180979980/

Ukraine Government (2017) Association Agreement between the European Union and Ukraine, *State sites of Ukraine.* Available at: https://www.kmu.gov.ua/en/yevropejska-integraciya/ugoda-pro-asociacyu.

Umland A. *et al.* (2021) *Damage Control: The Breach of the Budapest Memorandum and the Nuclear Non-Proliferation Regime.* Available at: https://www.academia.edu/45604934/ Damage_ Control_The_Breach_of_the_Budapest_Memorandum_and_ the_Nuclear_Non_Proliferation_Regime

UNHCR (2023) United Nations High Commissioner for Refugees (2023) Situation Ukraine Refugee Situation.. Available at: https:// data.unhcr.org/en/situations/ukraine.

UNRIC (2022) The UN and the war in Ukraine: key information, *United Nations Regional Information Centre for Western Europe.* Available at: https://unric.org/en/the-un-and-the-war-in-ukraine-key-information/.

Volten M.E. *et al.* (2007) Establishing Security and Stability in the Wider Black Sea Area: International Politics and the New and Emerging Democracies. IOS Press.

Weiss M. *et al.* (2022) "Horrifying footage appears to show Russian captors castrating a Ukrainian prisoner of war", *Yahoo! News..* Available at: https://news.yahoo.com/ horrifying-footage-appears-to-show-russian-captors-castrating-a-ukrainian-prisoner-of-war-221414554.html.

Wesolowsky T. (2021) "Thirty Years After Soviet Crackdown In Lithuania, Kremlin Accused Of Rewriting History", *Radio Free Europe, Radio Liberty.* Available at: https://www.rferl.org/a/lithuania-soviet-crackdown-1991-kremlin-rewriting history/31043914.htm.

White S. *et al.* (2008) "The Putin Phenomenon", *Journal of Communist Studies and Transition Politics*, vol. 24, no. 4.

White S. *et al.*, (2009) "Rethinking the 'Orange Revolution", *Journal of Communist Studies and Transition Politics,* vol. 25, no. 2-3.

Whiting K. (2022) "Here's how the food and energy crises are connected", *World Economic Forum.* Available at: https://www.weforum.org/agenda/ 2022/09/heres-how-the-food-and-energy-crises-are-connected/.

Yeung J. *et al.* (2022) "Russia attacks Ukraine", *CNN*. Available at: https://edition.cnn.com/ europe/live-news/ukraine-russia-news-02-23-22/h_ec5f24d5accb8 f8503aabdc63e3fd22d

Ziegler, Ch. E. (2009) The history of Russia. Greenwood Publishing Group.

CHAPTER 12

The impact of the war in Ukraine on a new arms race in the space domain

Łukasz Pokrywiecki

Abstract

This chapter explores the evolving dynamics of space militarization in the context of the ongoing war in Ukraine and its broader implications for a new arms race in space. The chapter investigates how the conflict has accelerated space-based technologies and defence systems, analyzing the strategies employed by Russia, the United States, and other global actors. It examines the role of satellite systems in intelligence gathering, surveillance, and communication, which have become increasingly vital for military operations. The study also delves into the legal frameworks governing space militarization, highlighting the challenges of enforcing international agreements such as the Outer Space Treaty amidst the rapid advancements in space defence technologies. Through this analysis, the research sheds light on the risks of escalating tensions and the potential consequences of an unregulated arms race in space. The findings suggest an urgent need for revising global governance in space to ensure long-term security and stability.

Keywords: space race, space militarization, war in Ukraine

Introduction

The 1957 launch of Sputnik initiated the space competition between the two nations: the United States and the Soviet Union. The two superpowers competed for the next three decades to explore space and develop space weapons. Currently, China, France, India, Japan, and South Korea are also participants in the space domain, and nations are once again competing to develop space weapons. In 2019, India joined the United States, China, and Russia in being able to obliterate orbiting satellites, and many nations have developed jamming technologies that could interfere with the satellites that enable GPS technology, high-speed internet, and weather forecasting. These satellites are used by the military for intelligence and communication. China is constructing sophisticated anti-satellite weapons. A new anti-satellite missile was tested, as was the launch of two satellites capable of destroying other satellites by Russia in 2020. China and Russia have been identified by the U.S. Defence Department as their principal adversaries. President Donald Trump, while in office, established the Space Force to safeguard U.S. and allied satellites and preserve the nation's ability to operate autonomously in space. Since the 24th of February 2022, we have been witnesses to the exploitation of the space domain, which has been central to warfare and has assisted civilians in their hard times. Lessons learned from the war in Ukraine can potentially shape the decisions and direct the paths of international superpowers in the new arms race in the space domain. Experts warn that this renewed emphasis on space defence could spark an escalation reminiscent of the Cold War.

The purpose of this research is to evaluate the effect that the conflict in Ukraine is having on the development of a new arms race in the space domain, with the specific question asked being weather the war in Ukraine will contribute to the acceleration and intensification of development of space militarization technology. This research provides an introduction to the attitude towards the militarization and weaponization of space in light of international law. The degree of advances in military space technology among world-leading nations, namely the People's Republic of China, the Russian Federation, and the United States of America, is discussed in this article. In addition to this, it offers an academic study of the space domain dimension of the continuing war in Ukraine, with the primary emphasis being the identification and examination of the predominant tendencies. It demonstrates the capabilities of the Ukrainian space industry as well as the future of the Ukrainian space sector. The study highlights possible future concerns about an arms race in the space domain and demonstrates the lessons gained from space-related military activities on all levels during the conflict in Ukraine. In addition, the research highlights the lessons learned from space-related military actions during the conflict in Ukraine and warns about vulnerable aspects of the space domain.

The objective of this research is to examine the potential correlation between the conflict in Ukraine and the emergence of a fresh arms race in the realm of space, with a particular focus on whether the ongoing war in Ukraine will serve as a catalyst for the hastened and heightened advancement of technology related to the militarization of space. This study examines the implications of international law on the militarization and weaponization of space, with a focus on altitude. The article provides an overview of the present state of the arms race in space in recent years, specifically military space capabilities in leading space-faring nations, with a particular focus on the United States of America, the Russian Federation, and the People's Republic of China. The text offers an academic assessment of the spatial dimensions of the ongoing conflict in Ukraine, concentrating on the identification and analysis of the dominant patterns. The display highlights the capabilities of Ukraine in the space sector and the potential of the Ukrainian space industry. The study presents insights gained from military operations related to space at all levels during the conflict in Ukraine. Additionally, it highlights possible future apprehensions regarding a potential arms race in the realm of space.

In order to attain the study's objectives, systematic analysis was employed. The purpose of the analysis is to provide a systemic perspective of the studied phenomenon, which is interconnected through a network of functional dependencies. The primary challenge refers to the limited accessibility of reliable information sources. The extensive coverage of the space aspect of the conflict in Ukraine has been observed to a certain degree. However, this has resulted in a proliferation of information that lacks reliability, thereby impeding the researcher's ability to construct an accurate representation of reality. The challenge of obtaining information can be attributed to various factors. Initially, it is noteworthy that military operations conducted in space are typically classified. The expansion of actors involved in conducting operations beyond just the armed forces and state agencies to include commercial entities has only partially resulted in increased transparency in the realm of information.

The portrayal of the conflict in Ukraine is significantly influenced by the propaganda tactics employed by both parties. Significantly, this activity frequently assumes more intricate manifestations than fabricating false information or negating established truths. It may materialise, for instance, through the highlighting or suppression of certain topics or by cultivating a suitable environment around specific issues. Lastly, it should be noted that the ongoing conflict in Ukraine is a contemporary occurrence. This implies that the various components of the subject are currently undergoing academic analysis, which is predominantly contemporary in nature and lacks the benefit of retrospective insight.

Militarization and weaponization of outer space

Some international agreements apply in space, including the 1967 Outer Space Treaty, but they do not address the majority of space weapons developed since then. According to some specialists, new agreements were desperately required to prevent conflict and collaboratively manage the use of outer space for everyone's benefit (Bielawski & Polkowska, 2020, p. 209). In 2008, the nations of Russia and China presented a formal proposal known as the Treaty on the Prevention of the Placement of Weapons in Outer Space and the Threat or Use of Force against Outer Space Objects to the United Nations Ad Hoc Committee on the Prevention of an Arms Race in Outer Space (PAROS). In 2014, an updated proposal was submitted by Russia and China with the aim of preventing the deployment of weapons in space. However, the proposal lacks a reliable verification mechanism, comprises ambiguous definitions, and omits ground-based weapons (IISS, 2022). On December 7th, 2020, the United Nations General Assembly passed four resolutions:

- Prevention of an arms race in outer space;
- Reducing space threats through norms, rules, and principles of responsible behaviour;
- No first placement of weapons in outer space;
- Transparency and confidence-building measures in outer space activities.

Moreover, during a UN meeting in October 2022, Russia cautioned that private facilities in outer space, which are implemented for military reasons, may be considered a justifiable attack for retaliatory measures.

The Biden Administration unilaterally announced on April 18th, 2022, the imposition of a self-imposed ban on the testing of anti-satellite (ASAT) weapons (Arms Control Association, 2022). The aforementioned declaration was released in reaction to the direct-ascent anti-satellite test conducted by Russia, which resulted in the targeting of the defunct Soviet surveillance satellite Cosmos 1408 and the creation of a vast cloud of debris (SPACE, 2021). The President has issued a call to action for other nations to collaborate in efforts to safeguard the security of outer space and establish a sustainable space ecosystem (U.S. Department of Defence, 2022).

Despite the presence of the term "peaceful uses of outer space" in the 1967 Outer Space Treaty and other multilateral treaties related to outer space, official government statements and state practise indicate that this term remains undefined and lacks authoritative interpretation; therefore, the existing system of international law does not protect against the militarization and weaponization of outer space (Kim, 2018, p. 275-276). The present paper cites the views of Professor Ivan A. Vlasic (1926–2011) on the distinction between the terms "militarization" and "weaponization" in the context of outer space. As per the professor's perspective, it is imperative to differentiate between the two concepts. The lack of internationally recognised definitions for the terms "militarization" and "weaponization" of outer space has led to ambiguity in their usage. The former relates to the utilisation of outer space by a substantial number of military space craft, whereas the latter applies to the deployment of any equipment intended to target human-made objects in outer space or on Earth for any duration. The weaponization of space encompasses the development of weaponry that can traverse the Earth's atmosphere and operate within the realm of outer space, as well as the deployment of armaments on celestial bodies. This includes the creation of weapons capable of penetrating outer space or engaging in offensive manoeuvres against targets within this domain. The term space weapon refers to the use of armaments with aggressive capabilities in outer space or on terrestrial surfaces to target entities situated in space.

The utilisation of outer space for military purposes has established it as militarised; however, it has not yet been weaponized. As of April 2023, there are no known operative orbital weapons systems designed to destroy other satellites or launch attacks on Earth's surface. Though successful tests have been conducted by Russia (SPACE, 2021) to demonstrate the capability of destroying satellites from the Earth's surface. The significance of space for state actors is crucial in terms of security and defence, particularly in the subsequent fields (NATO, 2023):

- Positioning, navigation, and timing technology that allows for accurate targeting, force tracking, and search and rescue operations;

- Early warning systems provide critical information on missile launches and ensure the safety of military personnel;

- Monitoring of the environment, weather forecasting, and mission planning;

- Secure satellite communications are imperative for effective mission consultation, command, and control;

- Earth observation is essential for situational awareness, planning, and decision-making processes.

In order to establish space as an effective domain, governmental authorities are augmenting their comprehension of the space environment, encompassing potential hazards and vulnerabilities, to improve their space domain awareness. The preservation of situational awareness and dependable access to space services is of utmost importance in guaranteeing the triumph of military operations. Taking all of these factors into account, it is presumed that a new space arms race is imminent.

The People's Republic of China

Beijing is advancing towards its goal of attaining parity with or exceeding the United States in the domain of space leadership by 2045 (IISS, 2022). Beijing has demonstrated its space heritage capabilities with hundreds of successful orbital launches to date and intends to launch more than 200 spacecraft by the end of 2023. The PRC has four facilities for launching space objects that have military and civil capabilities. Centres also have the capability to serve as ballistic and missile centres as well as carry out scientific research (DIA, 2022). In the year 2022, the nation of China executed a total of 64 space launches, of which two were unsuccessful. The launches were deemed successful, with a total of 150 satellites effectively placed into orbit, along with the deployment of both an orbital and suborbital spaceplane (McDowell, 2023).

Regarding Chinese space weaponry, it is noteworthy that the nation has achieved a significant level of advancement. This was demonstrated by the occurrence of cyberattacks that specifically targeted satellite objects. Cyberattacks resulted in disruptions in the functioning of satellites. According to available sources, it is likely that the cyberattacks were carried out by the Chinese hacking group known as Thrip. For the past 15 years, China has been actively engaged in the development of space kinetic weaponry. Specifically, the Direct-Ascent Antisatellite (DA-ASAT) surface-launched weaponry has been used in two successful tests in 2007 and 2018 (Bielawski, 2022). China is presently engaged in the development of non-kinetic weapons that are space-based, including laser and micro-laser technologies; moreover, China is working on Rendezvous and Proximity Operations (RPO) as a means of advancing its technological capabilities, potentially including the development of kinetic weapons for use in orbit. The Chinese have also reached the operational capability to use space-targeted jamming equipment via the J-16D aircraft.

Satellite technology is crucial for the development of a strategic early warning system that relies on it. The underlying rationale for its development is to furnish timely notification of potential risks emanating from the United States as well as from peripheral actors like Taiwan. The system possesses the capacity to facilitate aggressive military manoeuvres through the identification of targets and their missiles, the evaluation of combat casualties, and the provision of assistance in decision-making processes in the event of a requirement for subsequent strikes. The Space Situational Awareness (SSA) system of China has the ability to detect, track, and identify satellites in all Earth orbits. The system comprises a satellite tracking and control centre located in Xian, along with stationary land stations, a minimum of one mobile system, and seven Yuanwang tracking vessels that operate in the Pacific, Atlantic, and Indian Oceans (Stokes, 2022).

The People's Republic of China is currently making swift

progress in the development of an independent satellite navigation system known as BeiDou. The present iteration, which is the third generation of the system, provides two tiers of accessibility, namely, public and encrypted. The aforementioned entity possesses the capability to determine its location with a precision of up to 10 metres. The encrypted signal, designed for service in military contexts, offers a precision level of 10 centimetres.

China is making advancements in its pursuit of becoming the global leader in space exploration. China has sustained its position as the second-most proficient space nation, following the United States. The PRC has prioritised civil, intelligence, and military space capabilities as it invests in and strategizes for increased utilisation and accessibility of space in the forthcoming decade. The Tiangong space station was constructed by China and became operational in November 2022 (Spacenews, 2023). In 2016 and 2021, Beijing published two white papers pertaining to space activities. These documents not only articulate a vision for forthcoming space endeavours but also incorporate space into other strategic global initiatives (Bingen *et. al.,* 2023).

China is currently enhancing its diplomatic ties with various nations, with Russia being the most prominent among them. One example is the signing of an agreement with China's National Space Administration for cooperation in space activities for the period 2023–2027. The primary objectives of this partnership include the establishment of a lunar research station and the enhancement of the accuracy and reliability of the Chinese BeiDou and Russian GLONASS satellite navigation systems, which are in competition with the US-owned GPS. This agreement confirms Chinese support for Russia in the war in Ukraine, as both BeiDou and GLONASS can be used for military purposes, and GLONASS is currently being used in Ukraine. This system serves as the foundation for multiple aspects of contemporary conflict, encompassing surveillance drones, navigation, and missile targeting as the most popular. China and Russia assert their collaboration in two other crucial and sensitive areas, namely anti-ballistic missile and early warning systems. In 2009, an agreement was reached between two nations regarding the reciprocal notification of ballistic missile and launch vehicle launches, which was subsequently extended in 2020.

The Russian Federation

Moscow has acquired space heritage capabilities with regard to the launch of space objects. At present, it is operating multiple cosmodromes. The well-known Baikonur is a facility situated in Kazakhstan that is used for the launch of ballistic weapons and scientific satellites; however, the most extensive space cosmodrome in Russia is located in Plesetsk. Russian cosmodromes are able to launch full-spectrum space assets, encompassing a range of functions such as reconnaissance, meteorology, communication, early warning, natural resource surveying, navigation, scientific research, and other related activities.

Upon analysis of the capabilities of cyber weapons, it can be posited that Russia has attained a significant level of advancement in this domain. There exist at least two hacking groups, namely Turla (ESPI, 2018) and Fancy Bear (Vasquez, 2022), that conduct their operations on behalf of governmental entities. The nature of their conduct is marked by intricate modes of assault that result in sophisticated and persistent hazards to vital infrastructure and the governing entities of the targeted nation. Regarding the advancement of kinetic armaments, the Russian Federation possesses ballistic weaponry with the capability of targeting entities situated within low Earth orbit. One instance of this phenomenon can be observed in the PKO Nariad-W anti-satellite land-basing complex, which operates intercontinental ballistic missiles. The asset is outfitted with a warhead weighing two metric tonnes that has the ability to be utilised kinetically in outer space.

The development of non-kinetic weapons is also being pursued by Moscow. The Beriev A-60 system for satellite blinding is underway within the realm of laser weaponry. In 2009, efficacy tests were carried out on this substance, which demonstrated its effectiveness in countering a Japanese satellite orbiting at a height of 1,500 km (Butowski, 2023). The Peresvet ground-based laser weapon system, which Russia's deputy prime minister in charge of military development claims is operationally ready, but Laura Grego, an astrophysicist at the Massachusetts Institute of Technology, says that system is not sufficient to damage distant targets like orbiting satellites (Hitchens *et. al.,* 2022). Even though Russia said they were successful, advanced counter-space weapons like ground-based lasers were not seen as operational (Defence

News, 2022). The Krasukha-4 is electronic warfare equipment operated by the Russian Federation that has the ability to jam space elements situated in the Low Earth Orbit (LEO) up to a distance of 300 km from the surface of the Earth. Furthermore, the Russian Federation is currently in the process of developing the Ku-Pol early warning system. The primary objective of this system is to expeditiously detect and monitor ballistic missiles as well as missiles and hypersonic weaponry that may be deployed against Russia or its affiliated nations (Nightingale *et. al.,* 2016).

The Russian government is currently engaged in the development of a space situational awareness system with the capability to track objects in the cosmos situated in low-Earth orbit. The objective of this task is to oversee the debris orbiting in space. The extant system is designed to oversee a total of over twenty-two thousand celestial bodies. The envisaged configuration of the system comprises a total of 65 optical telescopes stationed on the ground, complemented by sensors that are strategically positioned on satellites orbiting the Earth and an optical sensor that is situated on the International Space Station (ISS). The implementation of artificial intelligence (AI) through machine learning techniques is being considered for the purpose of tracking space objects (Spacewatch.global, 2020). The GLONASS autonomous global navigation satellite system has been under development since 1982. The GLONASS-KM generation, an upgraded version of the existing GLONASS-K, is presently in the conceptual phase and is anticipated to be finalised by 2025. Furthermore, the latest iteration of the satellite system possesses the capability to convey the GPS L5 signal, thereby endowing it with a significant degree of immunity against interference (Shuai, 2022).

Russia is a significant player in the space race, and it still has a lot of space powers and forces. However, the country may face challenges in accomplishing its space objectives in the long run. Sanctions, restrictions on exports, an ageing population, and bribery are hurting the Russian space industry (IFRI, 2021). That resulted from its incursion into Ukraine. Moscow is at a turning point. Over the past year, Russia's space and counter-space powers have continued to be less advanced than expected. Russia's domestic space industry is beset with numerous issues, and there is mounting competition for programme resources within the country. It is likely that Russia will concentrate on prioritising and integrating space-based services that are considered crucial to its homeland's safety (Office of the Director of National Intelligence, 2023).

The United States of America

As the United States of America possesses sophisticated space capabilities, it is widely regarded as the preeminent military power in space. The US possesses a robust capacity for launching space objects, commonly referred to as its space heritage, which serves as a launch site for both rockets and shuttles in addition to functioning as a civilian launch pad.

Washington claims that its currently not engaged in the development of cyberwarfare capabilities that are based in space. The sole undertakings in this locality encompass the formulation of a cyberwarfare doctrine and the establishment of a governing body, namely the U.S. Cyber Command (USCYBERCOM), which bears the responsibility of enhancing cyber defence capabilities across the diverse factions of the United States military forces' locations, including among others European allies. The United States is advancing its capacity for space weaponry, encompassing kinetic and non-kinetic weaponry. An Exo-atmospheric Kill Vehicle (EKV) kinetic impact system has been devised as a component of the advancement of kinetic weaponry. In the event of an enemy missile attack, it can be transported to outer space by the ground-based interceptor missile. This object possesses the capacity to traverse through the expanse of outer space, monitor celestial bodies, and inflict damage upon them through the discharge of substantial kinetic energy resulting from a collision at a velocity of approximately 8 kilometres per second. As of 2022, there were 44 operational standby components in the United States.

Research and development efforts in the realm of non-kinetic space weaponry have been underway in the United States since the 1980s. Tests were conducted under the Mid-Infrared Advanced Chemical Laser programme and by the Airborne Laser System with positive results. The United States is currently engaged in the development of a space-based microwave weapon system (Hitchens, 2021). The predominant space-related electronic weaponry utilised by the United States is comprised of the

Counter Communications System (CCS) and Navigation Warfare (NAVWAR) systems (Bielawski, 2022). The aforementioned technology is a portable electronic warfare system designed for the purpose of disrupting adversary satellite communication systems that are stationed in geostationary orbit. The second system is used for both offensive and defensive purposes in influencing position, navigation, and timing services.

The development of early warning capabilities is also underway in order to support, among others, the Ballistic Missile Defence System, which is presently in development as a response to the swift advancement of missile technology, which poses an escalated risk of the deployment of these ballistic weapons, including nuclear warheads (U.S. Department of Defence, 2019). The US Space Situational Awareness Competency possesses the ability to conduct space monitoring and tracking of celestial bodies and man-made space objects. The system's functionality relies on the Space Surveillance Network (SSN), which comprises a collection of radiolocation stations as well as ground- and space-based telescopes. The United States is currently enhancing its system by increasing the deployment of its sensors and pursuing partnerships with commercial entities to establish reciprocal agreements for the exchange of information on space objects.

Washington is capable of providing worldwide navigation thanks to its satellite system, namely GPS-NAVSTAR. The ongoing development of GPS Block III represents the next iteration of this technology, boasting enhanced resistance to disruption, superior precision, heightened reliability, and improved data integrity. By the year 2030, it is projected that the current generation will be responsible for fulfilling the military and civilian requirements of the United States (Steigenberger, Thoelert & Montenbruck, 2020).

The United States of America remains the world's leading country in space, with approximately half of all satellites and space systems. Washington plans to return humans to the moon by 2024 (Butow *et. al.*, 2020). As long-lasting lunar infrastructure may allow for far-flung space excursions, even to Mars, the moon is seen as a stepping stone for future space exploration.

Space domain activities on the war in Ukraine

The invasion of the Russian Federation into Ukraine started on February 24, 2022. There is little question that the space domain, which, when employed effectively, greatly helps operations on the battlefield, has been playing a vital role in this struggle. The Russian military operation in Ukraine is conducted by both conventional and unconventional means, on land, in the air, at sea, and in cyberspace. The possibilities offered by space technologies—which not only assist other domains but are also an arena of warfare—play a crucial role from the very beginning of the conflict.

The conflict in Ukraine has demonstrated a diverse range of operations in the space domain. A great example is GPS-guided weaponry, such as HIMARS, which has been effectively implemented to accurately strike designated targets. In addition, satellites are capable of identifying and pinpointing GPS signal disruption origins, which cause alteration of the flight path of Ukrainian unmanned aerial vehicles (Hybrid CoE, 2023). The conflict has been characterised by certain analysts (Erwin & Erwin, 2022) as the "first commercial space war" as a result of the significant role played by Western space sector competences in bolstering Ukraine's struggle.

Nevertheless, since the very beginning, the Russian Federation has been using its capabilities in order to exceed in the space domain. Ukrainian government sources reported that a long-range unmanned aerial vehicle (UAV) encountered notable GPS interference, resulting in a momentary loss of control over the aircraft, just one day prior to the invasion (UK Space Agency, 2022). What is more, Russia executed a cyberattack aimed at disrupting the connectivity between the Viasat communications KA-SAT network and its numerous ground terminals just one hour in advance of the invasion of Russian troops. The use of jamming devices by Russia has persisted throughout the period of the military conflict. Russia has taken measures to impede Ukrainian command and control systems that rely on commercial communications satellites, in addition to engaging in electronic warfare against navigation systems. Multiple accounts suggest the utilisation of terrestrial electronic warfare apparatus in Ukraine, potentially encompassing the Krasukha-4, RB-109A "Bylina," R-330ZH Zhitel, Borisoglebsk-2, and Tirada-2, all of which possess the capacity to impede or interrupt GPS or satellite communications via uplink and downlink jamming.

Several trends have emerged about the militarization of space within the context of the conflict in Ukraine. The increase in the employment of commercial satellite communication systems for military purposes is the first one. The phenomenon in question is not a recent development. The military employment of commercial satellite communication systems has been demonstrated to present novel prospects, as evidenced by the conflict that has arisen in Ukraine. The aforementioned phenomenon is a result of the development of large-scale satellite constellations intended to facilitate worldwide internet dissemination, such as the Starlink system of the SpaceX company. According to Mykhailo Fedorov, Deputy Prime Minister for Innovation, Education, Science, and Technology Development, and Minister of Digital Transformation, as of April 26, 2023, a total of 42,000 Starlink internet kits had been transported to Ukraine (Ukrinform, 2023). This technology is operated not solely to preserve online communication channels in scenarios where terrestrial infrastructure has been damaged, which, taking into consideration the information operations being conducted by both sides, is crucial, but also to conduct strictly military actions. According to Tan's report (Business Insider, 2022), Starlink's communication services have been exploited for the coordination of artillery fire in combination with observation drones.

In contrast to conventional satellite communication systems that rely on a geostationary orbit, the Starlink network provides substantially greater bandwidth and reduced signal propagation times. That requires a great number of satellites, nevertheless, and has an undisputable advantage from a military point of view. Primarily, this implies a rise in system redundancy, rendering it arduous, if not unfeasible, to counteract its potential with conventionally destructive anti-satellite systems. However, the Starlink system has been subject to attempted jamming by Russian systems, and their effectiveness has been limited (Musk, 2022). Further instances of jamming have been noted during the course of the conflict and in regions proximate to the conflict zone and beyond.

The trend that has been emphasised refers to the growth of the exploitation of data acquired from commercial satellite remote sensing systems. The above-mentioned phenomenon was observable prior to the commencement of the conflict, as members of the general public were able to acquaint themselves with satellite-derived depictions of Russian activities in anticipation of the invasion. In addition to direct military benefits from the utilisation of such systems, which resulted in possessing reliable imagery intelligence data, Ukrainians had the opportunity to take support from open-source intelligence producers, which heavily rely on information provided by commercial platforms. The capabilities in the area of the conflict proved to be advantageous both before and during the hostilities phase in the context of the Ukrainian conflict (Kopeć, 2022). That demonstrates the feasibility of the potential presented by commercial imaging systems to furnish timely notification of an adversary's premeditated hostility, affording opportunities for both military and diplomatic intervention. What is more, the use of commercial imagery in information operations as well as psychologically directing public opinion by intensifying the message through the striking impact of images. Significantly, this was achieved without divulging visuals originating from military entities.

The third trend applies to the augmentation of radar satellite observation systems, which are designed to operate autonomously irrespective of weather conditions and regardless of the time of day, which multiplies opportunities to cover areas of interest. It is a verifiable fact that systems that rely on synthetic aperture radar do not provide a quantity of intelligence data that can be exploited on electro-optical images. Consequently, such systems are less suitable for propaganda purposes due to the less suggestive nature of the images they provide. However, the advantages of these systems are unparalleled. The capacity to conduct frequent surveillance, irrespective of meteorological circumstances and during the night, is especially advantageous in the context of the armed conflict in Ukraine, where the prevalence of cloud cover frequently renders electro-optical systems unfeasible. The ICEYE radar satellites' utility was deemed significant enough for Ukraine to procure an exclusive satellite in addition to obtaining data from the entire constellation. The contract stipulated unimpeded and sole entitlement to images acquired from the satellites, with the option to download image data from the complete constellation. In September 2022, Oleksii

Reznikov, the Defence Minister of Ukraine, provided a summary of the initial weeks of the contract. He emphasised the continuous operation of reconnaissance, even in autumn conditions, the capacity to identify concealed targets, including vehicles, and the rapidity of data transmission (Ukrinform, 2022).

Ukrainian space capabilities

The space industry of Ukraine was primarily built upon the lasting impact of the Soviet Union. This presented a favourable circumstance, yet it necessitates substantial financial commitments. Every aspect of the industry that was passed down through inheritance was solely focused on collaborating with Russia. During the Cold War, Ukrainian companies played a significant role in the production of rockets, especially those with military applications. Henceforth, particularly after 2014, the primary objective is to redirect attention towards western countries collaboration, implement novel paradigms in corporate governance, optimise technological resources, prioritise initiatives that yield the most effective advantages, and facilitate the advancement of space-related technologies (Ukraine's Space Assets, 2023).

According to Vladimir Taftai, President of the State Space Agency of Ukraine, in recent years, the Ukrainian space industry has experienced insufficient funding and therefore does not have enough resources for full development. At the same time, it has saved capabilities and largely introduced new technologies in the design and construction of launch vehicles, including continuing to participate in the Antares and Vega projects, developing satellite production, significantly expanding ground space infrastructure, and developing capabilities in receiving and processing Earth observation data (President of the State Space Agency of Ukraine, 2022).

However, although the Ukrainian Space Programme has not yet been implemented and Ukraine is facing extremely serious budget problems, it is still a space nation with a high level of ambition, focusing on the development of rocket technologies, the creation of the national surveillance satellite constellation, and increasing interoperability throughout participation in multinational programmes, principally Artemis. The Ukrainian Space Agency is almost as big as NASA, with 16,000 personnel. The organisation, a holdover from the Soviet period, manages 20 state-owned companies. Ukraine possesses the ability to manufacture space equipment of exceptional quality and exhibits promising potential for future advancements within the space technology sector.

The Cyclone-2 launch vehicle has demonstrated its reliability through the successful completion of all 106 test launches. The Cyclone-4M space rocket system, developed in collaboration with Maritime Launch Services, represents a new version of this series and is intended for conducting space launches from Nova Scotia, Canada. Simultaneously, Ukrainian enterprises have designed and initiated the production of the fundamental blueprint for the initial phase of the Antares spacecraft, which was contracted by Northrop Grumman Corporation of the United States. The proposed concept involves using a solid-fuel engine to launch microsatellites into orbit from a transport aircraft while in flight. In addition, the engineers are responsible for the development of rocket engines, such as the primary engine used in the Vega light rocket of the European Space Agency, engines for the Long March rocket series of China, and various undertakings for the Korean Aerospace Research Institute.

Ukrainian companies were responsible for the design and production of control and navigation systems used in launch vehicles and spacecraft during both the Soviet and post-Soviet periods. A number of enterprises that previously encompassed the entirety of the launch vehicle production process during the Soviet era are presently lacking in self-sufficiency. While Ukraine may not be able to rival space rocket powerhouses such as America's Space X, it is possible that its offerings could occupy specific niche positions, particularly within the American market for cost-effective space system solutions (Spacedotcom, 2022). Moreover, Ukraine has the capability to collaborate effectively with nations that are striving to execute domestic space initiatives. The utilisation of Ukrainian components in their space initiatives is of interest to the Turkish.

Nonetheless, Ukraine's status as a space-faring nation is not solely attributed to its hardware manufacturing capabilities. The successful functioning of spacecraft necessitates the existence of advanced terrestrial infrastructure that facilitates space observation as well as the control and processing of data obtained from orbit. The aforementioned functions have been designated to the National Space Surveillance and Analysis System and the Centre for the Reception and Processing of Special Information and Navigation Field Control. The PS-8.2 station is responsible for the reception and processing of information from remote Earth sensors via spacecraft.

Zbruch is a long-range radar system used for radio monitoring of objects located in outer space, specifically in the context of space situational awareness. The Zbruch station is a constituent of the National Centre for Space Management and Testing and has been specifically engineered to identify and track both man-made objects and space debris that are present in the Earth's orbit (State Space Agency of Ukraine, 2023). The computational aspect of the radar system is able to determine the path of descending debris, thereby anticipating any potential hazards to individuals or physical structures. Additionally, Zbruch has facilitated the categorization of over 12,000 celestial bodies to enable their trajectory surveillance.

However, the Ukrainian space sector encounters certain challenges. The space sector of Ukraine has faced hindrances in its further development due to the atrophy of several competencies from the Soviet era and the presence of inefficient government structures. The major reason for this phenomenon is the state's exclusive control over the space sector, which has persisted for a considerable duration. Nevertheless, a sector of international privately-owned aerospace corporations is presently conducting operations within the borders of Ukraine. Among other responsibilities, they oversee the prototype manufacturing of rocket elements.

Lessons learned

Taking into consideration the current state of space militarization as well as having analysed the space-related military actions on all levels during the war in Ukraine, but also including Ukrainian space capabilities the lessons learned presents as follow.

Firstly, commercial businesses and their space resources had unprecedentedly great contributions to space-related activities during the war. It has been causing a fusion of the distinction between civilian and military participants in the conflict. There may be a rise in the inclination towards incorporating double-purpose (military and civilian) space equipment in technological partnerships for the goal of enhancing crucial security to the space-related capabilities initiatives. Therefore, it is possible to give rise to the question of the readiness and capacity of authorities to safeguard private resources.

What is more, the advancement of space-related technologies has led to the emergence of novel combinations of capabilities that may be leveraged for space-related military-employed applications, and as a result, generate a strategic advantage over a militarily superior entity, namely:

- Earth observation – case ICEYE;
- Communication – case Starlink;
- Positioning, Navigation, Timing – case HIMARS;
- Electronic warfare – case Krasukha-4;
- Cyber Security – case Starlink and case Viasat.

On the other hand, the conflict between Russia and Ukraine has exposed notable weaknesses in the components of the space infrastructure. Space-related assets have been subjected to electronic and cyber-attacks. A prompt and effective response to potential attacks is crucial in mitigating the impact of cyberattacks or signal jamming in the space domain.

Furthermore, the challenges faced by the Russian command and control systems, the inadequacy of ultra-high resolution earth observation systems, and the significant errors associated with Russian precision arms, which are believed to be GLONASS-guided, suggest a comparatively less efficient utilisation of space systems in comparison to the United States (Massa, 2022). The imposition of technology sanctions in 2014 had a detrimental impact on the advancement of Russia's space capabilities.

Another significant lesson is that the conflict between Russia and Ukraine has facilitated the transformation of satellite-based technologies into daily-life devices for civilians, as evidenced by Starlink. The capacity to make a meaningful and practical impact during times of crisis and conflict can enhance and maintain people's resistance and preparation to safeguard each other. This is enabled by access to trusted sources of information, as individuals seek news concerning a crisis during such times. The utilisation of satellite-derived data is poised to fulfil this requirement. The utilisation of this approach may also prove advantageous in the context of information campaigns aimed at mitigating hybrid threats as well as bolstering individuals' ability to withstand persuasive efforts within the information sphere.

The effectiveness of some other satellite technologies designed for military purposes has not been proven so far in military operations on the battlefield. Principally, kinetic and laser weapons have not been evidenced during the conflict. Although Russia conducted a kinetic anti-satellite test in November 2021, the capability was not seen during the war. Ukraine lacks the necessary means to carry out such a course of action. In contrast, it is likely that Russia engages in this activity to a restricted extent. The feasibility of its utilisation, nonetheless, appears to be grossly insufficient in a scenario where potential objectives are abundant, owing to the constellation of satellites. The experimental nature of the satellite strike suggests that Russia lacks the capability to damage the constellation, even partially, as it is beyond its capabilities. Despite the claims of Russia's ability, there are no independently verified reports regarding the deployment of directed-energy capabilities against satellites in the ongoing conflict with Ukraine. Despite the availability of remote sensing satellites and other platforms that provide data and intelligence on Russian troop positions to the Ukrainian military, neither the Peresvet laser weapon system nor any other laser system has been utilised in the Ukrainian conflict (Bingen *et. al.*, 2023).

On the contrary, the efficacy of civilian imagery intelligence providers in enhancing situational awareness has been evidenced in the armed conflict in Ukraine. However, this source should be recognised as not fully reliable due to possible disinformation, and it should be confirmed on a case-by-case basis. Nevertheless, the private remote sensing sector has exhibited its potential, thereby showing the significance of not-classified data that may be disseminated worldwide by armed forces, which contributes to the significance of this sector as a crucial strategic asset.

Lastly, the Ukrainian space industry is able to contribute to the development of space-related technologies; therefore, it has not been a target of kinetic attacks by the Russian Federation as a potential target for a takeover. The Ukrainian space sector is a crucial part of the state's economy and an experienced source of know-how for building space capabilities. The potential profitability of the Ukrainian space industry is a valuable asset and a vital interest for all parties involved in the conflict.

Conclusion

The war, which started on February 24, 2022, is the first significant confrontation in which the two opponents conduct operations directly dependent on space capabilities (Massa, 2022). During the conflict, a wide spectrum of operations related to the space domain have been omnipresent. This includes operations conducted directly in the space domain as well as in every other domain (air, land, sea, and cyber) that rely on space technology and capabilities. The activities have been represented in the following areas (starting with the most relevant to the conflict):

- Satellite communication;
- Satellite-based earth observation;
- Positioning, Navigation and Timing;
- Electronic Warfare;
- Space-based early warning systems;
- Space situational awareness and tracking;
- Weather forecasting.

The remaining space capability has not yet been observed in the war in Ukraine, including these anti-satellite weapons. It is not an effective measure in terms of cost/effect ratio, and there is a high risk of Kessler syndrome as a result of the satellite strike, which constitutes the probable reasons for resigning the use of this technology during the conflict.

Cybersecurity is crucial for the space domain, as it is the most vulnerable part of the space system architecture. The probability of cyber-attacks and electronic jamming attacks is higher than that of physical space attacks due to various factors. Cyberattacks are a cost-effective alternative to constructing interceptor missiles, as they do not result in physical debris and may provide plausible deniability. Additionally, they may be less likely to provoke a military response.

Undoubtedly, the space domain has had a prodigious influence on the war in Ukraine. However, it works both ways, so the war in Ukraine has been influencing the space domain. Military applications and technologies that are strictly associated with the space domain have been used repeatedly and have contributed to operational leverage, consequently becoming a top priority domain in the context of the success of military operations. This conflict impacts the acceleration of the space militarization process and increases competition in the arms race in the space domain. The intensification of research and development efforts in the space sector is shifting the centre of gravity of the space domain from governmental assets closer to the private sector. The war showed that space technologies designed and intended for civilian use, like Starlink, can be quickly adopted for military purposes. The evolution of altitude to kinetic anti-satellite weapons will probably result in further focus on advances in laser anti-satellite weaponry that have not been evidenced either during the conflict or fully operational in any military forces all around the world due to an insufficient level of advancement. This makes laser anti-satellite technology an upcoming milestone in the space domain, and the run has already begun (DIA, 2022). Concurrently, the ongoing conflict has spurred endeavours to achieve vital independence, as exemplified by Europe's objective to establish an independent satellite communication network (EEAS, 2022), which is another proof of intense competition in the space arms race.

The long-term effects of the war will significantly influence the advancement of the space realm in contexts of cooperation and expanding the scope and adaptability of private services and equipment. As of February 15, 2023, a letter of intent (LOI) has been signed by sixteen members, including Finland and Sweden, to participate in the Alliance Persistent Surveillance from Space initiative. The objective of the agreement is to capitalise on the recent progress achieved in the commercial space sector with regard to geo-intelligence gathering as well as to achieve economic benefits by combining space systems, simplifying data collection procedures, and exploiting other available resources that are presently accessible to the alliance's constituents through the power of synergy (NATO, 2023). Chief of Space Operations Gen. B. Chance Saltzman also emphasises the importance of cooperation and coalition with countries that have capabilities in space. Support from the coalition partners is needed in order to fill the technology and capabilities gap (Space24, 2023).

The analysed space powers—the People's Republic of China, the Russian Federation, and the United States of America—have achieved a high level of militarization and weaponization of space and have developed their space capabilities. The United States is reasserting its aspiration to assume the position of the foremost global space authority. The conflict in Ukraine can be viewed as a catalyst for intensifying the phenomena of destabilisation and polarisation within the space domain. The initial indication of this development surfaced when the Russian government declared its intention to discontinue its participation in the International Space Station. At present, the extent of this declaration's scope remains ambiguous; currently, the Russians are upholding a level of activity within the station that is relatively typical. A discernible convergence between the Russian and Chinese powers has been observed, comparable to other domains, as evidenced even before the war by Russia's expressed desire to partake in the Chinese lunar space station in 2021 (Institut Montaigne, 2022). However, the imposition of technology sanctions and the anticipated reduction in government revenues in Russia cast doubt on the country's ability to bridge the gap in space capabilities.

Russia-China space cooperation can be divided into two distinct fields: technological progress and capacity building, and diplomatic activities related to space exploration. Notwithstanding China's 'win-win' rhetoric, a potential outcome of cooperation could be to make Russia more dependent on China. As such, it will provide an additional means of influencing the trajectory and extent of cooperation with regard to the development of China's space programme and broader aspirations in the space domain. Growing space cooperation between China and Russia raises security concerns for the transatlantic region. However, Russia's diminished global status due to its armed conflict in Ukraine could potentially hinder Chinese efforts to enlist the support of other nations for joint initiatives, given the growing rapprochement between Beijing and Moscow (Bergmann & Lohsen, 2022). The aforementioned dynamic could potentially lead to a divergence between China and Russia, thus creating an opportunity for further discussions on space security between Beijing and Western nations. The efficacy of the Chinese military's utilisation and assimilation of space capabilities in an actual conflict is yet to be determined. It is advisable to anticipate that China may employ space capabilities more efficiently in a prospective conflict than Russia has demonstrated in its actions in Ukraine, but it needs further research.

While private companies may play a role in enhancing security measures, it is important to note that the ultimate responsibility to guarantee safety lies with the governments that possess legal authority. It is highly recommended that governments provide increased support for safeguarding privately owned space systems, which are deemed critical strategic assets. Additionally, it is imperative for governments to establish a transparent plan of action in order to ensure their protection. The absence of clarity at present poses a potential danger of miscalculation by opposing parties.

Reference

Arms Control Association (2022) *U.S. Commits to ASAT Ban*. Available at: https://www.armscontrol.org/act/2022-05/news/us-commits-asat-ban.

Bergmann, M. & Lohsen, A. (2022) *Understanding the Broader Transatlantic Security Implications of Greater Sino-Russian Military Alignment*. Available at: https://www.csis.org/analysis/understanding-broader-transatlantic-security-implications-greater-sino-russian-military.

Bielawski, R. & Polkowska, M. (2020) *Organisational, Military and Legal Aspects of Space Security*. Akademia Sztuki Wojennej.

Bielawski, R. (2022) 'Rozwój zdolności w domenie kosmicznej przez potentatów kosmicznych', *Kultura Bezpieczeństwa*, 42, pp. 58–69. doi: 10.5604/01.3001.0015.9477.

Bingen, K. et al. (2023) *Space Threat Assessment 2023*. Available at: https://www.csis.org/ analysis/space-threat-assessment-2022.

Buisness Insider (2022) *Elon Musk's Starlink Satellites Are Helping Ukraine's Elite Drone Unit Destroy Russian Tanks and Trucks in the Night.* Business Insider. Available at: https://www.businessinsider.com/elon-musk-starlink-ukraine-drone-unit-russia-tanks-war-2022-3.

Butow, S.J., Cooley, T., Felt, E. & Mozer, J.B. (2020) *State of the Space Industrial Base 2020 Report.* Available at: https://www.aerospace.csis.org/wp-content/uploads/2020/07/ State-of-the-Space-Industrial-Base-2020-Report_July-2020_FINAL.pdf.

Butowski, P. (2023) *The Soviets Built Bespoke Balloon-Killer Planes During the Cold War.* The Drive. Available at: https://www.thedrive.com/the-war-zone/the-soviets-built-bespoke-balloon-killer-planes-during-the-cold-war.

Defence News (2022) *Russia Claims Its Zadira Laser Weapon Destroyed a Drone in Ukraine.* Available at: https://www.defencenews.com/global/europe/2022/05/19/russia-claims-its-zadira-laser-weapon-destroyed-a-drone-in-ukraine/.

DIA (2022) *2022 Challenges to Security in Space.* United States of America: Defence Intelligence Agency. Available at: https://www.dia.mil/Portals/110/ Documents/ News/Military_Power_Publications/Challenges_Security_Space_2022.pdf.

EEAS (2022) *A Strategic Compass for Security and Defence.* Available at: https://www.eeas.europa.eu/eeas/strategic-compass-security-and-defence-1_en.

Erwin, S. & Sandra, E. (2022) *On National Security: Drawing Lessons from the First "Commercial Space War".* SpaceNews. Available at: https://spacenews.com/on-national-security-drawing-lessons-from-the-first-commercial-space-war/.

ESPI (2018) *ESPI Report 64.* Available at: https://www.espi.or.at/reports/.

Hitchens, T. (2021) *What Satellite Attack Weapon Might the US Reveal Soon?* Breaking Defence. Available at: https://breakingdefence.com/2021/08/what-satellite-attack-weapon-might-the-us-reveal-soon/.

Hitchens, T. et al. (2022) *Don't Be Dazzled by Russia's Laser Weapons Claims: Experts.* Breaking Defence. Available at: https://breakingdefence.sites.Breaking-media.com/2022/05/dont-be-dazzled-by-russias-laser-weapons-claims-experts/.

Hybrid CoE (2023) *The Space Domain and the Russo-Ukrainian War: Actors, Tools, and Impact.* Available at: https://www.hybridcoe.

fi/publications/hybrid-coe-working-paper-21-the-space-domain-and-the-russo-ukrainian-war-actors-tools-and-impact/.

IFRI (2021) Russia's Space Policy: The Path of Decline? *IFRI – Institut français des relations internationales.* Available at: https://www.ifri.org/en/publications/etudes-de-lifri/russias-space-policy-path-decline.

IISS (2022) *The Strategic Survey 2022.* 1st edn. Taylor and Francis. Available at: https://www.perlego.com/book/3797245/the-strategic-survey-2022-pdf.

Institut Montaigne (2022) *Space: A Forgotten Battleground of the Ukraine War?* Institut Montaigne. Available at: https://www.institutmontaigne.org/en/expressions/space-forgotten-battleground-ukraine-war.

Kim, H.T. (2018) 'Militarization and Weaponization of Outer Space in International Law', *The Korean Journal of Air & Space Law and Policy*, 33(1), pp. 261-284.

Kopeć, R. (2022) 'Wykorzystanie systemów orbitalnych w wojnie Rosji z Ukrainą. Między militaryzacją a komercjalizacją kosmosu', *Roczniki Nauk Społecznych*, vol. 50, no. 4, pp. 115–131. doi: 10.18290/rns22504.5.

Massa, M. (2022) *Early Lessons from the Russia-Ukraine War as a Space Conflict.* Atlantic Council. Available at: https://www.atlanticcouncil.org/content-series/airpower-after-ukraine/early-lessons-from-the-russia-ukraine-war-as-a-space-conflict/.

McDowell, J. (2023) *Space Activities in 2022.* Available at: https://planet4589.org/ space/papers/space22.pdf.

Musk E. (2022) Twitter. Available at: https://twitter.com/elonmusk/status/15805943 79751686149.

NATO (2023) *NATO Official Website.* Available at: https://www.nato.int.

Nightingale, E.S. et al. (2016) *Evaluating Options for Civil Space Situational Awareness (SSA).* Science and Technology Policy Institute. Available at: https://www.ida.org/ research-and-publications/publications/all/e/ev/evaluating-options-for-civil-space-situational-awareness-ssa.

Office of the Director of National Intelligence (2023) *2023 Annual Threat Assessment of the U.S. Intelligence Community.* Available at: https://www.dni.gov/index.php/ newsroom/reports-publications/reports-publications-2023.

President of the State Space Agency of Ukraine (2022) 'Poland Provides Us with Outstanding Support during the War with Russia',

Defence24.com. Available at: https://defence24.com/geopolitics/president-of-the-state-space-agency-of-ukraine-poland-provides-us-with-outstanding-support-during-the-war-with-russia-interview.

Shuai, P. (2022) *Understanding Pulsars and Space Navigation.* Navigation: Science and Technology Ser.

SPACE (2021) Available at: https://space.com.

Space24 (2023) *Przeszłość i Przyszłość US Space Force [ANALIZA].* Space24. Available at: https://space24.pl/polityka-kosmiczna/swiat/przeszlosc-i-przyszlosc-us-space-force-analiza.

SPACEdotcom (2022) *Ukraine's Proud Space Industry Faces Obliteration, but Country's Former Space Chief Has Hope for the Future.* Space.com. Available at: https://www.space.com/ukraine-mighty-space-industry-faces-obliteration.

Spacenews (2023). Available at: https://spacenews.com.

Spacewatch.global (2020) *Russia to Develop Space Surveillance Satellite to Monitor Space Debris as Part of Milky Way SSA Network.* Available at: https:// spacewatch.global/2020/06/russia-to-develop-space-surveillance-satellite-to-monitor-space-debris-as-part-of-milky-way-ssa-network/.

State Space Agency of Ukraine (2023) *State Space Agency of Ukraine.* Available at: https://www.nkau.gov.ua/en/.

Steigenberger, P., Montenbruck, O., & Hauschild, A. (2014) 'Estimation of Satellite Antenna Phase Center Offsets using GPS Navigation Data', *Advances in Space Research*, 53(2), pp. 265–274. doi: 10.1016/j.asr.2013.10.031.

Stokes, M.J. (2022) *China's Strategic Intentions and Capabilities in Space.* Available at: https://www.uscc.gov/sites/default/files/2022-11/China_Strategic_Intentions_and_Capabilities_in_Space.pdf.

U.S. Department of Defence (2022) *DOD Releases 2022 National Defence Strategy.* Available at: https://www.defence.gov/News/Releases/Release/Article/3208292/dod-releases-2022-national-defence-strategy/.

Ukraine's Space Assets (2023) *Ukrainian Space Agency.* Available at: https:// www.nkau.gov.ua.

Ukrinform (2022) *ICEYE Satellite Imagery Yields First Results on Battlefield – Ukraine's Defence Minister.* Available at: https://www.ukrinform.net/rubric-ato/3581906-iceye-satellite-imagery-yields-first-results-on-battlefield-ukraines-defence-minister.html.

US Defence Intelligence Agency (2022) *Challenges to Security in Space 2022*. Available at: https://www.dia.mil/News/Publications/.

US Defence Intelligence Agency (2022) *Global Threat Assessment 2022*. Available at: https://www.dia.mil/News/Publications/.

CHAPTER 13

HUMINT as a weapon in Ukraine War

Mikołaj Schulz

Abstract

This chapter explores the critical role of Human Intelligence (HUMINT) in the ongoing war between Ukraine and Russia. It delves into how HUMINT has been employed as an instrumental weapon by both sides, particularly in gaining tactical and strategic advantages in a highly complex and rapidly evolving conflict. The chapter outlines the key elements of HUMINT operations, emphasizing its importance in counterintelligence, gathering information on enemy movements, and leveraging local populations. Through case studies, it analyzes the success and challenges faced by Ukrainian and Russian forces in employing HUMINT in a modern warfare context, where cyber capabilities and technological advancements play a major role. The findings indicate that while technological intelligence is increasingly dominant, HUMINT remains indispensable in providing on-the-ground realities that are often missed by remote surveillance. This chapter concludes by suggesting strategies to strengthen HUMINT capabilities in conflict scenarios, particularly in hybrid warfare environments like the one seen in Ukraine.

Keywords: HUMINT, counterintelligence, espionage, GRU, SVR, Ukraine

Introduction

The digital revolution has had a profound impact on society over the last two decades. However, its widespread use has not lessened the need for direct human interaction in the process of collection, analysis, evaluation and dissemination of intelligence. While there have been significant advances in artificial intelligence and machine learning, the direct involvement of humans in analysis and decision-making has not yet been discarded. In the context of human intelligence collection (HUMINT), the role of the person in establishing rapport with another person, building trust and confidence in the relationship and directing and tasking the person has not yet been replaced by a machine. As a consequence, this is why another person is so important in contacts with a person. Many significant pieces of information can be obtained during interpersonal conversations. This is precisely the power of HUMINT.

"Men are so simple and so ready to obey present necessities, that one who deceives will always find those who allow themselves to be deceived." – this quote from Niccolo Machiavelli's *The Prince* (Machiavelli, 1505, p.84) may indicate some human weaknesses that are particularly susceptible to influence. Another of his quotes, *"Hence it is necessary for prince, who wishes to maintain himself, to learn how not to be good, and to use this knowledge and not use it, according to the necessity of the case"* embodies intelligence activity. (Ibidem, p.71)

These quotes highlight two importance aspects of Human Intelligence or HUMINT. The first quote relates to the motivators of people to cooperate. The second quote relates to the need to undertake activity in a way that hides your true intent, specifically the collection of information while acting covertly. HUMINT though is just one collection discipline with others including open source intelligence (OSINT), geospatial intelligence (GEOINT), signals intelligence (SIGINT) and measure and signature intelligence (MASINT).

This article explores the issues associated with human intelligence sources including an analysis of the diverse categories of HUMINT motivation in relation to cooperation in covert collection of intelligence. It will primarily focus on the activities of the foreign intelligence services of the Russian Federation in its efforts to collect intelligence on states currently supporting the Armed Forces of Ukraine. The first part of the article introduces the concept of HUMINT and its associated definitions. Some of these have been constructed by bespoke legislation and others through the development of organisational field craft, policy and practice. The second part deals with specific identifiable motivators for cooperation, relevant to operational planning linked to HUMINT recruitment. Linked to this, it will explore and evaluate two commonly used motivational frameworks – MICE and FIREPLACES and how these both support HUMINT recruitment strategies. The last section outlines examples of the Russian Federation's intelligence activities across Europe during its war with the Ukraine. The article offers evidence of how, even in an increasingly complex technology rich environment, the role of human intelligence is still critical in providing insight and operational advantage during intelligence and military operations.

This research will draw upon a diverse range of material including academic journals and books, official government policy and announcements and judicial material. It will also draw from open-source material including social media, newspapers, and broadcast material. It acknowledges the limitations of researching in this area, for example, restricted access to classified material relating to espionage and also military activity, both covert and overt, small sample sizes and access constraints through a lack of government vetting of the author.

HUMINT – definitions

Covertly obtaining information from another person is the oldest of the intelligence collection disciplines that states and organisations have used to understand threats and risks. Its utility has meant it is still a major collection discipline today. While technology is starting to inform tradecraft and communication practice, much of the interaction is generally undertaken between handlers and informants. Technology those enables safe and quick opportunities for communication without the need for time consuming physical one to one interaction.

It may be helpful that prior to discussing some of the wider issues associated with HUMINT use, some consideration is given to associated definitions. Open-source research offers a multitude of definitions of this term.

According to the NATO dictionary, it is *"Intelligence data developed based on information collected by personal operators and fundamentally provided by personal sources"*. (NATO, 2017, p.233). Kamiński in his publication *"The Evolution of*

Intelligence as a State Institution" cites the definition from the *"National Intelligence a Consumer's Guides 2009"* of the American Intelligence Community (Kaminski, 2021, p.82). According to the Intelligence Association, HUMINT is *"The collection and delivery of information obtained through interpersonal contact by representatives of an organization"* (U.S. National Intelligence, p. 45-46). Minkina, the author of the publication *"The Art of Intelligence in the Modern State"*, stated that recruitment of a person holding a state official position, who has access to a special catalogue of information, is the most common. Of course, the most valuable are people with access to the critical information that determines the functioning of a given country, whether in civilian or military context (Minkina, 2022, p. 178–179).

With there is as diverse range of definitions associated with HUMINT, there are links of commonality. This is evidenced in the statement that HUMINT is *"The covert collection by humans of intelligence from other humans that is relevant to an organization's intelligence requirement."* is important though that any potential recruit who may have the requisite access to information are appropriately verified in terms of their identify, the receive appropriate training in tradecraft including information protection, and are checked any vulnerability to witting or unwitting disclosure of sensitive information to unauthorised individuals.

The higher the classification of the information, the more attractive it is to foreign intelligence. People who possess this information are more vulnerable to recruitment attempts by hostile states. Accordingly, the State needs to consider how it can deter people from passing on unauthorised information. Article 130 of the *Criminal Code of the Republic of Poland*, states *"Anyone who participates in foreign intelligence or acts on its behalf, providing intelligence with information whose transmission may harm the Republic of Poland, is liable to imprisonment for a term of not less than 3 years,"* This is an example of a statutory deterrent whose intention is to detere Polish citizens from cooperating with foreign intelligence services. However, legal provisions do not always have the effect of preventing people from offering their services to hostile states.

MICE and FIREPLACES – lockpicks for human beings?

The challenge for those persons charged with responsibility is to identify and then recruit a person to report against their own country or an organisation. One element of the recruitment process, it to identity the potential motivation or motivations that may persuade a person to take undertake a course of action, which would ordinarily conflict with their basic values and attitudes. Identifying and understanding motivation is a critical element of any recruitment operational planning and as a consequence has seen increasing research being undertaken to understand the range of motivational levers that could potentially be exploited.

Stanislav Levchenko, a KGB officer from 1971–1979, stated in an interview with *The New York Times* that "*the CIA used the MICE method to determine weaknesses of individuals who could be helpful in case of recruitment*" (The New York Times, 1988, p.33). MICE, mentioned by the former officer, is an acronym for:

- M – Money
- I – Ideology
- C – Compromise
- E – Ego

The first letter, 'M' reflects the financial factor. Intelligence officers may provide funds, the amount of which is often determined by the importance and quality of the disclosed intelligence. The money can be cash but it can also include other tangible rewards for example, clothes, vehicles, help with rent etc.

A CIA report from a media interview with Levchenko shows that he emphasizes that "*money as a motive for cooperation is increasingly important, not only for citizens of the United States but also for citizens of other countries.*" He also added that "the KGB is a very patient formation, which often spends even several years to obtain one personal source, but in the case of financial motivation, this process can be shortened to even a few days." (CIA, n.d., p.2). However, is Levchenko's statement supported by evidence? The author has not identified any academic material which supports his assertion that money is *increasingly* important although it is clearly one of the key motivators still. This is an area that required further research.

In his publication *"Rethinking an Old Approach: An Alternative Framework for Agent Recruitment: From MICE to RASCLS"*, Randy Burkett notes that in the case of financial motivation, individuals interested in this form of cooperation do not always need these funds for their expenses. Motivations can be different: the desire to improve living conditions for loved ones, the necessity of expensive treatment for family members, or financing education for their children. (CIA Intelligence Studies, 2013 p.9). However, Burkett offers two examples where money was a key factor, but not the only motivator. The first related to the case study of CIA officer Aldrich Ames, who sold secret CIA information to the Soviet Union until 1994. He was said to have earned 2.7 million dollars from this collaboration. The second example concerns GRU Colonel Pyotr Popov, a Soviet intelligence worker who sold Soviet secrets to the United States. and as a consequence, earned thousands of dollars.

Another letter of the acronym- 'I', represents Ideology. Ideological inspiration can be a strong driver human actions, a force for good but also for bad. This is particularly visible among communities associated with radicalism and terrorism (whether it's "Lone Actor", "Black Widows", or entire organizations). With the help of appropriate indoctrination, the subject can undertake actions that they would not have taken with other motivators. Psychological impact on basic human motivations can often distort the perceived reality.

In the case of profiling a person and detecting their sympathy for a particular country or organization, intelligence agencies may conduct recruitment under a "false flag". This is nothing more than recruitment in which the intelligence agency poses as the side that the potential "target" sympathizes with. After properly preparing the situation and circumstances, the person will believe in the presented version and will carry out their actions, convinced that they are doing it for the side they sympathize with. In the case of citizens of two doctrinally polarized countries, ideological premises can arise as a desire to leave one side for the other or to promote the political system that one of the sides possesses, and the person subject to the ideological factor favours. An example of such activity is the work of Oleg Penkovsky. As a colonel of Soviet GRU, in August 1960 he established cooperation with the American CIA. The main motivator of his actions was the desire to fight communism and support democracy. (Henriksen, 2015, p. 20) Ideology as a motivator was also an apparent driving force for the Cambridge spy, Kim Philby. While studying at Cambridge University, he became a supporter of communism and joined the Cambridge University Socialist Society. This institution was created (was it created by the Soviets or did they just exploit its membership?) by the Soviet intelligence and meticulously monitored its members and tried to recruit the best students. Kim Philby joined the ranks of the British foreign intelligence SIS (MI6), previously being recruited by the Soviet NKVD. In 1944, he took over the management of Section IX, responsible for combating espionage in the direction of the USSR (CIA Intelligence Studies, 2015, p. 41). Coercion or Compromise-The third of the four letters of the acronym MICE is 'C' and refers to coercion and includes blackmail. In this case, it may involve, among other things, the use of compromising materials on the potential target of recruitment or a threat to them, their close relatives or important things to them. During the Cold War, the Soviet intelligence utilised women employed by their organisations or prostitutes whose task was to seduce the "target", have sexual relations with them, and document these intimate encounters. The documentation was most often recorded in the form of photographs or films, which then served as a blackmail element. Of course, these "swallows" could also secretly plant drugs, illegal weapons or documents for the "target", which could also be used as a means of pressure. This phenomenon was called "sexpionage". According to former CIA officer Jason Matthews, the training center for female operatives assigned to these activities was a facility located in Kazan. Victims of these practices included Commander Anthony Courney and the British Ambassador to Moscow, Sir Geoffrey Harrison (Fisher, 2018). However, how successful is coercion as a means of building rapport and sustaining Handler-Informer relationships? How forthcomingare the sources going to be with their knowledge? The findings of research undertaken after the fall of the Berlin war, on the

Stasi's use of informant suggested coercion of potential informants was not a favoured motivation because of concerns over their long-term reliability.

The last letter of the acronym is E. It stands for "Ego/Excitement" and captures the potential informants need for excitement or adrenaline in this term. Additionally, the desire to be appreciated by a superior or even society can also be fitted into this term. A certain desire to become a hero or an object of admiration. In this case, if a person with a high ego level is mistreated by their superior, they may "in revenge" want to turn to the opposite side, in the way thinking "*maybe they will appreciate me.*"

The Cold War was called the "Golden Age of Soviet Espionage" because the intelligence services of global powers competed with each other, fought each other, and constantly sought ways to improve the effectiveness of their agencies. One example of such actions is the evolution of the MICE method.

Stanier and Nunan (2021 p. 2) propose a development of the MICE motivational framework. They introduce a mnemonic called FIREPLACES. The FIREPLACES framework expands MICE which they hold better explains the range and nuances of motivational reasons for informing. To Stanier and Nunan, the MICE framework, whilst useful in the Cold War period as a basic assessment tool is now somewhat dated. The increasing professionalisation of HUMINT practice and police, enhanced training and the increasing unit of dedicated HUMINT management resources means that a more sophisticated framework can be utilised to better understand motivations. Stanier and Nunan hold that the use of the FIREPLACES framework to identify and understand the range of motivations as play in an informants use means that there is a better opportunity to not only help identify a person's motives but also maintain and build on control and also to ensure continuity in the recruiter-target relationship. The expansion of the FIREPLACES acronym is as follows:

- F – Finance
- I – Ideology/Moral
- R – Revenge
- E – Excitement

- P – Protection
- L – Lifestyle
- A – Access
- C – Coercion
- E – Ego
- S – Sentence

The issues in this acronym, and MICE, may seem similar, but in this case, it is "a step further." In his publication, Stanier and Nunan clearly stated what is behind each letter:

F – Finance. It is not just about money as a form of payment, but also about objects, vehicles – all material goods. Additionally, this category also includes money to cover costs such as rent, education for oneself or family, and medical expenses for loved ones.

I – Ideology. This refers to providing information by a group/person who has conflicting interests with the group/person to whom the information relates. This is a factor that can clearly be driven by members of terrorist groups or organized crime, but also by intelligence officers who want to betray their country (including ideals that are at odds with the ideals of the person betraying) in favour of another country (e.g., a country with a communist system for one that adheres to democratic values).

R – Revenge. A very common driver for informing and action taking although not always openly disclosed at the recruitment stage. Revenge is an emotion that can be triggered by a single event but is painful for the person (e.g., the values they uphold). In the case of a lack of appreciation for an employee, humiliation of someone, or causing harm, strong emotions may come into play that will trigger the desire to "get back" at the perpetrator. Whether physically, mentally, or in other ways. One of these ways may be to cooperate with the enemies or competitors of a particular person, such as foreign intelligence services.

E- Excitement. Many people are not satisfied with their lives. Depression rates in society are increasing (Duszynski-Goodman, 2023). Therefore, one way to change such a state is to try to introduce something exciting into one's existence. People then try to find new hobbies or engage in extreme sports. To feel "something" because they don't feel much on a daily basis. Then some, wanting to break the monotony, turn to such diversification as providing adrenaline to their lives through cooperation with foreign intelligence agencies. The feeling of taking risks at the moment of stealing or copying important documents and passing them on to someone else releases a note of excitement and arousal that these people wanted to feel in their monotonous lives.

P – Protection. Individuals involved in organized crime or cooperating with foreign intelligence services are subject to criminal sanctions in their country. Therefore, one of the reasons why a person may undertake cooperation is to protect themselves from such sanctions. In the case of the criminal environment, a person who is, for example, a leader of a group, by informing on members of their own organization or its competition (if cooperation with law enforcement has been established) will receive a lesser prison sentence for themselves or will be able to continue their business activities under the supervision of the services. In the case of cooperation with foreign intelligence, a person may be guaranteed extraction in case of the threat of arrest and accusation of espionage.

L – Lifestyle. Ensuring a "goal" of a better life. Whether it's services, objects, or any kind of care. Access to foreign medical centers, expensive cosmetic procedures, expensive hotels, travel with exclusive means of transportation, and leading an extravagant lifestyle.

A – Access. The informant relationship provides an opportunity for counter-penetration to identify agency interest in offending networks and associates. This may include deliberate infiltration by criminals to understand the nature of police tasking and levels of interest in their or their competitor's criminal enterprises (Stanier & Nunan, 2021, p.3).

C – Coercion. Similar to the letter C in MICE.

E – Ego.

Another similarity to the MICE acronym, however, Dr Stanier points out a very important detail – the possible occurrence of a phenomenon among informants commonly referred to as "Walter Mitty". This term refers to a character with the same name from the movie "The Secret Life of Walter Mitty". In the movie, the character is a dreamer who leads a very calm life and comes up with different scenarios. He presents himself as someone very important or a person with impressive achievements. In reality, he works as an accountant (Welma, 2008, p. 1-2). The American

Heritage Dictionary defines Walter Mitty as "an ordinary often ineffectual person, who indulges in fantastic daydreams of personal triumphs" (American Heritage Dictionary, n.d.). The above phenomenon carries many risks for cooperation with the source of information, as the informant may significantly distort (or completely falsify) reality in order to present themselves as someone very influential or possessing important information, potentially leading to danger for the officer handling the informant, the exposure of the operation, or the entire intelligence activity in the area.

S – Sentence. People serving a prison sentence may agree to provide information in exchange for a reduced sentence or release from serving it. This is a very beneficial solution for people serving prison sentences for espionage, as they often receive long sentences in prisons, and by providing information, there is a possibility to significantly reduce or even completely end the sentence served.

The above presentation of the evolution of HUMINT methods shows that work is constantly being done to improve existing solutions. It is only a matter of time before newer methods of influencing human motivations are invented in order to establish cooperation in the recruiter-target field, but even the development of new methods will not render the current ones obsolete. It can be observed that new acronyms have many similarities to their older counterparts, which only shows that certain human motivations remain unchanged.

The War in Ukraine – intensification of intelligence operations in countries supporting the Ukrainian Armed Forces during the conflict with the Russian Federation.

On February 24th, 2022, the Russian Federation's forces carried out an armed aggression on the territory of Ukraine. The Russian authorities officially declared it a "special military operation," but in reality, it marked the beginning of a full-scale military conflict between the two countries. Over time, NATO countries began supporting the Ukrainian Armed Forces with their technology, military resources (vehicles, aircraft, weapons, ammunition), and training. To increase its chances of winning the conflict and weaken the cooperation between NATO and Ukraine, the Russian Federation decided to take action on their territory. For such operations, the Russian Federation currently has two intelligence agencies operating abroad: the Foreign Intelligence Service (SVR) and the Main Directorate of the General Staff of the Armed Forces of the Russian Federation (GU). These officers carry out operations abroad, under diplomatic cover or without it. One of the most effective weapons in their "arsenal" is HUMINT. HUMINT has the potential to help secure strategic information that could tip the balance of the war. Since the conflict with Ukraine began, media outlets around the world have systematically reported on the activity of Russian Federation's intelligence agencies, whose actions in this area have been uncovered.

1. Poland – expulsion of 45 Russian diplomats in March 2022

In March 2023, the authorities of the Republic of Poland, together with the Internal Security Agency (ABW), expelled 45 Russian diplomats because it was revealed that these 45 Russians were actually officers of the Russian intelligence operating under diplomatic cover (Republic of Poland, n.d.). In Poland, they appeared as representatives of Russian trading companies. The Coordinator of Special Services, Stanisław Żaryn, said that the goals of the expelled individuals were *"to undermine Poland's position on the international stage and threaten our country's interests"* (Gera, 2022). It has not been publicly disclosed which intelligence agency the above individuals belonged to or how long they carried out their activities on Polish territory.

2. Espionage in the Civil Registry Office in Warsaw, Poland – March 17, 2022

On March 17, 2022, the Internal Security Agency (ABW) arrested an employee of the Civil Registry Office in Warsaw who was collaborating with the Russian SVR. A person sitting in such an office had long-term access to very detailed personal data of the residents of the Polish capital, including their addresses and personal data of their partners. The man was a very valuable source of information for the Foreign Intelligence Agency of the Russian Federation (Sieniawski, 2022).

3. Spanish journalist in Poland, Pablo Gonzalez – night of 27-28 February 2022

Another arrest by the ABW, this time in the city of Przemyśl. The subject of the operation was a freelance journalist with dual citizenship – Spanish and Russian – working for the GRU. According to information, he was conducting espionage activities in Warsaw, several strategic border crossings (Przemyśl, Medyka), and on the territory of Ukraine. He was arrested in a hotel room in Przemyśl. He had two Russian passports and credit cards, which were issued under two different identities. It is not known how much information he managed to obtain and how significant it was (Tremlett, 2022).

4. Uncovering a spy network – Poland, March 2023

Minister Kamiński announced in March 2023 that a group of six people had been operating in Poland, preparing acts of sabotage and conducting espionage activities for the benefit of the Russian Federation. According to the Polish Minister, the arrested individuals were monitoring the supply chains of weapons to Ukraine (the railway line on which they were transported) and documenting this, as well as planning to disrupt the supply with acts of sabotage. According to ABW information, the Polish side has evidence that these individuals were paid by Russian intelligence services. Cameras were located near the Rzeszow-Jasionka airport (adapted for logistical purposes for military aid to Ukraine), which recorded the delivery process, the size of the supplies, and the type of weapons transported by Poland. These cameras were most likely installed by the aforementioned group of individuals (Easton, 2022).

5. Norway – 15 diplomats, March 2023

The Norwegian counterintelligence detected 15 people working undercover as diplomats who were in reality officers of the SVR, GRU, and FSB. They were involved in recruiting individuals and purchasing technology. The main areas of interest for Russian officers were the Norwegian defence sector and Norwegian aid delivered to Ukraine. The fact that Norway is the largest supplier of gas in Europe is also not insignificant, and information was sought in this area as well. According to the head of Norwegian counterintelligence, "the Russians wanted to learn as much as possible about gas and fuel technology because they themselves are the target of Western sanctions" (Polish Television, 2023).

6. *Germany – Spy in foreign intelligence – December 2022*

At the end of 2022, the German authorities announced the arrest of an intelligence employee who was conducting espionage activities for the Russian Federation. This person was Carsten L. He was accused of providing information to the Russian side that he obtained during his service. This was the first case of detecting espionage activities for another country since 2014 when it was discovered that Markus Reichel was providing information to both the CIA and the Russian Federation (Slow, 2022).

7. *Ukraine-Russia Informer 2022*

Ukrainian authorities have reported the arrest of a 43-year-old resident of the village of Slatyne who was providing the Russian side with information regarding the location of Ukrainian military positions. Communication took place through the Telegram application. His activity lasted from March to August 2022. The Kharkiv Oblast Prosecutor said that the information provided by the man contributed to the bombardments by the Russian Federation and to a significant number of casualties on the Ukrainian side (Majeed, 2022).

When trying to find the motives of recruited individuals, searches often end in failure. The same goes for data on the size and importance of stolen information. Such details are usually not revealed to public. The above examples show that recently an intensified amounts of actions conducted by the Russian Federation, aimed at obtaining strategic information, can be observed. Undoubtedly, the determinant of this is the ongoing conflict in Ukraine doubt course, the intelligence activities of the Russian Federation did not start just now, but took place significantly earlier. However, disclosing it to the public can properly align and often boost the morale of the population and the troops, which is crucial for citizens and soldiers fighting in Ukraine. The information policy should still be focused on maximalizing publicity of Ukrainian counterintelligence operation success. The role of the media should also involve showing the citizens the phenomenon of HUMINT and how they can become targets of its exploitation by enemy intelligence services. With social awareness, there will be a chance to recognize, report, and counter of possible recruitment of key individuals from the Ukrainian side.

Conclusion

During the war in Ukraine, intelligence activities are crucial, especially human intelligence. Even the mightiest armies that haven't access to strategic intelligence informations about the enemy are doomed to failure. Such informations can be obtained through the recruitment individuals holding positions on the enemy's side. Analysis of the cases presented in the article shows that sometimes acquiring single source can have a decisive impact on the construction of conflict strategies and their final outcome. The weakest link in all actions will always be the human factor and human nature. Negligence, greed, the desire for revenge, selfishness and human emotions are factors that technology does not possess, which at the same time, can annihilate the most organized and planned actions. However, technology also lacks factors such an empathy, understanding, reading motives and utilizing them appropriately.

The above article shows events that had or could have had a significant impact on the course of the conflict. They could have, as the details and scope of the acquired information are not known. Even the development of technology cannot replace human interaction and manipulation. Obtaining information often requires manipulation or a particular psychological game. This is demonstrated by the war in Ukraine and the actions of the Russian Federation in Europe. It seems necessary to take action to raise awareness of possible attempts to obtain critical information from individuals, particularly those with access to such data. Another key area is the implementation of knowledge in psychology for intelligence officers. This would allow for a much wider range of possible points of influence on potential targets and be a powerful weapon in every officer's arsenal. Only another person is capable of effectively using the above factors persuade some else to disclose valuable informations. As long as there are people on Earth, HUMINT will remain the most important and sometimes the only means of acquiring crucial informations, plans and details regarding enemy's past, present and future activities.

References

American Heritage Dictionary (n.d.) *Walter Mitty*. Available at: https:// ahdictionary. com/word/search.html?q=walter+mitty.

CIA   (n.d.)   *CIA-RDP90-00552R000403690002-9.*   Available at: https://www.cia.gov/   readingroom/docs/CIA-RDP90- 00552R000403690002-9.pdf.Charney, L.D., M.D., and Irvin, J.A. (2016) 'The Psychology of Espionage', in *Guide to the Study of Intelligence.*

CIA Intelligence Studies (2013) Unclassified Excerpts from Studies in Intelligence, Volume 57, No 1.

CIA Intelligence Studies (2015) Unclassified Excerpts from Studies in Intelligence, vol. 59, no. 1.

Duszynski-Goodman, L. (2023) *Mental Health Statistics.* Forbes. Available at: https://www.forbes.com/health/mind/ mental-health-statistics/.

Easton, A. (2023) *Entire Russian Spy Network Dismantled in Poland.* BBC. Available at: https://www.bbc.com/news/ world-europe-64975200.

Fisher, L. (2018) From Russia With Love: How Russian "Sexpionage" Agents and the Real-Life Red Sparrows Used the Art of Seduction to Wage a Very Hot War Against the West. The Sun. Available at: https://www.thesun.co.uk/news/ 5765043/ russian-sex-spies-red-sparrows/.

Gera, V. (2022) *Poland Orders Expulsion of 45 Russians Suspected of Spying.* AP News. Available at: https://apnews.com/article/ russia-ukraine-europe-poland-espionage-warsaw-b6d75f0e65287 f7d6bb68d5e64ecd926.

Henriksen, C.J. (2015) '"I Was": The Oleg Penkovsky Story and the Importance of Human Intelligence in Cold War Crises', *University of Wisconsin, Department of History.*

Kamiński, M. (2021) 'The Evolution of Intelligence as a State Institution', *Warsaw.*

Machiavelli, N. (1505) *The Prince.*

Majeed, Z. (2022) *Suspected Russian Informant Charged in Kharkiv for Spying on Ukraine Amid the Ongoing War*. Republic World. Available at: https://www. republicworld.com/world-news/ russia-ukraine-crisis/suspected-russian-informant-charged-in-kharkiv-for-spying-on-ukraine-amid-the-ongoing-war-articleshow.html.

Minkina, M. (2022) The Art of Intelligence in the Modern State.

National Intelligence (2009) *A Consumer's Guide*. Washington DC.

NATO (2017) NATO Glossary of Terms and Definitions.

Polish Television (2023) *Russian Diplomats Expelled by Norway Were Working for FSB, GRU*. TVP World, 14 April. Available at: https:// tvpworld.com/69183311/ russian-diplomats-expelled-by-norway-were-working-for-fsb-gru.

Republic of Poland (n.d.) *45 Russian Diplomats to be expelled*. Available at: https://www.gov.pl/web/special-services/45-russian-diplomats-to-be-expelled.

Sieniawski, B. (2022) *Alleged Russia Spy Believed to Have Accessed Polish Intelligence Data*. Euractiv. Available at: https://www. euractiv.com/section/politics/news/alleged-russia-spy-believed-to-have-accessed-polish-intelligence-data/.

Slow, O. (2022) *Suspected Russian Spy Held by German Intelligence*. BBC. Available at: https://www.bbc.com/news/world-64069977.

Stanier, I. & Nunan, J. (2021) 'FIREPLACES and Informant Motivation'.

The New York Times (1988) *Section 7*.

Tremlett, G. (2022) *Spanish Journalist Held in Poland on Suspicion of Pro-Russian Espionage*. The Guardian, 12 May. Available at: https://www.theguardian.com/ world/2022/may/12/spanish-journalist-held-in-poland-on-suspicion-of-pro-russian-espionage.

U.S. National Intelligence (2013) *An Overview*.

Welma, D. (2008) Politics of Walter Mitty, a Giant in His Own Mind.

The impact of Russian aggression against Ukraine and the management changes in Polish airspace

Wiktor Satkowski

Introduction

Even though Russia's aggression against Ukraine took place on February 24, 2022, Russian troops were touring the Ukrainian border much earlier and were monitored by NATO. Aid for Ukraine was increased by coalitions of countries not by NATO, and the central role was played by aviation, which ensured security for the walls of the Alliance as well as arming countries neighbouring the aggressor. Civilian companies were engaged in helping, and the entire theatre of these events took place in Polish airspace to this day. The functioning of Polish airspace as of February 22, 2022, has changed dramatically. Half of the airspace is reserved for the functioning of the army, air defence and allied forces aimed at creating a protective shield in the air against a potential conflict or attack to secure the entire Polish space, which is the border of the North Atlantic alliance. The movement of civil aircraft began to take place in the western part of the country. The barrier 180 kilometers from our eastern border has several restrictions and a ban on planning flights due to air defence operations. The primary limits on civil traffic affected the airport in Rzeszów since the local airport has become a base, a military hub for allied activities aimed at strengthening this part of the country. The airport in Lublin was also affected by restrictions, and the purpose of the airport changed to military and humanitarian operations.

Management of Polish airspace before the aggression

Protection of the state border and space of the Republic of Poland are priority tasks of the Air Force's aviation in peacetime and the crisis. According to Art. 7. Act of the day October 12, 1990, on the protection of the state border protection of the Polish border in the airspace, the Minister of National Defence is responsible, and the tasks The Minister in this respect are supervised by the Operational Commander Types of the Armed Forces through the executive body, i.e. Air Operations Center – Command Air Component (COP – DKP). Operational commanders, together with COP – DKP, play a crucial role from a security point of view in airspace because they are responsible for the functioning of the Polish Air Defence system and for direct command of resources and forces assigned by the Commanding General 39. Considering the primary function of the Air Force in peacetime – the defence and protection of space of the Polish Air Force – the Operational Commander, through COP-DKP, is, above all, responsible for the needs identification and maintenance of operational capabilities of the O.P. system and for control and command of the fighter air force assigned to performing combat duty (air policing). Military airspace surveillance (as well as ensuring its inviolability) is both a means of deterrence of a potential adversary and a guarantee of compliance with international agreements regulating the use of airspace. Fighter aircraft assigned to duty are, therefore, one of the critical elements of O.P. systems because they are not just one of the primary active means of combat but also allow you to react quickly in situations of crisis (such as, for example, civil abduction of passenger aircraft, the potential hazard from the side of a foreign military aircraft).

Currently, duty Combat tasks are performed in a rotational system by pairs of duty officers from the 22nd Tactical Air Base in Malbork (MiG-29), 23rd Tactical Air Base in Minsk Mazowiecki (MiG-29), 31st Air Base Tactical Station in Poznań-Krzesiny (F-16C/D) and 32. Tactical Air Base in Łask (F-16C/D). Duty hours are held 24 hours a day, seven days a week, and a couple of fighter planes are on standby "RS-15", which means the pilots are ready to take off armed machines within 15 minutes from the moment issuing the appropriate order. For practical execution tasks and aircraft preparation, the force personnel of the aircraft correspond directly to the commander units designated to perform duty. Belongs emphasizes that the officer in charge of the Duty Officer's activities Operational Service COP – DKP, i.e. the Duty Commander Air Defence, coordinates all activities of the Force Aircraft as part of the defence and protection of space of the air (its inviolability), and also performs a function representative of the Republic of Poland in the Integrated Defence System Air and Missile Treaty Organization North Atlantic (NATINAMDS). The scope of duties of the Duty Commander of Defence is regulated by the Regulation of the Council of Ministers of November 2, 2011, on determining the authority of air defence command and procedures when using air defence measures concerning foreign non-using aircraft to comply with calls from the state traffic management authority airline. According to the regulation at the discretion of the Duty Officer, The Air Defence Commanders make critical decisions related to, among others, intercepting foreign aircraft military and surveillance of civilian vessel aircraft that are subject to the "Renegade" procedure. Regulations in force in Poland related issues, including with interception and further dealing with both foreign aircraft military (in case of violation of space of the Republic of Poland) as well as for passengers aircraft subject to the "Renegade" procedure, are contained in the following documents – the Act of July 3, 2002 – Aviation Law; Act of October 12, 1990, on the protection of the state border; Regulation of the Council of Ministers of November 2 2011 on the determination of the defence command body and the Regulation of the Minister of Transport, Construction and Maritime Economy of July 31 2012 on the National Aviation Security Program civil.

Although air policing missions do not have to be, and usually are not combat missions, a scenario where the air force is responsible for implementing this type of task in the airspace of the Alliance deserves special attention. If we consider and allow the possibility of aggression against the Baltic States, one should consider the possibility that it takes place during the next shift of PKW Orlik. At the same time, the Polish Air Force may be involved in the future on similar missions over the territory of another member of NATO, threatened and, consequently, also affected by the conflict. Tasks set before PKW would result directly from the decisions of NATO bodies. However, it could happen in the initial phase of the contest to accidental fire contact with a forced aggressor. Depending on the region where air policing of the involved forces would be carried out by the other party to the conflict and the degree of threat to own territory, it could become a necessity to immediately evacuate the contingent or else carry out defensive tasks aimed at support of local air defence and operations land-based defences. The possibility of turning an air policing mission into a mission is relatively small.

Furthermore, such developments could likely happen suddenly, without any preceding stage of the growing crisis. For this reason, it should be assumed that the Polish contingent would be the only one available in the theatre, or rather, it would work as part of a broader allied component. In the case of this kind of mission, carried out in the conditions of the existing/growing crisis, it is necessary, first of all, to take into account the necessity of frequent preventing and counteracting aviation incidents in the form of airspace violations and escorting adversary aircraft performing flights near the border.

New types of aircraft and management after aggression

The Russian aggression against Ukraine made NATO decide to send a clear signal towards Moscow, further strengthening its eastern flank. This is why American Patriot batteries will be delivered to Poland and why the increased activity of NATO aircraft has been observed in our skies for several days. Initially, these were mainly aircraft of the USA, Great Britain and the Alliance itself, but recently, other units have joined them, including fighters from France. Various types of aircraft that appeared over the Polish sky:

- Boeing RC-135W Rivet Joint – British reconnaissance aircraft manufactured by Boeing. The sensors of this machine allow the crew to detect, identify and determine the location of signals in the field of electromagnetic radiation. In short, it is a plane for collecting information, e.g. intercepting messages sent by radio.

- Boeing KC-135R Stratotanker – An American-made tanker introduced into service in the 1950s. Initially, the aircraft was used mainly for refuelling strategic bombers, but since then, it has also been used by other military aircraft. Boeing KC-135R Stratotanker is operated by a crew of

3 and has a range of 2.4 thousand km. Km while carrying 68 t of fuel and flies at an altitude of up to 15 km.

- Airbus A330-MRTT – An American Stratotanker, a similar structure is also flying over Poland but strictly belonging to NATO. This is the Airbus A330-MRTT, or Multi Role Tanker Transport – a multi-role aircraft that can act as a tanker and a transporter. Its design was based on the civil Airbus A330.

- Boeing E-8C – The American aircraft present over Poland is the Boeing E-8C, i.e. a reconnaissance aircraft for monitoring objects on the ground and in the air, which can also operate as a flying command centre. The radar of this unit can track up to 600 targets simultaneously in an area of 50,000 km. sq km from a distance of up to 250 km.

- Airbus CC-150 Polaris – An Airbus CC-150 Polaris belonging to the Canadian Air Force also appeared over Poland. Polaris was built based on a civilian Airbus A310, which was turned into a multi-purpose long-range unit that serves transport purposes (from carrying cargo to ordinary passengers or injured) and an air tanker. This machine is in service only with the Canadian army.

- Airbus A400M – The Spanish-owned Airbus A400M, a four-engine transport aircraft with a wingspan of over 40 meters, also checked into our skies. The advantage of this model is that it has a greater payload than the famous C-130 Hercules; it can also take off from makeshift run-ways. The main task of these units is to transport people and goods, but the A400M can also serve as a medical transport unit and an air tanker.

- Boeing C-17 Globemaster III – The United States also sent a Boeing C-17 Globemaster III transport plane to the Polish sky, a massive machine with a 51-meter wingspan that can carry up to 77 tons of cargo, i.e. 100 paratroopers or one M1 Abrams tank. The plane has a range of almost 4.5 thousand km. Km with a 71-ton load and acceler-ates to a speed of 830 km per hour.

- Eurofighter Typhoon – NATO combat aircraft have also appeared in the Polish sky, which came to our country as part of the mission to patrol the airspace of the Alliance. The Germans and the British sent to our country Eurofighter Typhoon fighters, i.e. multi-task, extremely manoeuvrable structures designed mainly for high efficiency of air combat. Currently, however, it is a more versatile machine capable of effectively attacking targets on the ground and the water using a variety of missiles and bombs. Eurofighter also accelerates to a speed of 2,100 km per hour, and its combat range is almost 1,400 km and depends on the type of armament carried.

- Dassault Rafale – France also sends its planes to Poland in addition to German and British machines. The local Rafales take off from bases in France and come to Poland, patrolling our skies. This aircraft entered service in 2001 and was built from the beginning to perform a variety of missions – from intercepting enemy bombers through air combat to bombing raids deep into enemy territory and deterrence missions carrying nuclear warhead missiles. Interestingly, it is a unique machine almost entirely built in France. It was created after France withdrew from the European fighter program, which later became the Eurofighter mentioned above Typhoon. Rafale flies at a speed of 1,900 km per hour, its combat range is up to 1,850 km, and if necessary, the aircraft can survive overloads of over 11 g.

Despite the development of satellite reconnaissance, aerial survey remains one of the most important ways of collecting information about the enemy. This is especially true in the case of radio-electronic and radar studies. No wonder that even before the outbreak of war, NATO aircraft performed many reconnaissance missions in the Member States' airspace bordering Russia and Belarus, as well as over Ukraine itself and in the Baltic Sea zone. The Russian aggression against Ukraine caused the Alliance's aircraft to disappear from its airspace, but they intensified their operations in other regions not covered by direct military confrontation. Therefore, the USAF Boeing RC-135W / V Rivet Joint reconnaissance aircraft, used to detect, locate and recognize signals emitted by electronic, radar and communication systems of the enemy, began to be regular guests in Polish airspace.

These activities are generally referred to as SIGINT (Signal Intelligence), i.e. recognition of emitted signals, and can be divided into several subcategories: ELINT (Electronic Intelligence), i.e. detection and recognition of signals emitted by electronic military devices, radar stations and transponders; COMINT (Communications Intelligence), i.e. detection and recognition of communication, including voice; FISINT (Foreign Instrumentation Signals Intelligence), i.e. detection and recognition of signals generated by telemetry, tracking and data recording devices; MASINT (Measurement and Signature Intelligence), i.e. monitoring and measurement of emissions in the electromagnetic and infrared spectrum; and RADINT (Radar Intelligence), i.e. detecting and locating signals emitted by radar stations.

The USAF received a total of 17 RC-135V/W aircraft, most of which went to the 55th Wing stationed at the Offutt base in Nebraska, from where, if necessary, some of them are sent to allied bases, from where they conduct reconnaissance missions in the so-called inflamed regions. Occasionally, one of the three British RC-135W bearing the RAF designation Airseeker R Mk.1 could also be observed over Poland. These aircraft were rebuilt KC-135R (manufactured in 1964) by L-3 Communications (now L3Harris Technologies). These aircraft were delivered to the RAF between November 2013 and June 7, 2017, and are used by the 51st and 54th Squadron.

From time to time, patrols over Poland were carried out by the American RC-135U Combat Sent the E8C Joint STARS and even the unmanned RQ-4B. According to the RC-135U, it is necessary to perform ELINT-type missions, during which data on the operation of weapon systems are detected and recorded, in particular ground radars, airborne radars, radars and other systems mounted in ballistic missiles, cruise missiles and guided missiles. This data is used to develop warning systems and electronic warfare and to guide guided missiles, including anti-radar. The USAF has two such aircraft, which are in stock at the aforementioned 55th Wing. To ensure the inviolability of Polish airspace and to coordinate the activities protecting it by the Alliance's combat aircraft, the Boeing E-3A Sentry early warning and command aircraft, belonging to the international NATO E-3A component, stationed in Geilenkirchen, Germany, and the E-3F the air force of France.

The main element of the task system carried by the E-8C is the AN/APY-7 earth surface observation radar operating in the fixed target indication (FTI), synthetic aperture radar (SAR), wide-area surveillance and recognition and motion of moving ground targets (GMTI) modes. The radar is equipped with a 7.3 m longwall antenna with electronic beam control, located in a twelve-meter fairing under the front part of the fuselage.

The antenna with a field of view of 120° can be tilted to either side of the aircraft, allowing observation of 50,000 square kilometres. The radar can detect targets at a distance of up to 250 km. It also has limited detection capabilities for some low-flying aircraft. The USAF and the National Guard received 17 E-8s, which were created due to the conversion of used civilian Boeing 707-300s. In addition to reconnaissance aircraft belonging to the U.S. and Great Britain, missions were also performed in Polish airspace from the beginning of the war by other aircraft, including the RQ-4D crewless aircraft operating from the Italian Sigonella base belonging to the NATO Alliance Ground Surveillance, the Italian Gulfstream E- 550A CAEW and French C-160G Gabriel and Beech King Air 350ER/ALSR. The Italian Air Force currently has two E-550A CAEW (Conformal Airborne Early Warning & Control System) aircraft equipped with the airborne early warning and control multi-band radar system developed by Elta, a company belonging to the Israeli concern IAI cooperation with the Italian Leonardo concern. It can simultaneously detect and track nearly a hundred targets within a radius of 375 km and transmit the collected data.

The main element of the system is the antennae of the EL/W-2085 radiolocation station with Active Electronically Scanned Array (AESA) installed on the sides of the front part of the fuselage, enabling the detection of air, sea and land targets. The airframe also has antennae and devices detecting, locating and classifying radio emissions in a broad frequency spectrum. The first aircraft of this type was delivered to 14° Stormo stationed in Pratica di Mare in December 2016, and the second in January 2018. Flights performed over Poland and Romania in connection with the war in Ukraine were the first missions of the Italian E-550A CAEW over Eastern Europe. Shortly before the outbreak of war, on the morning of February 22, the only currently owned USAF Boeing WC-135W Constant Phoenix from the 55th Wing appeared over Poland, whose task is to collect samples from the atmosphere to detect and identify nuclear explosions, thanks to which this aircraft gained its unofficial name Sniffer (Sniffer). In addition to the RC-135 and E-3, much rarer alliance reconnaissance aircraft was also observed in Polish airspace. In the days preceding the outbreak of war and on February 24, the U.S. Army Bombardier Challenger 650 ARTEMIS (Airborne Reconnaissance and Targeting Multi-Mission Intelligence System) appeared in the Polish sky. The jet, which is still undergoing trials, bears civil registration marks N488CR and is formally registered to Lasai Aviation Inc., a company belonging to the Leidos concern. The aircraft is equipped with a radar mounted in the fairing under the fuselage, enabling terrain imaging and tracking objects in motion, e.g. tanks, as well as modern multi-range reconnaissance systems, combining various ISR, SIGINT functions, including COMINT and ELINT, allowing for the analysis of the situation in the field combat and real-time data transmission using hull-mounted satellite communication antennae.

It was not, after all, the first mission of this aircraft over Poland. Previously, it was tested in this area at the turn of May and June 2021, and in November, it flew over the Black Sea, Lithuania, Latvia and Poland, and even over Ukraine. The experience gained from operating the ARTEMIS prototype will be used in the target, larger aircraft based on Gulfstream or Boeing 737 airframes, which are scheduled to enter service around 2028. The American Northrop Grumman E-8C Joint STARS (Joint Surveillance Target Attack Radar System) aircraft also performed missions over Poland. Created as a result of cooperation between the USAF, the National Guard and the U.S. Army, the E-8C is a flying command and control centre with the ability to conduct observation of the earth's surface, surveillance and intelligence C2ISR (command and control, intelligence, administration, and watch – command and control, intelligence, supervision and recognition). The primary purpose of the aircraft is to provide ground and air commanders with information about enemy ground movements transmitted in near-real time.

In the Polish airspace, the Aérospatiale MBB C-160G Gabriel (Groupement aérien de brouillage, recherche et identification électronique – air group for jamming, search and electronic identification) belonging to the French Air and Space Forces, designed to perform the SIGINT mission, was also observed. France currently has two such aircraft, which were created in the second half of the 1980s from the reconstruction of standard transport copies with numbers F216 (serial number 219) and F221 (serial number 224), which in the new version received the designation G.T. and G.S., respectively, and was introduced into service in the late 1980s. As a result of the reconstruction of these aircraft, the rear loading ramps were fixed in the closed position, and soundproofed compartments closed with a bulkhead were installed in the cargo compartment in the fuselage for 12 operators operating SIGINT systems. These planes also have toilets, rest areas and kitchens.

The specialized equipment of the C-160G includes the antenna of the Thomson-CSF Epicéa system located in a retractable cover under the lower front part of the fuselage, used to find sources of U/VHF communication emissions, antennae on the top of the fuselage, pods at the wingtips of the Thomson-CSF ASTAC (Analyseur superhétérodyne tactique – Analyseur superhétérodyne tactique – tactical superheterodyne analyzer) for detecting, identifying and locating radar systems. These aircraft are also equipped with OMERA 51 panoramic cameras placed in the fairings on both sides of the rear part of the fuselage, thanks to which, in addition to the essential task of electronic survey, they can perform ROIM (Renseignement d'origine image) photo reconnaissance missions and the antenna of the H.F. communication system running from the rear part of the fuselage to the vertical stabilizer. In September 2008, the modernization carried out by Thales was completed, thanks to which the C-160G received the ability to process the collected data in real-time and transfer it to other aircraft or ships. The C-160G can perform missions lasting up to 6 hours, which, in the case of three-time refuelling in the air, can be extended up to 20 hours. Next year, the C-160Gs will be replaced with Dassault Falcon-7X Epicure jets. France also sent a Beech King Air 350ER/ALSR aircraft (Avion Léger de Surveillance et de Reconnaissance – light observation and reconnaissance aircraft) over Poland, intended for the IMINT (photographic reconnaissance) and SIGINT missions. Thales manufactured the specialized equipment installed on board, and Sabena Technics integrated the systems. The first of the two aircraft of this type currently operated by the French Air Force was delivered in July 2020, and according to the plan, six more aircraft are to enter service by 2030. The task of these aircraft is to gather intelligence for the Direction du Renseignement Militaire (French military intelligence) and the Direction Générale de la Sécurité Extérieure (foreign intelligence service). These aircraft can collect SIGINT data in an area of 517,847 square kilometers. The Russian aggression against Ukraine and the associated increase in threat caused the Alliance's combat aircraft to start air duty along the eastern borders of NATO countries. Air tankers support their activities. Among the planes of this type observed over Poland were both the most famous Boeing KC-135 Stratotanker and McDonnell Douglas KC-10A Extender, as well as Airbus A330 MRTT, Lockheed KC-130J and Boeing KC-767A, as well as the latest Boeing KC-46A Pegasus and customized for the role of Airbus A400M tankers.

Despite the passage of time, the KC-135R and KC-135T

operating over Poland remain the basic USAF tankers. Their range with 68 t of fuel intended for refuelling other aircraft is 2,420 km, and the maximum range for ferrying is 17,727 km. Power designed for transfer to other aircraft is carried in tanks in the lower part of the fuselage, where there are luggage hatches in communication aircraft and partially in the wings. Thanks to this, the KC-135 – depending on the amount of fuel taken – on the cargo deck can carry passengers and cargo with a total weight of up to 37,650 kg. From March 30, the latest American Boeing KC-46A Pegasus tankers operating from Spain began to appear over Poland, which have yet to reach full operational readiness. Airbus A330 MRTT tankers belonging to the Multinational Multi-Role Tanker Transport multi-role tanker/ transporter unit, the British Air Force, and – less frequently – France, also operated over Poland. In March and April, aerial refueling missions over Poland were carried out several times by the Italian Boeing KC-767A. Polish airspace has four military aerial refueling zones (TSA 29, TSA 22, TSA 28, TSA 26). Their exact data is provided and updated in MIL AIP POLAND. In 2002, Italy ordered four such aircraft that could perform aerial refueling and transport tasks. These machines, which are a version of the Boeing 767-200ER adapted to military needs, are equipped with a large cargo door with dimensions of 7.3 x 6 m located in the left front part of the fuselage, and their maximum reserve of fuel carried in standard tanks in the wings and the centre wing is 72 877 kg. This fuel can be transferred to recipients using a rigid probe mounted under the rear fuselage, with a capacity of up to 3,410 dm^3/min, or through flexible hoses installed in the under-wing tanks, with a total of up to 1,515 dm^3/min and in the rear fuselage (capacity of up to 2,275 dm^3/min). It is possible to transport up to 200 passengers or up to 19 463L pallets during transport tasks.

To strengthen the forces transferred to NATO's eastern flank and in connection with the Saber Strike exercises, American Sikorsky UH-60 and Boeing CH-47 and AH-64 helicopters, as well as VTOL Bell Boeing V-22 aircraft and support aircraft, appeared in Poland Special Operations Lockheed MC-130J Commando II. From 10 to February 28, 6 F-15C and 2 F-15D from the 493rd Fighter Squadron "Grim Reapers" stationed at RAF Lakenheath were also based in Łask, and on February 14, 8 F-15E from Seymour Johnson stationed daily at the base in North

Carolina, the 336th Fighter Squadron "Rocketeers", whose task was to strengthen the NATO Air Policing mission, consisting in protecting the airspace of Lithuania, Latvia and Estonia, which do not have their fighters. On the day the war broke out in the Polish airspace, one could observe e.g. belonging to the USAF F-15, KC135R, KC-10A, B-52H, E-8C and RC-135, A330 MRTT of the Multinational Multi-Role Tanker Transport Fleet and E-3A of the NATO Airborne Early Warning & Control Force (E- 3 Component). On the same day, during the ferrying operation to Bulgaria over Wielkopolska, 2 Dutch F-35s were refueled. From February 24, France engaged four Dassault Rafale multi-role combat jets stationed at their home base in Mont-de-Marsan in south-western France and two A330 MRTTs in operations on the eastern flank of the Alliance, including over Poland. On February 27, the French Armed Forces published information about the transfer to Poland of four Dassault Rafale F3R aircraft armed with MBDA Meteor air-to-air missiles, which, according to French media, was to be the operational debut of these missiles. On the same day, a USAF F-35A Lightning II from the 34th Fighter Squadron, belonging to the USAF, took off from the German Spangdahlem base and refueled over Poland with the KC-135 was observed in Polish airspace.

In the last days of February, the sky over Poland was patrolled by F-15, F-16, F-35 and Eurofighter Typhoon aircraft. On March 4, the U.K. Ministry of Defence announced that British Lockheed Martin F-35B Lightning II multi-role combat aircraft had started patrol flights over Poland and Romania. Eurofighter and A330 MRTT Voyagers support their operations. At the beginning of March, information also appeared that German Eurofighters were involved in patrols over Poland. At the same time, there was also information that, apart from the American F-15s, Łask probably also hosts French Rafales and American F-35s. In the first days of April, there were reports that the F/A-18C/D U.S. flew to the 32nd Tactical Air Base in Łask. Marine Corps from the 2nd Marine Aircraft Wing, after completing their participation in the Cold Response 22 exercises in Norway, were tasked with strengthening NATO's eastern flank. Until mid-April 2022, Poland also observed, among others, such NATO combat aircraft as the French Mirage 2000D, the British Eurofighter and the Belgian F-16. USAF B-52H and MC-130J reappeared from time to time, with the last of these aircraft even landing at some Polish airports. Currently, virtually every military and civil airport is used to help Ukraine. Aircraft of the Polish Air Force and other aircraft of NATO member countries constantly monitor what is happening in the Polish sky.

Conclusions

Summing up, Polish airspace played and still plays an essential role in the fight against the Russian invaders in Ukraine. To adequately fulfil its task, it is crucial to coordinate many authorities from air traffic control, approach control and guidance navigators. Another vital element is constant control over what is happening in the airspace and correct identification. In cases where the aircraft has its transponder turned off or does not respond to the controllers' calls for identification, the planes of the duty pair will undoubtedly be picked up. As a result of the tremendous amount of traffic in the air, both military and civilian, air traffic control authorities have much more work to do in recognizing aircraft and issuing their commands for separation in the air. Polish airspace is limited by a specific number of aircraft in the air. Still, as we know, when a war breaks out near the border of the North Atlantic Alliance, the army has priority to occupy separate zones in the air.

The restrictions introduced due to the flights of allied aircraft have already caused enormous financial losses for the Polish Agency dealing with air traffic; military conditions meant that some civil aviation flights were forced to change their flight routes, resulting in financial losses for Poland. Some of the paths of civil aircraft will go even further to the west because a large part of the Slovak space is also closed to civil traffic for security reasons. Air traffic is moving to Hungary, the Czech Republic and Germany. This arrangement is expected to continue for an extended period. Therefore, as in Poland, we must expect delays in air traffic because the limited capacity of Polish airspace is an essential aspect of air traffic, and an additional part is the work of air traffic controllers and their rest. The priority is the defence of our borders and the defence of the Polish sky, i.e. military actions and operations of military aircraft with the Polish checkerboard and allied forces. According to preliminary PANSA calculations, three months of conflict have caused 30-40 million losses. The airport in Lublin was also affected by restrictions, and the purpose of the airport changed to military and humanitarian operations. As a result of Russian aggression against Ukraine, the decrease in transit traffic decreased by 30%. The current situation is also affected by the closure of Ukraine's airspace for civil traffic and air traffic restrictions imposed mutually by the E.U. countries and the Russian Federation. It is necessary to introduce additional control bodies and create different air corridors for civil aircraft to recover from the financial losses incurred.

Conclusion

Vassilis (Bill) Kappis

The war in Ukraine has revealed deep vulnerabilities in the international security system, forcing the global community to confront a wide array of strategic, legal, and ethical challenges. As this Volume demonstrates, the conflict is not limited to a traditional battlefield but extends across domains such as information warfare, space militarization, hybrid attacks, and diplomatic realignment. These challenges call for an urgent reassessment of existing security frameworks and a recognition of the changing nature of modern warfare.

One of the central problems highlighted throughout the book is the vulnerability of NATO's Eastern Flank in the face of increasing Russian aggression. Magdalena Bugajny's in-depth exploration of NATO's deterrence capabilities emphasizes that the alliance must continually evolve to meet new threats. The precarious position of countries bordering Russia underscores the importance of NATO's collective defence mechanisms, which are tested by the current conflict.

The use of hybrid warfare is another key issue that emerges from this war. Dawid Kufel provides a thorough examination of how Russia has employed hybrid tactics, including cyber-attacks and disinformation campaigns, to weaken Ukraine and destabilize its institutions. His analysis points to the need for a comprehensive defence strategy that includes not only military strength but also resilience against non-conventional forms of warfare.

The humanitarian and legal consequences of warfare, particularly regarding the use of incendiary weapons, form a third major problem area. Szymon Boguski's chapter critically assesses the application of International Humanitarian Law (IHL) to these weapons, exposing the limitations of current legal frameworks in protecting civilians from such devastating effects. His call for stronger legal enforcement is a vital contribution to the global conversation on war crimes and the protection of non-combatants.

Technological advances in warfare, especially the rise of Artificial Intelligence (AI) on the battlefield, pose significant ethical dilemmas, as explored by Irena Diamentowicz. The increasing use of AI in military operations presents opportunities to improve efficiency and decision-making, but it also raises concerns about accountability, transparency, and the unintended consequences of autonomous systems. Diamentowicz's analysis signals a critical need for global standards and regulations to govern the deployment of AI in conflict.

Jarosław Drygowski highlights the power of strategic communication and rhetoric in warfare, particularly through his analysis of Vladimir Putin's 2022 Victory Day speech. The manipulation of public perception, both domestically and internationally, is a potent weapon that can justify aggression and influence global responses. Drygowski's work underscores the significance of language in mobilizing support for military actions and the need for strategic counter-narratives in conflicts.

The role of intelligence operations in modern warfare, particularly human intelligence (HUMINT), remains a cornerstone of successful military strategy. Krzysztof Górecki and Mikołaj Schulz both provide insights into the crucial part that intelligence plays in shaping military outcomes. Górecki's chapter on Ukraine's intelligence operations during the defence of Kyiv, and Schulz's broader examination of HUMINT, remind us that despite technological advancements, human intelligence remains indispensable in the theater of war.

The geopolitical rivalry in the Black Sea region is another important issue explored by Jarosław Łęski, who analyzes the strategic competition between Turkey and Russia. His work demonstrates that regional conflicts, such as the war in Ukraine, are often influenced by larger geopolitical rivalries that extend beyond the immediate belligerents. The Black Sea remains a critical flashpoint, with broader implications for NATO and European security.

As warfare extends into new domains, the militarization of space is becoming an increasingly significant challenge, as discussed by Łukasz Pokrywacki. The potential for space to become a new battleground in global conflicts is alarming, given the reliance on satellites for communication, intelligence, and navigation. Pokrywacki's chapter calls for urgent international agreements to prevent the weaponization of space and to ensure that it remains a peaceful domain.

On the political front, Maciej Grunt's analysis of the 2022 U.S. midterm elections highlights the political shifts that could influence NATO's strategic direction and support for Ukraine. His work demonstrates how domestic political developments in major powers, particularly the U.S., can have far-reaching effects on international security arrangements.

Finally, the management of airspace and the strategic importance of air defences, particularly in Poland, are discussed by Wiktor Satkowski. His chapter underscores the critical role of airspace management in protecting NATO's Eastern Flank from Russian aggression, emphasizing the need for enhanced coordination and preparedness in the face of evolving threats.

Taken together, the chapters in this Volume provide a comprehensive analysis of the complex problems arising from the war in Ukraine. The authors have explored the multidimensional nature of this conflict, from the battlefield to cyberspace, and from political rhetoric to space warfare. Their work not only highlights the immediate challenges but also points to the long-term implications for global security.

As we move forward, the lessons drawn from the war in Ukraine will continue to shape the future of global security. The issues raised in this volume—whether they concern NATO's readiness, hybrid warfare, technological advancements, or geopolitical rivalries – will remain central to international discussions on how to ensure peace and stability in an increasingly volatile world.

I extend my sincerest appreciation to all the authors who contributed their expertise and insights to this volume. Their comprehensive analyses and carefully considered perspectives have greatly deepened the understanding of the war in Ukraine, shedding light on its far-reaching implications for both regional and global security.

Dr hab. Vassilis (Bill) Kappis
Deputy Director of the Centre for Security and Intelligence Studies (BUCSIS)
University of Buckingham, Great Britain

FUTURE DISCUSSION

War in Ukraine: Challenges in Navigating Future Regional and Global Security

Marzena Żakowska

The war in Ukraine presents enormous challenges to European and global security. These challenges arise from the evolving nature of warfare, characterized by the increasing use of hybrid tactics that blur the lines between traditional and non-traditional forms of conflict. This multifaceted style of warfare creates a more complex and unpredictable security environment, requiring a comprehensive and coordinated response from Ukraine and its allies. States must be prepared to face hybrid threats in order to preserve national security. Given the complexities introduced by the conflict in Ukraine, several following key areas will require attention in future discussions.

Understanding the dynamics of hybrid warfare is essential in today's security landscape. Hybrid warfare is a complex strategy that merges conventional military power with irregular tactics such as terrorism, insurgency, cyberattacks, disinformation campaigns, and economic manipulation. It also includes the use of proxy forces, diplomatic and political pressure, psychological operations (PsyOps), orchestrated civilian protests, and covert operations. The ongoing war in Ukraine is a striking example of hybrid warfare in practice, where non-traditional tactics have been heavily employed alongside regular military operations. This approach has not only compromised national security and state sovereignty but has also had significant implications for regional and global security. The lessons drawn from this conflict emphasize the need for nations to focus on developing effective countermeasures and resilience strategies to mitigate the growing influence of hybrid threats. Particular attention should be given to bolstering cybersecurity, ensuring information integrity, enhancing strategic communications, and maintaining social cohesion in the face of such multifaceted challenges.

The role of strategic communications and propaganda in shaping public perception and influencing international opinion also requires in-depth discussion. State actors frequently use these tools to reinforce their strategic objectives and narratives. For instance, analyzing Vladimir Putin's speech during the Victory Day Parade in 2022 reveals how state leaders employ rhetoric to fuel nationalist sentiment, justify military actions, and construct a narrative that serves their interests. On the other hand, it is equally important to examine the speeches of Ukrainian President Volodymyr Zelensky. His addresses have become powerful instruments for fostering courage among citizens, strengthening social cohesion, and inspiring resilience in the face of adversity. These speeches play a crucial role in uniting the nation and cultivating the spirit to continue fighting. Beyond these examples, analyzing speeches from key ministers, media authorities, and influential religious figures can further enrich our understanding of how public opinion is shaped by prominent voices. This topic can explore the techniques used to craft persuasive messages, the psychological impact on both domestic and international audiences, and the role of the media in disseminating state-sponsored narratives. Moreover, it would be valuable to investigate the counter-strategies that other nations and international organizations can adopt to combat misinformation and promote balanced perspectives.

NATO's deterrence on its Eastern Flank is becoming increasingly important, especially in light of the ongoing war in Ukraine. This situation has underscored the need for a deeper discussion about NATO's evolving role in maintaining security across its Eastern Flank, which includes countries such as Poland, Estonia, Latvia, and Lithuania. Given their geographical proximity to Russia, these nations are particularly vulnerable to hybrid threats and destabilization efforts orchestrated by Russia and its allies. A key focus area is how these countries can bolster their defence capabilities and how NATO can enhance its deterrence posture. This could involve a range of strategic measures, including the deployment of rapid response forces, conducting joint military exercises, and integrating advanced defence technologies. These initiatives are crucial to ensuring swift and effective responses to any potential aggression. As the conflict in Ukraine continues, the need for Ukraine and its allies to improve their military readiness and modernization programs becomes more pressing. This includes not only upgrading military equipment but also enhancing rapid response mechanisms and expanding joint training exercises. Strengthening military alliances and partnerships, particularly within NATO's framework, will be vital in deterring future aggression and ensuring a coordinated and efficient response to emerging threats.

It is crucial to closely examine cyberspace as an emerging domain of state security, particularly for NATO and EU member states. The rapidly evolving nature of cyber threats underscores the urgent need for robust cybersecurity measures to safeguard both national and regional interests. This situation highlights the necessity of enhanced cooperation between NATO and European Union members. As a result, discussions on cybersecurity must focus on developing comprehensive strategies that foster collaboration among these international partners. Additionally, establishing clear norms and regulations to govern state behavior in cyberspace is essential for maintaining a stable and secure digital environment.

Another critical issue is the establishment of a robust intelligence information exchange system between NATO member states to effectively counter hybrid threats. To achieve this, NATO countries must strengthen their collective capability to share real-time intelligence and actionable information across borders. The creation of an intelligence-sharing platform within NATO would greatly enhance situational awareness, allowing member nations to detect early signs of hybrid threats such as cyber intrusions, political interference, or covert operations. This system should facilitate the seamless exchange of intelligence on hostile actors, their tactics, and potential vulnerabilities, ensuring that allies are well-informed and prepared to respond swiftly. It is essential to discuss key components of this intelligence-sharing system, which should include cybersecurity intelligence, disinformation monitoring, military intelligence, and economic intelligence, supported by artificial intelligence and data analytics. Furthermore, it is crucial to emphasize that this system allows for transparent collaboration among NATO members, fostering greater trust and operational efficiency.

Additionally, it is need to acknowledge the expanding role of Artificial Intelligence (AI) in military operations, as its integration offers transformative potential for future engagements. AI technologies are increasingly being embedded into various aspects of military strategies, enhancing capabilities in areas such as decision-making, predictive analytics, and the automation of combat systems. These innovations provide several advantages, such as improving the speed and accuracy of tactical decisions, enabling more precise targeting, and reducing the need for human intervention in high-risk situations. However, alongside these benefits come significant ethical considerations, particularly regarding the potential for autonomous weapons systems (commonly referred to as "killer robots") to operate independently of human control. These concerns must be addressed to ensure responsible and ethical use of AI in military contexts.

We should also point out that the war in Ukraine has prompted a reevaluation of global and regional security, highlighting vulnerabilities in defence policies, energy security, and diplomatic relations. The resurgence of armed conflict in Europe has emphasized the urgent need for enhanced international cooperation to address evolving threats. The conflict also calls for discussions on the changing global security landscape, particularly the roles of international organizations such as the United Nations and NATO. New security frameworks may need to emerge in response to these shifts. Additionally, the impact of the war on arms control, nuclear deterrence, and the prospects for future peace negotiations are critical aspects that must be addressed.

In light of the conflict, it is equally important to uphold international law, particularly concerning the norms surrounding aggression, state sovereignty, and the enforcement of strict rules for sanctioning entities that use aggression as a tool of foreign policy. Ensuring accountability for war crimes and violations of human rights is also essential in responding to the conflict. Discussions should focus on reforming international security mechanisms, particularly in redefining what constitutes war, aggression, and the legitimate use of military power in international relations. It is vital to strengthen mechanisms for documenting atrocities, pursuing justice, and reinforcing the international legal framework to prevent future conflicts.

Finally, the ongoing conflict has led to significant humanitarian crises, with large numbers of displaced people and refugees. This situation opens a discussion on how to effectively manage humanitarian aid, provide support for refugees, and coordinate rebuilding efforts in conflict-affected areas. These efforts are essential not only for maintaining stability but also for preventing further escalation. Humanitarian assistance must be at the fore-front of global response strategies as the international community works to mitigate the long-term effects of the war.

The war in Ukraine has reshaped the global and regional security landscape, introducing new complexities that demand comprehensive solutions. From the rise of hybrid warfare and cyber threats to the evolving role of NATO, the challenges ahead require international cooperation, strategic foresight, and techno-logical innovation. As you engage with this discussion, it becomes clear that these issues are not confined to Ukraine alone, but have far-reaching implications for global peace and stability.

In closing

I would like to sincerely thank the Autors of the chapters their remarkable contributions. Their deep expertise and thoughtful insights have significantly enhanced this Volume, offering perspectives that will undoubtedly influence future discussions on the shifting nature of warfare and the strategies required to face new global threats. Collectively, their work forms a solid foundation for comprehending the multifaceted nature of modern conflict and its far-reaching implications for global security.

Further, We invite the readers to engage in discussions around these critical issues presented in this book, as they offer valuable insights into the future of military strategies, cybersecu-rity, artificial intelligence in defence, and humanitarian efforts. Your participation is vital in helping to build more resilient and cooperative frameworks within the international community, enabling us to effectively address both current and future threats and safeguard regional and global security.

Join the discussion and contribute to navigating the path toward ending the war in Ukraine and creating a safer, more secure world.

Dr Marzena Żakowska

Director of The Postgraduate Diploma Studies of Global Affairs and Diplomacy
National Security Faculty
War Studies University
Warsaw, Poland

www.ingramcontent.com/pod-product-compliance
Lightning Source LLC
Chambersburg PA
CBHW050330270326
41926CB00016B/3388